WRITING ANALYTICALLY

EIGHTH EDITION

DAVID ROSENWASSER
Muhlenberg College

JILL STEPHEN
Muhlenberg College

Includes the
MLA 9th Edition
&APA 7th Edition
Updates

CENGAGE

Australia • Brazil • Canada • Mexico • Singapore • United Kingdom • United States

**Writing Analytically 8e
with 2021 MLA and
2020 APA Updates**
**David Rosenwasser and Jill
Stephen**

Product Manager: Laura Ross

Content Developer: Elinor Gregory

Product Assistant: Shelby
Nathanson

Marketing Manager: Kina Lara

Senior Content Project Manager:
Aimee Bear

Senior Art Director: Marissa Falco

IP Analyst: Ann Hoffman

IP Project Manager: Betsy
Hathaway

Manufacturing Planner: Betsy
Donaghey

Production Service: MPS Limited

Compositor: MPS Limited

Text Designer: MPS Limited

Cover Designer: Marissa Falco

Cover Image: Jorg Greuel/
DigitalVision/Getty Images

The content in this textbook for
which Cengage holds the copyright
has been updated to better fit MLA
and APA guidelines for language
that is inclusive and bias free. This
updating could not be applied to
content for which Cengage does
not own the copyright, including
excerpts from articles as well as
student papers.

For product information and technology assistance,
contact us at **Cengage Customer & Sales Support,
1-800-354-9706.**

For permission to use material from this
text or product, submit all requests online at
www.cengage.com/permissions.
Further permissions questions can be emailed to
permissionrequest@cengage.com.

Library of Congress Control Number: 2017954666

Student Edition:
ISBN: 978-1-337-55946-1

Loose-leaf Edition:
ISBN: 978-1-337-55947-8

Cengage
200 Pier 4 Boulevard
Boston, MA 02210
USA

Cengage is a leading provider of customized learning
solutions with employees residing in nearly 40 different
countries and sales in more than 125 countries around
the world. Find your local representative at:
www.cengage.com.

To learn more about Cengage platforms and services,
register or access your online learning solution, or
purchase materials for your course, visit
www.cengage.com.

Printed at CLDPC, USA, 08-22

CONTENTS

Preface   *xv*

UNIT I   The Analytical Frame of Mind   1

CHAPTER 1   2
The Five Analytical Moves   2

Writing as a Tool of Thought   2

Why Faculty Want Analysis   3

Analysis Is a Search for Meaning   3

Analysis Does More than Break a Subject into Its Parts   4

Distinguishing Analysis from Summary, Expressive Writing, and Argument   5

    Analysis and Summary   6

    Analysis and Expressive Writing   7

    Analysis and Argument   7

Counterproductive Habits of Mind   10

    Habit: The Judgment Reflex   10

    Cures for the Judgment Reflex   11

        TRY THIS 1.1: Experiment with Adjectives and Adverbs   11

    Habit: Naturalizing Our Assumptions (Overpersonalizing)   11

        VOICES FROM ACROSS THE CURRICULUM: Arguments vs. Opinions:

        A Political Scientist Speaks   12

    Habit: Generalizing   12

    Cures for the Problem of Generalizing   13

        TRY THIS 1.2: Distinguishing Abstract from Concrete Words   13

        VOICES FROM ACROSS THE CURRICULUM: Habits of Mind

        in Psychology: A Psychologist Speaks   13

    Get Comfortable with Uncertainty   14

    Habit: The Slot-Filler Mentality (Five-Paragraph Form)   14

    Learn to Notice   15

The Five Analytical Moves   16

Move 1: Suspend Judgment   16

Move 2: Define Significant Parts and How They Are Related   16

    NOTICE & FOCUS (RANKING)   17

    "Interesting," "Revealing," "Strange"   18

        TRY THIS 1.3: NOTICE & FOCUS Fieldwork   18

    Noticing and Rhetorical Analysis   18

        TRY THIS 1.4: Doing NOTICE & FOCUS with a Room   19

    Doing Exploratory Writing in the Observation Stage: Freewriting   19

Move 3: Make the Implicit Explicit. Push Observations to
    Implications by Asking "So What?"   21
    Asking "So What?"   23
    Asking "So What?" in a Chain   23
        TRY THIS 1.5: Track the "So What?" Question   24
        TRY THIS 1.6: Inferring Implications from Observations   25
Move 4: Look for Patterns of Repetition and Contrast and for Anomalies (The Method)   25
    The Steps of The Method   26
    Two Examples of The Method Generating Ideas   27
    Doing The Method on a Poem   29
        TRY THIS 1.7: Doing The Method on a Poem   31
    Troubleshooting The Method   31
        TRY THIS 1.8: Do The Method on a Visual Image   32
        TRY THIS 1.9: Do The Method on a Reading   32
Move 5: Keep Reformulating Questions and Explanations   32
Summing Up: Analyzing Whistler's Mother   33
Analysis and Personal Associations   35
Becoming a Detective   36
Assignments: The Five Analytical Moves   36

CHAPTER 2   38

Reading Analytically   38

Becoming Conversant Instead of Reading for the Gist   38
    Beyond the Banking Model of Education   39
    Rejecting the Transparent Theory of Language   39
    Seek to Understand the Reading Fairly on Its Own Terms   40
How to Write a Critique   41
    VOICES FROM ACROSS THE CURRICULUM: What Do We Mean
        by Critical Reading? A Music Professor Speaks   43
Focus on Individual Sentences   43
    Pointing   44
    Using Quotation   44
    Paraphrase × 3   45
        TRY THIS 2.1: Experiment with Paraphrase × 3   47
        TRY THIS 2.2: Paraphrase and Implication   47
    Passage-Based Focused Freewriting   47
        TRY THIS 2.3: Do Passage-Based Focused Freewriting   52
        TRY THIS 2.4: Writing and Reading with Others: A Sequence of Activities   52
    Keep a Commonplace Book   53
Situate the Reading Rhetorically   53
Find The Pitch, The Complaint, and The Moment   54
        TRY THIS 2.5: Locating The Pitch and The Complaint   56

Focus on the Structure of Thinking in a Reading   56

UNCOVERING ASSUMPTIONS   **56**

     TRY THIS 2.6: UNCOVERING ASSUMPTIONS Implied by a Statement   57

     TRY THIS 2.7: UNCOVERING ASSUMPTIONS: Fieldwork   58

TRACKING BINARIES in a Reading   58

REFORMULATING BINARIES   60

     TRY THIS 2.8: REFORMULATING BINARIES: Fieldwork   62

     TRY THIS 2.9: Practice TRACKING REFORMULATED BINARIES in a Reading   63

APPLY a READING as a LENS   63

Assignments: Reading Analytically   68

CHAPTER 3   70

Interpretation: Moving from Observation to Implication   70

The Big Picture   70

Making Interpretations Plausible: Interpretive Contexts   71

Context and the Making of Meaning   72

     Specifying an Interpretive Context: A Brief Example   73

     Intention as an Interpretive Context   74

     What Is and Isn't "Meant" to Be Analyzed   76

Avoiding the Extremes: Neither "Fortune Cookie" nor "Anything Goes"   77

     The Fortune Cookie School of Interpretation   77

     The Anything Goes School of Interpretation   77

Implications Versus Hidden Meanings   78

     Figurative Logic: Reasoning with Metaphors   79

       TRY THIS 3.1: Uncovering the Logic of Figurative Language   81

       TRY THIS 3.2: Analyzing the Figurative Language of Politics   81

SEEMS TO BE ABOUT X, BUT COULD ALSO BE (OR IS "REALLY") ABOUT Y   82

     SEEMS TO BE ABOUT X . . .: An Example   83

       TRY THIS 3.3: Apply the Formula SEEMS TO BE ABOUT X,

       BUT COULD ALSO BE (OR IS "REALLY") ABOUT Y   84

Making an Interpretation: The Example of a *New Yorker* Cover   84

     Description of a *New Yorker* Cover, Dated October 9, 2000   84

     Using THE METHOD to Identify Patterns of Repetition and Contrast   86

     Pushing Observations to Conclusions: Selecting an Interpretive Context   87

     Arriving at an Interpretive Conclusion: Making Choices   88

     Making the Interpretation Plausible   89

Making Interpretations Plausible Across the Curriculum   89

     Interpreting Statistical Data   90

       VOICES FROM ACROSS THE CURRICULUM:

       Interpreting the Numbers: A Psychology Professor Speaks   92

A Brief Glossary of Common Logical Fallacies   93

Assignments: Interpretation: Moving from Observation to Implication   97

CHAPTER 4   98

Responding to Traditional Writing Assignments More Analytically   98

Interpreting Writing Assignments   98

Find the Analytical Potential: Locate an Area of Uncertainty   99

Six Rules of Thumb for Responding to Assignments More Analytically   100

    Rule 1: Reduce Scope   100

    Rule 2: Study the Wording of Topics for Unstated Questions   100

    Rule 3: Suspect Your First Responses   101

    Rule 4: Begin with Questions, Not Answers   101

    Rule 5: Expect to Become Interested   101

    Rule 6: Write All of the Time About What You Are Studying   102

Summary   103

    Strategies for Making Summaries More Analytical   103

Personal Response: The Reaction Paper   105

    Strategies for Making Personal Responses More Analytical   106

Agree/Disagree   107

Comparison/Contrast   108

    Strategies for Making Comparison/Contrast More Analytical,

      Including DIFFERENCE WITHIN SIMILARITY   109

Definition   111

    Strategies for Making Definition More Analytical   112

Assignments: Responding to Traditional Writing Assignments More Analytically 113

CHAPTER 5   116

Thinking Like a Writer   116

Process and Product   116

    A Review of Some Strategies from *Writing Analytically*

      for Making Writing Happen   117

    Making Writing Happen   118

Freewriting Revisited   119

    TRY THIS 5.1: Freewriting on a Single Word or Phrase   120

    Observation Exercises: The Value of Close Description 120

    TRY THIS 5.2: Three Descriptive Freewrites   121

    TRY THIS 5.3: Hemingway's Five-Finger Exercise   121

Alternative Models of Revision: New Starts and the Back Burner   122

    Closing Your Eyes as You Speak   123

    When Class Members Become Audience: What Did You Hear?   124

    Writing on Computers vs. Writing on Paper   124

On Keeping a Writer's Notebook: Things to Try   126

    Collecting Possible Starting Points for Writing   126

    Collecting Words, Similes, and Metaphors: Not Just for Poets   128

"Three Minutes": An Ongoing, Essay-Writing Prompt 130
    TRY THIS 5.4: Three Minutes on Attention and Distraction 131
Writing from Life: The Personal Essay 132
    TRY THIS 5.5: Something You Know How to Do 133
    TRY THIS 5.6: Writing the Self 134
    TRY THIS 5.7: Reconstruct and Reflect 134
    TRY THIS 5.8: A Childhood Experience that Changed, Somehow,
        Your View of the World 135
Reading Like a Writer: Text Marking and Listing 135
Beyond Critique: Alternative Ways for Writers to Respond to Other Writers 136
    Procedures for Description-Based, Small-Group Peer Review 137
    Procedures for One-on-One Peer Review: The Writing Center Model 138
    A Word on Google Docs and Interactive Blogging 140
Writing with Other Writers 141
    Writing Marathons: Taking Writing on the Road 141
    Writers' Boot Camp 142
How to Assess Your Own Writing: Some Rubrics for Self-Evaluation 143
    Short List of Things That Go Wrong 144
    Some Do's and Don'ts of Good Writing 144
    Some Useful Mantras for Writers 146
Assignment: Thinking Like a Writer 146
    Write a Literacy Narrative 146

UNIT II   Writing the Analytical Paper 147

CHAPTER 6 148
Reasoning from Evidence to Claims 148

Linking Evidence and Claims 148
    The Functions of Evidence 149
    "Because I Say So": Unsubstantiated Claims 149
    Distinguishing Evidence from Claims 150
        TRY THIS 6.1: Distinguishing Evidence from Claims 151
    Giving Evidence a Point: Making Details Speak 151
More than Just "the Facts": What Counts as Evidence? 153
    VOICES FROM ACROSS THE CURRICULUM: Questions of Relevance
        and Methodology: A Political Science Professor Speaks 154
The Rules of Argument 155
    Syllogism and Enthymeme 156
    Toulmin's Alternative Model of the Syllogism 157
    Rogerian Argument and Practical Reasoning 159
Deduction and Induction: Two Ways of Linking Evidence and Claims 160
1 on 10 and 10 on 1 162
    DOING 10 ON 1 162

Organizing Papers Using 1 on 10   164

A Potential Problem with 1 on 10: Mere Demonstration   164

DOING 10 ON 1: Saying More About Less   164

A Potential Problem with 10 on 1: Not Demonstrating the
Representativeness of Your Example   165

TRY THIS 6.2: DOING 10 ON 1 with Newspaper Visuals   167

TRY THIS 6.3: DOING 10 ON 1 with a Reading   167

10 on 1 and Disciplinary Conventions   168

Larger Organizational Schemes: Writing Papers Based on 1 on 10 and 10 on 1   168

The Problem of Five-Paragraph Form: A Reductive Version of 1 on 10   168

Rehabilitating Five-Paragraph Form   171

Outline for a Viable Version of Five-Paragraph Form   171

Pan, Track, and Zoom: "Directing" Your Paper   172

A Template for Organizing Papers Using 10 on 1   173

DOING 10 ON 1 to Find an Organizing Claim: A Student Paper   174

TRY THIS 6.4: Marking Claims, Evidence, and Complications in a Draft   175

Assignments: Reasoning from Evidence to Claims   176

CHAPTER 7   178

Finding and Evolving a Thesis   178

The Big Picture   179

What a Good Thesis Is and Does   180

Potential Problems with Thesis-Driven Writing   182

Making a Thesis Evolve   182

Developing a Thesis Is More than Repeating an Idea   182

The Thesis as Camera Lens: The Reciprocal Relationship
Between Thesis and Evidence   183

Induction and Deduction: Two Paths a Thesis May Take   184

Making a Thesis Evolve: A Brief, Inductive Example   185

Making a Thesis Evolve: A Brief, Deductive Example   186

The Evolving Thesis as Hypothesis and Conclusion
in the Natural and Social Sciences   187

VOICES FROM ACROSS THE CURRICULUM: The Hypothesis
in the Natural and Social Sciences: Three Professors Speak   187

Evolving a Working Thesis in an Exploratory Draft: The Example of *Las Meninas*   188

From Details to Ideas: Arriving at a Working Thesis in an Exploratory Draft   191

Six Steps for Finding and Evolving a Thesis in an Exploratory Draft   192

Knowing When to Stop: How Much Revising Is Enough?   198

Practice Tracking Thesis Statements in Finished Drafts   199

Tracking the Thesis in a Final Draft: The Example of *In Bruges*   199

Introductions, Conclusions, and the Thesis   202

Setting Up the Thesis: Two Tasks   202

Making the Thesis Matter: Providing an Interpretive Context   203

How Much of the Thesis Belongs in the Introduction?   204

The Conclusion: Returning the Thesis to the Larger Conversation 204
VOICES FROM ACROSS THE CURRICULUM: Recognizing Your
Thesis: A History Professor Speaks 205
How to Word Thesis Statements 205
Put X in Tension with Y 205
TRY THIS 7.1: Spotting the Tension in Good Thesis Statements 206
Is It Okay to Phrase a Thesis as a Question? 207
VOICES FROM ACROSS THE CURRICULUM: Getting Beyond
the All-Purpose Thesis: A Dance Professor Speaks 207
Recognizing and Fixing Weak Thesis Statements 207
Weak Thesis Type 1: The Thesis Makes No Claim 208
Weak Thesis Type 2: The Thesis Is Obviously True or Is a Statement of Fact 209
Weak Thesis Type 3: The Thesis Restates Conventional Wisdom 209
Weak Thesis Type 4: The Thesis Bases Its Claim on Personal Conviction 210
Weak Thesis Type 5: The Thesis Makes an Overly Broad Claim 211
Assignment: Finding and Evolving a Thesis 212

CHAPTER 8   213
Conversing with Sources: Writing the Researched Paper   213

The Big Picture 213
Using Sources Analytically 214
"Source Anxiety" and What to Do About It 215
The Conversation Analogy 216
Conversing with a Source: A Brief Example 217
Ways to Use a Source as a Point of Departure 218
Six Strategies for Analyzing Sources 219
Strategy 1: Make Your Sources Speak 219
Strategy 2: Attend Carefully to the Language of Your Sources by
Quoting or Paraphrasing 220
Strategy 3: Supply Ongoing Analysis of Sources (Don't Wait Until the End) 221
VOICES FROM ACROSS THE CURRICULUM:
Bringing Sources Together: A Psychology Professor Speaks 222
Strategy 4: Use Your Sources to Ask Questions, Not Just Provide Answers 222
Strategy 5: Put Your Sources Into Conversation with One Another 225
Strategy 6: Find Your Own Role in the Conversation 227
VOICES FROM ACROSS THE CURRICULUM:
Engaging Sources in the Sciences: A Biology Professor Speaks 230
Using Sources Analytically: An Example 230
Integrating Quotations Into Your Paper 231
Preparing an Abstract 234
What Does Plagiarism Do to the Conversation? 235
Frequently Asked Questions (FAQS) about Plagiarism 236
Assignments: Conversing with Sources: Writing the Researched Paper 238

CHAPTER 9   242

Finding, Evaluating, and Citing Sources   **242**

Three Rules of Thumb for Getting Started with Research   242

Start with Scholarly Indexes, Abstracts, and Bibliographies   243

Specialized Dictionaries and Encyclopedias   244

Finding Your Sources: Articles and Books   244

     VOICES FROM ACROSS THE CURRICULUM: Finding
       Quality Sources: Two Professors Speak   245

Finding Quality on the Web   246

   Understanding Domain Names   246

   Print Corollaries   247

   Web-Published Gems   247

   Wikipedia, Google, and Blogs   248

   Asking the Right Questions   249

   Subscriber-Only Databases   250

     TRY THIS 9.1: Tuning in to Your Research Environment: Four Exercises   251

Eight Tips for Locating and Evaluating Electronic Sources   251

   Tip #1: Backspacing   251

   Tip #2: Using WHOIS   251

   Tip #3: Beware of the ~ in a Web Address   251

   Tip #4: Phrase Searching   252

   Tip #5: Title Searching   252

   Tip #6: Wikipedia Talk Tab   252

   Tip #7: Full Text from Library Databases   252

   Tip #8: Archives of Older Published Periodicals   252

Four Steps Toward Productive Research Across the Disciplines   253

The Four Documentation Styles: Similarities and Differences   255

APA Style, 7th Edition   257

Chicago Style, 17th Edition   258

CSE Style Employing Name-Year (Author-Date) System, 8th Edition   260

CSE Style Employing Citation Sequence System, 8th Edition   261

MLA Style, 9th Edition   262

Guidelines for Finding, Evaluating, and Citing Sources   263

UNIT III   Matters of Form   265

CHAPTER 10   266

From Paragraphs to Papers: Forms and Formats Across the Curriculum   **266**

The Two Functions of Formats   266

   Using Formats Heuristically: An Example   267

The Common Structure of Most Academic Writing 268

    Science Format Compared with Other Kinds of Writing 268

        VOICES FROM ACROSS THE CURRICULUM: Writing in the Sciences:

          A Biochemistry Professor Speaks 269

        VOICES FROM ACROSS THE CURRICULUM: How to

          Write—and Read—Scientific Formats: Two Professors Speak 270

Three Organizing Strategies 271

    Climactic Order: Saving the Best for Last 271

    Comparison/Contrast: Two Formats 271

    Concessions and Refutations: Giving and Taking Away 272

        TRY THIS 10.1: Locating Concessions and Refutations 273

What Introductions Do: "Why What I'm Saying Matters" 273

    How Much to Introduce Up Front: Typical Problems 274

        VOICES FROM ACROSS THE CURRICULUM: Avoiding Strong

          Claims in the Introduction: An Economics Professor Speaks 276

    Some Good Ways to Begin a Paper 276

What Conclusions Do: The Final "SO WHAT?" 278

        VOICES FROM ACROSS THE CURRICULUM: Beyond

          Restatement: A Business and a Political Science Professor Speak 279

    Solving Typical Problems in Conclusions 279

Introductions and Conclusions Across the Curriculum 281

    Introductory Paragraphs in the Humanities 281

    Using Procedural Openings: Introductions and Conclusions

      in the Social Sciences 282

        VOICES FROM ACROSS THE CURRICULUM: Using Procedural

          Openings: A Political Science Professor Speaks 283

    Putting an Issue or Question in Context 283

        VOICES FROM ACROSS THE CURRICULUM: Providing an

          Introductory Context: A Political Science Professor Speaks 283

        VOICES FROM ACROSS THE CURRICULUM: Framing Research

          Questions and Hypotheses: A Political Science Professor Speaks 284

    Writing Introductions in the Sciences 284

        VOICES FROM ACROSS THE CURRICULUM:

          Introductions in the Sciences: Three Professors Speak 284

    Integration of Citations in a Literature Review: A Brief Example 286

    Introductions in Scientific Papers: A Brief Example 286

    Writing Conclusions in the Sciences: The Discussion Section 286

        VOICES FROM ACROSS THE CURRICULUM:

          Writing Conclusions in the Sciences: Two Professors Speak 287

    Conclusions in Scientific Papers: A Brief Example 288

        VOICES FROM ACROSS THE CURRICULUM: Ethos and

          Style in Scientific Writing: A Biochemistry Professor Speaks 288

The Idea of the Paragraph 288

    How Long?: Paragraphs, Readers, and Writers 289

Linking the Sentences in Paragraphs: Minding the Gaps   **290**

What a Paragraph Does: The Paragraph as Movement of Mind   **291**

TRY THIS 10.2: Label the Function of the Sentences in a Paragraph   292

TRY THIS 10.3: Identify the Structure of a Paragraph   294

The Shaping Force of Transitions   295

TRY THIS 10.4: Tracking Transitions   297

Assignments: From Paragraphs to Papers: Forms and Formats
Across the Curriculum   297

CHAPTER 11   299

Style: Choosing Words, Shaping Sentences   299

Seeing Style as Inseparable From Meaning   299

About Prescriptive Style Manuals: A Word of Warning   300

Sentence Logic: Seeing How the Parts of a Sentence Are Related   301

Finding the Spine of a Sentence: Subjects and Predicates   302

Kinds of Verbs: Transitive, Intransitive, and Linking   303

Verbals: Verb Forms that Function as Other Parts of Speech   304

Sentence Combining: Coordination   305

Sentence Combining: Subordination   307

TRY THIS 11.1: Identify Clauses and Conjunctions   309

Seeing the Shape of Sentences: Why Commas Matter   310

TRY THIS 11.2: Find and Explain Commas in a Piece of Writing   311

What Punctuation Marks Say: A Quick-Hit Guide   312

Emphasis and the Order of Clauses: The Importance of What Comes Last   313

TRY THIS 11.3: Order Clauses in a Sentence for Emphasis   314

Embedding Modifiers: Relative Clauses, Words, and Phrases   314

Periodic and Cumulative Styles: Two Ways of Locating Closure   316

The Periodic Sentence: Delay Closure to Achieve Emphasis   317

The Cumulative Sentence: Start Fast to Build Momentum   318

TRY THIS 11.4: Write Periodic and Cumulative Sentences   319

Symmetry and Sense: Balance, Antithesis, and Parallelism   320

Parallel Structure: Put Parallel Information into Parallel Form   320

TRY THIS 11.5: Correct Errors in Parallelism   321

Two Powerful Forms of Parallelism: Antithesis and Chiasmus   321

"Official Style"   322

Finding the Action in a Sentence: "To Be" Or Not "To Be"   322

TRY THIS 11.6: Find Active Verbs in Your Sentences   324

Active and Passive Voice: Emphasizing the Doer or the Action   324

TRY THIS 11.7: Analyze the Effect of Passive Voice   325

TRY THIS 11.8: Write Passive and Active Voice Sentences   325

Expletives: Beginning with "It Is" or "There Is"   326

Concrete vs. Evaluative Adjectives and Intensifiers:
What's Bad About "Good" and "Bad"   326

Concrete and Abstract Diction   327

Latinate Diction 328

Etymology: Finding a Word's Physical History 329

TRY THIS 11.9: Tracing Word Histories 329

"Right" and "Wrong" Words: Shades of Meaning 330

Tone 331

TRY THIS 11.10: Analyze Prose with Questionable Tone 332

TRY THIS 11.11: Analyze Effective Tone 332

Bias-Free Language 332

Make Sure Identity Terms Used Are Relevant 332

Aim for Gender Neutrality 332

Be Specific 333

Show Respect via Terms Used and Their Capitalization and Styling 333

Avoid Pronouns That Exclude 333

Avoid Judgments 333

Check the Dictionary 333

The Politics of Language 334

Ethos, Audience, and Levels of Style 335

Transparent vs. Opaque Styles: Knowing When to Be Visible 335

The Person Question: When and When Not to Use "I" 336

VOICES FROM ACROSS THE CURRICULUM: Using the First-Person "I":
Two Professors Speak 337

VOICES FROM ACROSS THE CURRICULUM: Sentence Style in Science
Writing: A Biochemistry Professor Speaks 337

Formal vs. Colloquial Styles 338

The Problem of Inflated Diction 339

Jargon: When to Use Insider Language 339

Style Analysis: A Summary of Things to Look For 340

Assignments: Style: Choosing Words, Shaping Sentences 341

CHAPTER 12 343

Nine Basic Writing Errors (BWEs) and How to Fix Them 343

The Concept of Basic Writing Errors (BWEs) 343

Nine Basic Writing Errors 344

BWE 1: Sentence Fragments 345

Noun Clause (No Predicate) as a Fragment 345

Verbal as a Fragment 345

Subordinate Clause as a Fragment 346

Using Dashes and Colons to Correct Fragments 346

BWE 2: Comma Splices and Fused (or Run-On) Sentences 347

Comma Splice 347

Comma Splice 347

Cures for the Perpetual Comma Splicer 348

Fused (or Run-on) Sentence 348

Comma Splices with Conjunctive Adverbs 349

BWE 3: Errors in Subject–Verb Agreement 350
    Agreement Problem: Plural Subject, Singular Verb 350
    Agreement Problem: Singular Subject, Plural Verb 350
    Agreement Problem: "Each" Must Take Singular Verb 351
    A Note on Dialects and Standard Written English 351
BWE 4: Shifts in Sentence Structure (Faulty Predication) 352
    Faulty Predication 352
    Faulty Predication 352
BWE 5: Errors in Pronoun Reference 353
    Pronoun-Antecedent Agreement 353
    Pronoun Error: Plural Pronoun with Singular Antecedent 353
    Gender-Neutral "They" and Pronoun Usage 353
    Pronoun Error: Ambiguous Reference 354
    Pronoun Error: Broad Reference 355
BWE 6: Misplaced Modifiers and Dangling Participles 356
    Misplaced Modifier: Modifier Appears to Modify Wrong Word 356
    Misplaced Modifier: Modifier Appears to Modify Wrong Word 356
    Dangling Participle: Subject That Participle Modifies Does
        Not Appear in the Sentence 356
BWE 7: Errors in Using Possessive Apostrophes 357
    Apostrophe Error 357
    Apostrophe Error 357
BWE 8: Comma Errors 358
    Comma Error: Comma Missing After Introductory Phrase 358
    Comma Error: Comma Missing After Introductory Phrase 358
    Comma Error: Two Commas Needed Around Parenthetical Element 358
    A Note on Restrictive versus Nonrestrictive Elements 359
    Comma Error: Two Commas Needed Around Parenthetical Element 359
    Comma Error: Restrictive Elements Should Not Be Enclosed Within Commas 359
BWE 9: Spelling/Diction Errors That Interfere with Meaning 360
    Spelling/Diction Error: "It's" versus "Its" 360
    Spelling/Diction Error: "Their" versus "There" versus "They're" 361
    Spelling/Diction Error: "Then" versus "Than" 361
    Spelling/Diction Error: "Effect" vs. "Affect" 361
Correctness vs. Usage: Grammar Rules and Social Convention 362
    Usage: How Language Customs Change 362
    Usage: Examples of Right and Wrong vs. Etiquette 363
    When Usage Begins to Change Grammar 364
    Usage as Cultural Marker 365
        TRY THIS 12.1: Discover the Rationale for Usage Choices 366
Glossary of Grammatical Terms 366
Assignments: Nine Basic Writing Errors (BWEs) and How to Fix Them 370

APPENDIX 371

INDEX 378

PREFACE

Nearly three decades ago, we started writing the book that would become *Writing Analytically*. It is, as far as we know, still the only book-length text available focused on analytical writing. Analysis is not the only form of writing that students need to learn, but it is the one they will most often be called on to do in college and beyond. We continue to believe in the goal of helping students adopt analytical habits of mind, because we see this as the best way to help students become adults who are capable of sustained acts of reflection in a culture that doesn't sufficiently promote this goal.

Our aim in this book has been to evolve a common language for talking about writing, one that can move beyond the specialized vocabularies of different academic disciplines. We have worked to isolate and define the specific, writing-based cognitive skills that effective writers have at their disposal, skills that many students lack or simply don't recognize in their own thinking. These skills have become "the heuristics"—the moves and strategies—at the heart of the book.

Writing Analytically was something of an accident for us, one of those things you think will be a short detour in life that turns out to be a main road. The college at which we had just arrived was in the process of developing a Writing Across the Curriculum (WAC) program in which all faculty, not just English department faculty, would be teaching writing-intensive courses. Since we were the only ones on campus with training in writing pedagogy, we were asked to offer a week-long seminar for faculty on how to teach writing.

During the early years offering the seminar, we asked faculty to read the usual essays about writing that graduate students in English, Rhetoric, and Composition normally read. We asked our colleagues to freewrite about these materials and to keep a journal of their responses to the reading and to seminar discussion—and, if they were willing, to share these with us. And share they did. Their responses were filled with insecurity and self-doubt ("You want me to immerse myself in the welter of confusion that my students are experiencing as they try to learn?") and sometimes with anger ("So you want my students to sit in a circle and share their feelings about DNA?"). Prompted by this kind of honest talk across disciplinary lines, we started out on our project of studying what faculty wanted from student writing, and what students might not readily understand about the kinds of writing they were being asked to do in their college courses—something that our lives inside an English department might not have inspired us to do.

The clearest consensus we have found among college faculty is, in fact, on the kind of writing they say they want from their students: not issue-based argument, not personal reflection (the "reaction" paper), not passive summary, but analysis, with its patient and methodical inquiry into the meaning of information. Here, in brief, is what we have learned about what faculty want:

- Analysis rather than passive summary
- Analysis before argument: understanding in depth before taking a stand
- Alternatives to agree-disagree & like-dislike responses
- Tolerance of uncertainty
- Respect for complexity
- Ability to apply theories from reading, using them as lenses
- Ability to use secondary sources in ways other than plugging them in as "answers."

We also discovered that there was no common language out there for talking about analysis with students and faculty beyond the simple definition of dividing a subject into its parts. Books on writing tended to devote a chapter at most to the subject, and sometimes as little as a couple of paragraphs in a chapter on rhetorical modes. Brief guides on writing in particular subject areas (for example, writing about economics, writing about film) tended to do a better job of explaining analytical habits of mind. As useful as they are, however, these books don't easily help students recognize common methods and values, as they move from course to course and department to department.

Here, in brief, are some definitions of analysis that we have derived from our work with faculty across the curriculum:

- Analysis seeks to discover what something means. An analytical argument makes claims for how something might be best understood, and in what context.
- Analysis deliberately delays evaluation and judgment.
- Analysis begins in and values uncertainty rather than starting from settled convictions.
- Analytical arguments are usually pluralistic; they tend to try on more than one way of thinking about how something might be best understood.

But these definitions alone are not enough. We thought, and still do, that the key to improving students' writing is helping them to become more aware of their own habits of mind. We thought, and still do, that this was a matter of attitude, not just of skills and knowledge of rules about writing. We believed, and still do, that process-oriented pedagogy need not be implicitly Romantic in theory and practice, but could instead—in keeping with the ideas of John Dewey—be methodical, consisting of teachable mental activities that students could consciously develop and practice, both individually and together.

Going into its eighth edition, *Writing Analytically* has been through many changes, but it is still what we hoped it would be in the beginning: a process-oriented guide to analytical writing that can serve students' needs at different stages in their college careers and in different disciplines. We hope this new edition will continue to provide a basis for conversation—between faculty and students, between students and students, and, especially, between writers and their own writing. When students and teachers can share the means of idea production, class discussion and writing become better connected, and students can more easily learn to see that good ideas don't just happen—they're made.

New to This Edition

- The biggest change in this edition is a new chapter called "Thinking Like a Writer" (Chapter 5). The chapter's aim is to help writers become more confident about and more engaged with their own writing. After a brief review of the heuristics in the book's first four chapters, the chapter offers a variety of writing prompts including description-based observation exercises, ways of keeping a Writer's Notebook, and experiments with personal writing as a means of learning to use writing as a mode of inquiry. The emphasis throughout the chapter is on making the writing classroom a collaborative space. Toward that end, the chapter suggests alternatives to the usual ways of prompting revision and of working in groups with other writers.

- We have located the book's chapters in three units in order to better distinguish different phases of the writing process and different levels of concern. **Unit One** contains the book's primary observation heuristics along with definition of the aims and methods of analysis. **Unit Two** addresses issues relevant to writing analytical papers such as finding and developing a thesis, finding and evaluating sources, and putting sources into conversation in research-based writing. **Unit Three** explains forms and formats across the curriculum, basic writing errors and how to fix them, and ways of becoming more adept at seeing sentence shapes and understanding the impact of various style choices.

- We have relocated the "Interpretation" chapter (now Chapter 3) so that it comes immediately after and is better connected with the book's opening two chapters, "The Five Analytical Moves" and "Reading Analytically."

- We have rearranged the thesis chapter to better foreground its primary heuristic—the six steps for making a thesis evolve.

- We have extensively rewritten the chapter on research-based writing ("Conversing with Sources"), adding new and more accessible examples of effective student writing about sources.

- The chapter on finding, evaluating, and citing sources (including online sources) has been revised and updated by its author, a reference librarian.

- The table of contents more clearly flags each chapter's heuristics, "Try This" exercises, and "Voices from Across the Curriculum."

- There is now a two-page chart of many of the book's heuristics located inside the back cover.

- We have done what we could to correct infelicities of style and to make the book's explanations more concise—while still respecting students' need for rationale in support of our advice on how to become smarter, more observant, and more independent thinkers and writers.

How to Use This Book

For a quick introduction to the ideas and activities that the book offers, read the "Overview" paragraphs at the beginning of each chapter.

For a compact guide to the book's heuristics, see the two-page chart inside the back cover. *Writing Analytically* is activity-based; it offers a variety of ways to make writing happen in the classroom and to help students function collaboratively as learning communities.

To sample the kind of writing-to-learn assignments the book suggests, browse the "Try This" exercises dispersed throughout the book's chapters. These can be used to generate class discussion and as prompts for short writing assignments to be done in class or as homework.

There is also an extensive Instructor's Manual for *Writing Analytically* that is available to teachers of the book. It contains a wealth of materials on writing pedagogy as well as detailed discussions of how to work with each chapter in the book. If you are teaching the book, contact your Cengage representative to get access to a copy.

Although we assume that users of this book will most often wish to provide their own writing assignments and readings, we have provided writing assignments at the end of each chapter that can be adapted to various kinds of course content and various levels of student readiness for college writing. (*Writing Analytically with Readings*, 3rd edition, contains a series of analytical readings arranged into five thematic units.)

The following features of *Writing Analytically* should eliminate, in most cases, the need for an additional handbook:

- A concise but thorough guide to finding, evaluating, and citing sources—both print and digital (Chapter 9)

- A chapter with exercises, a punctuation guide, and a compact glossary of grammatical terms that teaches students how to recognize, understand, and correct nine basic writing errors (Chapter 12)

- A chapter on syntax and word choice that teaches students how to discern different sentence shapes and understand them not in terms of a single one-size-fits-all set of rules but as a range of options with different rhetorical effects (Chapter 11)

- A chapter on conversing with sources in research-based writing (Chapter 8)
- Extended discussion of various organizational schemes and discipline-specific formats across the curriculum (Chapters 6, 7, and 10).

Using Unit One: The Analytical Frame of Mind

Spend as much time as you can afford to spend on **Chapter 1** ("The Five Analytical Moves") and **Chapter 2** ("Reading Analytically"), giving students the necessary practice to make these chapters' observation heuristics habitual before moving on to the more paper-oriented focus of Unit Two. The rest of the book rests on the assumption that students have learned to apply these heuristics informally to everything they are asked to read and think about.

The primary goal of the heuristics is to habituate students to being more observant, less quick to move to judgments, and more able to move from observations to implications—which is not the same thing as selecting pieces of evidence solely for the purpose of supporting some single claim. These goals require hands-on practice. Students are asked to recognize that observation is not natural, but learned.

When students are first learning to do THE METHOD (looking for patterns of repetition and contrast), we often ask them to produce the lists and the single analytical paragraph that the exercise calls for as a regular homework assignment. In this way, they get repeated, low-stakes practice in thinking and writing analytically before being asked to present the results of their thinking in a more formal, thesis-driven or disciplinary format-driven mode.

For those instructors who need to assign papers from an early point in the semester, the writing prompts that are part of the heuristics called THE METHOD and NOTICE & FOCUS in Chapter 1 can easily generate a series of short papers.

The heuristics in Chapter 2, form a sequence that students can use with reading that they are asked to prepare for class: Commonplace Book, POINTING, PARAPHRASE × 3, PASSAGE-BASED FOCUSED FREEWRITING, FINDING THE PITCH AND THE COMPLAINT, UNCOVERING ASSUMPTIONS, REFORMULATING BINARIES.

As these practices become habitual, students become increasingly comfortable doing the work for themselves, rather than expecting teachers to explain the readings and other course materials for them. The chapter's heuristics, like others in the book, help students learn to find their own starting points for writing and discussion, which we think is an important skill for them to learn as part of learning to write.

Chapter 3, "Interpretation," follows from and further develops the move from observation to implication stressed in Chapters 1 and 2. The chapter answers two questions: What makes some interpretations better than others? and What makes interpretation more than a matter of opinion? The chapter's primary concept is that interpretation always takes place within some context that a conscientious writer takes care to specify along with the writer's reasons for choosing it.

Chapter 4, "Responding to Traditional Writing Assignments More Analytically," shows students how to achieve greater analytical depth on traditional kinds of college writing topics, such as summary, comparison/contrast, and personal response. See, for example, the heuristic we call DIFFERENCE WITHIN SIMILARITY for sharpening the focus of comparing and contrasting.

Chapter 5, "Thinking Like a Writer" (new to this edition) offers a variety of writing assignments and exercises designed to encourage students to use the writing process as a source of ideas and personal growth. The chapter contains projects, such as keeping a Writer's Notebook (not the same thing as a diary or a journal) and doing descriptive (observational) freewriting. The assignment at the end of this chapter, "Writing a Literacy Narrative," is one that many writing courses start with. This chapter also contains rubrics for students' self-evaluation and offers two formats for conducting small group peer review that rely on description rather than critique.

Using Unit Two: Writing the Analytical Paper

Early in a writing course, while students are learning to use the heuristics in Unit One, you might have students read about and try in **Chapter 6** ("Reasoning from Evidence to Claims") the practice we call 10 on 1 (saying 10 things about a single, representative example) as an alternative to 1 on 10—attaching the same, usually overly general claim to a series of examples. The chapter offers alternatives to rigidly deductive formats (such as five-paragraph form) that inhibit analyzing evidence in depth. The chapter explains the problem with mustering evidence only in order to prove that "I am right."

Chapter 7, "Finding and Developing a Thesis," confronts the idea that a thesis is an unchanging (static) claim and shows students how to use complicating evidence to make a thesis evolve. The chapter emphasizes the importance of qualifying claims. This orientation toward thesis-driven writing is challenging for students, and so we usually delay teaching it until students have learned in Unit One how to use writing in order to arrive at ideas. A good way to ease students into the methods prescribed in this chapter (under "Six Ways of Making a Thesis Evolve") is to have them track the evolution of a thesis in things they are reading.

Chapter 8, "Conversing with Sources," offers alternatives to agreeing or disagreeing with sources and to plugging them in as answers. It shows students how to do more than simply assemble sources in support of (or against) some point of view. A good place to start is to ask them to choose a single sentence from source A and a single sentence from source B and use these to determine what each author would say to the point of view implicit in the other's statement.

Chapter 9, "Finding, Evaluating and Citing Sources," was written by a college reference librarian, Kelly Cannon. It takes students on a tour of the research process, introducing them to useful indexes and bibliographies, showing them how to evaluate the relative value of both print and online sources, and explaining the logic of standard citation methods. Students can use this chapter just as they would use a handbook in order to cite sources according to the most recent citation guidelines in MLA, AP, Chicago, and CSE Styles. The chapter aims to make sense of the increasingly complex world of information in which students find themselves.

Using Unit Three: Matters of Form

Chapter 10, "From Paragraphs to Papers: Forms and Formats Across the Curriculum," helps students see both the logic and the heuristic value of disciplinary formats such as IMRAD (the report format required in the natural and social sciences). The chapter emphasizes common denominators among the methods of organization prescribed in disciplines across the curriculum. The chapter also offers practical help with introductions, conclusions, and paragraph development.

Chapter 11, "Style: Choosing Words, Shaping Sentences," teaches students how to look at sentences as the shapes that thought takes. The chapter gives students the vocabulary they need in order to analyze sentences and begin to think about what makes a sentence good. Rather than prescribing one set of style rules, the chapter shows students how to think in terms of the effects of various stylistic choices. The chapter explains, for example, that whatever comes at the end of a sentence tends to get the most emphasis, which offers a useful revision guideline.

Chapter 12, "Nine Basic Writing Errors (BWEs) and How to Fix Them," offers students a self-help guide to finding and correcting errors in grammar and punctuation. The chapter offers proofreading advice based on Mina Shaughnessy's concepts of hierarchy of error, pattern of error, and logic of error.

About the Authors

David Rosenwasser and Jill Stephen are professors of English at Muhlenberg College in Allentown, Pennsylvania. They teach writing, rhetoric, and literature and have co-directed Muhlenberg's Writing Across the Curriculum (WAC) Program and Writing Center for many years. David started teaching as a graduate student at the University of Virginia and then at the College of William and Mary. Jill started teaching as a graduate student at New York University and then at Hunter College (CUNY). They have offered seminars on writing and writing instruction to faculty and graduate students across the country, and they regularly teach a semester-long training course to undergraduates preparing to serve as peer tutors in their college's Writing Center and as Writing Assistants embedded in first-year seminars.

Acknowledgments

We owe much to the conversations about writing we have had over the years with colleagues and to their ongoing support of us and our book. Without

Christine Farris's early support, we might not have gotten through the long process of turning our ideas into a book. Without Christine's adoption of the book for the first-year writing program she directed at Indiana University, Writing Analytically might not have lasted beyond its first edition. Thanks also to John Schilb and Ted Leahey at Indiana and to the teachers across the state of Indiana who use our book for the dual credit writing course they offer in high schools.

Colleagues in the Writing Program at The Ohio State University offered us many learning opportunities during the years our book has served the university's first-year writing course. Thanks especially to Scott DeWitt, Wendy Hesford, and Eddie and Lynn Singleton, whom we count as both colleagues and friends.

In recent years, we have benefitted from and greatly enjoyed our collaborations with Noreen Groover Lape and Sarah Kersh at Dickinson College, where Noreen is Director of the Writing Program and Writing Center, and with Janet Carl, Director of the Writing Lab at Grinnell College, and her colleague in the English Department, Tim Arner. They are inspired and inspiring program directors and teachers.

We thank the faculty members at Dickinson, Grinnell, Kenyon (especially Jeanne Griggs, who brought us there to present to the Center for Innovative Pedagogy), Ramapo (with special thanks to Todd Barnes for inviting us to speak at the college), Indiana University, Ohio State, and at our own college, Muhlenberg, who have participated in our writing workshops over the years. They asked the questions we needed to hear.

We appreciate Jill Gladstein, who directs the Writing Associates Program at Swarthmore College, for her friendship and support and for her invention and nurturing of the Small Liberal Arts College-Writing Program Administrators consortium (SLAC), where we have had the opportunity to learn from colleagues who direct writing programs at small liberal arts colleges across the country.

We owe special thanks to present and past members of the Writing Program Committee at Muhlenberg College, including Chris Borick, Keri Colabroy, Ted Conner, Jessica Cooperman, Amy Corbin, Will Gyrc, Brian Mello, Pearl Rosenberg, Jordanna Sprayberry, and Lynda Yankaskas. Thanks as well to Provost Kathleen Harring for her continued support of the Writing Program, and to Dean Bruce Anderson for his generous support of travel grants for our tutors.

The cross-curricular dimension of this book would be sadly impoverished without the interest and support of our faculty colleagues who participate in the writing cohort at our college, many of whom are included in the Voices from Across the Curriculum boxes in the book. These colleagues (along with those on the Writing Program Committee) have shared with us examples of good student and professional writing in their fields, writing assignments from their writing-intensive classes, examples of their own writing, and responses to our question on what constitutes an analytical question. These colleagues include James Bloom, Susan Clemens-Bruder, Karen Dearborn, Daniel Doviak, Laura Edelman, Joseph Elliott, Chuck French, Jack Gambino, Barri Gold, William Gruen, Kimberley Heiman, Daniel Leisawitz, Dawn Lonsinger, John Malsberger, Eileen McEwan, Linda McGuire, Holmes Miller, Matt Moore, Marcia Morgan, Richard Niesenbaum, Dustin Nash, Jim Peck, Jefferson Pooley, Tad Robinson, Danielle Sanchez, Grant Scott, Beth Schachter, Jeremy Teissere, Alan Tjeltveit, Kevin Tuttle, and Bruce Wightman. We are also grateful to Katherine Kibblinger Gottschalk of Cornell University for permission to quote her paper on the correspondence of E. B. White.

For significant contributions to our book we offer much thanks to Kelly Cannon, reference librarian at Muhlenberg, for his chapter on finding, evaluating, and citing sources; to Keri Colabroy, for her contributions on writing in the natural sciences to our chapter on forms and formats across the curriculum, and for her amazing distillation of our book's heuristics into a two-page chart; to Chris Borick, for helping us clarify our thinking on thesis evolution in deductive writing and for writing an entertaining and informative guide to political labels for our essay anthology, *Writing Analytically with Readings*; to Sarah Kersh, for her writing and drawing, for her excellent work on the Instructor's Manual for *Writing Analytically*, and for her research on analytical essays for *Writing Analytically with Readings* (along with Robert Saenz di Viteri); and to the many faculty colleagues who have contributed their thinking on writing for the Voices Across the Curriculum pieces in the book.

We are grateful to our students, especially those who serve as peer tutors in Muhlenberg's Writing Center and in first-year seminars and upper-level writing courses at the college. We appreciate their enthusiasm, their integrity, and their dedication to writers and writing, and we admire the excellent research a number of them have done and presented at the International Writing Center Association's annual conferences. Special thanks go to students and former students who have recently contributed their writing to our book: Emily Casey, Kate O'Donoghue, James Patefield, Patrick C. Smith, Steven Poirier, Anna Whiston.

We benefitted much from the guidance of many people at Cengage. For this edition, we wish to thank Laura Ross, Leslie Taggart, Alison Duncan, Lynn Huddon, Aimee Bear, Mary Stone, and especially Elinor Gregory. Thanks as well to past editors who contributed much to previous editions: Karl Yambert, Dickson Musslewhite, Margaret Leslie, Michael Rosenberg, Aron Keesbury, John Meyers, Michell Phifer, and Karen R. Smith.

We cannot forget our longtime friends and inspiring colleagues from whom we have learned so much: Richard Louth, Dean Ward, Kenny Marotta, and Emily Stockton-Brown.

Over the past seven years, we could not have managed without the intelligence, resourcefulness, tact, and good humor of Brian Borosky, who served as Writing Assistant in each of our first-year seminars while he was an undergraduate, and who served for three years after graduation as Assistant Director of the Writing Center, in which role he essentially co-directed the Muhlenberg writing program with us—mentoring and managing our staff of fifty peer tutors, directing student research, soliciting and directing the review process for first-year seminars, assigning tutors to faculty members, arranging students' participation at national conferences, and more. We wish him all the best in graduate school and in wherever that and his many talents lead him.

We wish to dedicate this edition of the book to the memory of our friend and colleague, Linda Bips, who, as Professor of Psychology and Writing Program Liaison for Student Development, tirelessly supported us and our tutors, helping them to shape their research on tutoring practices and keeping them calm in the face of the inevitable pressures of working closely with faculty and students on writing. Linda always knew the right thing to say. We will never forget her mantra for working collaboratively with others: silence is the sound of people thinking.

Special thanks to our families: Elizabeth Rosenwasser, and Lesley and Sarah Stephen.

We would also like to thank the colleagues who reviewed the book; we are grateful for their insights:

Jared Abraham, Weatherford College
Diann Ainsworth, Weatherford College
Todd Barnes, Ramapo College of New Jersey
Darla Branda, Stephens College
Lisa Johnson, Casper College
Gary Leising, Utica College
Steven Plunkett, Brandeis University
Erika Sutherland, Muhlenberg College
Geoffrey Trumbo, Louisiana State University
Afton Wilky, Louisiana State University

Online Resources

MindTap® English for Rosenwasser/Stephen, *Writing Analytically*, 8th Edition, is the digital learning solution that powers students from memorization to mastery. It gives you complete control of your course—to provide engaging content, and to challenge every individual and build their confidence. Empower students to accelerate their progress with MindTap. MindTap: Powered by You.

MindTap gives you complete ownership of your content and learning experience. Customize the interactive assignments, emphasize the most important topics, and add your own material or notes in the eBook.

- Interactive activities on grammar and mechanics promote application to student writing.
- An easy-to-use paper management system helps prevent plagiarism and allows for electronic submission, grading, and peer review.

- A vast database of scholarly sources with video tutorials and examples supports every step of the research process.
- A collection of vetted, curated student writing samples in various modes and documentation styles to use as flexible instructional tools.
- Professional tutoring guides students from rough drafts to polished writing.
- Visual analytics track student progress and engagement.
- Seamless integration into your campus learning management system keeps all your course materials in one place.
- Additional thematic readings with questions for analysis.
- Downloadable worksheets for in-class activities or homework.

MindTap® English comes equipped with the diagnostic-guided JUST IN TIME PLUS learning module for foundational concepts and embedded course support. The module features scaffolded video tutorials, instructional text content, and auto-graded activities designed to address each student's specific needs for practice and support to succeed in college-level composition courses.

The Resources for Teaching folder provides support materials to facilitate an efficient course setup process focused around your instructional goals: the MindTap Planning Guide offers an inventory of MindTap activities correlated to common planning objectives, so that you can quickly determine what you need. The MindTap Syllabus offers an example of how these activities could be incorporated into a 16-week course schedule. The *Instructor's Manual* provides suggestions for additional activities and assignments.

UNIT 1

The Analytical Frame of Mind

CHAPTER 1

The Five Analytical Moves

Overview   In this chapter, we define analysis and explain why it is the kind of writing you will most often be asked to do in college and beyond. We explain the characteristics that college teachers look for in student writing and the changes in orientation this kind of writing requires: the analytical frame of mind. The chapter identifies the counterproductive habits of mind most likely to block good writing and offers in their place the book's first set of strategies for becoming a more observant and more confident writer: Notice & Focus, free-writing, Asking "So What?," and The Method. These strategies are embedded in a discussion of what we call the Five Analytical Moves.

Writing as a Tool of Thought

Of all the skills you acquire as a writer and thinker, analysis is likely to have the greatest impact on the way you learn. This is so because the more that you write analytically, the more actively and patiently you will think. The patience comes from recognizing that ideas and understanding are a product not just of sudden flashes of insight but of specific mental skills. Thinking is a process, an activity. Ideas don't just happen; they are made.

This book will make you much more aware of your own acts of thinking and will show you how to experiment more deliberately with ways of arriving at ideas—for example, by sampling kinds of informal and exploratory writing that will enhance your ability to learn. As the next few chapters will show, the analytical process consists of a fairly limited set of basic moves. People who think well have these moves at their disposal, whether they are aware of using them or not. *Writing Analytically* describes and gives names to these moves, which are activities you can practice and use systematically in order to become a more confident, more resourceful, and more independent thinker and writer.

Learning to write well means more than learning to organize information in appropriate forms and to construct clear and correct sentences. Learning to write well means learning ways of using writing in order to think well. This means that writing can make you smarter. But first, you have to learn to feel comfortable with the activity. Since so much writing instruction concentrates on what writers do wrong, it is difficult for many people to find the necessary level of comfort and trust to make writing happen. Clearly, rules governing matters of form are important, and we will have much to say about these in the third part of this book, but rules governing such things as paper organization and style don't easily translate into the ability to get words onto the page in the first place—the stage of writing that classical rhetoric called "invention."

In classical rhetoric, procedures and forms that served as aids to discovery were called "heuristics." The term comes from the Greek word *heuriskein*, which means "to find out" or "to discover." This book's analytical methods, such as the ones you will find in this chapter, are heuristics. These offer alternatives to what might be called the light bulb theory of inspiration, wherein ideas simply come to people, like a light bulb turning on in their heads. Writers do, of course, sometimes have ideas in this way—suddenly and unexpectedly and seemingly with little conscious effort. But, as we hope to show, this is more often the exception than the rule.

Why Faculty Want Analysis

For over two decades, we've co-directed a Writing Across the Curriculum program in which writing is taught by our colleagues from all the other disciplines. They have helped us to see why analysis is what they expect from student writing. They want analysis because of the attitudes toward learning that come along with it—the way it teaches learners to cultivate curiosity, to tolerate uncertainty, to respect complexity, and to seek to understand a subject before they attempt to make arguments about it.

Overall, what faculty want is for students to learn to do things with course material beyond merely reporting it on the one hand, and just reacting to it (often through like-dislike, agree-disagree responses) on the other (see Figure 1.1). This is the issue that *Writing Analytically* addresses: how to locate a middle ground between passive summary and personal response. That middle ground is occupied by analysis.

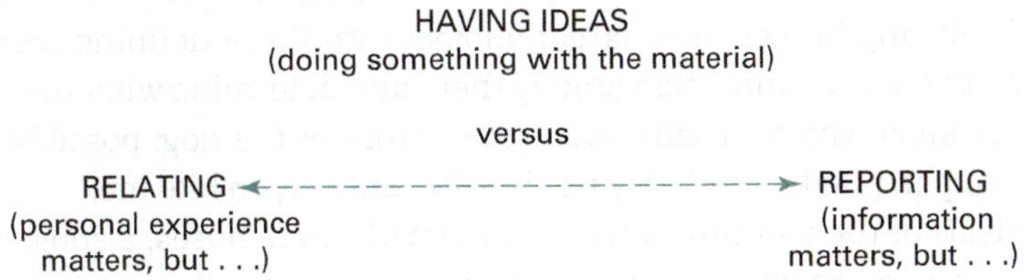

HAVING IDEAS
(doing something with the material)

versus

RELATING ◄ – ► REPORTING
(personal experience   (information
matters, but . . .)   matters, but . . .)

FIGURE 1.1
What Faculty Want from Student Writing

Analysis Is a Search for Meaning

To analyze something is to ask what that something means. It is to ask how something does what it does or why it is as it is. Analysis is a form of detective work. It typically pursues something puzzling, something you are seeking to understand rather than something you believe you already have the answers to. Analysis finds questions where there seemed not to be any, and it makes connections that might not have been evident at first. Analysis is, then, more than just a set of skills: it is a frame of mind, an attitude toward experience.

Analysis is the kind of thinking you'll most often be asked to do in college, the mainstay of serious thought. Yet it's also among the most common of our mental activities. The fact is that most people already analyze all of the time, but they often don't realize that this is what they're doing.

If, for example, you find yourself being followed by a large dog, your first response—other than breaking into a cold sweat—will be to analyze the situation. What does being followed by a large dog mean for me, here, now? Does it mean the dog is vicious and about to attack? Does it mean the dog is curious and wants to play? Similarly, if you are losing at a game of tennis, have just left a job interview, or are looking at a large painting of a woman with three noses, you will begin to analyze. How can I play differently to increase my chances of winning? Am I likely to get the job, and why or why not? Why did the artist give the woman three noses?

Analysis Does More than Break a Subject into Its Parts

Whether you are analyzing an awkward social situation, an economic problem, a painting, a substance in a chemistry lab, or your chances of succeeding in a job interview, the process of analysis is the same:

- Divide the subject into its defining parts, its main elements or ingredients.
- Consider how these parts are related, both to each other and to the subject as a whole.

In the case of the large dog, for example, you might notice that he's dragging a leash, has a ball in his mouth, and is wearing a bright red scarf around his neck. Having broken your larger subject into these defining parts, you would try to see the connection among them and determine what they mean, what they allow you to decide about the nature of the dog: possibly somebody's lost pet, playful, probably not hostile, unlikely to bite me.

Analysis of the painting of the woman with three noses, a subject more like the kind you might be asked to write about in a college course, would proceed in the same way. Your end result—ideas about the nature of the painting—would be determined, as with the dog, not only by noticing its various parts, but by your familiarity with the subject. If you knew little about painting, scrutiny of its parts would not tell you, for instance, that it is an example of the movement called "cubism." You would, however, still be able to draw some analytical conclusions—ideas about the meaning and nature of the subject. You might conclude, for example, that the artist is interested in perspective or in the way we see, as opposed to being interested in realistic depictions of the world.

One common denominator of all effective analytical writing is that it pays close attention to detail. We analyze because our global responses, say, to a play or a speech or a social problem are too general. If you try, for example, to comment on an entire football game, you'll find yourself saying things like "great game," which is a generic response, something you could say about almost anything. This "one-size-fits-all" comment doesn't tell us very much except that you probably liked the game.

In order to say more, you would necessarily become more analytical—shifting your attention to the significance of some important piece of the game as a whole—such as "they won because the offensive line was giving the quarterback all day to find his receivers" or "they lost because they couldn't defend against the safety blitz." This move from generalization to analysis, from the larger subject to its key components, is a characteristic of the way we think. In order to understand a subject, we need to discover what it is "made of," the particulars that contribute most strongly to the character of the whole.

If all analysis did was take subjects apart, leaving them broken and scattered, the activity would not be worth very much. The student who presents a draft to their professor with the encouraging words, "Go ahead, rip it apart," reveals a disabling misconception about analysis—that, like dissecting a frog in a biology lab, analysis takes the life out of its subjects.

Analysis means more than breaking a subject into its parts. When you analyze a subject, you ask not just "What is it made of?" but also "How do these parts help me to understand the meaning of the subject as a whole?" A good analysis seeks to locate the life of its subject, the aims and ideas that energize it.

Distinguishing Analysis from Summary, Expressive Writing, and Argument

How does analysis differ from other kinds of thinking and writing? A common way of answering this question is to think of communication as having three possible centers of emphasis: the writer, the subject, and the audience. Communication, of course, involves all three of these components, but some kinds of writing concentrate more on one than on the others (see Figure 1.2). Autobiographical writing, for example, such as diaries or memoirs or stories about personal experience, centers on the writer and the writer's desire for self-expression. Argument, in which the writer takes a stand on an issue, advocating or arguing for or against a policy or attitude, is reader-centered; its goal is to bring about a change in its readers' actions and beliefs. Analytical writing is more concerned with arriving at an understanding of a subject than it is with either self-expression or changing readers' views.

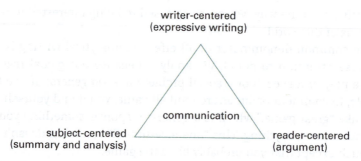

writer-centered
(expressive writing)

communication

subject-centered
(summary and analysis)

reader-centered
(argument)

FIGURE 1.2

The Communication Triangle

These three categories of writing are not mutually exclusive. For example, expressive (writer-centered) writing is also analytical in its attempts to define and explain a writer's feelings, reactions, and experiences. Analysis is a form of self-expression because it inevitably reflects the ways a writer's experiences have taught him or her to think about the world. Similarly, analysis is a close cousin of argument in its emphasis on logic and the dispassionate scrutiny of ideas ("What do I think about what I think?"). But as we shall see, analysis and argument are not the same.

Analysis and Summary

One of the most common kinds of writing you'll be asked to do in college, in addition to analysis, is summary. Summary differs from analysis, because the aim of summary is to recount in reduced form someone else's ideas. But summary and analysis are also clearly related and usually operate together. Summary is important to analysis, because you can't analyze a subject without laying out its significant parts for your reader. Similarly, analysis is important to summary, because summarizing is more than just shortening someone else's writing. To write an accurate summary, ask analytical questions such as:

- Which of the ideas in the reading are most significant? Why?

- How do these ideas fit together? What do the key passages in the reading mean?

Like an analysis, an effective summary doesn't assume that the subject matter can speak for itself: the writer needs to play an active role. A good summary provides perspective on the subject as a whole by explaining, as an analysis does, the meaning and function of each of that subject's parts. So, summary, like analysis, is a tool of understanding and not just a mechanical task. But a summary stops short of analysis because summary typically makes much smaller interpretive leaps.

Laying out the data is key to any kind of analysis, not simply because it keeps the analysis accurate but also because, crucially, it is *in the act of carefully describing a subject that analytical writers often have their best ideas*. The writer who can offer a careful description of a subject's key features is likely to arrive at conclusions about possible meanings that others would share.

Here are two guidelines to be drawn from this discussion of analysis and summary:

1. Describe with care. The words you choose to summarize your data will contain the germs of your ideas about what the subject means.

2. In moving from summary to analysis, scrutinize your language, asking "Why did I choose this word?" and "What ideas are implicit in the language I have chosen?"

Analysis and Expressive Writing

At their extremes, analysis and expressive writing differ significantly in method and aim. The extreme version of expressive writing focuses on the self, with other subjects serving only to evoke greater self-understanding. The extreme version of analytical writing banishes the "I" and, although its insights may derive from personal experience, it foregrounds the writer's reasoning, not the writer's experiences.

In practice, though, the best versions of analysis and expressive writing can overlap a lot. Although most analytical writing done in the academic disciplines is about a subject other than the self, all writing is, in a sense, personal, because there is an "I" doing the thinking and selecting the details to consider.

Virtually all forms of description are implicitly analytical. When you choose what you take to be the three most telling details about your subject, you have selected significant parts and used them as a means of getting at what you take to be the character of the whole. This is what analysis does: it goes after an understanding of what something means, its nature, by zeroing in on the function of significant detail.

Analysis and Argument

Analysis and argument proceed in the same way. They offer evidence, make claims about it, and supply reasons that explain and justify the claims. In other words, in both analysis and argument you respond to the questions "What have you got to go on?" (evidence) and "How did you get there?" (the principles and reasons that caused you to conclude what you did about the evidence).

Although analysis and argument proceed in essentially the same way, they differ in the kinds of questions they try to answer. Argument, at its most dispassionate, asks, "What can be said with truth about x or y?" In common practice, though, the kinds of questions that argument more often answers are more committed and directive, such as "Which is better, x or y?"; "How can we best achieve x or y?"; and "Why should we stop doing x or y?"

Analysis, by contrast, asks, "What does x or y mean?" In analysis, the evidence (your data) is something you wish to understand, and the claims are assertions about what that evidence means. The claim that an analysis makes is usually a tentative answer to a *what, how,* or *why* question; it seeks to explain why people watch professional wrestling, or what a rising number of sexual harassment cases might mean, or how certain features of government health care policy are designed to allay the fears of the middle class.

The claim that an argument makes, however, is often an answer to a *should* question. For example, readers should or shouldn't vote for bans on smoking in public buildings, or they should or shouldn't believe that gays can function effectively in the military. The writer of an analysis is more concerned with discovering how each of these complex subjects might be defined and explained than with convincing readers to approve or disapprove of them.

Analysis versus Debate-Style Argument Many of you may have been introduced to writing arguments through the debate model—arguing for or against a given position, with the aim of defeating an imagined opponent and convincing your audience of the rightness of your position. The agree/disagree mode of writing and thinking that you often see in editorials, hear on radio or television, and even practice sometimes in school may incline you to focus all your energy on the bottom line—aggressively advancing a claim for or against some view—without first engaging in the exploratory interpretation of evidence that is so necessary to arriving at thoughtful arguments. But as the *American College Dictionary* says, "to argue implies reasoning or trying to understand; it does not necessarily imply opposition." It is this more exploratory, tentative, and dispassionate mode of argument that this book encourages you to practice. It sounds more civil, more open-minded, and more educated—and it usually is.

Adhering to the more restrictive, debate-style definition of argument can create problems for careful analytical writers:

1. By requiring writers to be oppositional, it inclines them to discount or dismiss problems on the side or position they have chosen; they cling to the same static position rather than testing it as a way of allowing it to evolve.

2. It inclines writers toward either/or thinking rather than encouraging them to formulate more qualified (carefully limited, acknowledging exceptions, etc.) positions that integrate apparently opposing viewpoints.

3. It overvalues convincing someone else at the expense of developing understanding.

If you approach an argument with the primary goals of convincing others that you are right and defeating your opponents, you may neglect the more important goal of arriving at a fair and accurate assessment of your subject. In fact, you will be able to argue much more effectively from evidence if you first take the time to really consider what that evidence means and, thereby, to find valid positions to argue about it.

Ethos and Analysis Analysis, as we have been arguing, is interested in how we come to know things, how we make meaning. This focus privileges not just conclusions about a subject, but also sharing with readers the thought process that led to those conclusions. Rather than telling other people what to think, the best analytical writers encourage readers to think collaboratively with them. This is true of the best writers in the civic forum as well as in colleges and universities.

It follows that the character of the speaker (*ethos*) in an analysis will serve to create a more collaborative and collegial relationship with readers than might be the case in other kinds of writing.

Classical rhetoric thought of the impact that writers/speakers had on audiences in terms of three categories: *logos, pathos,* and *ethos.* The word *logos* (from Greek) refers to the logical component of a piece of writing or speaking. *Pathos* refers to the emotional component in writing—the ways that it appeals to feelings in an audience. *Ethos* may be familiar to you as a term because of its relation to the word "ethics." In classical rhetoric, *ethos* is the character of the speaker, which is important in determining an audience's acceptance or rejection of the speaker's arguments.

Much of this book is concerned with the *logos* of academic writing, with ways of deriving and arguing ideas in colleges, universities, and the world of educated discourse. *Ethos* matters too. The thinking you do is difficult to separate from the sense the audience has of the person doing the thinking. In fact, the personae (versions of ourselves) we assume when we write have a formative impact on what we think and say. *Ethos* is not just a mask we assume in order to appeal to a particular audience. The stylistic and thinking moves prescribed by the *ethos* of particular groups become, with practice, part of who we are and thus of how we think and interact with others.

Eventually, college writers need to learn how to adopt different self-representations for different academic disciplines. So the acceptable *ethos* of a chemistry lab report differs in significant ways from the one you might adopt in a political science or English paper. Nevertheless, in most academic disciplines, *ethos* is characterized by the following traits:

- nonadversarial tone—not looking for a fight
- collaborative and collegial—treats readers as colleagues worthy of respect who share your interest
- carefully qualified—not making overstated claims
- relative impersonality in self-presentation—keeps focus primarily on the subject, not the writer.

Counterproductive Habits of Mind

Analysis, we have been suggesting, is a frame of mind, a set of habits for observing and making sense of the world. There is also, it is fair to say, an anti-analytical frame of mind with its own set of habits. These habits shut down perception and arrest potential ideas at the cliché stage. Having ideas depends on noticing things in a subject that we wish to better understand rather than glossing things over with a quick and too-easy understanding.

The nineteenth-century poet, Emily Dickinson, wrote that "Perception of an object/Costs precise the object's loss." When we leap prematurely to our perceptions about a thing, we place a filter between ourselves and the "object," shrinking the amount and kinds of information that can get through to our minds and our senses. The point of the Dickinson poem is a paradox—that the ideas we arrive at deprive us of material with which to have more ideas. We have to be careful about leaping to conclusions, because if we are not careful, this move will lead to a form of mental blindness—loss of the object.

Here, then, are the four habits that most interfere with analysis—along with explanations of why they are a problem, and some suggestions for how to unlearn them.

THE PROBLEM

leaps to

data ———→ evaluative claims (like/dislike; agree/disagree)

leaps to

data (words, images, other detail) ———→ broad generalization

Habit: The Judgment Reflex

In its most primitive form—most automatic and least thoughtful—judging is like an on/off switch. When the switch gets thrown in one direction or the other, the resulting judgment predetermines and over-directs any subsequent thinking we might do. Rather than thinking about what X is or how X operates, we lock ourselves prematurely into proving that we were right to think that X should be banned or supported.

The psychologist Carl Rogers has written at length on this problem of the judgment reflex. He claims that our habitual tendency as humans—virtually a programmed response—is to evaluate everything and do so very quickly.

When people leap to judgment, they usually land in the mental pathways they've grown accustomed to traveling, guided by family or friends or popular opinion. The fact that you liked or didn't like a movie probably says more about you—your tastes, interests, biases, and experiences—than it does about the movie. What makes a movie boring: that it doesn't have enough car chases? that its plot resembles half the plots on cable channels? that the leading man was miscast, or the dialogue was too longwinded? At the very least, in such cases, you'd need to share with readers your *criteria* for judgment—your reasons and your standards of evaluation.

This is not to say that all judging should be avoided—only delayed. A writer needs to take into account how the writer's judgment has been affected by the details of a situation (context) and to acknowledge how thinking about these details has led to restricting (qualifying) the range of the judgment: X is sometimes true in these particular circumstances. Z is probably the right thing to do but only when A and B occur.

As a general rule, try to figure out what your subject means before deciding how you feel about it. If you can break the judgment reflex and press yourself to analyze before judging a subject, you will often be surprised at how much your initial responses change.

Cures for the Judgment Reflex

- Become conscious of the like/dislike switch in your thinking, and try to avoid it altogether.
- Neither agree nor disagree with another person's position until you can repeat that position in a way the other person would accept as fair and accurate. Carl Rogers recommends this strategy to negotiators in industry and government.
- Try eliminating the word "should" from your vocabulary for a while. Judgments often take the form of *should* statements.
- Try eliminating evaluative adjectives—those that offer judgments with no data.

"Jagged" is a descriptive, concrete adjective. It offers something we can experience. "Beautiful" is an evaluative adjective. It offers only judgment. Sometimes the concrete-abstract divide is complicated. Consider for example the word "green," a literal color with figurative associations (envious, innocent, ecological, etc.).

TRY THIS 1.1: Experiment with Adjectives and Adverbs

Write a paragraph of description on anything that comes to mind without using evaluative adjectives or adverbs. Alternatively, analyze and categorize the adjectives and adverbs in a piece of your own recent writing, a book review, or an editorial.

Habit: Naturalizing Our Assumptions (Overpersonalizing)

The word "naturalize" in this context means we are representing—and seeing— our own assumptions as natural, as simply the way things are *and ought to be*. "Individualism is good." Even on a lifeboat where collaboration is necessary to survive? "People are entitled to their own opinions." Even if those opinions belittle others and express hatred and aim to provoke violence? Writers who naturalize their own assumptions—a version of the judgment reflex—tend to make personal experiences and prejudices an *unquestioned* standard of value.

It is surprisingly difficult to break the habit of treating our points of view as self-evidently true—not just for us, but for everyone. The overpersonalizer assumes that because they experience or believe X, everyone else does, too. But what is "common sense" for one person, and so not even in need of explaining, can be quite uncommon and not so obviously sensible to someone else. More often than not, "common sense" is a phrase that really means "what seems obvious to me and therefore should be obvious to you."

VOICES FROM ACROSS THE CURRICULUM

Arguments vs. Opinions: A Political Scientist Speaks

Writers need to be aware of the distinction between an argument, which seeks support from evidence, and mere opinions and assertions. People too often assume that in politics one opinion is as good as another. (Tocqueville thought this was a peculiarly democratic disease.) From this perspective, any position a person might take on controversial issues is simply his or her opinion to be accepted or rejected by another person's beliefs/prejudices. The key task, therefore, is not so much the substitution of knowledge for opinions, but substituting well-constructed arguments for unexamined opinions. An argument presupposes a willingness to engage with others. To the extent that a writer operates on the assumption that everything is in the end an opinion, they have no reason to construct arguments; they are locked into an opinion.

— JACK GAMBINO, PROFESSOR OF POLITICAL SCIENCE

Habit: Generalizing

"What it all boils down to is . . ."; "What this adds up to is . . ."; "The gist of her speech was . . ." We generalize from our experience because this is one way of arriving at ideas. The problem with generalizing as a habit of mind is that it removes the mind—usually much too quickly—from the data that produced the generalization in the first place.

Most of us tend to remember our global impressions and reactions. The dinner was dull. The house was beautiful. The music was exciting. But we forget the specific, concrete causes of these impressions (if we ever fully noticed them). As a result, we deprive ourselves of material to think with—the data that might allow us to reconsider our initial impressions or to share them with others.

The problem comes when generalizations omit supporting details. Consider for a moment what you are really asking others to do when you offer them a generalization such as "The proposed changes in immigration policy are a disaster." Unless the recipients of this observation ask a question—such as "Why do you think so?"—they are being required to take your word for it: the changes are a disaster because you say so.

What happens instead if you offer a few details that cause you to think as you do? Clearly, you are on riskier ground. Your listener might think that the details you cite lead to different conclusions and a different reading of the data, but at least conversation has become possible.

Cures for the Problem of Generalizing

- The simplest antidote to the problem of generalizing is to train yourself to be more conscious of where your generalizations come from. *Press yourself to trace your general impressions back to the particulars that caused them.* Deciding to become more aware of your own responses to the world and their causes counteracts the inevitable numbing that takes place as habit takes control of our daily lives.

- Here's another strategy for bringing your thinking down from high levels of generality. Think of the words you use as steps on an abstraction ladder, and consciously climb down the ladder from abstract generalization to concrete detail.

"Mammal," for example, is higher on the abstraction ladder than "cow." A concrete word appeals to the senses. Abstract words are not available to our senses of touch, sight, hearing, taste, and smell. "Peacekeeping force" is an abstract phrase; it conjures up a concept. "Submarine" is concrete. We know what people are talking about when they say there is a plan to send submarines to a troubled area. We can't be so sure what is up when people start talking about peacekeeping forces. George Orwell offers an eloquent attack along these lines in his famous essay, "Politics and the English Language," which is discussed in Chapter 11.

TRY THIS 1.2: Distinguishing Abstract from Concrete Words

Make a list of the first ten words that come to mind and then arrange them from most concrete to most abstract. Then repeat the exercise by choosing key words from a page of something you have written recently.

VOICES FROM ACROSS THE CURRICULUM

Habits of Mind in Psychology: A Psychologist Speaks

Psychologists who study the way we process information have established important links between the way we think and the way we feel. Some psychologists, such as Aaron Beck, have identified common "errors in thinking" that parallel the habits of mind discussed in this chapter. Beck and others have shown that falling prey to these counterproductive habits of mind is associated with a variety of negative outcomes. For instance, a tendency to engage in either/or thinking, overgeneralization, and personalization has been linked to higher levels of anger, anxiety, and depression. Failure to attend to these errors in thinking chokes off reflection and analysis. As a result, the person becomes more likely to "react" rather than think, which may prolong and exacerbate the negative emotions.

—MARK SCIUTTO, PROFESSOR OF PSYCHOLOGY

Get Comfortable with Uncertainty

Most of us learn early in life to pretend that we understand things even when we don't. Rather than ask questions and risk looking foolish, we nod our heads. Soon, we even come to believe that we understand things when really we don't, or not nearly as well as we think we do. This understandable but problematic human trait means that to become better thinkers, most of us have to cultivate a more positive attitude toward not knowing. Prepare to be surprised at how difficult this can be.

Start by trying to accept that uncertainty—even its more extreme version, confusion—is a productive state of mind, a precondition to having ideas. The poet John Keats coined a memorable phrase for this willed tolerance of uncertainty. He called it *negative capability*.

> I had not had a dispute but a disquisition with Dilke, on various subjects; several things dovetailed in my mind, & at once it struck me, what quality went to form a Man of Achievement especially in Literature & which Shakespeare possessed so enormously—I mean *Negative Capability*, that is when man is capable of being in uncertainties, Mysteries, doubts, without any irritable reaching after fact & reason.

— LETTER TO GEORGE AND THOMAS KEATS, DECEMBER 1817

The key phrases here are "capable of being in uncertainties" and "without any irritable reaching." Keats is not saying that facts and reason are unnecessary and therefore can be safely ignored. But he does praise the kind of person who can remain calm (rather than becoming irritable) in a state of uncertainty. He is endorsing a way of being that can stay open to possibilities longer than most of us are comfortable with. Negative capability is an essential habit of mind for productive analytical thinking.

Actively search out possible alternative interpretations. Look for ambiguity. Tell yourself that you don't understand, even if you think that you do. You'll know that you are surmounting the fear of uncertainty when the meaning of your evidence starts to seem less rather than more clear to you, and perhaps even strange. You will begin to see details that you hadn't seen before and a range of competing meanings where you had thought there was only one.

Habit: The Slot-Filler Mentality (Five-Paragraph Form)

Can a format qualify as a counterproductive habit of mind? Yes, if you consider how many high school students have naturalized five-paragraph form as the structure for organizing the writing they do in school.

The shift from high school to college writing is not just a difference in degree but a difference in kind. The changes it requires in matters of form and style are inevitably also changes in thinking. The primary change in thinking for many students demands saying good-bye to five-paragraph form.

Of course, it can be anxiety-producing to bid farewell to this one-size-fits-all writing format and replace it with a set of different forms for different situations. But it is essential to let go of this security blanket.

So, what's wrong with five-paragraph form? Its rigid, arbitrary, and mechanical organizational scheme values structure over just about everything else, especially in-depth thinking.

The formula's defenders claim that essays need to be organized, and that the simple three-part thesis and three body paragraphs (one reason and/or example for each) and repetitive conclusion meet that need. They also say that five-paragraph form is useful for helping writers to get started.

But the problem with treating five-paragraph form as a relatively benign aid to clarity is that, like any habit, it is very hard to break. The form actually discourages thinking by conditioning writers to be afraid of looking closely at evidence. If they look too closely, they might find something that doesn't fit, at which point the prefabricated organizational scheme falls apart. And it is precisely the something-that-doesn't-seem-to-fit, the thing writers call a "complication," that triggers good ideas.

We will return in Chapter 6 to the problems created by five-paragraph form and how to remedy them. For now, keep in mind that if you can't break the slot-filler habit, you'll remain handicapped because five-paragraph form runs counter to virtually all of the values and attitudes that you need in order to grow as a writer and a thinker.

Learn to Notice

Some people, especially the very young, are good at noticing things. They see things that the rest of us don't see or have ceased to notice. Growing up, we all become increasingly desensitized to the world around us; we tend to forget the specific things that get us to feel and think in particular ways.

Why is this? Is it just that people become duller as they get older? The poet William Wordsworth thought so: he argued that we aren't the victims of declining intelligence, but of habit. That is, as we organize our lives so that we can function more efficiently, we condition ourselves to see in more predictable ways and to tune out things that are not immediately relevant to our daily needs.

You can test this theory by considering what you did and did not notice this morning on the way to work or class or wherever you regularly go. Following a routine for moving through the day can be done with minimal engagement of either the brain or the senses. Moving along the roadway in cars, we periodically realize that miles have gone by while we were driving on automatic pilot, attending barely at all to the road or the car or the landscape. Arguably, even when we try to focus on something that we want to consider, the habit of not really attending to things stays with us.

The deadening effect of habit on seeing and thinking has long been a preoccupation of artists as well as philosophers and psychologists. Some people have even defined the aim of art as "defamiliarization." "The essential purpose of art," writes the novelist David Lodge, "is to overcome the deadening effects of habit by representing familiar things in unfamiliar ways." The man who coined the term *defamiliarization*, Victor Shklovsky, wrote

"Habitualization devours works, clothes, furniture, one's wife, and the fear of war. . . . And art exists that one may recover the sensation of life" (David Lodge, *The Art of Fiction*. New York: Penguin, 1992, p. 53).

We all know the buzz phrase "thinking outside the box," which appears to mean getting beyond outworn ways of thinking about things. The phrase assumes that most of the time most of us are trapped inside the box—inside a set of prefabricated answers (clichés) and like/dislike responses.

In this context, we come to the Five Analytical Moves that thinkers regularly make when they analyze things. To become a more confident and observant writer, you will need to become more aware of these moves in your thinking and practice them systematically.

The Five Analytical Moves

The act of analyzing can be broken down into five essential moves:

> Move 1: Suspend judgment.
> Move 2: Define significant parts and how they are related.
> Move 3: Make the implicit explicit. Push observations to implications
>   by ASKING "SO WHAT?"
> Move 4: Look for patterns of repetition and contrast and for anomalies
>   (THE METHOD).
> Move 5: Keep reformulating questions and explanations.

Move 1: Suspend Judgment

Much of what passes for thinking is merely reacting: right/wrong, good/bad, loved it/hated it, couldn't relate to it, boring. As we noted in our discussion of Counterproductive Habits of Mind, responses like these are habits, reflexes of the mind. And they are surprisingly tough habits to break. As an experiment, eavesdrop on people walking out of a movie. Most of them will immediately voice their approval or disapproval, usually in either/or terms: "I think it was a good movie and you are wrong to think it was bad." And so on.

A first move in conducting analysis—in fact, a precondition—is to delay judgment, especially of the agree-disagree, like-dislike kind. In the opening pages of *The Great Gatsby*, Nick Carraway cites as the one piece of wisdom he learned from his father the following statement: "Reserving judgments is a matter of infinite hope." In analysis, the goal is always to understand before you judge.

Move 2: Define Significant Parts and How They Are Related

In order to define significant parts and figure out how they are related, writers need to train themselves to attend closely to details. Becoming observant is not natural; it's learned. Toward that end, this book offers a series of observation and interpretation strategies to equip you to see more and to make more of what you see.

The first of these is a strategy we call NOTICE & FOCUS, which will help you to stay open longer to what you can notice in your subject matter. Do this by starting not with "What do I think?" or, worse, with "What do I like/dislike?," but with "What do I *notice*?". This small shift in words will engineer the major conceptual shift this chapter asks you to make: to locate more of your time and attention in the observation stage, which necessarily precedes formulating a thesis.

NOTICE & FOCUS (Ranking)

NOTICE & FOCUS: SLOW DOWN

Not "What do you think?" &

Not "What do you like or dislike?"

but

"What do you notice?"

A few prompts:

What do you find most INTERESTING?

What do you find most STRANGE?

What do you find most REVEALING?

This exercise is governed by repeated return to the question, "What do you notice?". Most people's tendency is to generalize and thus rapidly move away from whatever it is they are looking at. The question "What do you notice?" redirects attention to the subject matter, itself, and delays the pressure to come up with answers (see Figure 1.3).

1. **Repeatedly answer the question, "What do you notice?,"** being sure to cite actual details of the thing being observed rather than moving to more general observations about it. (This is more difficult than it sounds.) This phase of the exercise should produce an extended and unordered list of details—features of the thing being observed—that call attention to themselves for one reason or another.

2. **Rank (create an order of importance) for the various features you have noticed.** Answer the question "What three details (specific features of the subject matter) are most interesting (or significant or revealing or strange)?" The purpose of relying on "interesting" or one of the other suggested words is that these will help to deactivate the like/dislike switch, which is so much a reflex in all of us, and replace it with a more analytical perspective.

3. **Say why the three things you selected struck you as the most interesting.** Remember to start by noticing as much as you can about what you are looking at. Dwell with the data. Record what you see. Don't move to generalization or judgment. What this procedure will begin to demonstrate is how useful description is as a tool for arriving at ideas. Stay at the description stage longer (in that attitude of uncertainty we've recommended) and have better ideas. Training yourself to notice is fun. It will improve your memory as well as your ability to think.

FIGURE 1.3

NOTICE & FOCUS + Ranking

Start by noticing as much as you can about what you are looking at. Dwell with the data. Record what you see. It will improve your memory as well as your ability to think.

"Interesting," "Revealing," "Strange"

These three words are triggers for analysis. Often, we are interested by things that have captured our attention without our clearly knowing why. To say that something is interesting is not the end but the beginning of analysis. If you press yourself to explain why something is interesting, revealing, or strange, you will be prompted to make an analytical move.

"Revealing" (or "significant") requires you to make choices that can lead to interpretive leaps. If something strikes you as revealing or significant, even if you're not yet sure why, you will eventually begin producing some explanation. The word "strange" gives us permission to notice oddities and things that initially seem not to fit. Strange, in this context, is not a judgmental term, but one denoting features of a subject that aren't readily explainable. Where you locate something strange, you isolate something to figure out—what makes it strange and why.

TRY THIS 1.3: NOTICE & FOCUS Fieldwork

Try this exercise with a range of subjects: an editorial, the front page of a newspaper, a website, a key paragraph from something you are reading, the style of a favorite writer, conversations overheard around campus, looking at people's shoes, political speeches, a photograph, a cartoon, and so forth. (The speech bank at americanrhetoric.com is an excellent source.) Remember to include all three steps: notice, rank, and say why.

Noticing and Rhetorical Analysis

When you become attuned to noticing words and details rather than registering general impressions, you inevitably focus not only on the message—what gets said—but on how it gets said. To notice how information is delivered is to focus on its rhetoric. To analyze the rhetoric of something is to assess how that something persuades or positions us as readers or viewers or listeners.

Rhetorical analysis is an essential skill because it reveals how voices in the world are perennially seeking to enlist our support and shape our behavior.

Everything has a rhetoric, not just political speeches and not even just words: classrooms, churches, supermarkets, department store windows, Starbucks, photographs, magazine covers, your bedroom, this book. Intention, by the way, is not the issue. It doesn't matter whether the effect of a place or a piece of writing on its viewers (or readers) is deliberate and planned or not. What matters is that you can notice how the details of the thing itself encourage or discourage certain kinds of responses in the "consumers" of whatever it is you are studying.

What, for example, does the high ceiling of a Gothic cathedral invite in the way of response from people who enter it? How might the high ceilings make people feel about their places in the world? What do the raised platform at the front of a classroom, and the tidy rows of desks secured to the floor, say to the students who enter there?

To get you started on rhetorical analysis, here is a brief example on the layout of our college campus.

> The campus is laid out in several rows and quadrangles. It is interesting to observe where the different academic buildings are located relative to the academic departments they house. It is also interesting to see how the campus positions student housing. The campus is set up as a series of quadrangles— areas of space with four sides. One dormitory, for example, forms a quadrangle. Quadrangles invite people to look in, rather than out. They are enclosed spaces, the center of which is a kind of blank. The center serves as a shared space, a safely walled-off area for the development of a separate community. The academic buildings also form a quadrangle of sorts, with an open green space in the center. On one side of this quadrangle are the buildings that house the natural and social sciences. Opposite these—on the other side of a street that runs through the center of campus—are the modern brick and glass structures that house the arts and the humanities . . .

What might these details lead us to conclude about the rhetoric of the campus layout?

- that the campus is inward-looking and self-enclosed
- that it invites its members to feel separate and safe
- that it announces the division of the sciences and the social sciences from the arts and humanities, arguably creating the sense of a divided community.

TRY THIS 1.4: Doing NOTICE & FOCUS with a Room

List a number of details about a room, then rank the three most important ones. Use as a focusing question any of the three "trigger" words: interesting, revealing, or strange. Or come up with your own focus for the ranking, such as the three aspects of the room that seem most to affect the way you feel and behave in the space.

Doing Exploratory Writing in the Observation Stage: Freewriting

What is especially useful about so-called "prewriting" strategies such as NOTICE & FOCUS is freedom—freedom to experiment without worrying about readers saying that you are wrong, freedom to just pay attention to what you notice and see where these observations might lead you. But NOTICE & FOCUS and other forms of listing can also arrest you in the list stage: you have your column of ranked observations, but now what?

The answer to that last question is to start writing consecutive sentences explaining why you found particular details especially interesting and revealing. Your goal at this stage is not to produce a finished paper, but to start some trains of thought on features of your subject that seem worth writing about.

The name most often attached to this kind of exploratory writing—which can, by the way, happen at various points in the writing process, not just at the beginning—is "freewriting."

"How Do I Know What I Think Until I See What I Say?" Freewriting is a method of arriving at ideas by writing continuously about a subject for a limited period of time without pausing to edit or revise. The rationale behind this activity can be understood through a well-known remark by the novelist E.M. Forster (regarding the "tyranny" of prearranging everything): "How do I know what I think until I see what I say?" Freewriting gives you the chance to see what you'll say.

The writer Anne Lamott writes eloquently (in *Bird by Bird*) about the censors we all hear as nasty voices in our heads that keep us from writing. These are the internalized voices of past critics whose comments have become magnified to suggest that we will never get it right. Freewriting allows us to tune out these voices long enough to discover what we might think.

Freewriting opens up space for thinking by enabling us to catch different thoughts as they occur to us, without worrying prematurely about how to communicate these to a reader. The order in which ideas occur to us is not linear. Things rarely line up in a straight forward sequence. As we try to pursue one thought, others press on our attention. The act of writing allows us to follow our mental trails and to experiment with alternate routes without losing track of where we've been. Without writing, in all but the most carefully trained memories, the trails keep vanishing, sometimes leaving us stranded.

Paper-writing requires you to develop ideas sequentially. Freewriting gives you the freedom to make sudden, often unanticipated leaps. These frequently take you from a bland, predictable statement to an insight. You learn what you think by seeing what you say.

Freewriting seeks to remove what the rhetorician Peter Elbow saw as the primary cause of much poor writing: the writer's attempt to conduct two essentially opposed activities—drafting and editing, inventing and arranging—at the same time. Freewriting helps you to separate these activities until you've generated enough material to actually be worth arranging for an audience.

In general, only the most practiced analytical thinkers can arrive at their best ideas before they begin to write. The common observation, "I know what I want to say, I'm just having trouble getting it down on paper," is a half-truth at best. Getting words on paper almost always alters your ideas, and leads you to discover thoughts you didn't know you had. If you expect to have all the answers before you begin to write, you are more likely to settle for relatively superficial ideas. And when you try to conduct all of your thinking in your head, you may arrive at an idea but be unable to explain to your readers how you got there.

When you make the shift from freewriting to writing a first draft, you may not—and most likely will not—have all of the answers, but you will waste significantly less time chasing ill-focused and inadequately considered ideas than might otherwise have been the case.

The Rules for Freewriting There aren't many rules to freewriting.

The first is: pick a concrete starting point. Find *something specific* to be interested in. NOTICE & FOCUS works well for locating that focus, as do "interesting" and "strange."

Write your focus at the top of the page—a few lines or a short list of details or a short passage. Then launch the freewrite from there.

Commit to an allotted time in which you will write continuously. Ten minutes is a minimum. You may be surprised at how much you can find to say in this amount of time. The more you do freewriting, the better you will get at it, and the longer you will be able to go.

Most importantly, keep your pen (or fingers on the keyboard) moving. Don't reread as you go. Don't pause to correct things. Don't cross things out. Don't quit when you think you have run out of things to say. Just keep writing.

Move 3: Make the Implicit Explicit. Push Observations to Implications by ASKING "SO WHAT?"

NOTICE & FOCUS, "interesting," and "strange," as well as freewriting—these moves aim to keep writers dwelling longer in the observation phase of analysis, to spend more time exploring and amassing data before they leap to making some kind of claim. It's time now to shift our focus to the leap itself.

One of the central activities and goals of analysis is to make explicit (overtly stated) what is implicit (suggested). When we do so, we are addressing such questions as "What follows from this?" and "If this is true, what else is true?" The pursuit of such questions—drawing out implications—moves our thinking and our writing *forward.*

MOVING FORWARD

Observation $\longrightarrow$ So what? $\longrightarrow$ Implications
Implications $\longrightarrow$ So what? $\longrightarrow$ Conclusions

This process of converting suggestions into direct statements is essential to analysis, but it is also the feature of analyzing that, among beginning writers, is least well understood. The fear is that, like the emperor's new clothes, implications aren't really "there," but are instead the phantasms of an over-active imagination. "Reading between the lines" is the common and telling phrase that expresses this anxiety. Throughout this book, we will have more to say about the charge that analysis makes something out of nothing—the spaces between the lines rather than what is there in black and white. But for now, let's look at a hypothetical example of this process of drawing out implications, to suggest not only how it's done, but how often we do it in our everyday lives.

Imagine that you are driving down the highway and find yourself analyzing a billboard advertisement for a particular brand of beer. Such an analysis might begin with your noticing what the billboard photo contains, its various "parts"—six young, athletic-looking and scantily clad men and women drinking beer while pushing kayaks into a fast-running river. If you were to stop at this point, you would have produced not an analysis but a summary—a description of what the photo contains. If, however, you went on to consider what the particulars of the photo imply, your summary would become more analytical.

You might say, for example, that the photo implies that beer is the beverage of fashionable, healthy, active people, not just of older men with large stomachs dozing in armchairs in front of the television. Thus, the advertisement's meaning goes beyond its explicit contents; your analysis would lead you to convert to direct statement meanings that are suggested but not overtly stated, such as the advertisement's goal of attacking a common, negative stereotype about its product (that only fat, lazy, men drink beer). The naming of parts that you do in analysis is not an end unto itself, is not an exercise in making something out of nothing; it serves the purpose of allowing you to better understand the nature of your subject. The implications of the "parts" you name are an important part of that understanding.

The word "implication" comes from the Latin *implicare*, which means "to fold in." The word "explicit" is in opposition to the idea of implication. It means "folded out." An act of mind is required to take what is folded in and to fold it out for all to see. This process of drawing out implications is also known as making inferences. Inference and implication are related but not synonymous terms. The term implication describes something that might follow from the material itself. The term "inference" describes your thinking process. In short, you infer what the subject implies.

PUSHING OBSERVATIONS TO CONCLUSIONS: Asking "So What?"

(shorthand for)
What does the observation imply?
Why does this observation matter?
Where does this observation get us?
How can we begin to theorize the significance of the observation?

Asking "So What?"

Asking "So What?" is a universal prompt for spurring the move from observation to implication and ultimately to interpretation. Asking "So What?"—or its milder cousin, "And so?"—is a calling to account, a way of pressing yourself to confront that essential question, "Why does this matter?" The tone of "So what?" can sound rude or at least brusque, but that directness can be liberating. Often writers will go to great lengths to avoid stating what they take something to mean. After all, that leaves them open to attack, they fear, if they get it wrong. But Asking "So What?" is a way of forcing yourself to take the plunge without too much hoopla. And when you are tempted to stop thinking too soon, Asking "So What?" will press you onward.

Asking "So What?" in a Chain

Experienced analytical writers develop the habit of Asking "So What?" repeatedly. That is, they ask "So what?," answer, and then ask "So what?" of that answer, and often keep going (see Figure 1.4). The repeated asking of this question causes writers to move beyond their first attempt to arrive at a claim.

By sustaining their pursuit of implications, seasoned writers habitually reason in a chain rather than settling prematurely for a single link, as the next example illustrates.

1	Describe significant evidence
2	Begin to query your own observations by making what is implicit explicit
3	Push your observations and statements of implications to interpretive conclusions by *again* Asking "So What?"

FIGURE 1.4
Asking "So What?"

The following is the opening paragraph of a talk given by a professor of political science at our college, Dr. Jack Gambino, on the occasion of a gallery opening featuring the work of two contemporary photographers of urban and industrial landscapes. We have located in brackets our annotations of his turns of thought, as these pivot on "strange" and "So what?" (Note: images referred to in the example are available from Google Images—search for Camilo Vergara fern street 1988, and also for Edward Burtynsky.)

If you look closely at Camilo Vergara's photo of Fern Street, Camden, 1988, you'll notice a sign on the side of a dilapidated building:

Danger: Men Working

W. Hargrove Demolition

Perhaps that warning captures the ominous atmosphere of these very different kinds of photographic documents by Camilo Vergara and Edward Burtynsky: "Danger: Men

Working." Watch out—human beings are at work! But the work that is presented is not so much a building-up as it is a tearing-down—the work of demolition. **["strange": tearing down is unexpected; writer asks "So what?" and answers]**

Of course, demolition is often necessary in order to construct anew: old buildings are leveled for new projects, whether you are building a highway or bridge in an American city or a dam in the Chinese countryside. You might call modernity itself, as so many have, a process of creative destruction, a term used variously to describe modern art, capitalism, and technological innovation. The photographs in this exhibit, however, force us to pay attention to the "destructive" side of this modern equation. **["strange": photos emphasize destruction and not creation; writer asks "So what?" and answers]**

What both Burtynsky and Vergara do in their respective ways is to put up a warning sign—they question whether the reworking of our natural and social environment leads to a sustainable human future. And they wonder whether the process of creative destruction may not have spun recklessly out of control, producing places that are neither habitable nor sustainable. In fact, a common element connecting the two photographic versions is the near absence of people in the landscape. **[writer points to supporting feature of evidence, about which he will further theorize]**

While we see the evidence of the transforming power of human production on the physical and social environment, neither Vergara's urban ruins nor Burtynsky's industrial sites actually show us "men working." **[writer continues to move by noticing strange absence of people in photographs of sites where men work]** Isolated figures peer suspiciously out back doors or pick through the rubble, but they appear out of place. **[writer asks a final "So what?" and arrives at a conclusion]** It is this sense of displacement—of human beings alienated from the environments they themselves have created—that provides the most haunting aspect of the work of these two photographers.

The Gambino opening is a good example of how Asking "So What?" generates forward momentum for the analysis. Notice the pattern by which the paragraph moves: the observation of something strange, about which the writer asks and answers "So what?" several times until arriving at a final "So what?"—the point at which he decides what his observations ultimately mean. We call the final "So what?" in this chain of thinking the ultimate "So what?" because it moves from implications to the writer's culminating point.

TRY THIS 1.5: Track the "So What?" Question

The aim of this exercise is to sensitize you to the various moves a writer makes when presenting and analyzing information. Locate any piece of analytical prose—perhaps an article from *Arts & Letters Daily* online (aldaily .com)—and identify in the margins the writer's moves as we have done for the Gambino example.

TRY THIS 1.6: Inferring Implications from Observations

Write a list of as many plausible implications as you can think of for each statement. Insofar as the statement is true, what might it suggest that is not explicitly included? What assumptions are implicit, for example, in the quotation from Robert Frost's poem "Mending Wall"? After you have made your list of implications for each item, consider how you arrived at them. You might find it useful to do this exercise along with other people, because part of its aim is to reveal the extent to which different people infer the same implications.

1. The sidewalk is disappearing as a feature of the American residential landscape.

2. New house designs are tending increasingly toward open plans in which the kitchen is not separated from the rest of the house.

3. "Good fences make good neighbors." — Robert Frost

4. An increasing number of juveniles—people under the age of eighteen—are being tried and convicted as adults, rather than as minors, in America, with the result that more minors are serving adult sentences for crimes they committed while still in their teens.

5. Neuroscientists tell us that the frontal cortex of the brain, the part that is responsible for judgment and especially for impulse control, is not fully developed in humans until roughly the age of twenty-one. What are the implications of this observation relative to observation four?

6. Shopping malls and grocery stores rarely have clocks.

7. List as many plausible implications as you can for this statement (which has been contested by other researchers):

   "In the eye-tracking test, only one in six subjects read Web pages linearly, sentence by sentence. In this study, Nielsen found that people took in hundreds of pages 'in a pattern that's very different from what you learned in school.' It looks like a capital letter F. At the top, users read all the way across, but as they proceed their descent quickens and horizontal sight contracts, with a slowdown around the middle of the page. Near the bottom, eyes move almost vertically, the lower-right corner of the page largely ignored."

   — MARK BAUERLEIN, "ONLINE LITERACY IS A LESSER KIND," *THE CHRONICLE REVIEW*

Move 4: Look for Patterns of Repetition and Contrast and for Anomalies (THE METHOD)

We have been defining analysis as the understanding of parts in relation to each other and to a whole. But how do you know which parts to attend to? What makes some details in the material you are studying more worthy of your attention than others?

The procedure we call THE METHOD offers a tool for uncovering significant patterns. Like NOTICE & FOCUS, THE METHOD orients you toward significant
detail; but whereas NOTICE & FOCUS is a deliberately unstructured activity, THE
METHOD applies a matrix or grid of observational moves to a subject. In its
most reduced form, it organizes observation and then prompts interpretation
by asking the following sequence of questions.

QUESTIONS FROM THE METHOD

What repeats?

What goes with what? (strands)

What is opposed to what? (binaries)

(for all of these) $\longrightarrow$ So what?

What doesn't fit? (anomalies) So what?

In virtually all subjects, repetition and close resemblance (strands) are
signs of emphasis. In a symphony, for example, certain patterns of notes repeat
throughout, announcing themselves as major themes. In Shakespeare's play
King Lear, references to seeing and eyes call attention to themselves through
repetition, causing us to recognize that the play is *about* seeing. Binary oppositions, which often consist of two strands or repetitions that are in tension
with each other, suggest what is at stake in a subject. We can understand *King
Lear* by the way it opposes kinds of blindness to ways of seeing.

Along with looking for pattern, it is also fruitful to attend to anomalous
details—those that seem not to fit the pattern. Anomalies help us to revise
our assumptions. Picture, for example, a TV ad featuring a baseball player
reading Dostoyevsky in the dugout. In this case, the anomaly—a baseball
player who reads serious literature—subverts the stereotypical assumption
that sports and intellectualism don't belong together.

People tend to avoid information that challenges (by not conforming
to) views they already hold. They screen out anything that would ruffle
the pattern they've begun to see, and ignore the evidence that might lead
them to a better theory. Most advances in thought have arisen when someone has observed some phenomenon that does not fit within a prevailing
theory.

The Steps of THE METHOD

THE METHOD of looking for patterns works through a series of steps. Hold yourself initially to doing the steps one at a time and in order. Later, you will be able
to record your answers under each of the five steps simultaneously. Although
the steps of THE METHOD are discrete and modular, they are also consecutive.
They proceed by a kind of narrative logic. Each step leads logically to the
next, and then to various kinds of regrouping, which is actually rethinking
(see Figure 1.5).

1	**List exact repetitions and the number of each (words, details).** For example, if forms of the word *seems* repeat three times, write "seems × 3." With images, the repeated appearance of high foreheads would constitute an exact repetition. Concentrate on substantive (meaning-carrying) words. Only in rare cases will words like "and" or "the" merit attention as a significant repetition. At the most literal level, whatever repeats is what the thing is about.
2	**List repetitions of the same or similar kind of detail or word—which we call strands** (for example, *polite, courteous, decorous*). Be able to explain the strand's connecting logic with a label: *manners.*
3	**List details or words that form or suggest binary oppositions**—pairs of words or details that are opposites—and select from these the most important ones, which function as **organizing contrasts** (for example, *open/closed, ugly/beautiful, global/local*). Your goal here is not to engage in either/or thinking but to locate what is at stake in the subject, the tensions and issues that it is trying to resolve.
4	**Choose ONE repetition, strand, or binary as a starting point for a healthy paragraph** (or two) in which you discuss its significance in relation to the whole. (This ranking, as in Notice & Focus, prompts an interpretive leap.)
5	**Locate anomalies: exceptions to the pattern, things that seem not to fit.** Once you see an anomaly, you will often find that it is part of a strand you had not detected (and perhaps one side of a previously unseen binary).

FIGURE 1.5

THE METHOD

Expect ideas to suggest themselves to you as you move through the steps of THE METHOD. Strands often begin to suggest other strands that are in opposition to them. Words you first took to be parts of one strand may migrate to different strands. This process of noticing and then relocating words and details into different patterns is one aspect of doing THE METHOD that can push your analysis to interpretation.

It may be helpful to think of this method of analysis as a form of mental doodling. Rather than worrying about what you are going to say, or about whether or not you understand, you instead get out a pencil and start tallying up what you see. Engaged in this process, you'll soon find yourself gaining entry to the logic of your subject matter.

Two Examples of THE METHOD Generating Ideas

In the paragraph below you can see how the writer's noticing strands and binaries direct his thinking.

The most striking aspect of the spots is how different they are from typical fashion advertising. If you look at men's fashion magazines, for example, at the advertisements for the suits of Ralph Lauren or Valentino or Hugo Boss, they almost always consist of a beautiful man, with something interesting done to his hair, wearing a gorgeous outfit. At the most, the man may be gesturing discreetly, or smiling in the demure way that a man like that might smile after, say, telling the supermodel at the next table no thanks he has to catch an early-morning flight to Milan. But that's all. The beautiful face and the clothes tell the whole story. The Dockers ads, though, are almost exactly the opposite. There's no face. The camera is jumping around so much that it's tough to concentrate on the clothes. And instead of stark simplicity, the fashion image is overlaid with a constant, confusing pattern. It's almost as if the Dockers ads weren't primarily concerned with clothes at all—and in fact that's exactly what Levi's intended. What the company had discovered, in its research, was that baby-boomer men felt that the chief thing missing from their lives was male friendship. Caught between the demands of the families that many of them had started in the eighties and career considerations that had grown more onerous, they felt they had lost touch with other men. The purpose of the ads—the chatter, the lounging around, the quick cuts—was simply to conjure up a place where men could put on one-hundred-percent-cotton khakis and reconnect with one another. In the original advertising brief, that imaginary place was dubbed Dockers World.

— MALCOLM GLADWELL, "LISTENING TO KHAKIS"

First Gladwell notes the differences in two kinds of fashion ads aimed at men, high-fashion ads and the Dockers ads. In the first of these, the word "beautiful" repeats twice as part of a strand (including "gorgeous," "interesting," "supermodel," "demure"). The writer then poses traits of the Dockers ads as an opposing strand. Instead of a beautiful face there is no face; instead of "gorgeous outfit," "it's tough to concentrate on the clothes." These oppositions cause the writer to make his interpretive leap, that the Dockers ads "weren't primarily concerned with clothes at all" and that this was intentional.

In the student essay, below, Lesley Stephen develops a key contrast between two thinkers, Sigmund Freud and Michel Foucault, by noticing the different meanings that each attaches to some of the same key words. THE METHOD helps to locate the key terms and define them by seeing what other words they suggest (strands).

Freud defines civilization as serving two main purposes. The first is to protect men against nature, and the second is to adjust their mutual relations. Freud seems to offer returning to nature as a possible solution for men's sexual freedom. I think Freud might believe that returning to nature by rejecting civilization could bring about sexual freedom, but that sexual freedom does not necessarily equal happiness.

Foucault completely defies Freud's idea that sexuality is natural and that repression exists as anti-sexuality. He believes that everything is created from discourse; nothing is natural. And because nothing is natural, nothing is repressed. There is no such thing as a natural desire; if the desire exists, it is because it is already part of the discourse.

By focusing on repetitions of the words "nature" and "natural," and then seeing what goes with what, the writer creates a succinct and revealing comparison.

Doing THE METHOD on a Poem

Here is an example of how one might do THE METHOD on a piece of text—in this case a student poem. We use a poem because it is compact and allows us to illustrate efficiently how THE METHOD works.

> Brooklyn Heights, 4:00 A.M.
> Dana Ferrelli
>
> sipping a warm forty oz.
>
> Coors Light on a stoop in
>
> Brooklyn Heights. I look
>
> across the street, in the open window;
>
> Blonde bobbing heads, the
>
> smack of a jump rope, laughter
>
> of my friends breaking
>
> beer bottles. Putting out their
>
> burning filters on the #5 of
>
> a hopscotch court.
>
> We reminisce of days when we were
>
> Fat, pimple faced—
>
> look how far we've come. But tomorrow
>
> a little blonde girl will
>
> pick up a Marlboro Light filter, just to play.
>
> And I'll buy another forty, because
>
> that's how I play now.
>
> Reminiscing about how far I've come

Here are the steps of THE METHOD, applied to the preceding poem.

1. *Words that repeat exactly:* forty × 2, blonde × 2, how far we've (I've) come × 2, light × 2, reminisce, reminiscing × 2, filter, filters × 2, Brooklyn Heights × 2

2. *Strands:* jump rope, laughter, play, hopscotch (connecting logic: childhood games, the carefree worldview of childhood), Coors Light, Marlboro Light filters, beer bottles (connecting logic: drugs, adult "games," escapism?), smack, burning, breaking (connecting logic: violent actions and powerful emotion: burning)

3. *Binary oppositions:* how far we've come/how far I've come (a move from plural to singular, from a sense of group identity to isolation, from group values to a more individual consideration)

   Burning/putting out

   Coors Light, Marlboro Lights/jump rope, hopscotch

   How far I've come (two meanings of *far?*, one positive, one not)

   Heights/stoop

   Present/past

4. *Ranked repetitions, strands, and binaries plus paragraph explaining the choice of one of these as central to understanding.*

   Most important repetitions: forty, how far we've/I've come

   Most important strands: childhood games and adulthood games

   Most important binaries: Burning versus putting out, open and laughter versus putting out

5. *Anomaly:* Fat, pimple faced—This detail does not fit with the otherwise halcyon treatment of childhood.

ANALYSIS (HEALTHY PARAGRAPHS) The repetition of *forty* (forty-ounce beer) is interesting. It signals a certain weariness—perhaps with a kind of pun on *forty* to suggest middle age and thus the speaker's concern about moving toward being older in a way that seems stale and flat. The beer, after all, is warm—which is not the best state for a beer to be in, once opened, if it is to retain its taste and character. Forty ounces of beer might also suggest excess—"supersizing."

The most important (or at least most interesting) binary opposition is *burning versus putting out.* This binary seems to be part of a more intense strand in the poem, one that runs counter to the weary prospect of moving on toward a perhaps lonely ("how far *I've* come") middle-aged feeling. Burning goes with breaking and the smack of the jump rope, and even putting out (a strand), if we visualize putting out not just as a fire extinguished but in terms of putting a cigarette out by pushing the burning end of it into something (the number 5 on the Hopscotch court). The poem's language has a violent and passionate edge to it, even though the violent words are not always in a violent context (for example, the smack of the jump rope).

This is a rather melancholy poem in which, perhaps, the speaker is mourning the passing, the "putting out" of the passion of youth ("burning"). In the poem's more obvious binary—the opposition of childhood games to more "adult" ones—the same melancholy plays itself out, making the poem's refrain-like repetition of "how far I've come" ring with unhappy irony. The little blonde girl is an image of the speaker's own past self (since the poem talks about reminiscing), and the speaker mourns that little girl's (her own) passing into a more uncertain and less carefree state. It is 4:00 A.M. in Brooklyn Heights—just about the end of night, the darkest point perhaps before the daybreak. But windows are open, suggesting possibility, so things are not all bad. The friends make noise together, break bottles together, revisit hopscotch square 5 together, and contemplate moving on.

Note: the reference to "Fat, pimple faced—" in the poem is an anomaly in the otherwise idealized representation of childhood in terms of games and laughter. The young women in the poem are sad that they can re-enact childhood games but they can't recover childhood's innocent happiness. The anomaly usefully reminds us of adults' desire to idealize the past by forgetting that the past has pimples as well as hopscotch. "Fat, pimple faced—" goes with what we might also be able to see as an anomaly—the open windows in what the poem otherwise describes as a steady closing down of hope.

Notice how this discussion moves from analysis of a key repetition and a key binary to a series of claims about the meaning of the poem as a whole. Writing about the data that THE METHOD has gathered leads us to see how the significant parts are related (Move 2 of the Five Analytical Moves).

TRY THIS 1.7: Doing THE METHOD on a Poem

Locate online "The Crowd at the Ballgame," by William Carlos Williams (a famous American poet). A useful site for finding poems is poetryfoundation. org. Do THE METHOD on the poem individually or in groups, using our treatment of "Brooklyn Heights, 4:00 A.M." as a model. Be sure to do the steps, including the healthy paragraph, in writing.

Troubleshooting THE METHOD

THE METHOD is a means to an end, not an end in itself. Deciding what goes with what is an analytical move. It's not just listing. One aim of THE METHOD is to induce you to pay more attention, and a different kind of attention, to what you are studying.

Don't let the procedure turn into tedious or superficial data gathering. Look for the *interesting* repetitions, strands, and binaries, not just the most prevalent ones. Let this activity generate ideas.

In applying THE METHOD to longer texts, don't try to cover everything, and don't start making your lists until you have done a chunk of the reading. After all, you can't be expected to recognize a repetition in an extended essay until it has reappeared several times. Keep informal lists in the margins as you read, or in the inside cover of a book. When you become aware of an opposition, you can mark it with a +/− next to the paragraph where you were struck.

THE METHOD is designed to prompt thinking. You should be able to offer your reasons for why you think a given repetition or strand is most important. You should be able to express what issue you think is at stake in the organizing contrast you choose as most important.

As you look over your binaries, choose the binary that you think organizes the thinking in the subject as a whole—the *organizing* contrast. Which binary contains, implicitly or explicitly, the central issue or question or problem that is being addressed?

To make THE METHOD spark ideas, remember to ask "So what?" as a way of moving from observation to implication.

TRY THIS 1.8: Do THE METHOD on a Visual Image

We recommend using an image by Adrian Tomine, a frequent contributor to *The New Yorker* magazine and a graphic novelist. Use Google Images for "New Yorker covers + Tomine" to obtain a range of possibilities. We suggest his August 24, 2009, cover, "Double Feature"—an image of a crowd at dusk beneath the Brooklyn Bridge. Then, for homework repeat the exercise alone, using a second Tomine cover—we suggest the November 8, 2004, cover, "Missed Connection," featuring a man and a woman looking at each other from passing subway cars.

TRY THIS 1.9: Do THE METHOD on a Reading

Select any article from *Arts & Letters Daily* (aldaily.com), and do THE METHOD on it. Or use THE METHOD on the front page of the newspaper, a speech from the American Rhetoric website, or perhaps a series of editorials on the same subject. You can work with as little as a few paragraphs or as much as an entire article, chapter, or book.

Move 5: Keep Reformulating Questions and Explanations

The preceding four analytical moves can be thought of in question form. The process of posing and answering such questions—the analytical process—is one of trial and error. Learning to write well is largely a matter of learning how to frame questions. Whatever questions you ask, the answers you propose won't always turn out to be answers, but may instead produce more questions. It follows that you need to keep the process of understanding open, often longer than feels comfortable. You do so by repeatedly reformulating your questions and explanations and going back to the original data for nourishment.

The following three groups of questions (organized according to the analytical moves they're derived from) are typical of what goes on in an analytical writer's head while attempting to understand a subject. These questions will work with almost anything that you want to think about. As you will see, the questions are geared toward helping you locate and try on explanations for the meaning of various patterns of details.

Which details seem significant? Why?
What does each detail mean?
What else might it mean?
　　(Moves: Define Significant Parts; Make the Implicit Explicit)
How do the details fit together? What do they have in common?
What does this pattern of details mean?
What else might this pattern mean? How else could it be explained?
　　(Move: Look for Patterns)
What details don't seem to fit? How might they be connected with other
　details to form a different pattern?
What does this new pattern mean? How might it cause me to read the
　meaning of individual details differently?
　　(Moves: Look for Anomalies and Keep Asking Questions)

We conclude this chapter with an analysis of the famous painting that has come to be known as *Whistler's Mother*.

Summing Up: Analyzing *Whistler's Mother*

Throughout this chapter we have emphasized the importance of slowing down leaps to conclusions in order to spend more time dwelling with the data, carefully describing what you notice. We have stressed the importance of focusing on the details, looking for questions rather than answers, and telling yourself you don't understand even when you think you might. We have also said that summary and description are close cousins of and necessary to analysis, but that analysis provides more interpretive thinking—making the implicit explicit.

Key to any kind of analysis is laying out the data, not simply because it keeps the analysis accurate, but also because, crucially, it is in the act of carefully describing a subject that analytical writers often have their best ideas. What might an analysis of Whistler's painting include, and why? (see Figure 1.6).

The first step is to describe with care. Look for the painting's significant parts and how they're related (Move 2) and for patterns of repetition and contrast (Move 4). The words you choose to describe your data will contain the germs of your ideas about what the subject means. In moving from description to analysis, scrutinize the language you have chosen, asking, "Why did I choose this word?" and "What ideas are implicit in the language I have used?" This attention to your own language will help you to make the implicit explicit (Move 3).

FIGURE 1.6

Arrangement in Grey and Black: The Artist's Mother, by James Abbott McNeill Whistler, 1871

Figure 1.7 is a depiction of this analytical process in outline form. What does this analysis tell us? It might tell us that the painter's choice to portray his subject in profile contributes to our sense of her separateness from us and of her nonconfrontational passivity. We look at her, but she does not look back at us. Her black dress and the fitted lace cap that obscures her hair are not only emblems of her self-effacement, shrouds disguising her identity like her expressionless face, but also the tools of her self-containment and thus of her power to remain aloof from prying eyes.

What is the attraction of this painting (this being one of the questions that an analysis might ask)? What might draw a viewer to the sight of this austere, drably attired woman, sitting alone in the center of a mostly blank space? Perhaps it is the very starkness of the painting, and the mystery of self-sufficiency at its center, that attracts us.

You may not agree with the terms by which we have summarized the painting, and thus you may not agree with such conclusions as "the mystery

Data	Analytical Moves	Interpretive Leaps ("So What?")
subject in profile, not looking at us	make implicit explicit (speculate about what the detail might suggest)	figure strikes us as separate, nonconfrontational, passive
folded hands, fitted lace cap, contained hair, expressionless face	locate pattern of same or similar detail; make what is implicit in pattern of details explicit	figure strikes us as self-contained, powerful in her separateness and self-enclosure— self-sufficient?
patterned curtain and picture versus still figure and blank wall; slightly frilled lace cuffs and ties on cap versus plain black dress	locate organizing contrast; make what is implicit in the contrast explicit	austerity and containment of the figure made more pronounced by slight contrast with busier, more lively, and more ornate elements and with little picture showing world outside
slightly slouched body position and presence of support for feet	anomalies; make what is implicit in the anomalies explicit	these details destabilize the serenity of the figure, adding some tension to the picture in the form of slightly uneasy posture and figure's need for support: she looks too long, drooped in on her own spine

FIGURE 1.7
Summary and Analysis of *Whistler's Mother* Diagram

of self-sufficiency." Nor is it necessary that you agree, because there is no single, right answer to what the painting means. But the process of careful observation and description and repeated tries at interpretation by ASKING "SO WHAT?" has produced claims about what and how the painting communicates that others would at least find reasonable and fair.

Analysis and Personal Associations

Although observations like those offered in the "Interpretive Leaps" column in Figure 1.7 go beyond simple description, they serve the task of explaining the painting rather than moving to private associations that the painting might prompt, such as effusions about old age or rocking chairs or the character and situation of the writer's own mother. Such associations could well be valuable unto themselves as a means of prompting a searching piece of expressive writing. They might also help a writer to interpret some feature of the painting that they were working to understand. But the writer would not be free to use pieces of their personal history as conclusions about what the painting communicates, unless these conclusions could also be reasonably inferred from the painting itself.

Analysis is a creative activity, a fairly open form of inquiry, but its imaginative scope is governed by logic. The hypothetical analysis we have offered is not the only reading of the painting that a viewer might make, because the same pattern of details might lead to different conclusions. But a viewer would not be free to conclude anything the viewer wished, such as that the woman is mourning the death of a son or is patiently waiting to die. Such conclusions would be unfounded speculations, because the black dress is not sufficient to support them. Analysis often operates in areas where there is no one right answer, but like summary and argument, it requires the writer to reason from evidence.

Becoming a Detective

As we began this chapter by saying, analysis is a form of detective work. It can surprise us with ideas that our experiences produce once we take the time to listen to ourselves thinking. But analysis is also a discipline; it has rules that govern how we proceed and enable others to judge the validity of our ideas.

A few rules are worth highlighting here:

1. The range of associations for explaining a given detail or word must be governed by context.

2. It's fine to use your personal reactions as a way into exploring what a subject means, but take care not to make an interpretive leap stretch further than the actual details will support.

3. Because the tendency to transfer meanings from your own life onto a subject can lead you to ignore the details of the subject itself, you need always to be asking yourself: "What other explanations might plausibly account for this same pattern of detail?"

A good analytical thinker needs to be the attentive Dr. Watson to their own Sherlock Holmes. That is what the remainder of this book will teach you to do. (See Chapter 3 for more on the rules governing interpretation, again using *Whistler's Mother* as a primary example.)

Assignments: The Five Analytical Moves

1. **Do The Method on a reading.** Look for repetitions, strands, and binaries in the paragraph below, the opening of an article entitled "The End of Solitude" by William Deresiewicz, which appeared in *The Chronicle of Higher Education* on January 30, 2009, and at www.chronicle.com /article/The-End-of-Solitude/3708. After selecting the repetition, strand,

or organizing contrast that you find most important, try writing several paragraphs about it.

> What does the contemporary self want? The camera has created a culture of celebrity; the computer is creating a culture of connectivity. As the two technologies converge—*broadband* tipping the Web from text to image, social-networking sites spreading the mesh of interconnection ever wider—the two cultures betray a common impulse. Celebrity and connectivity are both ways of becoming known. This is what the contemporary self wants. It wants to be recognized, wants to be connected: It wants to be visible. If not to the millions, on Survivor or Oprah, then to the hundreds, on Twitter or Facebook. This is the quality that validates us, this is how we become real to ourselves—by being seen by others. The great contemporary terror is anonymity. If Lionel Trilling was right, if the property that grounded the self, in Romanticism, was sincerity, and in modernism it was authenticity, then in *postmodernism* it is visibility.

If you can, visit this article online and include the paragraph that follows as well in your analysis.

2. **Analyze an image in relation to text.** The Adrian Tomine *New Yorker* covers that we referred to in TRY THIS 1.8 could produce a good short paper. You could either do THE METHOD on the two covers in order to write a comparative paper. Or you could do THE METHOD on the Tomine cover called "Double Feature" and the paragraph from "The End of Solitude" above, and write about them comparatively. (Note: the entire article is available online.)

   What do you think Tomine's cover says about the issues raised in "The End of Solitude" by William Deresiewicz? How might Tomine see the issues differently? And how might Deresiewicz interpret Tomine's cover, and "So what?"

3. **Analyze a portrait or other visual image.** Locate any portrait, preferably a good reproduction from an art book or magazine, one that shows detail clearly. Then do a version of what we've done with *Whistler's Mother*. Your goal is to produce an analysis of the portrait with the steps we included in analyzing *Whistler's Mother*. First, summarize the portrait, describing accurately its significant details. Do not go beyond a recounting of what the portrait includes; avoid interpreting what these details suggest.

   Then use the various methods offered in this chapter to analyze the data. What repetitions (patterns of same or similar detail) do you see? What organizing contrasts suggest themselves? In light of these patterns of similarity and difference, what anomalies do you then begin to detect? Move from the data to interpretive conclusions.

   This process will produce a set of interpretive leaps, which you may then try to assemble into a more coherent claim of some sort—a short essay about what the portrait "says."

CHAPTER 2

Reading Analytically

Overview Virtually all college-level writing assignments call for students to write about reading and to use writing in order to better understand reading. The chapter suggests skills that will help writers become more active and more confident readers.

The chapter's strategies include a sequence for writing and talking about reading, including POINTING, PARAPHRASE × 3, and PASSAGE-BASED FOCUSED FREEWRITING. The chapter demonstrates how to unearth the logical structure of a reading by UNCOVERING ASSUMPTIONS and TRACKING BINARIES, and it explains how to apply a reading as a lens for understanding other material. For more extended discussion of summary and other traditional, reading-based writing assignments, see Chapter 4. On using secondary sources in research-based writing, see Chapter 8.

Becoming Conversant Instead of Reading for the Gist

This chapter will teach you how to do these things with readings:

- find the questions rather than just the answers,
- put key passages from readings into conversation with each other,
- use an idea or methodology in a reading in order to generate thinking about something else, and
- gain control of complex ideas on your own, rather than needing others (such as teachers) to do this work for you.

These tasks require you to change your orientation to reading. How, you might ask, do I make this change, given that I am reading difficult material produced by experts?

The challenge of reading well is to become conversant rather than reading for the gist. Many readers operate under the mistaken impression that they are to read for the gist—for the main point, to be gleaned through a glancing speed-reading. Reading for the gist causes readers to leap to global (and usually unsubstantiated) impressions, attending only superficially to what they are reading. Although there are virtues to skimming, the vast majority of writing tasks that you will encounter in college and in the workplace require your *conversancy* with material that you have read.

To become conversant means that you should be able to:

- talk about the reading conversationally with other people and answer questions about it without having to look everything up, and
- converse with the material—be in a dialogue with it, to see the questions the material asks and pose your own questions about it.

Few people are able to really understand things they read or see without making the language of that material in some way their own. We become conversant, in other words, by finding ways to actively engage material rather than moving passively through it.

If you are to play this more active role in writing about reading, you must accept that you need to:

1. *Learn to speak the language of the text.* Every course is in some sense a foreign language course: if a writer wishes to be heard, the writer needs to acquire the vocabulary of the experts. That's why it is so important to pay attention to the actual words in a reading and to use them when you write.

2. *Treat reading as a physical as well as a mental activity.* Passing your eyes or highlighter over the text, generalizing about it, or copying notes from someone else's PowerPoint will not teach you the *skills* to become an independent thinker. These activities are too passive; they don't trigger your brain into engaging the material. To get physical with the reading, focus on particular words and sentences, copy them out, restate them, and clarify for yourself what you do and do not understand.

Beyond the Banking Model of Education

The educational theorist Paolo Friere famously criticized a model of education that he compared to banking. In the banking model of education, students are like banks, accepting deposits of information from their teachers and then withdrawing them to give back on exams. Friere argued that an education consisting entirely of "banking"—information in/information out—does not teach thinking. Being able to recite other people's ideas does not automatically render a person capable of thinking about these ideas or producing them. So how can a reader accomplish the goal of acquiring new information from a reading while also learning to think about it—to be more than a passive conduit through which ideas pass? In a word, you multitask. This chapter will offer strategies to help you assimilate the information in a reading as you begin to formulate ways of responding to it. To start, let's look at how the way the information is presented contributes to its meaning.

Rejecting the Transparent Theory of Language

Any child psychology textbook will tell you that as we acquire language, we acquire categories that shape our understanding of the world. Words allow us to ask for things, to say what's on our mind. To an enormous extent, we understand the world and our relation to it by working through language.

Considering how central language is in our lives, it's amazing how little we think about words themselves. We tend to assume that things mean simply or singly, but virtually all words have multiple meanings, and words mean differently depending on context. Consider the following examples of memorably silly headlines: "Teacher Strikes Idle Kids," "New Vaccines May Contain Rabies," "Local High School Drop-outs Cut in Half," and "Include Your Children When Baking Cookies" (or if you prefer, "Kids Make Nutritious Snacks"). Language is always getting away from us—in such sentences as "The bandage was wound around the wound," or in the classic, "Time flies like an arrow; fruit flies like a banana." The meanings of words and the kinds of sense a sentence makes are rarely stable.

The transparent theory of language assumes the opposite—that words are more like clear windows opening to a meaning that can be separated from language. It also assumes that the meanings of words are obvious and self-evident. This theory is roundly rejected by linguists and other language specialists. They know that to change a word is inevitably to change meaning. This view, known as the constitutive theory of language, holds that what we see as reality is shaped by the words we use. What we say is inescapably a product of how we say it. And so, failure to arrest attention on the words causes us as readers to miss all but the vaguest impression of the ideas that the words constitute.

Seek to Understand the Reading Fairly on Its Own Terms

Most good reading starts by giving the reading the benefit of the doubt: this is known as producing a sympathetic reading, or reading with the grain. This advice applies whether or not you are inclined to agree with the claims in the reading. When you are seeking to entertain the reading on its own terms, first you have to decide to suspend judgment as an act of mind, trying instead to think *with* the piece.

Reading with the grain does not mean passive restatement. A sympathetic reading can and should also be *an active reading*. When you are writing about a reading with the grain, your goal is to help the reader (and yourself) gain some understanding of the piece. Chapter 1 has already given you some tools for accomplishing this task: Notice & Focus (ranking), and The Method to find patterns and uncover tensions (what is opposed to what). These tools allow you to answer the crucial questions, "What is at stake in the piece, and why?" And as we will discuss later in this chapter, you also ask the standard rhetorical questions, "What is this piece inviting us to think, and by what means?"

This chapter will add several new strategies, beginning with ways of focusing more closely on key words and sentences. But first let us take up briefly what writers are being asked to do when instructed to write a critique of a reading.

How to Write a Critique

We have just said that good reading starts by seeking to understand a piece on its own terms, regardless of your point of view on the subject. Does understanding a piece on its own terms mean that your role as a writer is limited to supportive restatement of what another writer has said?

In a critique, you still are expected to help readers to understand a reading as an author might wish it to be understood, but you are also expected to provide some thinking of your own on the reading. This does not mean your thinking about the subject of the reading, but instead your thinking about the writer's thinking about the subject.

Because people take critique to mean "criticize," they usually assume that they should find ways of being oppositional. An effective critique usually does not sit in judgment. You are not being asked to follow the model of talk-show, big-opinion culture—to go in and demolish the piece. Critique does not mean to attack. Instead, you are trying to put the piece into some kind of perspective, often more than one possible perspective, for your readers. This task is known as contextualizing the reading.

It helps to remember that a reading's ways of presenting its ideas (the "how") is part of its content (the "what"). A good critique includes attention to both what the reading says and how it says it. Here is a list of *some* of the things that you might choose to do in a critique (you can't do them all). These include strategies from Chapter 1 as well as moves you will encounter later in this or subsequent chapters.

- Explain what is at stake in the piece. What, in other words, is opposed to what, and why, according to the writer (implicitly, explicitly, or both), and why does the writer think it matters?

- Determine what the reading seems to wish to accomplish, which is not always the same thing as that which it explicitly argues. Do this in the context of what this chapter will later define as THE PITCH, THE COMPLAINT, AND THE MOMENT.

- Make the implicit explicit. What might the piece be saying that goes beyond what it overtly argues? This is Move #3 of the Five Analytical Moves.

- Try to figure out the possible consequences of the piece. That is, if we think in the way that the reading suggests, what might follow? What might we gain? What might we lose?

- Locate the reading in the context of other, similar readings as part of an ongoing conversation.

- Consider how well the evidence in the piece seems to support its claims and how well the writer explains her reasons for saying the evidence means what she says it does. See Chapter 6.

- Consider the logical structure of the piece by UNCOVERING ASSUMPTIONS and TRACKING BINARIES, which are discussed later in this chapter. In this way, you might locate arguments the piece is having with itself, and potentially conflicting or contradictory assumptions upon which the piece is built. Revealing such tensions need not launch an attack on the piece. Rather, it establishes perspective on the way that the reading goes about making its case.

Consider the following rhetorical analysis of a commencement address delivered by novelist David Foster Wallace at Kenyon College in 2005 (later published as "This Is Water"). Notice how the writer uses description to arrive at ideas about the speech. Description is essential in a critique, just as it is in any analytical writing. You need to start by offering your reader some significant detail in order to ground your thinking. When you select particular details and call attention to them by describing them, you are likely to begin noticing what these details suggest. Description presents details so that analysis can make them speak.

Consider how the writer of this analysis makes implicit tensions in the speech explicit. As a result, we get some perspective on the character of the speech as a whole, and on the character of its writer (*ethos*), which goes beyond simple restatement. We are given some critical distance on the piece, which is what critique does, without inviting us to approve or disapprove. The writer begins with four short quotations to get the evidence before the reader.

"I am not the wise old fish."

"Please don't worry that I am getting ready to lecture you about compassion."

"Please don't think that I am giving you moral advice."

"Please don't dismiss it as just some finger-wagging Dr. Laura sermon."

A recurrent feature of the address is the author's imploring his audience ("Please") not to assume that he is offering moral instruction. The sheer repetition of this pattern suggests that he is worried about sounding like a sermonizer, that the writer is anxious about the didacticism of his speech.

But obviously the piece does advance a moral position; it does want us to think about something serious, which is part of its function as a commencement address. What's most interesting is the final apology, offered just as the piece ends (7). Here Wallace appears to shift ground. Rather than denying that he's "the wise old fish" (1), he denies that he is Dr. Laura, or rather, he pleads not to be dismissed as a Dr. Laura. So he's saying, in effect, that we should not see him as a TV personality who scolds ("finger-wagging") and offers moral lessons for daily life ("sermon").

Why is he so worried about the didactic function? Obviously, he is thinking of his audience, fearful of appearing to be superior, and fearful that his audience does not want to be preached at. But he cannot resist the didactic impulse the occasion bestows.

In these terms, what is interesting is the divided nature of the address: on the one hand, full of parables—little stories with moral intent—and on the other hand, full of repeated denials of the very moral impulse his narratives and the occasion itself generically decree.

VOICES FROM ACROSS THE CURRICULUM

What Do We Mean by Critical Reading? A Music Professor Speaks

As a first step, we consider what we mean by a "critical reading." Because the term itself has become so ingrained in our consciousness, we rarely think critically about what it means. So, we discuss moving beyond a summary of the content and cursory judgment. I ask students to take notes on each reading (content and commentary) and conclude with three points. These points may include a main idea of the article or a part of the author's argument they found particularly interesting. We try to locate insights into the author's reason for writing the essay and rhetorical gestures or techniques used by the author to influence the reader.

Does the author make his or her objectives and biases explicit? If not, we examine the rhetorical strategies authors employ to convince us of their objectivity. We observe the ways that language colors the presentation of facts—how "a bitter civil war that pitted the slaveholding Southern states against the rest of the country" was probably not written by an author sympathetic to the Confederacy.

Much of our time is spent investigating how authors construct their narratives: the way the argument is formed and its ideological position. These ways of viewing the reading help us to move beyond restatement, delay judgment, and evaluate readings on a more sophisticated level.

—TED CONNER, PROFESSOR OF MUSIC

Focus on Individual Sentences

Analyzing needs to be anchored. Anchoring to a general impression—a global sense of what the reading is about—is like putting a hook in a cloud. There is nothing specific to think about, to rephrase, to nudge toward implications or back to assumptions. The best way to remember what you read and to have ideas about it is to start with the local: focus on individual sentences and short passages, and build up a knowledge base from there.

It does not matter which sentences you start with. What matters is to choose sentences that strike you as especially interesting, revealing, or strange. (See NOTICE & FOCUS, Chapter 1.) Good reading is *slow* reading: it stops your forward momentum long enough to allow you to dwell on individual sentences and make the effort necessary to explore and expand your understanding of them.

A second and related way that people neglect the actual words is that they approach the reading *looking to react*. They are so busy looking to respond to other people's statements that they don't listen to what the other person is saying. A well-known article on reading by the literary and educational theorist Robert Scholes suggests that people read badly because they substitute for the words on the page some association or predetermined idea that the words accidentally trigger in them. As a result, they replay their own perceptions rather than taking in the writer's actual words. (See Robert Scholes, "The Transition to College Reading," *Pedagogy*, volume 2, number 2, Duke UP, 2002, pp. 165–172.)

We will now survey a few techniques for focusing on individual sentences.

POINTING

POINTING is a practice (associated with two writing theorists and master teachers, Peter Elbow and Sheridan Blau) in which members of a group take turns reading sentences aloud. POINTING provides a way of summarizing without generalizing, and it is one of the best ways to build community and to stimulate discussion (see Figure 2.1).

1	**Select sentences from a reading that you are willing to voice.**
2	**Take turns reading individual sentences aloud.** No one raises hands or comments on the sentences during the pointing. Read only one of your chosen sentences at a time. Later in the session, you may read again.
3	**Let the recitation build.** Some sentences repeat as refrains; others segue or answer previous sentences. POINTING usually lasts about five minutes and ends more or less naturally, when people no longer have sentences they wish to read.

FIGURE 2.1
POINTING

POINTING stirs our memories about the particular language of a piece. In reading aloud, and hearing others read, you hear key words and discover questions you'd not noticed before; and the range of possible starting points for getting at what is central in the reading inevitably multiplies. POINTING is an antidote for the limiting assumption that a reading has only one main idea. It also remedies the tendency of group discussion to veer into general impressions and loose associations.

POINTING is most productive when participants focus on listening to others' sentences. Have everyone take notes about what they hear—the key words—as the POINTING proceeds. Once the activity is finished, class members can respond to the prompt "What did you hear?" by taking turns reading the key words aloud from their notes.

Using Quotation

Quoting key words and sentences from a reading keeps you focused on specific words and ideas rather than general impressions. It is not enough, however, to quote key sentences from a reading without discussing what you take them to mean, for what a sentence means is never self-evident. A mantra of this book is that analytical writers quote *in order to* analyze. That is, they follow up quotation by voicing what specifically they understand that quote to mean. The best way to arrive at that meaning is to paraphrase. (Some disciplines, it must be acknowledged, refrain from quoting and include only the paraphrase.) In any case, a quote alone cannot serve as your "answer" by itself; you can't use a quote in place of your own active explanation of what a reading is saying. Quotes only help you to focus and launch that explanation. (For more on this subject, see Chapter 8.)

PARAPHRASE × 3

Paraphrasing is one of the simplest and most overlooked ways of discovering ideas and stimulating interpretation. Like POINTING, PARAPHRASE × 3 seeks to locate you in the local, the particular, and the concrete rather than the global, the overly general, and the abstract. Rather than make a broad claim about what a sentence or passage says, a paraphrase stays much closer to the actual words.

The word "paraphrase" means to put one phrase next to ("para") another phrase. When you recast a sentence or two—finding the best synonyms you can think of for the original language, translating it into a parallel statement—you are thinking about what the original words mean. The use of "× 3" (times 3) in our label is a reminder to paraphrase key words more than once, not settling too soon for a best synonym (see Figure 2.2).

1. **Select a short passage** (as little as a single sentence or even a phrase) from whatever you are studying that you think is interesting, perhaps puzzling, and especially useful for understanding the material. Assume you *don't* understand it completely, even if you think you do.

2. **Find synonyms for all of the key terms.** Don't just go for the gist, a loose approximation of what was said. Substitute language virtually word-for-word to produce a parallel version of the original statement.

3. **Repeat this rephrasing several times** (we suggest three). This will produce a range of possible implications that the original passage may possess.

4. **Contemplate the various versions you have produced.** Which seem most plausible as restatements of what the original piece intends to communicate?

5. **Decide what you now recognize about the meaning of the original passage.** What do you now recognize about the passage on the basis of your repeated restatements? What now does the passage appear to mean? What implications have the paraphrasings revealed?

FIGURE 2.2

PARAPHRASE × 3

When you paraphrase language, whether your own or language you encounter in your reading, you are not just defining terms but opening out the wide range of implications those words inevitably possess. When we read, it is easy to skip quickly over the words, assuming we know what they mean. Yet when people start talking about what particular words mean—the difference, for example, between *assertive* and *aggressive* or the meaning of ordinary words such as *polite* or *realistic* or *gentlemanly*—they usually find less agreement than expected.

Note: Different academic disciplines treat paraphrase somewhat differently. In the humanities, it is essential first to quote an important passage and then to paraphrase it. In the social sciences, however, especially in Psychology, you paraphrase but rarely if ever quote. In more advanced writing in the social sciences, paraphrase serves the purpose of producing the literature review—survey of relevant research—that forms the introduction to reports.

How PARAPHRASE × 3 Unlocks Implications: An Example Like the "So what?" question, paraphrasing is an effective way of bringing out implications—meanings that are there in the original but not overt. And especially if you paraphrase the same passage repeatedly, you will discover which of the words are most "slippery"—elusive, hard to define simply and unambiguously.

Let's look at a brief example of PARAPHRASE × 3 from the book *The Literature Workshop* by Sheridan Blau. We have paraphrased it three times.

> "A conviction of certainty is one of the most certain signs of ignorance and may be the best operational definition of stupidity."

1. Absence of doubt is a clear indication of cluelessness and is perhaps the top way of understanding the lack of intelligence.

2. A feeling of being right is one of the most reliable indexes of lack of knowledge and may show in action the meaning of mental incapacity.

3. Being confident that you are correct is a foolproof warning that you don't know what's going on, and this kind of confidence may be an embodiment of foolishness.

Having arrived at these three paraphrases, we can use them to explore what they suggest—i.e., their implications. Here is a short list. Once you start paraphrasing, you discover that there's a lot going on in this sentence.

- One implication of the sentence is that as people come to know more and more, they feel less confident about what they know.

- Another is that ignorance and stupidity are probably not the same thing, though they are often equated.

- Another is that there's a difference between feeling certain about something and being aware of this certainty as a conviction.

- Another implication is that stupidity is hard to define—perhaps it can only be defined in practice, "operationally," and not as an abstract concept.

As we paraphrased, we were struck by the repetition of "certainty" in "certain," which led us to wonder about the tone of the sentence. Tone may be understood as the implicit point of view, the unspoken attitude of the statement toward itself and its readers. The piece overtly attacks "a conviction of certainty" as "a sign of ignorance" and perhaps ("may be") "a definition of stupidity." By implication, being less sure you are right would be a sign of wisdom. But the statement itself seems extremely sure of itself, brimming with confidence: it asserts "a certain sign."

One implication of this apparent contradiction is that we are meant to take the statement with a grain of salt—that is, read it as poking fun at itself (ironically), demonstrating the very attitude it advises us to avoid.

TRY THIS 2.1: Experiment with Paraphrase × 3

Recast the substantive language of the following statements using Paraphrase × 3:

- "I am entitled to my opinion."
- "We hold these truths to be self-evident."
- "That's just common sense."

What do you come to understand about these remarks as a result of paraphrasing? Which words, for example, are most slippery (that is, difficult to define and thus rephrase) and why?

It is interesting to note, by the way, that Thomas Jefferson originally wrote the words "sacred and undeniable" in his draft of the Declaration of Independence, instead of "self-evident." So what?

TRY THIS 2.2: Paraphrase and Implication

Consider for a moment an assignment a former student of ours, Sean Heron, gave to a class of high school students he was student-teaching during a unit on the Civil War. He asked students to paraphrase three times the following sentence: "The South left the country." His goal, he reported, was to get them to see that "because language is open to interpretation, and history is conveyed through language, history must also be open to interpretation." Use Paraphrase × 3 to figure out how Sean's sentence slants history.

Passage-Based Focused Freewriting

Passage-Based Focused Freewriting increases your ability to learn from what you read. It is probably the single best way to arrive at ideas about what you are reading. The passage-based version differs from regular freewriting (see Chapter 1) by limiting the focus to a piece of text. It prompts in-depth analysis of a representative example, on the assumption that you'll attain a better appreciation of the whole after you've explored how a piece of it works.

The more you practice Passage-Based Focused Freewriting, the better you will get and the easier you will find things to say about your chosen passage. Ask yourself:

- "What one passage in the reading do you think most needs to be discussed—is most useful and interesting for understanding the material?"

- "What one passage seems puzzling, difficult to pin down, anomalous, or even just unclear—and how might this be explained?"

The impromptu nature of PASSAGE-BASED FOCUSED FREEWRITING encourages you to take chances, to think out loud on the page. It invites you to attend to what you notice in the moment and take some stabs at what the passage might mean without having to worry about formulating a weighty thesis statement or maintaining consistency. It allows you to worry less about what you don't understand and instead start to work things out as you write.

Many great papers start not as outlines but as freewrites, written in class or out (see Figure 2.3).

1	**Choose a short passage to focus on and write about it without stopping for 10 to 20 minutes.** Pick a passage you find interesting and that you probably don't quite understand. Copy out the passage at the beginning of your freewrite. This act will encourage attention to the words and induce you to notice more about the particular features of your chosen passage.
2	**Contextualize the passage.** Where does the passage come from in the text? Of what larger discussion is it a part? Briefly answering these questions will prevent you from taking things out of context.
3	**Focus on what the passage is inviting readers to think**—its point of view—not your point of view of that subject.
4	**Make observations about the passage.** Stay close to the language you've quoted, paraphrasing key phrases and teasing out the possible meanings of these words. Then reflect on what you've come to better understand through paraphrasing. Remember to share your reasoning about what the evidence means.
5	**Address how the passage is representative, how it connects to broader issues in the reading.** Move from your analysis of local details to consider what the work as a whole may plausibly be "saying" about this or that issue or question. It's okay to work with the details for almost the entire time and then press yourself to an interpretive leap with the prompt, "I'm almost out of time but my big point is. . . ."

FIGURE 2.3
PASSAGE-BASED FOCUSED FREEWRITING

Note: It's okay to work with the details for almost the entire time and then press yourself to an interpretive leap with the prompt, "I'm almost out of time, but my big point is. . . ." One aim of PASSAGE-BASED FOCUSED FREEWRITES is to get you to a claim.

Some Moves to Make (or Avoid) in PASSAGE-BASED FOCUSED FREEWRITING

PASSAGE-BASED FOCUSED FREEWRITING incorporates a number of the methods we have been discussing in these first two chapters. So, for example:

- Don't start with a claim begin by describing carefully what you notice in the language of the passage (review our description of the painting *Whistler's Mother* in Figure 1.7).

- Start with observations discovered by doing NOTICE & FOCUS or "interesting, revealing, or strange" (Move 2 of the Five Analytical Moves discussed in Chapter 1).

- It often grows out of doing THE METHOD, further developing the paragraph that explains why you chose one repetition, strand, or binary as being most important.

- In analyzing the chosen passage, use PARAPHRASE × 3 to interrogate the key words, opening up interpretive possibilities.

- Keep the writing going by insistently ASKING "SO WHAT?" at the ends of paragraphs.

The best PASSAGE-BASED FOCUSED FREEWRITING usually arrives at one or more of the following:

- **Interpretation**, which uses restatement to figure out what the sentence from the text means.

- **Implication**. A useful (and logical) next step is to go after implication. If X or Y is true, then what might follow from it? ("So what?")

- **Application**. A passage that is resonant in some way for the reader might lead him or her to write about some practical way of applying the reading—for example, as a lens for understanding other material.

- **Assumptions**. We lay out implications by moving forward (so to speak). We unearth assumptions by moving backwards. If a text asks us to believe X, what else must it already believe? From what unstated assumptions, in other words, would X follow?

- **Queries**. What questions, interpretive difficulties, and struggles are raised by the reading?

Notice how the writers use these moves in the examples that follow.

From PASSAGE-BASED FOCUSED FREEWRITING to Formal Essay It is often productive to take a focused freewrite and type it, revising and further freewriting until you have filled the inevitable gaps in your thinking that the time limit has created. (One colleague of ours has students revise and expand in a different font, so both can see how the thinking is evolving.) Eventually, you can build up, through a process of accretion, the thinking for an entire paper in this way.

An especially useful way of making PASSAGE-BASED FOCUSED FREEWRITING productive academically is to freewrite for fifteen minutes every day on a different passage as you move through a book. If, for example, you are discussing a book over four class periods, prepare for each class by giving fifteen minutes to a passage before you attend. You will not only discover things to say, but also you will begin to write your way to an essay.

One way to get from a freewrite to an essay is to keep starting new free-writes from the best ideas in your earlier ones. Try putting an asterisk in the margin next to your best idea or question, and start another PASSAGE-BASED FOCUSED FREEWRITE from there.

PASSAGE-BASED FOCUSED FREEWRITING: An Example Below is an example of a student's exploratory writing on an essay by the twentieth-century African American writer Langston Hughes. The piece is a twenty-minute reflection on two excerpts. Most notable about this piece, perhaps, is the sheer number of interesting ideas. That may be because the writer continually returns to the language of the original quotes for inspiration. She is not restricted by maintaining a single, consistent thread. Notice, however, that as the freewrite progresses, a primary focus (on the second of her two quotes) seems to emerge.

Passages from "The Negro Artist and the Racial Mountain,"
by Langston Hughes

"But jazz to me is one of the inherent expressions of negro life in America; the eternal tom-tom beating in the Negro soul—the tom-tom of revolt against weariness in a white world, a world of subway trains, and work, work, work; the tom-tom of joy and laughter, and pain swallowed in a smile. Yet the Philadelphia clubwoman is ashamed to say that her race created it and she does not like me to write about it. The old subconscious 'white is best' runs through her mind. . . . And now she turns up her nose at jazz and all its manifestations—likewise almost everything else distinctly racial."

"We build our temples for tomorrow, strong as we know how, and we stand on top of the mountain, free within ourselves."

Langston Hughes's 1926 essay on the situation of the Negro artist in America sets up some interesting issues that are as relevant today as they were in Hughes's time. Interestingly, the final sentence of the essay ("We build our temples. . .") will be echoed some four decades later by the Civil Rights leader, Martin Luther King, but with a different spin on the idea of freedom. Hughes writes, "we stand on top of the mountain, free within ourselves." King says, "Free at last, free at last, my God almighty, we're free at last." King asserts an opening out into the world—a freeing of black people, finally, from slavery and then another century of oppression.

Hughes speaks of blacks in a more isolated position—"on top of the mountain" and "within ourselves." Although the mountain may stand for a height from which the artist can speak, it is hard to be heard from the top of mountains. It is one thing to be free. It is another to be free within oneself. What does this phrase mean? If I am free within myself I am at least less vulnerable to those who would restrict me from without. I can live with their restrictions. Mine is an inner freedom. Does inner freedom empower artists? Perhaps it does. It may allow them to say what they want and not worry about what others say or think. This is one thing that Hughes seems to be calling for. But he is also worried about lack of recognition of Negro artists, not only by whites but by blacks. His use of the repeated phrase, tom-tom, is interesting in this respect. It, like the word "mountain," becomes a kind of refrain in the essay—announcing both a desire to rise above the world and its difficulties (mountain) and a desire to be heard (tom-tom and mountain as pulpit).

The idea of revolt, outright rebellion, is present but subdued in the essay. The tom-tom is a "revolt against weariness" and also an instrument for expressing "joy and laughter." The tom-tom also suggests a link with a past African and probably Native American culture—communicating by drum and music and dance. White culture in the essay stands for a joyless world of "work work work." This is something I would like to think about more, as the essay seems to link the loss of soul with the middle and upper classes, both black and white.

And so the essay seeks to claim another space among those he calls "the low down folks, the so-called common element." Of these he says ". . .they do not particularly care whether they are like white folks or anybody else. Their joy runs, bang! into ecstasy. Their religion soars to a shout. Work maybe a little today, rest a little tomorrow. Play awhile. Sing awhile. O, let's dance!" In these lines Hughes the poet clearly appears. Does he say then that the Negro artist needs to draw from those of his own people who are the most removed from middle class American life? If I had more time, I would start thinking here about Hughes's use of the words "race" and "racial". . . . (Reprinted with permission from the June 23, 1926 issue of *The Nation*. For subscription information, call 1-800-333-8536. Portions of each week's *Nation* magazine can be accessed at http://www.thenation.com.)

PASSAGE-BASED FOCUSED FREEWRITING: Another Example PASSAGE-BASED FOCUSED FREEWRITING is especially well suited to doing rhetorical analysis, as in the following example. As we explained in Chapter 1, rhetorical analysis seeks to understand how a writer's word choice reveals the writer's way of appealing to a target audience. Sometimes in-class writings are done in response to a prompt. The prompt for this freewrite was, "How does Obama's first inaugural address compare with his election night victory speech?"

What was most interesting to me about Obama's inaugural speech was his use of the collective first person—"we," "our," "us," etc.—as opposed to the singular "I." This is especially different from his victory speech, which did make use of the singular "I" and addressed the audience as "you." These pronoun choices are actually very conducive to the tone of each speech. Obama's victory speech was a *victory* speech—it was meant to be joyful, hopeful, optimistic, and, of course, thankful... so every use of "you" is not accusatory but rather congratulatory and proud—e.g. "this is because of you," "you have done this," "this is your victory."

On the other hand, Obama's inaugural speech was by and large a more somber piece of writing—as the President said to George Stephanopolous, he wanted to capture that moment in history as exactly as possible. "You" here is not the American public as in the victory speech; rather, "you" is any "enemy" of America. And "I," it seems, has become "we." This choice automatically makes Obama the voice of society, as though speaking for every American. This is a really subtle but smart choice to make, because the listener or reader is hearing everything he says as his or her own position. Using that collective first person also puts Obama on the same level as everyone else, and when he does blame America for its own problems, the "our's" and "we's" soften the blow. The "you's" here are harsh and accusatory but meant for that great, terrible, unnamed enemy to "our" freedom and happiness.

I found a lot more obvious echoes to Lincoln in this speech as compared to the victory speech, coupled with earth imagery—for example, "we cannot hallow this ground" (Lincoln) vs. "what the cynics fail to understand is that the ground has shifted" (Obama). This ties America to the actual physical land. It romanticizes and makes permanent the ideas of our country—a nice setting behind all of the nation's troubles—while simultaneously adding to the so-desired degree of "timelessness" of Obama's first inaugural address.

You can sense the writer, Molly Harper, gathering steam here as she begins to make connections in her evidence, yet her rhetorical analysis started from a simple observation of Obama's pronouns and then the significance of the contrast between them in the two speeches she is comparing.

TRY THIS 2.3: Do Passage-Based Focused Freewriting
Select a passage from any of the material that you are reading and copy it at the top of the page. Remember to choose the passage in response to the question, "What is the single sentence that I think it is most important for us to discuss and why?" Then do a twenty-minute focused freewrite, applying the steps offered above. Discover what you think by seeing what you say.

TRY THIS 2.4: Writing and Reading with Others: A Sequence of Activities
1. Spend five to ten minutes Pointing on some piece of reading. Remember that no one should comment on their choice of sentences during the Pointing exercise.

2. Without pausing for discussion, spend ten minutes doing Passage-Based Focused Freewriting on a sentence or several similar sentences from the reading. It is important to write nonstop and to keep writing throughout the appointed time.

3. Volunteers then take turns reading all or part of their freewrites aloud to the group, without comment. It is useful for people to read, rather than describe or summarize, what they wrote. As each person reads, listeners should jot down words and phrases that catch their attention.

4. After each freewrite is read, listeners call out what they heard in the freewrite by responding to the question, "What did you hear?" Alternatively, writers can meet in small groups (of three or four) and then report to the entire group in the last fifteen minutes of class.

Note: This sequence works best when it is practiced frequently—perhaps once a week. The more you practice in-class writing, the better you'll get; and if it becomes a regular feature of a course, it can turn a class of individuals into a community of writers.

Keep a Commonplace Book

Professional writers have long kept commonplace books—essentially, records of their reading. Most such books consist primarily of quotations that the writers have found striking and memorable. This practice is closely related to Pointing, Paraphrase × 3, and Passage-Based Focused Freewriting.

The word "place" comes from the Latin *locus* in classical rhetoric and is related to places that rhetoricians thought of as reliable starting points from which a writer could launch arguments. A commonplace book is a collection of ideas, a storehouse for thinking that a writer might later draw on to stimulate their own writing.

The goal of keeping a commonplace book in a course is to bring you closer to the language you find most interesting, which you inscribe in your memory as you copy it onto the page. (Aim for two quotations with citation from each reading.) It's remarkable what you will notice about a sentence if you copy it out, rather than just underlining or highlighting it. Moreover, you will find yourself remembering the original language that has struck you most forcefully in the reading. That way you can continue to ponder key words and phrases and stay engaged, almost physically, with what the writers have said.

In addition to being a record of your reading, the commonplace book is also a record of your thinking about the reading. Try to write a sentence or two after most of your quotes, noting what you find of interest there, perhaps paraphrasing key terms. Alternatively, you might append a paragraph after your collected quotes from the reading, responding to them as a group. Remember not to judge the passages you select in like-dislike terms.

Situate the Reading Rhetorically

There is no such thing as "just information." Virtually all readings possess what speech-act theorists call "illocutionary force," which means the goal of an utterance. Everything you read, to varying degrees, is aware of you, the audience, and is dealing with you in some way.

One of the most productive ways of analyzing a reading is to consider the frame within which a piece is presented: who its intended audience is, what it seeks to persuade that audience about, and how the writer presents himself or herself to appeal to that audience. Readings virtually never treat these questions explicitly, and thus, it is a valuable analytical move to infer a reading's assumptions about audience.

Find THE PITCH, THE COMPLAINT, and THE MOMENT

An element of situating a reading rhetorically is to locate what it seeks to accomplish and what it is set against at a given moment in time. We address these concerns as a quest to find what we call THE PITCH, THE COMPLAINT, AND THE MOMENT:

- THE PITCH, what the piece wishes you to believe.

- THE COMPLAINT, what the piece is reacting to or concerned about.

- THE MOMENT, the historical and cultural context within which the piece is operating.

Here's a bit more on each.

THE PITCH: *A reading is an argument*, a presentation of information that makes a case of some sort, even if the argument is not explicitly stated. Look for language that reveals the position or positions the piece seems interested in having you adopt.

THE COMPLAINT: *A reading is a reaction to some situation*, some set of circumstances that the piece has set out to address, even though the writer may not say so openly. An indispensable means of understanding someone else's writing is to figure out what seems to have caused the person to write the piece in the first place. Writers write, presumably, because they think *something* needs to be addressed. What is that something? Look for language in the piece that reveals the writer's starting point. If you can find the position or situation the writer is worried about and possibly trying to correct, you will more easily locate the pitch, the position the piece asks you to accept.

THE MOMENT: *A reading is a response to the world conditioned by the writer's particular moment in time*. In your attempt to figure out not only what a piece says but also where it is coming from (the causes of its having been written in the first place and the positions it works to establish), history is significant. When was the piece written? Where? What else was going on at the time that might have shaped the writer's ideas and attitudes?

Rhetoricians sometimes use a term from classical rhetoric, *kairos*, for what this book calls THE MOMENT. This Greek word has been translated roughly as "the right time." Another useful term for the concept of the moment is exigence, which refers to a writer's reasons for writing, such as a problem that requires immediate attention.

THE PITCH, THE COMPLAINT, AND THE MOMENT: Two Brief Examples Here are two examples of student writing in response to the request that they locate THE PITCH, THE COMPLAINT, AND THE MOMENT for a famous essay in the field of Composition and Rhetoric, "Inventing the University," by David Bartholomae.

> Bartholomae's complaint seems to center around the idea that writing is typically taught at a grammatical, not intellectual, level. "Basic" writers are identified by their

sentence level compositional errors, not by the content of their ideas or ability to present a complex argument. Bartholomae argues that students must be drawn into the language and mindset of academia before they have the authority to confidently expand upon more complicated ideas. Students are expected to fluently participate in academic discourse long before they have the authority to pull it off with ease. Therefore, students should be familiarized with the world of academia and led through the preliminary steps towards becoming proficient in its language. This is the only way to make them more authoritative writers.

This example treats the moment in particular:

The moment, or the specific time in which the essay was written, offers some valuable insight into what might have shaped Bartholomae's perspective. First, it is important to note the other writers and thinkers Bartholomae cites throughout the essay. Take the author's frequent mention of writer Pat Bizzell whom Bartholomae deems "one of the most important scholars now writing on basic writers" and whom he recognizes as "owing a great debt to." He credits Bizzell with seeing how difficult it is for young writers to learn the complex vocabularies and conventions of academic discourse.

There are most likely other, more broadly cultural, influences at work as well, such as the American political scene in 1985. In 1984 Ronald Reagan was re-elected president. His presidency and the conservative climate it fostered sparked change in Americans' attitude toward education. Reagan's policies mandated spending cuts and, it can reasonably be assumed, invited certain anti-academic and more pre-professional attitudes. In this moment, then, Bartholomae's concerns about higher education and the need for students to gain access into the privileged world of the educated begins to make more sense.

Audience Analysis: A Brief Example Consider the following paragraph of student writing on the same essay, this time focused on how the essay's author establishes his relationship with his target audience. The writer was responding to this assignment: Write a brief analysis of the essay's rhetoric— the various methods it employs to gain acceptance with its target audience: a) who is the target audience? How can you tell? Cite and analyze evidence; b) what decisions has the author made on how best to "sell" his argument to this audience? How do you know?

Bartholomae often uses the inclusive "us" to describe academia, putting the reader (presumably, academics) above the level of those being discussed. Students must be taught "to speak our language, to speak as we do, to try on the peculiar ways of knowing, selecting, evaluating, reporting, concluding and arguing that define the discourse of our community." He effectively builds up the reader, perhaps making him or her more open to absorbing the argument that follows. He refrains from criticizing, including his audience in his idea and putting them on the same level as he is. He refers to the students as "our students" and writes almost as though the reader is separate from any flaws in the current system. He writes to colleagues, with the tone of one sharing something new and interesting.

TRY THIS 2.5: Locating The Pitch and The Complaint

At aldaily.com (Arts & Letters Daily, the website sponsored by the *Chronicle of Higher Education*) locate an article on a topic you find interesting. It should be a substantive piece of thinking, as opposed to an editorial or a piece of popular commentary. Find language that you think reveals The Pitch and The Complaint in your chosen article. Type out these sentences and be ready to explain your choices.

Focus on the Structure of Thinking in a Reading

Readers sometimes get lost because they lack perspective: they're trying so hard to understand what a text is saying word by word and sentence by sentence that, as the old saying goes, they can't see the forest for the trees. It can often be immensely useful to read for the larger cognitive structure of a piece, and two of the best ways to see this structure are to focus on its underlying assumptions or track its use of binary oppositions. The first uncovers its premises; the second reveals its preoccupations. (For more on logical analysis, see Chapter 6, "Reasoning from Evidence to Claims".)

Uncovering Assumptions

To read well requires you to see the writer's reasoning process, especially the assumptions (the premises) upon which the writer's thinking rests. An assumption is an underlying belief from which other statements spring. Assumptions are often left unstated, which is why they need to be uncovered.

Uncovering Assumptions is a version of Move 3 of the Five Analytical Moves from Chapter 1: it renders the implicit explicit. But in this case, what is revealed is not what follows from a given statement, but rather, what precedes it.

Uncovering Assumptions is a powerful analytical procedure that gives you insight into the root, the basic givens that a piece of writing has assumed are true. When you locate assumptions in a text, you understand the text better—where it's coming from, what else it believes that is more fundamental than what it is overtly declaring. The essential move is to ask, *"Given its overt claim, what must this reading also already believe?"* To answer this question, you need to make inferences from the primary claims to the ideas that underlie them. In effect, you are reasoning backwards, reinventing the chain of thinking that led the writer to the position you are now analyzing (see Figure 2.4).

The practice of Uncovering Assumptions will also help you to develop and revise your own work. When you work back to your own premises, you will often find what else you believe, at a more basic level, that you did not realize you believed.

1	Determine the key terms in a statement and paraphrase them.
2	**Ask what assumptions the statement rests on,** the implicit ideas underlying it that the writer seems to assume to be true.
3	**Consider how these underlying assumptions contribute to your understanding of the reading as a whole.**

FIGURE 2.4

UNCOVERING ASSUMPTIONS

UNCOVERING ASSUMPTIONS: An Example Consider the claim, "Tax laws benefit the wealthy."

We might paraphrase the claim as "The rules for paying income tax give rich people monetary advantages" or "The rules for paying income tax help the rich get richer."

Now let's look at the implicit ideas that the claim assumes to be true:

Tax laws don't treat people equally.

Tax laws may have unintended consequences.

If we assume that the speaker is worried about tax laws possibly benefiting the wealthy, then a few more assumptions can be inferred:

Tax laws shouldn't benefit anybody.

Tax laws shouldn't benefit those who are already advantaged.

This process of definition will reveal the key concepts upon which the claim depends. Regardless of the position you might adopt—attacking tax laws, defending them, showing how they actually benefit everyone, and so on—you risk arguing blindly if you fail to question the purpose of the tax law in the first place.

The wording of this claim seems to conceal an egalitarian premise: the assumption that tax laws should not benefit anyone, or, at least, that they should benefit everyone equally. But what is the purpose of tax laws? Should they redress economic inequities? Should they spur the economy by rewarding those who generate capital? Our point here is that you would need to move your thesis back to this point and test the validity of the assumptions upon which it rests.

TRY THIS 2.6: UNCOVERING ASSUMPTIONS Implied by a Statement

In the reference application sent to professors at our college for students who are seeking to enter the student-teaching program, the professor is asked to rank the student from one to four (unacceptable to acceptable) on the following criterion: "The student uses his/her sense of humor appropriately." Use the three-step procedure for UNCOVERING ASSUMPTIONS to explore what the authors of this criterion must also already believe—about education, about humor, and about anything else the evidence suggests—if they think this category of evaluation is important.

TRY THIS 2.7: Uncovering Assumptions: Fieldwork

You can practice Uncovering Assumptions with all kinds of material—newspaper editorials, statements you see on billboards, ideas you are studying in your courses, jokes, and so forth. Try a little fieldwork: spend a week jotting down in your notebook interesting statements you overhear. Choose the best of these from the standpoint of the implied (but unstated) premises upon which each statement seems to rest. Then make a list of the assumptions.

Reading Against the Grain Earlier in the chapter we counseled that you should start by reading with the grain. When you begin Uncovering Assumptions, however, you may discover interesting ways in which a reading seems to say things it may not have intended to communicate.

When we ask ourselves what a work (and, by implication, an author) might not be aware of communicating, we are doing what is called *reading against the grain*. When we ask ourselves what a work seems aware of, what its (and, by implication, its author's) conscious intentions are, we are *reading with the grain*.

Writers can never be fully in control of what they communicate; our words always, inescapably, communicate more (and less) than we intend. Any of us who has had what we thought to be a perfectly clear and well-intentioned e-mail misinterpreted (or so we thought) by its recipient can understand this idea. When we look at the letter again we usually see what it said that we hadn't realized (at least not consciously) we were saying.

Communication of all kinds takes place both directly and indirectly. Reading against the grain—looking for what a work is saying that it might not know it is saying, that it might not mean to say—requires us to notice and emphasize implicit patterns and make their significance explicit. So, for example, in the classic novel *Jane Eyre*, the narrator Jane repeatedly remarks on her own plain appearance, with the implication that physical beauty is transient and relatively insignificant. Reading against the grain, we'd see the novel's very obsession with plainness as a symptom of how worried it is about the subject, how much it truly believes (but won't admit) that looks matter.

Tracking Binaries in a Reading

Once you begin looking at chains of thought—Uncovering Assumptions—you will often discover that key binaries rise to the surface. We have encountered binaries before—pairs of words or details that are opposites (for example, *open/ closed, ugly/beautiful, global/local*). In Chapter 1, locating binaries was introduced as a key component of looking for pattern using The Method.

The assumption that underlies binaries is that we understand that which is in terms of that which is not. In other words, fundamental contrasts and oppositions are sites of uncertainty, places where there is a struggle among various points of view.

Thus, the swiftest way to apprehend what is at stake in a reading is to discern its organizing contrasts. To track the thinking in a piece is to track how it moves among its various binary formulations.

Writers think through binaries, consciously or unconsciously reformulating them, as we can see when we TRACK THE BINARIES through a reading. Notice how James Howard Kunstler develops his thinking in the following excerpt:

> Civic life is what goes on in the public realm. Civic life refers to our relations with our fellow human beings—in short, our roles as citizens. Sometime in the past forty years we ceased to speak of ourselves as citizens and labeled ourselves consumers. That's what we are today in the language of the evening news—*consumers*—in the language of the Sunday panel discussion shows—*consumers*—in the blizzard of statistics that blows out of the U.S. Department of Commerce every month. Consumers, unlike citizens, have no responsibilities, obligations, or duties to anything larger than their own needs and desires, certainly not to anything like the common good. How can this be construed as anything other than an infantile state of existence? In degrading the language of our public discussion this way—labeling ourselves consumers—have we not degraded our sense of who we are? And is it any wonder that we cannot solve any of our social problems, which are problems of the public realm and the common good? [From James Howard Kunstler, *Home From Nowhere: Remaking Our Everyday World for the Twenty-First Century* (Simon & Schuster, 1996).]

The implicit binary that organizes the thinking in this paragraph is public versus private. Here is a rough approximation of how this binary generates a range of opposing terms as the paragraph progresses:

PUBLIC	PRIVATE
civic life	
our relations with/ fellow humans	labeled ourselves consumers
our roles as citizens	panel discussion tv shows and govt statistics
responsibilities to others	no responsibilities beyond own needs and desires
the common good	
implicitly, adult	infantile state of existence
the public realm	implicitly, the private realm

Kunstler doesn't just settle for a simple binary; he develops, expands and clarifies it by renaming it. In this way, the thinking grows and develops to arrive, at the end, in an explanation of why "we cannot solve any of our social problems."

If you leap too quickly to a binary, however, one that is too general or inaccurate, you can get stuck in oversimplification, in rigidly dichotomized points of view. At that point, you are in the grasp of a reductive habit of mind called either/or thinking. The solution is to keep in mind that the binaries you discover in a reading are sites at which the piece is arguing with itself, figuring out in some qualified way what ultimately it believes.

REFORMULATING BINARIES

We wish now to focus on a related use of binaries, one that takes place in higher order analysis. This move we call REFORMULATING BINARIES.

Thinking is not simply linear and progressive, moving from point A to point B to point C like stops on a train. Careful thinkers are always retracing their steps, questioning their first—and second—impressions, assuming that they've missed something. All good thinking is *recursive*—that is, it repeatedly goes over the same ground, rethinking connections. And that's why REFORMULATING BINARIES is an essential analytical move.

You know that a writer is REFORMULATING BINARIES when a reading does one or more of the following:

- Discovers that the binary has not been named adequately, and that another formulation of the opposition would be more accurate.

- Values both sides of the binary (rather than seeing the issue as all or nothing), but weights one side of the binary more heavily than the other.

- Discovers that the two terms of the binary are not so separate and opposed after all, but are actually parts of one complex phenomenon or issue. (This key analytical move is known as "collapsing the binary.")

When you formulate a binary opposition in your own analytical prose—the place where something is at issue—your next step is to begin to ask questions about and complicate the binary. To "complicate" a binary is to discover evidence that unsettles it and formulate alternatively worded binaries that more accurately describe what is at issue in the evidence (see Figure 2.5).

1	**Locate a range of opposing categories (binaries).** Finding binaries will help you find the questions around which almost anything is organized. Use THE METHOD to help you uncover the binary oppositions in your subject matter that might function as organizing contrasts.
2	**Define and analyze the key terms.** By analyzing the terms of most binaries, you should come to question them and ultimately arrive at a more complex and qualified position.
3	**Question the accuracy of the binary and rephrase the terms.** Think of the binary as a starting point—a kind of deliberate overgeneralization—that allows you to set up positions you can then test in order to refine.
4	**Substitute "to what extent?" for "either/or."** The best strategy in using binaries productively is usually to locate arguments **on both sides** of the either/or choice that the binary poses and then choose a position somewhere between the two extremes. Once you have arrived at what you consider the most accurate phrasing of the binary, you can rephrase the original either/or question in the more qualified terms that asking "To what extent?" allows.

FIGURE 2.5

REFORMULATING BINARIES

REFORMULATING BINARIES: An Example Suppose you are analyzing the following topic in a management course: Would the model of management known as Total Quality Management (TQM), widely used in Japan, function effectively in the American automotive industry?

Step 1: A range of opposing categories are suggested by the language of the topic, the most obvious being function versus not function. But there are also other binaries here: Japanese versus American, and TQM versus more traditional and traditionally American models of management. These binaries imply further binaries. The question requires a writer to consider the accuracy and relative suitability of particular traits commonly ascribed to Japanese versus American workers, such as communal and cooperative versus individualistic and competitive.

Step 2: Questions of definition might concentrate on what it means to ask whether TQM *functions effectively* in the American automotive industry. Does that mean make a substantial profit? Produce more cars more quickly? Improve employee morale? You would drown in vagueness unless you carefully argued for the appropriateness of your definition of this key term.

Step 3: How accurate is the binary? To what extent do American and Japanese management styles actually differ? Can you locate significant differences between these management styles that correspond to supposed differences between Japanese and American culture that might help you formulate your binary more precisely?

Step 4: To complicate the either/or formulation, you might suggest the danger of assuming that all American workers are rugged individualists and all Japanese workers are communal bees. Insofar as you are going to arrive at a qualified claim, it would be best stated in terms of *the extent to which* TQM might be adaptable to the auto industry.

COLLAPSING THE BINARY: A Brief Example In his essay "In Defense of Distraction," writer Sam Anderson argues that contemporary American culture is suffering from what he terms "a crisis of attention." He initially proposes a binary between attention (focus) and distraction. But as the essay progresses, he comes to argue that the two are not entirely opposed but in fact comprise one complex phenomenon: focused distraction. He finds value in both, he finds limitation in both, and he discovers that they rely on each other.

Tracking the Thinking Through Complication and Qualification: An Example In the following excerpt from "On Political Labels," political scientist Christopher Borick complicates the definition of liberalism by tracking it historically. Look in the first paragraph for the historical roots of liberalism as favoring public control over government actions. In the second paragraph, see how this emphasis moves almost to its opposite—the belief that "government intervention in society is necessary." You'll learn a lot from the excerpt by seeing how it pivots around more than one sense of the word "freedom."

Let's look at liberalism for a start. The term liberal can be traced at least back to 17th-Century England, where it evolved from debates dealing with the voting franchise among English citizens. Proponents of including greater numbers of Englishmen in elections came to be known as liberals, thanks in part to the writings of John Locke, whose ideas about the social contract helped to build the philosophical underpinnings of this political ideology. Over time, liberalism has maintained its focus on public control over government actions, but there have been splits that have led to its current manifestation. In the 18th and 19th Centuries, liberalism began to stress the importance of individual freedom and broader rights of the citizenry in terms of limits on government. In essence, this type of liberalism focused on "negative rights" or the restrictions on what government could do to its citizens. The First Amendment of the Constitution includes numerous examples of negative rights. The granting of the right to freedom of speech or the press is achieved through the prohibition of government from creating laws that abridge such freedoms. Thus negating an action of government creates rights for the people.

In the 20th Century, however, liberalism became synonymous with the view that government had to be much more active in helping citizens get to the point where they would be able to truly live a free life. In this expanding view of liberalism, government intervention in society is necessary to create a more level playing field on which individuals can then use their freedom to achieve desired goals. Such beliefs have been at the roots of government expansion into social welfare policies such as public housing, food stamps, and affirmative action, and have formed the core of government agendas such as Franklin Roosevelt's New Deal and Lyndon Johnson's Great Society.

As this piece progresses, you can expect that it will either resolve the significant gap between the two historical definitions of liberalism, or that it will in various ways show us how the gap has continued to produce tensions or misunderstandings that it may rename.

In the case of most academic writing, it is usually a mistake to assume that the piece is making a single argument. A smarter assumption is that the piece is interested in exploring an issue or a problem from multiple points of view.

TRY THIS 2.8: REFORMULATING BINARIES: Fieldwork
Locate some organizing contrasts in anything—something you are studying, something you've just written, something you saw on television last night, something on the front page of the newspaper, something going on at your campus or workplace, and so forth. Consider, for example, the binaries suggested by current trends in contemporary music or by the representation of women in birthday cards. Having selected the binaries you want to work with,

pick one and transform the either/or thinking into more qualified thinking using the "to-what-extent" formula (step 4).

TRY THIS 2.9: Practice Tracking Reformulated Binaries in a Reading

In the following paragraph, writer Jonathan Franzen explores a problem by locating, defining, analyzing, and Reformulating Binaries. Track the thinking in the Franzen paragraph. How does it engage readers' expectations? What happens to the binary *public* versus *private*?

> Walking up Third Avenue on a Saturday night, I feel bereft. All around me, attractive young people are hunched over their StarTacs and Nokias with preoccupied expressions, as if probing a sore tooth, or adjusting a hearing aid, or squeezing a pulled muscle; personal technology has begun to look like a personal handicap. All I really want from a sidewalk is that people see me and let themselves be seen, but even this modest ideal is thwarted by cell-phone users and their unwelcome privacy. They say things like "Should we have couscous with that?" and "I'm on my way to Blockbuster." They aren't breaking any laws by broadcasting these breakfast-nook conversations. There's no PublicityGuard that I can buy, no expensive preserve of public life to which I can flee. Seclusion, whether in a suite at the Plaza or in a cabin in the Catskills, is comparatively effortless to achieve. Privacy is protected as both commodity and right; public forums are protected as neither. Like old-growth forests, they're few and irreplaceable and should be held in trust by everyone. The work of maintaining them gets only harder as the private sector grows ever more demanding, distracting, and disheartening. Who has the time and energy to stand up for the public sphere? What rhetoric can possibly compete with the American love of "privacy"? [From Jonathan Franzen, "Imperial Bedroom," in *How to Be Alone* (Farrar, Straus, and Giroux, 2003).]

Apply a Reading as a Lens

This final section of the chapter discusses how to apply a reading to other material you are studying. Using a reading as a lens means literally looking at things as the reading does, trying to think in its terms.

In college, students are expected to be able to take readings often complex, theoretical readings and use them in order to understand other material. This is one of the biggest differences between writing about reading in high school versus college. As a lens, the reading shapes how we come to understand whatever it is being applied to.

Your first goal when working with a reading as a lens is to explore its usefulness for explaining features of your subject. Because the match between lens and new material will never be perfect, you need to remember that whenever you apply the lens A to a new subject B, you are taking lens A from its original context and using its ideas in somewhat different circumstances for at least somewhat different purposes. Using the lens in a different context upon a different kind of information will often require you to adjust the lens—to refocus it a bit to bring this new content into clear focus.

Let's say, for example, that you have read a smart review essay on the representation of Black/White race relations in contemporary films in the 1970s, and you decide to use the review as a lens for exploring the spate of Black/White buddy films that emerged in the 1990s.

"Yes, but. . . ," you find yourself responding: there are places where the 1990s films appear to fit within the pattern that the article claims, but there are also exceptions to the pattern. What do you do? What *not* to do is either choose different films that "fit better" or decide that the article is wrong-headed. Instead, start with the "yes": talk about how the films accord with the general pattern. Then focus on the "but," the claims in the reading (the lens) that seem not to fit, or material in your subject not adequately accounted for by the lens.

Because cultural climates and trends are constantly shifting and reconfiguring themselves, particularly in popular culture, you will learn from examining the films how the original review might be usefully extended to account for phenomena that were not present when it was originally written.

Using a Reading as a Lens: An Extended Example In the following example of Applying a Reading as a Lens, one of our students, Anna Whiston, applies her lens (the theories of socio-linguist Deborah Tannen on gender and conversation styles) to her subject: the conversational tactics of male celebrities on late-night talk shows. The assignment was to use concepts from two books by Tannen—*You Just Don't Understand: Women and Men in Conversation* and *That's Not What I Meant: How Conversational Style Makes or Breaks Relationships*—to explore a conversational topic of the student's choice.

In her essay, excerpted here from a longer draft, Whiston shows how to do more with a theoretical reading than use it in a matching exercise. Rather than simply demonstrating the match between her evidence and Tannen's theories, she extends their range. She also shows how seemingly contradictory evidence can be seen actually to support Tannen's primary claims.

"'I think my cooking, uh, sucks:' Self-Deprecation on Late-Night Television," by Anna Whiston

In *You Just Don't Understand*, linguist Deborah Tannen explores conversation as a process affected largely by the gender of the speaker. For men, according to Tannen, "... life is a contest in which they are constantly tested and must perform, in order to avoid the risk of failure." This sense of competition often manifests itself in "one-upsmanship," a strategy in which men attempt to outdo each other in order to achieve a superior position within a conversation. There are, however, certain situations in which being on top of the hierarchy is not necessarily desirable. The interactions between men on late night talk shows provide examples of such situations.

Low confidence is not exactly typical in Hollywood. Celebrities are known just as much for their egos as they are for the movies that they headline and the scandals that they induce. And yet, late-night talk shows, such as *The Tonight Show with Jay Leno, Late Night with Conan O'Brien, The Late Show with David Letterman,* and *Jimmy Kimmel Live,* include endless examples of self-deprecation on the parts of both the male hosts and the male celebrity guests.

Self-deprecation is, on the surface, a way of belittling oneself. However, examination of the conversations that take place on these television programs helps show that this strand of apparent humility is actually a much more nuanced conversational technique. Conversations on late night talk shows reveal that self-deprecation does not necessarily pit one man as inferior to another. Instead, it actually serves to maintain rather than diminish a speaker's higher status in the conversation.

In another one of her works on conversation, *That's Not What I Meant,* Tannen discusses framing, the idea that "everything about the way we say something contributes to establishing the footing that frames our relationships to each other" (75). The guests on talk shows are entering a frame, or conversational alignment, that is inherently asymmetrical. Though both guest and host are technically celebrities, the guest is presented as the centerpiece of the program, the one who answers the questions, while the host is simply the asker.

This frame is not always one that is appealing for the guest, who may want to create a persona that is not that of an elite star, but of a likable and approachable everyman. In order to cultivate this persona, the guest can use conversation to downplay his star status and success in order to establish a more symmetrical alignment to the host, thereby changing the frame of the conversation. As we will see, however, this reframing is complicated, since it essentially shifts the asymmetry to a different ground. An example of this technique can be found in actor Paul Rudd's interview with former NBC late-night talk show host Conan O'Brien:

Rudd: I'm great, how are you?
O'Brien: I'm very good. You know things are going very well for you. You've been in so many successful movies. You have this new film *Role Models*. People love this movie, very funny, big hit for you, you've gotta be excited. I mean you you're a big, big star.
Rudd: It...I don't know about that, but it's very exciting. Oh God, I'm still out of breath! I swear to God.

By negating O'Brien's compliment, Rudd downplays his fame and thus reframes the conversation. By saying, "Oh God, I'm still out of breath," Rudd draws attention away from his stardom to some goofy dancing that O'Brien and Rudd did at the beginning of the interview. When O'Brien again tries to draw attention to Rudd's star power, Rudd again dodges the compliment.

O'Brien: But I would have to think by now that it's reaching critical mass, so many successful movies you must be getting the star treatment now. I bet you're treated like—

Rudd: I met Bruce Springsteen. I met him but it wasn't a…I snuck backstage at a Police concert and he was there.

Rudd's move, which allows him to segue into a self-deprecating anecdote about his encounter with Bruce Springsteen, represents an effort to resist the frame that O'Brien attempts to establish. Instead of accepting the frame that situates Rudd as a star and O'Brien as an average fan, Rudd strategically reframes the conversation by invoking a third party, a star whom both O'Brien and Rudd admire. Now, the conversation is not taking place between a "big star" and his fan, but rather between two fans.

To help understand Rudd's move, we can use Tannen's conversational categories of "report-talk" and "rapport-talk," the former being a way of "exhibiting knowledge and skill" and the latter being a way of "establishing connections" by "displaying similarities and matching experiences" *(Understand 77)*. While men are generally associated with report talk rather than rapport talk, the two categories are not necessarily gender exclusive. Humility, which often takes the form of self-deprecation, can help to remove asymmetry from a conversation. Such a move allows the men to capitalize on their similarities rather than emphasize their differences. We see Rudd do just that by transforming his conversational role from that of the star to that of the fan, a fan that must sneak backstage to meet his musical idols, just like the proverbial rest of us.

[…]

One possible explanation for the desire to dismiss and minimize praise is that compliment-giving is not the selfless act it may appear to be, but is, in fact, pure one-upmanship. According to Tannen, "Giving praise, like giving information, is also inherently asymmetrical. It too frames the speaker as one-up, in a position to judge someone else's performance" *(Understand 69)*. Thus, accepting praise may force the man on the receiving end of the praise to surrender supremacy to the praise-giver. By negating or avoiding praise, hierarchy can be reserved.

[…]

If this is so, then perhaps self-deprecating humor functions as a sort of preemptive move in which one man points out his own flaws before the other man has the chance to do so. If a man makes fun of himself, he still has control. He refuses to surrender this power to another man and thus surrender a hierarchical position in the conversation. Take, for example, this excerpt from Senator John McCain's conversation with NBC host Jay Leno:

Leno: And you went up to the mountains too?
McCain: We went up to our place near Sedona and had a very nice time and—
Leno: Now which house is that, number twel—
McCain: You know that's uh let's see it's a very … let's see … twenty-seven.

Leno was on the verge of making a dig about the senator's many homes, but McCain, seeing this coming, beat Leno to the punch, cutting him off before he even finished the word "twelve." McCain then goes on to exaggerate the number of homes that he owns. This shows that McCain not only understands the public's perception of him, he also is aware that his surplus of homes is a funny, and perhaps even embarrassing, subject. Thus, McCain uses self-deprecation to control the conversation, taking away Leno's opportunity to laugh at him before he laughs at himself.

Perhaps the most frequent and telling place in which self-deprecation pops up is in stories. Late night television is an excellent medium through which to study storytelling; in addition to the release dates of the projects they are promoting, celebrities always come equipped with an anecdote or two. Tannen includes a study of the differences found in stories told by men from those told by women. Her findings indicated that "the stories the men told made them look good" while the women were more likely to tell stories "in which they [women] violate social norms and are scared or embarrassed as a result" (Understand 177).

The behavior of men on late-night talk shows would seem to contradict these findings: the men's stories usually involve them telling of an incident in which, they were, indeed, "embarrassed as a result." When we look at the content of these stories, however, it becomes apparent that these stories function on a more sophisticated level than simple self-effacement.

Whether it is Paul Rudd's story about showing an embarrassing movie at a friend's wedding or Steve Carrell's anecdote about his parents flying on a plane with a Thanksgiving turkey because his cooking "sucks," the men doing the self-deprecating do not ultimately portray themselves in an embarrassing or pathetic light. The stories that they tell at their own expense draw laughs—and the storyteller is laughing with them.

In this regard, the stories told are actually more flattering than they are embarrassing. The stories send the message, or metamessage, that the storyteller is able not only to laugh at himself, but also to draw laughs from his audience, all the while coming across as likable and humble. What appears to be humility or lack of self-confidence actually serves a purpose more akin to a joke. And when a joke is told, conversational asymmetry is unavoidable as one man is doing the joke telling while the other functions as the audience (Understand 90). Thus, what seems like a way to put one's self down is, in fact, one-upmanship.

Self-deprecation is a complex conversational tool. On the surface, it seems to be simply a way for the speaker to disparage himself. It also, however, can function as a tool for humility and compromise, a way to create conversational symmetry from a situation of asymmetry. The most subtle and fascinating way in which self-deprecation functions, however, is a bit of a paradox: by putting himself down, a man can actually build himself up. Conversation is not merely a straightforward exchange of words; it is a skill, that when used strategically and with great awareness, can help a speaker to get ahead—often without anyone else realizing that he is doing it.

Assignments: Reading Analytically

1. **Analyze a Piece of Writing Using One or More of the Chapter's Methods:**
   a. PARAPHRASE × 3
   b. Finding the underlying structure by UNCOVERING ASSUMPTIONS and TRACKING BINARIES
   c. Attending to THE PITCH, THE COMPLAINT, and THE MOMENT
   d. PASSAGE-BASED FOCUSED FREEWRITING

2. **Paraphrase a Complicated Passage.** Paraphrasing can help you to understand sophisticated material by uncovering the implications of the language. As a case in point, consider this passage from an article about *Life* magazine by Wendy Kozol, "The Kind of People Who Make Good Americans: Nationalism and *Life*'s Family Ideal." Try PARAPHRASE × 3 with this passage. Paraphrase each sentence at least twice. Then rewrite the paragraph based on the understanding you have arrived at through paraphrasing.

   Traditional depictions of the family present it as a voluntary site of intimacy and warmth, but it also functions as a site of consumption. At the same time capitalism lauds the work ethic and the family as spheres of morality safe from the materialism of the outside world. These contradictions produce a "legitimation crisis" by which capitalist societies become ever more dependent for legitimacy on the very sociocultural motivations that capitalism undermines. (186; rpt in *Rhetorical Visions* by Wendy Hesford, pp 177–200.)

3. UNCOVER ASSUMPTIONS **and Read Against the Grain.** Take a paragraph from an analytical essay you are reading in one of your courses, or from a feature article from a newspaper or website such as Slate or aldaily. com, and do the following:

   - First, UNCOVER ASSUMPTIONS by reasoning back to premises. Ask yourself, if the piece believes this, what must it also already believe? Answer that question and share your reasoning (why you think so).

   - Try reading against the grain. What if anything is the piece saying that it might not know it is saying?

   Or you could also UNCOVER ASSUMPTIONS regarding a policy decision at your school or place of work. This works best if you have not just the policy but also a written manifesto on it.

4. **Use a Reading as a Lens for Examining a Subject.** For example, look at a piece of music or a film through the lens of a review that does not discuss the particular piece or film you are writing about. Or you might read about a particular theory of humor and use that as a lens for examining a comic play, film, story, television show, or stand-up routine.

5. **Put the Tools to work: Compose an Analytical Portfolio.** Select a subject—which could be a film, an advertising campaign, a political campaign, a television series, something that you are currently reading for a course or on your own, and so on—and do a series of Passage-Based Focused Freewriting as a way of generating ideas.

CHAPTER 3

Interpretation: Moving from Observation to Implication

Overview This chapter examines the move from observation to interpretation to address some of the issues that interpretation typically raises. What makes some interpretations better than others? What makes an interpretation more than a matter of personal opinion? The chapter's strategies include specifying an interpretive context, interpreting figurative language, and the heuristic we call SEEMS TO BE ABOUT X. The chapter concludes with a brief glossary of logical fallacies.

The Big Picture

Analysis, we have been suggesting, enriches understanding. In the opening two chapters, we have concentrated on ways to expand activities in the observation phase, so that you can notice more. These chapters also flashed forward on what a writer does with these observations: organizing them to see more clearly what they might reveal.

Although this chapter is titled "Interpretation," we have actually been talking about interpretation from the start of the book—seeding the move to ideas. We have been using a set of related words to name this step in the process: invention (Aristotle's term), meaning-making, implication. In the first two chapters, we have introduced the move to ideas in the following contexts:

- Ranking (what is most important, or interesting, or revealing, and why?), the second part of NOTICE & FOCUS, as a step toward interpretation

- ASKING "SO WHAT?" as the way to prompt Move 3 of the Five Analytical Moves—making the implicit explicit—designed to spur the leap to a claim, especially at the end of doing THE METHOD

- PASSAGE-BASED FOCUSED FREEWRITING, also aiming to take writer swiftly from what they notice about a chosen passage to what they make of it—some culminating claim or "big idea" at the end

- PARAPHRASE × 3, as a first step in interpretation, enabling writers to see that what words mean is never self-evident, and inviting them to use rephrasing as a way of rethinking.

Making Interpretations Plausible: Interpretive Contexts

So you already have the tools for prompting the move from observation to implication. But ideas don't operate in a vacuum. We now wish to add another necessary move: specifying and arguing for a context in which the evidence might be best understood—the *interpretive context*. Here are two key principles:

- *Everything means,* which is to say that everything in life calls on us to interpret, even when we are unaware of doing so.
- *Meaning is contextual,* which is to say that meaning-making always occurs inside of some social, cultural, or other frame of reference.

1	Organize the data (do THE METHOD).
2	Move from observation to implication (ASK "SO WHAT?").
3	Select an appropriate interpretive context.
4	Determine a range of plausible interpretations.
5	Assess the extent to which one interpretation explains the most about the data.

FIGURE 3.1
How to Interpret

Your readers' willingness to accept an interpretation is powerfully connected to their ability to recognize its *plausibility*—that is, how it follows from both the supporting details that you have selected and the language you have used to characterize those details. *An interpretive conclusion is not a fact, but a theory.* Interpretive conclusions stand or fall not so much on whether they can be proved right or wrong, but on whether they are demonstrably plausible. Often, the best that you can hope for with interpretive conclusions is not that others will say, "Yes, that is obviously right," but "Yes, I can see where it might be possible and reasonable to think as you do."

Meanings must be reasoned from sufficient evidence if they are to be judged plausible. Meanings can always be refuted by people who find fault with your reasoning or can cite conflicting evidence. Let's refer back briefly to a hypothetical interpretation raised in the Chapter 1 discussion of *Whistler's Mother*: that the woman in the painting who is clad in black is mourning the death of a loved one, perhaps a person who lived in the house represented in the painting on the wall. True, black clothes often indicate mourning—this is a culturally accepted sign. But with only the black dress and perhaps the sad facial expression (if it is sad) to go on, this "mourning theory" gets sidetracked from what is actually in the painting and moves into storytelling. Insufficient evidence would make this theory implausible.

Now, what if another person asserted that Whistler's mother is an alien astronaut, for example, her long black dress concealing a third leg? Obviously, this interpretation would not win wide support, and for a reason that points up another of the primary limits on the meaning-making process: meanings, to have value outside one's own private realm of experience, have to make sense to other people. This is to say that the relative value of interpretive meanings is to some extent socially (culturally) determined. The assertion that Whistler's mother is an alien astronaut is unlikely to be deemed acceptable by enough people to give it currency.

Although people are free to say that things mean whatever they want them to mean, saying doesn't make it so. The mourning theory has more evidence than the alien astronaut theory, but it still relies too heavily on what is not there, on a narrative for which there is insufficient evidence in the painting itself.

In experimental science, it is especially important that a writer/researcher be able to locate their work in the context of other scientists who have achieved similar results. Isolated results and interpretations not corroborated by others' research have much less credibility. In this respect, the making of meaning is collaborative and communal. The collaborative nature of scientific and scholarly work is one of the reasons that writing about reading is so important at the college level. In order to interpret evidence in a way that others will find plausible, you first need to have some idea of what others in the field are talking about.

Context and the Making of Meaning

Most interpretations that people are willing to accept as plausible occur inside a social or cultural context. They are valid according to a given point of view—what the social commentator Stanley Fish has called an "interpretive community." The participants inside these communities have shared interests, a shared language set, and for the most part a shared understanding of the range of plausible interpretations for addressing the questions and problems that are common to that community. The existence of interpretive communities for just about everything, from academic disciplines to sports to antiques to cuisine, is yet another pressing reason why it is essential for you as a writer to become aware of what others are saying about your subject. Your credibility depends, at least in part, on your ability to talk the talk.

We will now try to answer questions posed at the chapter's opening— what makes some interpretations better than others? And what makes interpretations more than a matter of personal opinion?

Regardless of how the context is arrived at, an important part of getting an interpretation accepted as plausible is to argue for the appropriateness of the interpretive context you use, not just the interpretation it takes you to. *An interpretive context is a lens.* Depending on the context you choose—preferably a context suggested by the evidence itself—you will see different things.

Different interpretations will account better for some details than others—which is why it enriches our view of the world to try on different interpretations. Ultimately, you will have to decide which possible interpretation, as seen through which plausible interpretive context, best accounts for what you think is most important and interesting to notice about your subject.

Consider, for example, an interpretation of *Whistler's Mother* that a person might produce while noticing the actual title, *Arrangement in Grey and Black: The Artist's Mother*. From this starting point, a person might focus exclusively on the disposition of color and arrive at an interpretation that the painting is about painting (which might then explain why Whistler includes in his portrait a painting on the wall).

The figure of the mother then would have meaning only insofar as it contained the two colors mentioned in the painting's title, black and gray, and the painting's representational content (the aspects of life that it shows us) would be assigned less importance. This is a promising and plausible idea for an interpretation. It makes use of details that are different from previous interpretations we've suggested, but it would also address some of the details already targeted (the dress, the curtain) from an entirely different context.

To generalize: two equally plausible interpretations can be made of the same thing. It is not the case that our first reading (in Chapter 1), focusing on the profile view of the mother and suggesting the painting's concern with mysterious separateness, is right, whereas the painting-about-painting (or aesthetic) view, building from the clue in the title, is wrong. They operate within different contexts.

It should be acknowledged before we move to another example that there is no such thing as interpretation without an interpretive context. We are always looking through one lens or another, even if we are not aware of it—the lens of cultural cliché, or of our religious or class or other group orientation. It should also be acknowledged that often we are not aware of a particular interpretive context when we begin to analyze a subject. Only after our interpretation begins to gain strength by the details that have attracted our attention (and these details, by a process of subliminal association are prone to attract other, similar details) do we recognize that we are situating the subject under analysis within a particular frame of reference. We will only add that it is an advantage for writers to become aware of their interpretive context. Once you recognize the frame, you can derive the benefits of a given interpretive community: the vocabulary and the assumptions that members of that community share, as well as the general kinds of conclusions or answers that members of that community tend to subscribe to.

Specifying an Interpretive Context: A Brief Example

Notice how in the following analysis the student writer's interpretation relies on his choice of a particular interpretive context, post-World War II Japan.

Had he selected another context, he might have arrived at different conclusions about the same details. Notice also how the writer perceives a pattern in the details and queries his own observations ("So what?") to arrive at an interpretation.

> The series entitled "Kamaitachi" is a journal of the photographer Eikoh Hosoe's desolate childhood and wartime evacuation in the Tokyo countryside. He returns years later to the areas where he grew up, a stranger to his native land, perhaps likening himself to the legendary Kamaitachi, an invisible sickle-toothed weasel, intertwined with the soil and its unrealized fertility. "Kamaitachi #8" (1956), a platinum palladium print, stands alone to best capture Hosoe's alienation from and troubled expectation of the future of Japan. [**Here the writer chooses the photographer's life as his interpretive context.**]
>
> The image is that of a tall fence of stark horizontal and vertical rough wood lashed together, looming above the barren rice fields. Straddling the fence, half-crouched and half-clinging, is a solitary male figure, gazing in profile to the horizon. Oblivious to the sky above of dark and churning thunderclouds, the figure instead focuses his attentions and concentrations elsewhere. [**The writer selects and describes significant details.**]
>
> It is exactly this *elsewhere* that makes the image successful, for in studying the man we are to turn our attention in the direction of the figure's gaze and away from the photograph itself. He hangs curiously between heaven and earth, suspended on a makeshift man-made structure, in a purgatorial limbo awaiting the future. He waits with anticipation—perhaps dread?—for a time that has not yet come; he is directed away from the present, and it is this sensitivity to time which sets this print apart from the others in the series. One could argue that in effect this man, clothed in common garb, has become Japan itself, indicative of the post-war uncertainty of a country once-dominant and now destroyed. What will the future (dark storm clouds) hold for this newly humbled nation? [**Here the writer notices a pattern of in-between-ness and locates it in an historical context in order to make his interpretive leap.**]

Remember that regardless of the subject you select for analysis, you should directly address not just "What does this say?" but also, as this writer has done, "What are we invited to make of it, and in what context?"

Intention as an Interpretive Context

An interpretive context that frequently creates problems in analysis is intention. People relying on authorial intention as their interpretive context typically assert that the author—not the work—is the ultimate and correct source of interpretation.

Look at the drawing titled *The Dancers* in Figure 3.2. Then read the artist's statement about how the drawing came about and what it came to mean to her.

FIGURE 3.2

The Dancers, by Sarah Kersh

> This piece was created completely unintentionally. I poured some ink onto paper and blew on it through a straw. The ink took the form of what looked like little people in movement. I recopied the figures I liked, touched up the rough edges, and ended with this gathering of fairy-like creatures. I love how in art something abstract can so suddenly become recognizable.

In this case, interestingly, the artist initially had no intentions beyond experimenting with materials. As the work evolved, she began to arrive at her own interpretation of what the drawing might suggest. Most viewers probably would find the artist's interpretation plausible, but this is not to say that the artist must have the last word and that it is somehow an infraction for others to produce alternative interpretations.

Suppose the artist had stopped with her first two sentences. Even this explicit statement of her lack of intention would not prohibit people from interpreting the drawing in some of the ways that she later goes on to suggest. The artist's initial absence of a plan doesn't require viewers to interpret *The Dancers* as only ink on paper.

Whenever an intention is ascribed to a person, an act, or a product, this intention contributes significantly to meaning; but the intention, whatever its source, does not outrank or exclude other interpretations. It is simply another context for understanding.

Here is another example. In the early 1960s, the popular domestic sitcom *Leave It to Beaver* portrayed the mother, June Cleaver, usually impeccably dressed in heels, dress, and pearls, doing little other than dusting the mantelpiece and making tuna fish sandwiches for her sons. Is the show then intentionally implying that the proper role for women is that of domestic helper? Well, in the context of post-women's movement thinking, the show's representation of Mrs. Cleaver might plausibly be read this way, but not as a matter of intention. To conclude that *Leave It to Beaver* promoted a particular stereotype about women does not mean that the writers got together every week with the intention of oppressing her.

It is interesting and useful to try to determine from something you are analyzing what its makers might have intended. But, by and large, you are best off concentrating on what the thing itself communicates, as opposed to what someone might have wanted it to communicate.

What Is and Isn't "Meant" to Be Analyzed

What about analyzing things that were not intended to "mean" anything, like blockbuster films and everyday things like blue jeans and shopping malls? Some people believe that it is wrong to bring out unintended implications. Let's take another example: Barbie dolls. These are just toys intended for young girls, people might say. Clearly, the intention of Mattel, the makers of Barbie, is to make money by entertaining children. Does that mean Barbie must remain outside of interpretive scrutiny for such things as her built-in earrings and high-heeled feet? What the makers of a particular product or idea intend is only a part of what that product or idea communicates.

The urge to cordon off certain subjects from analysis on the grounds that they weren't meant to be analyzed unnecessarily excludes a wealth of information—and meaning—from your range of vision. It is right to be careful about the interpretive contexts we bring to our experience. It is less right—and less useful—to confine our choice of context in a too literal-minded way to a single category. To some people, baseball is only a game, and clothing is only there to protect us from the elements.

What such people don't want to admit is that things communicate meaning to others whether we wish them to or not, which is to say that the meanings of most things are socially determined. What, for example, does the choice of wearing a baseball cap to a staff meeting or to a class "say"? Note, by the way, that a communicative gesture such as the wearing of a hat need not be premeditated to communicate something to other people. The hat is still "there" and available to be "read" by others as a sign of certain attitudes and a culturally defined sense of identity—with or without intention.

Baseball caps, for example, carry different associations from berets or wool caps because they come from different social contexts. Baseball caps convey a set of attitudes associated with the part of American culture from which they come. They suggest, for example, popular rather than high culture, casual rather than formal, young—perhaps defiantly so, especially if worn backward—rather than old, and so on.

We can, of course, protest that the "real" reason for turning our baseball cap backward is to allow more light in, making it easier to see than when the bill of the cap shields our faces. This practical rationale makes sense but does not explain away the social statement that the hat and a particular way of wearing it might make, whether or not this statement is intentional. Because meaning is to a significant extent socially determined, we can't entirely control what our clothing, our manners, our language, or even our way of walking communicates to others.

The social contexts that make gestures like our choice of hats carry particular meanings are always shifting, but some such context is always present. As we asserted at the beginning of this chapter, everything means, and meaning is always contextual.

Avoiding the Extremes: Neither "Fortune Cookie" nor "Anything Goes"

Two of the most common missteps in producing an interpretation are the desire for a single, right answer and, at the opposite extreme, the conviction that all explanations are equally acceptable (or equally lame!). The first of these we call the Fortune Cookie School of Interpretation, and the latter we label the Anything Goes School.

The Fortune Cookie School of Interpretation

Proponents of the Fortune Cookie School believe that if a person can only "crack" the thing correctly—the subject, the problem—it will yield an extractable and self-contained "message." There are several problems with this conception of the interpretive process.

First, the assumption that things have single, hidden meanings interferes with open-minded and dispassionate observation. Adherents of the Fortune Cookie School look solely for clues pointing to *the* hidden message and, having found these clues, discard the rest, like the cookie in a Chinese restaurant once the fortune has been extracted. The fortune cookie approach forecloses on the possibility of multiple plausible meanings, each within its own context. When you assume that there is only one right answer, you are also assuming that there is only one proper context for understanding and, by extension, that anybody who happens to select a different starting point or context and thus arrives at a different answer is necessarily wrong.

Most of the time, practitioners of the fortune cookie approach aren't even aware that they are assuming the correctness of a single context, because they don't realize a fundamental truth about interpretations: they are always limited by contexts. In other words, we are suggesting that claims to universal truths are problematic. Things don't just mean in some simple and clear way for all people in all situations; they always mean within a network of beliefs, from a particular point of view. The person who claims to have access to some universal truth, beyond context and point of view, is either naïve (unaware) or, worse, a bully—insisting that their view of the world is obviously correct and must be accepted by everyone.

The Anything Goes School of Interpretation

At the opposite extreme from the Fortune Cookie School lies the completely relativist Anything Goes School. The problem with the "anything goes" approach is that it tends to assume that *all* interpretations are equally viable, and that meanings are simply a matter of individual choice, regardless of evidence or plausibility. Put another way, it overextends the creative aspect of interpretation to absurdity, arriving at the position that you can see in a subject whatever you want to see. Such unqualified relativism is not logical. It is simply not the case that meaning is entirely up to the individual; some readings are clearly better than others. The better interpretations have more evidence and rational explanation of how the evidence supports the interpretive claims—qualities that make these meanings more public and negotiable.

Implications Versus Hidden Meanings

While some people search for a single right answer and dismiss the rest, others dismiss the interpretive project altogether. Those who adopt this latter stance are excessively literal minded; they see any venture into interpretation as a benighted quest to impose "hidden meanings" on the reader.

The phrase itself, "hidden meaning," carries implications. It assumes that meanings exist in places other than the literal words on the page: they are to be found either "under" or "between" the lines of text.

Another phrase with which such people disparage the interpretive process is "reading between the lines," suggesting that we have to look for meanings elsewhere than in the lines of text themselves. At its most skeptical, the phrase "reading between the lines" means that an interpretation has come from nothing at all—from the white space between the lines—and therefore has been imposed on the material by the interpreter.

Neither of these positions is a wholly unreasonable response because each recognizes that meanings are not always overt. But responding with these phrases misrepresents the process of interpretation. To understand why, let's spell out some of the assumptions that underlie these phrases.

The charge that the meaning is hidden can imply for some people an act of conspiracy on the part of either an author, who chooses to deliberately obscure their meaning, or on the part of readers, who conspire to "find" things lurking below the surface that other readers don't know about and are unable to detect. A further assumption is that people probably know what they mean most of the time but, for some perverse reason, they are unwilling to come out and say so.

Proponents of these views of analysis are, in effect, committing themselves to the extreme literalist position that everything in life means what it says and says what it means. It is probably safe to assume that most writers try to write what they mean and mean what they say. That is, they try to control the range of possible interpretations that their words could give rise to, but there is always more going on in a piece of writing (as in everyday conversation) than can easily be pinned down and controlled. It is, in fact, an inherent property of language that it always means more than, and thus other than, it says. This discussion recalls a memorable exchange at the mad tea party in *Alice's Adventures in Wonderland*:

"Then you should say what you mean," the March Hare went on.

"I do," Alice hastily replied; "at least—at least I mean what I say—that's the same thing, you know."

"Not the same thing a bit!" said the Hatter.

It is also true that a large part of human communication takes place indirectly. A good example of this is metaphor, to which we now turn.

Figurative Logic: Reasoning with Metaphors

Metaphor, it has been said, is one of the few uses of language in which it is okay to say one thing and mean another. It is, in other words, a way of communicating things via association and implication rather than direct statement. If metaphors were found only in poems, as some people assume to be the case, then interpreting them would be a specialized skill with narrow application. But, in fact, metaphors are deeply engrained in the language we use every day, which becomes evident as soon as we take the time to notice them.

George Lakoff, Professor of Linguistics and Cognitive Science, and English Professor Mark Turner, among others, have demonstrated that metaphors are built into the way we think. (See Lakoff and Turner's book, *More than Cool Reason: A Field Guide to Poetic Metaphor*, University of Chicago Press, 1989.) As such, metaphors routinely constitute our assumptions about the world and our place in it. Life, for example, is a journey. To become successful you climb a ladder. Being up is a good thing. To be down is to be unhappy (or blue). These are all metaphors.

If we accept their implicit arguments in an unexamined way, metaphors can call the shots in our lives more than we should allow them to. For example, if you believe that success involves climbing a ladder, you will be more likely to feel compelled to constantly climb higher than others in an organization rather than take a chance on a horizontal move that might lead you to something more personally rewarding (and in that respect, more successful). And if you have absorbed from the culture the idea that life is a race, then you will be worried about not moving fast enough and not competing effectively with others, as opposed to collaborating or doing something different that most others are not doing—perhaps something with no obvious prize attached.

THE LOGIC OF METAPHOR

- Metaphors pervade our way of thinking.
- Metaphor is a way of thinking by analogy.
- The logic of metaphors is implicit.

- The implicit logic of metaphors can be made explicit by scrutinizing the language.
- We can recast figurative language to see and evaluate its arguments.

The fact that metaphors require interpretation—as do most uses of language—does not take away from the fact that metaphors are a way of thinking. Being able to articulate the implicit arguments embodied in metaphors—making their meanings explicit so that they can be opened to discussion with others—is an important skill to acquire.

Although figurative logic does not operate in the same way as claims-based (propositional) logic, it nevertheless produces arguments, the reasoning of which can be analyzed and evaluated *systematically*. Let's start with a definition. Metaphors and similes work by **analogy**—a type of comparison that often finds similarities between things that are otherwise unlike.

Consider the simile "My love is like a red, red rose." A simile, identifiable by its use of the words "like" or "as," operates like a metaphor except that both sides of the analogy are explicitly stated. The subject of the simile, love, is called the *tenor*; the comparative term brought in to think about love, rose, is called the *vehicle*.

In metaphors, the thought connection between the vehicle (rose) and the tenor (my love) is left unstated. But for our purposes the clearer and more explicit simile will do. It is the nature of the resemblance between the speaker's love and roses that we are invited to infer.

Here is where the process of interpreting figurative language becomes systematic. The first step in interpreting this simile is to list the characteristics of the vehicle, a red rose—especially a red, red (very red) rose—that might be relevant in this piece of thinking by analogy. Most people find roses to be beautiful. Most people associate red with passion. In fact, science can now measure the body's response to different colors. Red produces excitement and can even increase the pulse rate Roses are also complicated flowers. Their shape is convoluted. Roses are thought of as female. Rose petals are fragile. Many roses have thorns. So, the simile is actually a piece of thinking about love and about women.

It is not a very deep piece of thinking, and probably many women would prefer that the thorn part not be made too prominent. In fact, a reader would have to decide in the context of other language in the poem whether thorniness, as a characteristic of some roses, is significant and ought to be considered. The point is that the simile does make an argument about women that could be stated overtly, analyzed, and evaluated. The implication that women, like roses, might have thorns—and thus be hard to "pick," defending them from male intruders, and so on—is part of the argument.

Figure 3.3 represents the procedure for exploring the logic of metaphor.

1	**Isolate the vehicle**—the language in the metaphor that states one side of the analogy.
2	**Articulate the characteristics of the vehicle, its defining traits.**
3	**Select the characteristics of the vehicle that seem most significant in context.**
4	**Make interpretive leaps to what the metaphor communicates.** Use significant characteristics of the vehicle to prompt these leaps.

FIGURE 3.3
Interpreting Figurative Language

Notice how, in the rose example, our recasting of the original simile has made explicit the implicit meanings suggested by the figurative language. This recasting is a useful act of thinking that makes evident the thought process set in motion by a metaphor.

What such recasting reveals is not only that metaphors do, in fact, make claims, but that they are remarkably efficient at doing so. A metaphor can say a lot in a little by compressing a complex amalgam of thought and feeling into a single image.

TRY THIS 3.1: Uncovering the Logic of Figurative Language

Uncover the figurative logic in the following statements by making what is implicit explicit in each. Follow the Steps for Interpreting Figurative Language (Figure 3.3).

- Conscience is a man's compass. *Vincent Van Gogh*

- All religions, arts and sciences are branches of the same tree. *Albert Einstein*

- All the world's a stage, and all the men and women merely players. They have their exits and their entrances. *William Shakespeare*

- America has tossed its cap over the wall of space. *John F. Kennedy*

- I am the good shepherd . . . and I lay down my life for the sheep. *The Bible, John 10:14–15*

TRY THIS 3.2: Analyzing the Figurative Language of Politics

Figurative language is especially pervasive in politics. Find some online examples of arguments between Democrats and Republicans being carried out through metaphors and similes. Here is an example of Obama speaking about the midterm elections in September 2010:

> They drove our economy into a ditch. And we got in there and put on our boots and we pushed and we shoved, and we were sweatin'. And these guys were standing, watching us, and sipping on a Slurpee . . . And then when we finally got the car

up—and it's got a few dings and a few dents, it's got some mud on it, we're going to have to do some work on it . . . they got the nerve to ask for the keys back!

What are Trump's favorite metaphors—or the metaphors his critics favor in their attempts to reconfigure these for their own ends? Unpack the logic of your examples, and write a paragraph or two on why you think a particular strand of figurative language has become prominent at this time.

SEEMS TO BE ABOUT X, BUT COULD ALSO BE (OR IS "REALLY") ABOUT Y

When people begin to interpret something, they usually find that less obvious meanings are cloaked by more obvious ones, and so they are distracted from seeing them. In most cases, the less obvious and possibly unintended meanings are more telling and more interesting than the obvious ones they have been conditioned to see.

The person who is doing the interpreting too often stops with the first "answer" that springs to mind while moving from observation to implication, often landing upon a cliché. One way to block this premature leap to a claim is to apply the heuristic we call SEEMS TO BE ABOUT X. If the first response becomes the X, then the writer is prompted to come up with other, probably less commonplace interpretations, as the Y. (See Figure 3.4.)

This prompt is based on the conviction that understandings are rarely simple and overt. Completing the formula by supplying key terms for X and Y, writers get practice in making the implicit explicit and accepting the existence of multiple plausible meanings for something. SEEMS TO BE ABOUT X is especially useful when considering the rhetoric of a piece: its complex and various ways of targeting and appealing to an audience. It's also useful for "reading against the grain"—seeking out what something is about that it probably does not know it's about. (See the treatment of this tactic in the discussion of uncovering assumptions in Chapter 2.)

1	Start the interpretive process by filling in the blank (the X) in the statement "This subject SEEMS TO BE ABOUT X." X should be an interpretive leap, not just a summary or description.
2	Pose another interpretive possibility by finishing the sentence, "but it could also be (or is really) about Y."
3	Repeat this process a number of times to provoke new interpretive leaps. In effect, you are brainstorming alternative explanations for the same phenomenon.
4	Choose what you think is the best formulation for Y and write a paragraph or more explaining your choice.

FIGURE 3.4

Doing "SEEMS TO BE ABOUT X, BUT COULD ALSO BE (OR IS "REALLY") ABOUT Y"

Don't be misled by our use of the word *really* in this heuristic into thinking that there should be some single, hidden, right answer. The aim is to prompt you to think recursively—to come up with a range of possible landing sites for your interpretive leap rather than just one. You will get the most out of this move if you make X something sophisticated, a plausible and complex interpretive possibility rather than a simplistic straw man. The better the X, the better the Y.

Seems To Be About X . . .: An Example

A classic television ad campaign for Nike Freestyle shoes contains sixty seconds of famous basketball players dribbling and passing and otherwise handling the ball in dexterous ways to the accompaniment of court noises and hip-hop music. The ad Seems to Be About X (basketball or shoes) but could also be about Y. Once you've made this assertion, a rapid-fire (brainstormed) list might follow in which you keep filling in the blanks (X and Y) with different possibilities. Alternatively, you might find that filling in the blanks (X and Y) leads to a more sustained exploration of a single point. This is your eventual goal, but doing a little brainstorming first will keep you from shutting down the interpretive process too soon.

Here is one version of a rapid-fire list, any item of which might be expanded:

Seems to be about basketball but is "really" about dance.
Seems to be about selling shoes but is "really" about artistry.
Seems to be about artistry but is "really" about selling shoes.
Seems to be about basketball but is "really" about race.
Seems to be about basketball but is "really" about the greater acceptance of
  Black culture in American media and society.
Seems to be about individual expertise but is "really" about working as a group.

Here is one version of a more sustained exploration of a single Seems to Be About X statement.

> The Nike Freestyle commercial seems to be about basketball but is really about the greater acceptance of Black culture in American media. Of course it is a shoe commercial and so aims to sell a product, but the same could be said about any commercial.

> What makes the Nike commercial distinctive is its seeming embrace of African American culture. The hip-hop sound track, for example, which coincides with the rhythmic dribbling of the basketball, places music and sport on a par, and the dexterity with which the players (actual NBA stars) move with the ball—moonwalking, doing 360s on it, balancing it on their fingers, heads, and backs—is nothing short of dance.

> The intrinsic cool of the commercial suggests that Nike is targeting an audience of basketball lovers, not just African Americans. If I am right, then it is selling blackness to White as well as Black audiences. Of course, the idea that Black people are cooler than White people goes back at least as far as the early days of jazz and might be seen as its own strange form of prejudice.

TRY THIS 3.3: Apply the Formula Seems to Be About X, But Could Also Be (Or Is "Really") About Y

Try it as the first sentence of an in-class writing or as a way of drafting an essay or to lead off a paragraph of writing to prepare for class discussion. The formula is helpful for revision as well.

Making an Interpretation: The Example of a *New Yorker* Cover

A major point of this section is that interpretive contexts are suggested by the material you are studying; they aren't simply imposed. Explaining why you think a subject should be seen through a particular interpretive "lens" is an important part of making interpretations reasonable and plausible. Our discussion illustrates a writer's decision-making process in choosing an interpretive context, and how, once that context has been selected, the writer goes about analyzing evidence to test as well as support the usefulness of that context.

The example upon which we are focusing is a visual image, a cover from *The New Yorker* magazine by Ian Falconer titled *The Competition*; it appeared on the October 9, 2000, issue (Figure 3.5). Producing a close description of the thing you are analyzing is one of the best ways to begin because the act of describing causes you to notice more and triggers analytical thinking. Here is our description of *The New Yorker* cover.

Description of a *New Yorker* Cover, Dated October 9, 2000

The picture contains four women, visible from the waist up, standing in a row in semi-profile, staring out at some audience other than us, since their eyes look off to the side. All four gaze in the same direction. Each woman is dressed in a bathing suit and wears a banner draped over one shoulder in the manner of those worn in the swimsuit competition at beauty pageants. Three of the women are virtually identical. The banners worn by these three women show the letters *gia*, *rnia*, and *rida*, the remainder of the letters being cut off by the other women's shoulders, so that we have to fill in the missing letters to see which state each woman represents.

The fourth woman, who stands third from the left in line, tucked in among the others who look very much alike, wears a banner reading YORK. This woman's appearance is different in just about every respect from the other three. Whereas they are blonde with long flowing hair, she is dark with her hair up in a tight bun. Whereas their mouths are wide open, revealing a wall of very white teeth, her mouth is closed, lips drawn together. Whereas their eyes are wide open and staring, hers, like her mouth, are nearly closed, under deeply arched eyebrows.

The dark woman's lips and eyes and hair are dark. She wears dark eye makeup and has a pronounced dark beauty mark on her cheek. Whereas the other three women's cheeks are high and round, hers are sharply angular. The three blonde women wear one-piece bathing suits in a nondescript gray

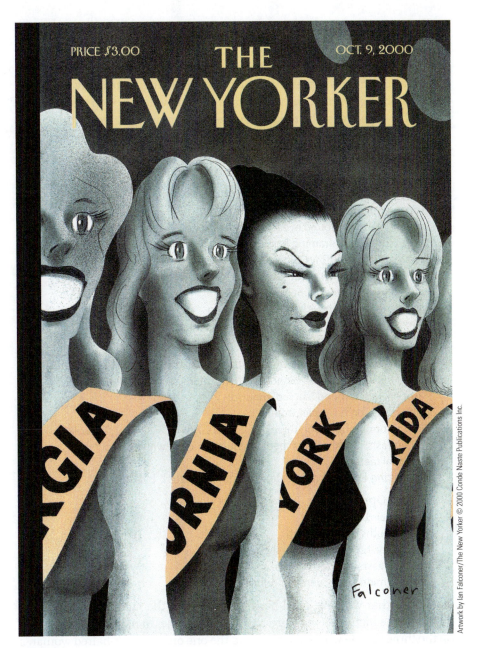

PRICE $3.00   OCT. 9, 2000

THE NEW YORKER

Falconer

FIGURE 3.5
The Competition, by Ian Falconer

color. The dark-haired woman, whose skin stands out in stark contrast to her hair, wears a two-piece bathing suit, exposing her midriff. Like her face, the dark-haired woman's breast, sticking out in half profile in her bathing suit, is pointed and angular. The other three women's breasts are round and quietly contained in their high-necked gray bathing suits.

Using THE METHOD to Identify Patterns of Repetition and Contrast

As we discussed in Chapter 1, looking for patterns of repetition and contrast (using THE METHOD) is one of your best means of getting at the essential character of a subject. It will prevent you from generalizing, instead involving you in hands-on engagement with the details of your evidence. Step 1, looking for things that repeat exactly, tends to suggest items for step 2, repetition of the same or similar kinds of words or details (strands), and step 2 leads naturally to step 3, looking for binary oppositions and organizing contrasts.

Here are partial lists of exact repetitions and strands and binary oppositions in *The New Yorker* cover:

Some Details that Repeat Exactly
Large, wide-open, round eyes (3 pairs)
Long, blonde, face-framing hair (3)
Small, straight eyebrows (3 pairs)
Wide-open (smiling?) mouths with expanses of white teeth (3)
   (but individual teeth not indicated)
banners (4) but each with different lettering
round breasts (3)
states that end in *a* (3)

Some Strands (groups of the same or similar kinds of details)
Lots of loose and flowing blonde hair/large, fully open, round eyes/large, open, rather round (curved) mouths:
Connecting logic = open, round
Skin uniformly shaded on three of the figures/minimal color and shading contrasts/mouths full of teeth, but just a mass of white without individual teeth showing:
Connecting logic = homogenous, undifferentiated, indistinct

Binary Oppositions
Blonde hair/black hair
Open mouths/closed mouth
Straight eyebrows/slanted (arched) eyebrows
Round breasts/pointed breasts
Covered midriff/uncovered midriff

Notice that we have tried hard to "stick with the facts" here—concrete details in the picture. If we were to try, for example, to name the expression on the three blonde women's faces, and the one on the black-haired woman's face—(expressionless versus knowing? vapid versus shrewd? trusting versus suspicious? and so on), we would move from data gathering—direct observation of detail—into interpretation. The longer you delay interpretation in favor of noticing patterns of like and unlike detail, the more thoughtful and better grounded your eventual interpretation will be.

Anomalies
Miss New York

Pushing Observations to Conclusions: Selecting an Interpretive Context

As we have argued throughout this chapter, the move from observations to conclusions depends on context. You would, for example, come up with different ideas about the significance of particular patterns of detail in *The New Yorker* cover if you were analyzing them in the context of the history of *New Yorker* cover art than you might if your interpretive context was other art done by Ian Falconer, the cover's artist. Both of these possibilities suggest themselves, the first by the fact that the title of the magazine, *The New Yorker*, stands above the women's heads, and the second by the fact that the artist's last name, Falconer, runs across two of the women.

What other interpretive contexts might one plausibly and fairly choose, based on what the cover offers us? Consider the date—October 9, 2000. Some quick research into what was going on in the country in the early fall of 2000 might provide some clues about how to read the cover in a historical context. November 2000 was the month of a presidential election. At the time the cover was published, the long round of presidential primaries, with presidential hopefuls courting various key states for their votes, had ended, but the last month of campaigning by the presidential nominees—Al Gore and George W. Bush—was in full swing.

You might wish to consider whether and how the cover speaks to the country's political climate during the Gore/Bush competition for the presidency. The banners and the bathing suits, and the fact that the women stand in a line staring out at some implied audience of viewers, perhaps judges, reminds us that the picture's narrative context is a beauty pageant, a competition in which women representing each state compete to be chosen the most beautiful of them all. Choosing to consider the cover in the context of the presidential campaign would be reasonable; you would not have to think you were imposing a context on the picture in an arbitrary, ungrounded way. Additionally, the Table of Contents identifies the title of Falconer's drawing as *The Competition*.

Clearly, there is other information on the cover that might allow you to interpret the picture in some kind of political and/or more broadly cultural context. A significant binary opposition is New York versus Georgia, California, and Florida. The three states having names ending in the same letter are represented by look-alike, virtually identical blondes. The anomalous state, New York, is represented by a woman who, despite standing in line with the others, is about as different from them as a figure could be. *So what* that the woman representing New York looks so unlike the women from the other states? And why those states?

If you continued to pursue this interpretive context, you might want more information. Which presidential candidate won the primary in each of the states pictured? How was each state expected to vote in the election in November? Because timing matters in the case of a topical interpretive context, it would also be interesting to know when the cover art was actually produced and when the magazine accepted it. If possible, you could also try to discover whether other of the artist's work is in a similar vein. (He has a website.)

Arriving at an Interpretive Conclusion: Making Choices

As we have been arguing, the picture will "mean" differently, depending on whether we understand it in terms of American presidential politics in the year 2000 or in terms of American identity politics at the same point—specifically, attitudes of and about New Yorkers.

Let's try on one final interpretive context, and then see which of the various contexts (lenses) through which we have viewed the cover produces the most credible interpretation, the one that seems to best account for the patterns of detail in the evidence. We will try to push our own interpretive process to a choice by selecting one interpretive context as the most revealing: *The New Yorker* magazine itself.

In this context, the dark-haired figure wearing the New York banner stands, in a sense, for the magazine or, at least, for a potential reader—a representative New Yorker. What, then, does the cover "say" to and about New Yorkers, and to and about the magazine and its readers?

So what that the woman representing New York is dark when the other women are light, is closed (narrowed eyes, closed mouth, hair tightly pulled up and back) when the others are open (wide-open eyes and mouths, loosely flowing hair), is pointed and angular when the others are round, sports a bared midriff when the others are covered?

As with our earlier attempt to interpret the cover in the context of the 2000 presidential campaign, interpreting it in the context of other *New Yorker* covers would require a little research. How do *New Yorker* covers characteristically represent New Yorkers? What might you discover by looking for patterns of repetition and contrast in a set of *New Yorker* covers rather than just this one?

The covers are all online. A cursory review of them would make evident the magazine's fondness for simultaneously sending up and embracing the stereotype of New Yorkers as sophisticated, cultured, and cosmopolitan. How does the cover read in the context, for example, of various jokes about how New Yorkers think of themselves relative to the rest of the country? (One well-known cover depicts the United States as two large coastlines, east and west, connected by an almost nonexistent middle.)

Armed with the knowledge that the covers are not only characteristically laughing at the rest of the country, but also at New Yorkers themselves, you might begin to make explicit what is implicit in the cover.

Here are some attempts at making the details of the cover speak. Is the cover in some way a "dumb blonde" joke in which the dark woman with the pronounced beauty mark and calculating gaze participates in but also sets herself apart from some kind of national beauty contest? Are we being invited (intentionally or not) to invert the conventional value hierarchy of dark and light so that the dark woman—the sort that gets represented as the evil stepmother in fairy tales such as "Snow White"—becomes "the fairest of them all," and nobody's fool?

Let's end this sample analysis and interpretation with two possibilities—somewhat opposed to each other, but both plausible, at least to certain audiences (East and West Coast Americans, and readers of *The New Yorker*). At its most serious, *The New Yorker* cover may speak to American history, in which New York has been the point of entry for generations of immigrants, the "dark" (literally and figuratively) in the face of America's blonde northern European legacy.

Within the context of other *New Yorker* covers, however, we might find ourselves wishing to leaven this dark reading with comic overtones—that the magazine is also admitting, yes America, we do think that we're cooler and more individual and less plastic than the rest of you, but we also know that we shouldn't be so smug about it.

Making the Interpretation Plausible

What makes an interpretation plausible? Your audience might choose not to accept your interpretation for a number of reasons. They might, for example, be New Yorkers and, further, inclined to think that New Yorkers are cool and that this is what the picture "says." They might be from one of the states depicted on the cover in terms of look-alike blondes and, further, inclined to think that New Yorkers are full of themselves and forever portraying the rest of the country as shallowly conformist and uncultured.

But none of these personal influences ultimately matters. What matters is that you share your data, show your reasons for believing that it means what you say it means, and do this well enough for readers to find your interpretation reasonable (whether they actually believe it or not).

Making Interpretations Plausible Across the Curriculum

As we note at various points in this book, the practices governing data gathering, analysis, and interpretation differ as you move from one academic division to another. In the humanities, the data to be analyzed are usually textual—visual or verbal details. In the social sciences, data are sometimes textual, as would be the case, for example, if you were analyzing the history of a particular political theory or practice, such as free speech. But much analytical thinking in the social sciences and the natural sciences involves arriving at plausible conclusions about the significance of quantitative (numerical) and experimental data. This book's primary interpretive prompt, "So what?" (where do these research data get me, and why does this data set mean what I say it means?), still applies in the sciences, though the interpretive leaps are typically worded differently.

Interpretation in the natural and social sciences considers the extent to which data either confirm or fail to confirm the expectations defined in a hypothesis, which is a theory the writer proposes in response to a research question. In the remainder of this section, we will look briefly at procedures for interpreting evidence in the sciences. As you will see, the guidelines that direct interpretation across the curriculum are similar. The emphases on careful description of evidence and on arguing for the appropriateness of a particular interpretive context are common to all three academic divisions.

Interpreting Statistical Data

Statistics are a primary tool—a virtual language—for those writing in the natural, and especially the social, sciences. Depending on how they are used, they can have the advantage of greater objectivity, and, in the social sciences, of offering a broad view of a subject. Remember, though, that like other forms of evidence, statistics do not speak for themselves; their significance must be overtly interpreted. It should never simply be assumed that statistics are valid representations of the reality they purport to measure.

When writers seek to interpret numerical data, they must decide the extent to which the data confirm or fail to confirm an expectation defined in the study's hypothesis. In order to make a case for their interpretation, writers need to demonstrate the appropriateness and relevance of their chosen context, including their reasons for choosing one possible interpretive context over another.

Here is a brief example of statistical analysis from a political science course on Public Opinion Research. The study uses a data set generated to test the hypothesis that "Republican defectors who have been members of the party for over 11 years are less likely to change party affiliation to Democrat because of the Republican Party's policies than Republican defectors registered with the party for under 10 years." Note how the writer integrates quantitative data into her discussion of the findings—a move characteristic of interpretation in the social sciences—and how she establishes the context in which this data might be best understood.

> The data suggest that long-standing Republican party members are less likely to switch party affiliation than party members registered for under 10 years. However, the data also reveal something else: that the longer a Republican defector was a member of the Republican Party, the more likely that person was to switch party affiliation to Democrat because of the Republican Party's policies as opposed to changes in his or her own belief system. For example, 35% of Republican defectors who had been members of the party for 1–5 years agreed with the statement "the Republican Party's policies led me to leave the party," while 35% said it was due to changes in their personal beliefs. Thus, it appears as though both reasons have equal influence on an individual's decision to switch parties.

However, when you look at the defectors who were members of the party for over 6 years, roughly 20% more of them left because of the party's policies than because of a change in their personal beliefs. This suggests that long-time party members are more likely to change their party affiliation because of party policy than because of changes in their own beliefs.

In the case of statistical data, an interpretive problem arises when writers attempt to determine whether a statistical *correlation* between two things—blood cholesterol level and the likelihood of dying of a heart attack, for example—can be interpreted as *causal*. Does a statistical correlation between high cholesterol levels and heart attack suggest that higher levels of cholesterol cause heart attacks, or might it only suggest that some other factor associated with cholesterol is responsible? Similarly, if a significantly higher percentage of poor people treated in hospital emergency rooms die more often than do their more affluent counterparts, do we conclude that emergency room treatment of the poor is at fault? What factors, such as inability of poor people to afford regular preventive health care, might need to be considered in interpretation of the data? (See "Mistaking Correlation for Cause" in the next section, "A Brief Glossary of Common Logical Fallacies.")

In interpretation, as in other kinds of analytical thinking, it is always important to qualify (limit) claims. Notice how the authors in the following example speculate about, but are careful not to endorse any single cause for, the statistically significant phenomenon they analyze. Rather, they use it to ask new questions.

Since the 1980s, there has been a growing body of data that examines the perceptions of Americans regarding the issue of global warming. This data paints a picture of generally increasing recognition, acceptance, and concern in the United States regarding atmospheric heating of the earth (Nisbet and Myers, 2007). In the past two decades, the number of Americans who have heard of the "greenhouse effect" has steadily increased. In 1986, less than one in four respondents said they had heard of global warming. By 2006, over nine out of ten recognized the issue (Nisbet and Myers, 2007). A growing number of Americans believe that the Earth is already experiencing increased heating as Table One shows. [. . .]

Public opinion research shows Americans are increasingly acknowledging global warming (Nisbet and Myers, 2007); however, what isn't seen are the underlying causes of these beliefs. In particular, what type of evidence do Americans cite as having an important effect on their perceptions of global warming? Recent Pew Research Center polls have shown fairly significant short-term shifts in the number of Americans who believe there is evidence of global warming. Between June 2006 and January 2007, there was a 7% increase (70% to 77%) among U.S. residents who indicated there was "solid evidence" that the Earth is warming. However, between January 2007 and April 2008, the percentage decreased by 6% (77% to 71%). This decline in public acceptance of the evidence of global warming may be an aberration in a long-term trend of increasing belief. However, the shift does raise questions regarding the underlying factors affecting public acknowledgement of global warming. What types of evidence are individuals reacting to?

(Christopher Borick and Barry Rabe, "A Reason to Believe: Examining the Factors That Determine Americans' Views on Global Warming." *Issues in Governance Studies*, No.18, July, 2008).

In the following Voice from Across the Curriculum, Professor of Psychology Laura Edelman offers advice on how to read statistically. She expresses respect for the value of numbers as evidence, as opposed to relying on one's own experience or merely speculating. But she also advises students to be aware of the various problems of interpretation that statistical evidence can invite.

VOICES FROM ACROSS THE CURRICULUM

Interpreting the Numbers: A Psychology Professor Speaks

The most important advice we offer our psychology students about statistical evidence is to look at it critically. We teach them that it is easy to misrepresent statistics and that you really need to evaluate the evidence provided. Students need to learn to think about what the numbers actually mean. Where did the numbers come from? What are the implications of the numbers?

In my statistics course, I emphasize that it is not enough just to get the "correct" answer mathematically. Students need to be able to interpret the numbers and the implications of the numbers. For example, if students are rating satisfaction with the textbook on a scale of one (not at all satisfied) to seven (highly satisfied) and we get a class average of 2.38, it is not enough to report that number. You must interpret the number (the class was generally not satisfied) and again explain the implications (time to choose a new text).

Students need to look at the actual numbers. Let's say I do an experiment using two different stat texts. Text A costs $67 and text B costs $32. I give one class text A and one class text B, and at the end of the semester I find that the class using text A did statistically significantly better than the class using text B. Most students at this point would want to switch to the more expensive text A. However, I can show them an example where the class using text A had an average test grade of 87 and the class with text B had an average test grade of 85 (which can be a statistically significant difference): students see the point that even though it is a statistical difference, practically speaking it is not worth double the money to improve the class average by only two points.

There is so much written about the advantages and limitations of empirical information that I hardly know where to begin. Briefly, if it is empirical, there is no guesswork or opinion (Skinner said "the organism is always right"—that is, the data are always right). The limitations are that the collection and/or interpretation can be fraught with biases and error. For example, if I want to know if women still feel that there is gender discrimination in the workplace, I do not have to guess or intuit this (my own experiences are highly likely to bias my guesses): I can do a survey. The survey should tell me what women think (whether I like the answer or not). The limitations occur in how I conduct the survey and how I interpret the results. You might remember the controversy over the Hite Report on sexual activities (whom did she sample, and what kind of people answer those kinds of questions, and do they do so honestly?).

Despite the controversy over the problems of relying on empirical data in psychology, I think that it is the only way to find answers to many fascinating questions about humans. The patterns of data can tell us things that we have no other access to without empirical research. It is critically important for people to be aware of the limitations and problems, but then to go on and collect the data.

—LAURA EDELMAN, PROFESSOR OF PSYCHOLOGY

A Brief Glossary of Common Logical Fallacies

What follows is a brief discussion of common fallacies—false moves—that can subvert argument and interpretation. The logical fallacies share certain characteristics. They offer cheap and unethical ways of "winning" an argument—usually at the cost of shutting down the possibility of negotiation among competing views and discovery of common ground.

The most noticeable feature of arguments based on the logical fallacies is sloganizing. In sloganizing, each side tries to lay claim to various of a culture's honorific words, which then are repeated so often and so much out of context that they evoke little more than a warm glow that each side hopes to attach to its cause. Words and phrases often used in this way are "liberty," "freedom," "the individual," and "the American people," to name a few.

Words like these, along with "natural" and "real," are sometimes referred to as "weasel" words. The analogy with weasels owes to the notion that weasels suck out the contents of eggs, leaving empty shells behind. The words have become, in effect, empty shells.

The sloganizing move gets made when each side tries to attach to the other side various labels that evoke fear—even though the words have been repeated so often, in reference to so many different things, that they have become virtually meaningless. Sloganizing almost always reduces complex circumstances to clear-cut goods and evils. Prominent examples in the current contentious political environment are "socialist," "big government," "neoliberal," and "capitalist."

As you will see, many of these logical fallacies involve the root problem of oversimplification.

1. *Ad hominem.* Literally, this Latin phrase means "to the person." When an argument is aimed at the character of another person rather than at the quality of the person's reasoning or performance, one is engaging in

an *ad hominem* argument. If a political candidate is attacked because they are rich, rather than because of their political platform, they are the victim of an *ad hominem* attack. In some cases, an *ad hominem* argument might be somewhat pertinent—e.g., if a political candidate is discovered to have mob or treasonous connections.

2. **Bandwagon (*ad populum*).** Bandwagon arguments appeal to the emotions of a crowd, as in "everyone's doing it." A bandwagon argument is a bad argument from authority, because no reasons are offered to demonstrate that "everybody" is an informed and reliable source.

3. **Begging the question (circular reasoning).** When you beg the question, you attempt to prove a claim by offering an alternative wording of that claim. To beg the question is to argue in a circle by asking the audience to accept without argument a contestable point. This kind of fallacious argument hides its conclusion among its assumptions. For example, "*Huckleberry Finn* should be banned from school libraries as obscene because it uses dirty language" begs the question by presenting as obviously true issues that are actually in question: the definition of obscenity and the assumption that the obscene should be banned because it is obscene.

4. **Equivocation.** Equivocation confuses an argument by using a single word or phrase in more than one sense. For example: "Only man is capable of religious faith. No woman is a man. Therefore, no woman is capable of religious faith." Here the first use of "man" is generic, intended to be gender neutral, while the second use is decidedly masculine.

5. **False analogy.** A false analogy misrepresents matters by making a comparison between two things that are more unlike than alike. The danger that false analogy poses is that an inaccurate comparison—usually one that oversimplifies—prevents you from looking at the evidence. Flying to the moon is like flying a kite? Well, it's a little bit like that, but . . . in most ways that matter, sending a rocket to the moon does not resemble sending a kite into the air.

An analogy can also become false when it becomes overextended: there is a point of resemblance at one juncture, but the writer then goes on to assume that the two items compared will necessarily resemble each other in most other respects. To what extent is balancing your checkbook really like juggling? On the other hand, an analogy that first appears overextended may not be: how far, for example, could you reasonably go in comparing a presidential election to a sales campaign, or an enclosed shopping mall to a village main street?

When you find yourself reasoning by analogy, ask yourself two questions: (1) are the basic similarities greater and more significant than the obvious differences?, and (2) am I overrelying on surface similarities and ignoring more essential differences?

6. **False cause**. This is a generic term for questionable conclusions about causes and effects. Here are three versions of this fallacy:

   a. **Simple cause/complex effect.** This fallacy occurs when you assign a single cause to a complex phenomenon that cannot be easily explained. A widespread version of this fallacy is seen in arguments that blame individual figures for broad historical events; for example, "Eisenhower caused America to be involved in the Vietnam War." Such a claim ignores the Cold War ethos, the long history of colonialism in Southeast Asia, and a multitude of other factors. When you reduce a complex sequence of events to a single, simple cause—or assign a simple effect to a complex cause—you will almost always be wrong.

   b. **Post hoc, ergo propter hoc.** This term is Latin for "after this, therefore because of this." The fallacy rests in assuming that because A precedes B in time, A causes B. For example, it was once thought that the sun shining on a pile of garbage caused the garbage to conceive flies.

      This error is the stuff that superstition is made of. "I walked under a ladder, and then I got hit by a car" becomes "Because I walked under a ladder I got hit by a car." A more dangerous form of this error goes like this:

      Evidence: A new neighbor moved in downstairs on Saturday. My television disappeared on Sunday.
      Conclusion: The new neighbor stole my TV.

      As this example also illustrates, typically in false cause some significant alternative has not been considered, such as the presence of flies' eggs in the garbage. Similarly, it does not follow that if a person watches television and then commits a crime, television watching necessarily causes crime; there are other causes to be considered.

   c. **Mistaking correlation for cause.** This fallacy occurs when a person assumes that a correlation between two things—some kind of connection—is necessarily causal. The philosopher David Hume called this problem "the constant conjunction of observed events." If you speed in a car and then have a minor accident, it does not follow that speeding caused the accident. If an exit poll reveals that a large number of voters under the age of 25 voted for candidate X, and X loses, it does not follow that X lost because he failed to appeal to older voters. There is a correlation, but the candidate may have lost for any number of reasons.

7. **Hasty generalization.** A conclusion derived from only one or two examples produces the fallacy known as hasty generalization. It is also known as an unwarranted inductive leap because the conclusion lacks sufficient evidence. When a child concludes that all purple food tastes bad because she dislikes eggplant, she has run afoul of this fallacy; give her a grape popsicle.

8. *Non sequitur.* Latin for "it does not follow," *non sequiturs* skip logical steps in arriving at a conclusion. For example: if we mandate a new tax on people who work downtown but do not live there, businesses will all leave the city. Really?

9. **Oversimplification/overgeneralization.** An inadequately qualified claim is to blame for the fallacy of oversimplification or overgeneralization. It may be true that some heavy drinkers are alcoholics, but it would not be fair to claim that all heavy drinking is or leads to alcoholism. As a rule, be wary of "totalizing" or global pronouncements; the bigger the generalization, the more likely it will admit of exceptions.

10. **Poisoning the well.** This fallacy occurs when a person uses loaded language to trivialize or dismiss an argument before even mentioning it. For example: no reasonable person would swallow that left-wing, tax-and-spend position.

11. **Red herring.** The name comes from the practice of using herring, a smelly fish, to distract dogs from the scent they are supposed to be tracking. A red herring diverts the attention of the audience, often by provoking them with some loaded or controversial topic not really related to the matter at hand. For example, if you are talking about the quality of different brands of computers, the issue of whether or not they were made in America would be a red herring.

12. **Slippery slope.** This error is based on the fear that once a move is made in one direction, we will necessarily continue to "slide" in that direction. So, for example, if the U.S. approves medicinal uses of marijuana, soon there will be no control of illicit drug use across the nation. A classic case of slippery slope is offered by the Vietnam War: if a single country was allowed to fall under communist rule, soon all the other countries in the region would follow.

13. **Straw man.** This move involves oversimplifying and even caricaturing another person's argument or position in order to make it easier to refute. For example, opponents of health care reform treat it as a straw man when they claim that such reform would deny benefits to the elderly and perhaps even result in so-called "death panels"—groups who would choose which people will live and which will die.

14. **Weasel word.** As we noted in our earlier discussion of sloganizing, a specialized form of equivocation results in what are sometimes called weasel words. A weasel word is one that has been used so much and so loosely that it ceases to have much meaning. The word "natural," for example, can mean good, pure, and unsullied, but it can also refer to the ways of nature (flora and fauna). Such terms as "love," "reality," and "experience" invite equivocation because they mean so many different things to different people.

Assignments: Interpretation: Moving from Observation to Implication

1. **Build a paper from implications.** Begin this assignment by making observations and drawing out possible implications for one of the topics below. Then use your list as the starting point for a longer paper.

   - Changing trends in automobiles today
   - What your local newspaper chooses to put on its front page (or editorial page) over the course of a week
   - Shows (or advertisements) that appear on network television (as opposed to cable) during one hour of evening prime time
   - Advertisements for scotch whiskey in highbrow magazines

2. **Analyze a magazine cover by researching an interpretive context.** Choose a magazine that, like *The New Yorker*, has interesting covers. Write an analysis of one such cover by studying other covers from the same magazine. Follow the model offered at the end of this chapter:

   a. Apply THE METHOD—looking for patterns of repetition and contrast—to the cover so that you arrive at key repetitions, strands, and organizing contrasts. Begin to ponder a range of possible interpretive leaps as to what they signify.

   b. Use these data to suggest plausible interpretive contexts for the cover. Remember that interpretive contexts are not simply imposed from without; they're suggested by the evidence.

   c. Move to the other covers. Perform similar operations on them to arrive at an awareness of common denominators among the covers, and to analyze what those shared traits might reveal or make more evident in the particular cover you are studying. You will be trying to figure out how the magazine conceives of itself and its audience by the way that it characteristically represents its "face."

   It might be illuminating to survey a range of covers by a single artist, such as Ian Falconer, who created the cover we analyzed in the chapter.

CHAPTER 4

Responding to Traditional Writing Assignments More Analytically

Overview This brief chapter is a companion to the previous chapters, applying strategies from them in the service of making your response to traditional kinds of writing assignments more analytical. These frequently assigned types of writing include:

- Summary
- Personal Response (reaction paper)
- Agree/disagree
- Comparison/contrast (similarity despite difference)
- Definition

Each of these conventional topics can invite problems for writers, or rather a shared problem: oversimplification. The chapter that follows will offer some basic and easy-to-follow solutions to this problem. Most of these involve small changes in wording or approach. See, for example, the strategy called DIFFERENCE WITHIN SIMILARITY as a means of giving comparison and contrast depth and focus. Rather than leading you to a single or obvious answer, an analytical topic aims to define a space in which you can have ideas about (explore the questions in) what you've been learning.

Interpreting Writing Assignments

One fact of college writing is that someone is usually telling you not only what to write about, but also what form to write it in. This situation is not, however, as straightforward as it sounds. Consider, for example, an assignment to discuss how a supply-side economist might respond to the idea of eliminating most tariffs on imported goods. How do you interpret the word "*discuss*"? Should you confine your response to summarizing (restating) the reading you've done on the subject? Should you analyze the reading by, for example, drawing out its unstated assumptions or pointing to inconsistencies in its position? Should you write an argument about the reading, revealing the extent to which you agree or disagree with the supply-side view? And what do you do about the other most common writing situation, the open topic, wherein the assignment is essentially to go write your own assignment?

By the time you reach college, you will have learned to recognize certain kinds of instructions that writing assignments characteristically contain: compare and contrast, define, agree or disagree. The key words of a topic trigger different kinds of writing. Some topics call for *argument*—for taking a firm stand on one side of an issue and making a case for that stand. Some call for *summary*—for restating ideas and information in a focused and concise way. Some call for *personal response*—for testing an idea or attitude or question against your own life experience.

These kinds of writing assignments have a significant analytical component, though this fact is often overlooked. This chapter will show you how to make your responses to common kinds of topics more analytical.

Find the Analytical Potential: Locate an Area of Uncertainty

The best way to become more analytical in your response to topics is to actively search out an area of your subject where there are no clear and obvious answers—to look for something that needs explaining, rather than reiterating the obvious. The analytical component in a topic is often not apparent. You have to actively look for it.

Although disciplines vary in the kinds of questions they characteristically ask, every discipline is concerned with asking questions, exploring areas of uncertainty and attempting to solve, or at least clarify, problems. An analytical response to a topic calls on you, in other words, to *deliberately situate yourself among sites of potential ambiguity or conflict,* so that your writing can explore the complexity of your subject. In order to learn how to enter this uncertain space, you will first have to get over the fear that you are doing something wrong if you cannot arrive quickly at a clear and obvious answer. Many high school students enter college believing that paper-writing is about providing answers. Most of the time, though, it actually has to do with finding the questions. This shift in orientation can be profound. It means that as you read, you are consciously trying to locate elements in the reading that you don't understand, that you genuinely question. Those are the sites where the best potential papers are to be found—places where your writing will have real analytical work to do.

We now turn to six rules of thumb that can help you discover and respond to the complexities that are there but not always immediately apparent in your subject matter, nor explicitly asked for in the writing assignments you encounter. All of our suggestions have in common the single requirement that you train yourself to look for questions rather than leaping too quickly to answers. It is this orientation toward topics that will move you beyond merely reporting information and lead you to think with and about it.

Six Rules of Thumb for Responding to Assignments More Analytically

The following rules of thumb can help you discover and respond to the complexities of the topics that you encounter, rather than oversimplifying or evading them.

Rule 1: Reduce Scope

Whenever possible, reduce drastically the scope of your inquiry. Resist the temptation to include too much information. Even when an assignment calls for broad coverage of a subject, an effective and usually acceptable strategy is for you to begin with an overview and then analyze one or two key points in greater depth.

For example, if you were asked to write on President Franklin Roosevelt's New Deal, you would obviously have to open with some general observations, such as what it was and why it arose. But if you tried to stay on this general level throughout, your paper would have little direction or focus. You could achieve a focus, though, by moving quickly from the general to some much smaller, more specific part of the subject, such as attacks on the New Deal. You would then be able to limit the enormous range of possible evidence to a few representative figures, such as Huey Long, Father Coughlin, and Alf Landon. Once you began to compare the terms and legitimacy of their opposition to the New Deal, you would be much more likely to manage a complex analysis of the subject than if you had remained at the level of broad generalization. Typically, you will find that some mixture of wide-angle coverage with more narrowly focused discussion is the best way to cover the ground without sacrificing depth.

Rule 2: Study the Wording of Topics for Unstated Questions

Nearly all formulations of an assigned topic contain one or more overt questions, and also other questions that are implied by the topic's wording. Taking the time to ponder the wording and to articulate the questions that wording implies is often the first step to having an idea—to finding an angle of approach.

Consider, for instance, a topic question such as "Is feminism good for Judaism?" The question itself seems to invite you simply to argue yes or no, but the wording implies preliminary questions that you would need to articulate and answer before you could address the larger issue. What, for example, does "good for Judaism" mean? That which allows the religion to evolve? That which conserves its tradition? The same kinds of questions, defining and contextualizing and laying out implications, might be asked of the term "feminism." And what of the possibility that feminism has no significant effect whatsoever?

As this example illustrates, even an apparently limited and straightforward question presses writers to make choices about how to engage it. So don't leap from the topic question to your plan of attack too quickly. One of the best strategies lies in smoking out and addressing the unstated assumptions implied by the wording of the topic. (See the discussion of uncovering assumptions in Chapter 2.)

Rule 3: Suspect Your First Responses

If you settle for your first responses, the result is likely to be superficial, obvious, and overly general. A better strategy is to examine your first responses for ways in which they are inaccurate and then to develop the implications of these overstatements (or errors) into a new formulation. In many cases, writers go through this process of proposing and rejecting ideas ten times or more before they arrive at an angle or approach that will sustain an essay.

A first response is okay for a start, as long as you don't stop there. For example, many people might agree, at first glance, that no one should be denied health care, or that a given film or novel that concludes with a marriage is a happy ending, or that the American government should not pass trade laws that might cause Americans to lose their jobs. On closer inspection, however, each of these responses begins to reveal its limitations. Given that there is a limited amount of money available, should everyone, regardless of age or physical condition, be accorded every medical treatment that might prolong life? And might not a novel or film that concludes in marriage signal that the society offers too few options, or more cynically, that the author is feeding the audience an implausible fantasy to blanket over problems raised earlier in the work? And couldn't trade laws resulting in short-term job loss ultimately produce *more* jobs and a healthier economy?

As these examples suggest, first responses—usually pieces of conventional wisdom—can blind you to rival explanations. Try not to decide on an answer to questions too quickly.

Rule 4: Begin with Questions, Not Answers

Whether you are focusing an assigned topic or devising one of your own, you are usually better off to begin with something that you don't understand very well and want to understand better. Begin by asking what kinds of questions the material poses. For example, if you are already convinced that Robinson Crusoe changes throughout Defoe's novel, and you write a paper cataloguing those changes, you will essentially be composing a selective plot summary. If, by contrast, you wonder why Crusoe walls himself within a fortress after he discovers a footprint in the sand, you will be more likely to interpret the significance of events rather than just report them.

Rule 5: Expect to Become Interested

Writing gives you the opportunity to cultivate your curiosity by thinking exploratively. Rather than approaching topics in a mechanical way or putting them off to the last possible moment and doing the assignment grudgingly, try giving yourself and the topic the benefit of the doubt. If you can suspend judgment and start writing, you will often find yourself uncovering interests where you had not seen them before. In other words, accept the idea that interest is a product of writing—not a prerequisite.

Rule 6: Write All of the Time About What You Are Studying

Because interest is so often a product and not a prerequisite of writing, it follows that writing informally about what you are studying while you are studying it is probably the single best preparation for developing interesting topics. Writing spontaneously about what you read accustoms you to being a less passive consumer of ideas and information, and you will have more ideas and information available to think actively with and about. In effect, you will be formulating possible topics long before an actual topic is assigned. In any case, you should not wait to start writing until you think you have an idea around which you can organize a paper. Instead, use writing to get you to the idea.

Using Freewriting to Find and Interpret Topics As we have argued in previous chapters, freewriting offers one of the best antidotes to both superficial writing and writer's block. It also enables you to develop and organize your ideas when you begin drafting more formally because you already will have explored some possible paths you might travel and rejected others as dead ends.

Passage-Based Focused Freewrites (see Figure 2.3 in Chapter 2) are an especially useful way to move from a broad topic to one that is more carefully directed and narrowed. Start by choosing passages in response to the question, "What in the reading needs to be discussed; poses a question or a problem; or seems in some way difficult to pin down, anomalous, or even just unclear?" You can vary this question infinitely, selecting the passage that you find most puzzling, most important, most dissonant, or the like. Then write without stopping for fifteen minutes or so.

One advantage of Passage-Based Focused Freewrites is that it forces you to articulate what you notice as you notice it. There is no set procedure for such writing, but it usually involves the following:

- It selects key words or phrases in the passage and paraphrases them, trying to tease out their possible meanings.

- It addresses how the passage is representative of broader issues in the reading; perhaps it will refer to another, similar passage.

- It attends, at least briefly, to the context surrounding the passage, identifying the larger section of which the passage is a part.

If you assign yourself several Passage-Based Focused Freewrites on a given topic, you can build up, through a process of accretion, the thinking for an entire paper.

The remainder of this chapter offers strategies for upping the analytical quotient in your response to traditional writing assignments.

Summary

All analytical topics require a blend of two components: a thinking component and an information component. Summary provides the information component. Summarizing is basically a translation process, and as such it is an essential part of learning. It is the way that not just facts and figures but also other people's theories and observations enter your writing.

Summary performs the essential function of contextualizing a subject accurately. It creates a fair picture of what's there. Summarizing isn't simply the unanalytical reporting of information; it's more than just condensing someone else's words. To write an accurate summary, you have to ask analytical questions, such as the following:

- Which ideas in the reading are most significant? Why?
- How do these ideas fit together?
- What do the key passages in the reading mean?

Like paraphrasing, summarizing is a tool of understanding, not just a mechanical task. (They are not the same, however: paraphrase expands the original; summary condenses.)

Ineffectual summaries are mere lists in a simple "this and then this" sequence. Often they are random, like a shopping list compiled from the first thing you think of to the last. The problem is that lists do very little logical connecting among the parts beyond "next." They omit the *thinking* that the piece is doing.

Writing analytical summaries can teach you how to read for the connections, the lines that connect the dots. And when you're operating at that level, you are much more likely to have ideas about what you are summarizing. This invention-oriented component of writing summaries is particularly helpful when you are working on an extended research project, because you will be encouraged to have ideas about the subject as you amass information about it.

Strategies for Making Summaries More Analytical

Strategy 1: Look for the underlying structure. Use THE METHOD to find patterns of repetition and contrast (see Chapter 1). If you apply it to a few key paragraphs, you will find the terms that get repeated, and these will suggest strands, which in turn make up organizing contrasts. This process works to categorize and then further organize information and, in so doing, to bring out its underlying structure. See also UNCOVERING ASSUMPTIONS and TRACKING BINARIES in Chapter 2.

Strategy 2: Select the information that you wish to discuss on some principle other than general coverage. Use NOTICE & FOCUS to rank items of information in some order of importance (see Chapter 1). Let's say that you are writing a paper on major changes in the tax law or on recent developments in U.S. policy toward the Middle East. Rather than simply collecting the information, arrange it into hierarchies. What are the least or most significant changes or developments, and why? Which changes or developments are most overlooked or most overrated or most controversial or most practical, and why? All of these terms—significant, overlooked, and so forth—have the effect of focusing the summary, guiding your decisions about what to include and exclude.

Strategy 3: Reduce scope to say more about less. Reducing scope is an especially efficient and productive strategy when you are trying to understand a reading you find difficult or perplexing. It will move you beyond passive summarizing and toward having ideas about the reading. You can still begin with a brief survey of major points to provide context before narrowing the focus.

If you read Chaucer's *Canterbury Tales* and catalog what makes it funny, you are likely to end up with unanalyzed plot summary—a list that arranges its elements in no particular order. But narrowing the question to "How does Chaucer's use of religious commentary contribute to the humor of 'The Wife of Bath's Tale'?" reduces the scope to a single tale and the humor to a single aspect of humor. Describe those as accurately as you can, and you will begin to notice things.

Strategy 4: Get some detachment: shift your focus from *what?* to *how?* and *why?* Most readers tend to get too single-minded about absorbing information. That is, they attend only to the *what*: what the reading is saying or is about. They take it all in passively. But you can deliberately shift your focus to *how* it says what it says and *why*.

If you were asked to discuss the major discoveries that Darwin made on *The Beagle*, you could avoid simply listing his conclusions by redirecting your attention to *how* he proceeded. You could choose to focus, for example, on Darwin's use of the scientific method, examining how he built and, in some cases discarded, hypotheses. Or you might select several passages that illustrate how Darwin proceeded from evidence to conclusion and then *rank* them in order of importance to the overall theory. Notice that in shifting the emphasis to Darwin's thinking—the how and why—you would not be excluding the what (the information component) from your discussion.

One way to focus on the how and the why—whether it be a sign on a subway or the language of a presidential speech—is to situate the reading rhetorically. Like analysis in general, rhetorical analysis asks what things mean, why they are as they are, and how they do what they do. But rhetorical analysis asks these questions with one primary question always foregrounded: how does the thing achieve its effects on an audience? Rhetorical analysis asks not just "What do I think?," but "What am I being invited to think (and feel), and by what means?" See "Noticing and Rhetorical Analysis" in Chapter 1 and "Find The Pitch, The Complaint, and The Moment" in Chapter 2.

Personal Response: The Reaction Paper

How do you know when you are being asked for a personal response? And what does it mean to respond personally? When asked for your reactions to a particular subject, or for what you think is most important or interesting or revealing in it, you are being asked to select your own starting point for discussion, for the initial impressions that you will later analyze more systematically. You will often discover in such reactions the germ of an idea about the subject.

The biggest advantage of personal response topics is that they give you the freedom to explore where and how to engage your subject. Such topics often bring to the surface your emotional or intuitive response, allowing you to experiment with placing the subject in various contexts. You might, for example, offer your personal response to an article on the abuses of hazing in fraternity and sorority life in the context of your own experience. Or you might think about it in connection to some idea about in-groups and out-groups that you read about in a sociology course, or as it relates to what you read about cultural rituals in an anthropology course.

Another advantage of personal response questions is that they often allow you to get some distance from your first impressions, which can be deceiving. If, as you reexamine your first reactions, you look for ways they might be inaccurate, you will often find places where you now disagree with yourself, in effect stimulating you to think in new ways about the subject. In such cases, the first reaction has helped to clear the way to a second, better response.

Personal response becomes a problem, however, when it distracts you from analyzing the subject. In most cases, you will be misinterpreting the intent of a personal response topic if you view it as an invitation either to assert your personal opinions unreflectively, or substitute narratives of your own experience for careful consideration of the subject.

In a sense, all analysis involves your opinions insofar as you are choosing the evidence and arguments upon which to focus. But, at least in an academic setting, an opinion is more than an expression of your beliefs—it is a conclusion that you validate through a careful examination of evidence.

When invited to respond personally, you are being asked for more than your endorsement or critique of the subject. If you find yourself constructing a virtual list—"I agree with this point," or "I disagree with that point"—you are probably doing little more than matching your opinions with the points of view encountered in a reading. At the very least, look for places in the reaction paper where you find you are disagreeing with yourself.

Strategies for Making Personal Responses More Analytical

Strategy 1: Trace your responses back to their causes. As the preceding discussion of problems with personal response topics suggests, *you need to bring your reactions back to the subject so you can identify and analyze exactly what in the reading has produced your reaction, how, and why.* If you find an aspect of your subject irritating or interesting, disappointing or funny, you will be able to use—rather than simply indulge—such responses if you then examine the piece of evidence that has provoked them.

Tracing your impressions back to their causes (the phrasing was Ernest Hemingway's, his advice to young writers) is the key to making personal response analytical—because you focus on the details that gave you the response rather than on the response alone. In the planning stage, you may find it useful to brainstorm some of your reactions/responses—the things you might say about the material if asked to talk about it with a sympathetic friend. You would then take this brainstorm and use it to choose the key sentences, passages, etc. in the reading that you want to focus on in your analysis.

Say that you are responding to an article on ways of increasing the number of registered voters in urban precincts. You find the article irritating; your personal experience working with political campaigns has taught you that getting out the vote is not as easy as this writer makes it seem. From that starting point, you might analyze one (to you) overly enthusiastic passage, concentrating on how the writer has not only overestimated what campaign workers can actually do, but also condescends to those who don't register—assuming, perhaps, that they are ignorant, rather than indifferent or disillusioned. Tracing your response back to its cause may help to defuse your emotional response and open the door to further investigation of the other writer's rationale. You might discover that the writer has in mind a much more long-term effect, or that urban models differ significantly from the suburban ones of your experience.

Strategy 2: Assume that you may have missed the point. It is difficult to see the logic of someone else's position if you are preoccupied with your own. Similarly, it is difficult to see the logic, or illogic, of your own position if you already assume it to be true.

Although an evaluative response (approve/disapprove) can sometimes spur analysis, it can also lead you to prejudge the case. If, however, you habitually question the validity of your own point of view, you will sometimes recognize the possibility of an alternative point of view, as was the case in the voter registration example (see Figure 4.1). Assuming that you have missed the point is a good strategy in all analytical writing. It causes you to notice details of your subject that you might not otherwise have registered.

> **Evaluative Personal Response:** *"The article was irritating."* This response is too broad and dismissively judgmental. Make it more analytical by tracing the response back to the evidence that triggered it.
>
> **A More Analytical Evaluative Response:** *"The author of the article oversimplifies the problem by assuming the cause of low voter registration to be voters' ignorance rather than voters' indifference."* Although still primarily an evaluative response, this observation is more analytical. It takes the writer's initial response ("irritating") to a specific cause.
>
> **A Non-evaluative Analytical Response:** *"The author's emphasis on increased coverage of city politics in local/neighborhood forums such as the churches suggests that the author is interested in long-term effects of voter registration drives and not just in immediate increases."* Rather than simply reacting ("irritating") or leaping to evaluation ("oversimplifies the problem"), the writer here formulates a possible explanation for the difference between the writer's point of view on voter registration drives and the article's.

FIGURE 4.1

Making Personal Response More Analytical

Strategy 3: Locate your response within a limiting context. Suppose you are asked in a religion course to write about your religious beliefs. Although this topic would naturally lead you to think about your own experiences and beliefs, you would probably do best to approach it in a more limiting context. The reading in the course could provide this limit. Let's say that thus far you have read two modern religious thinkers, Martin Buber and Paul Tillich. Using these as your context, "What do I believe?" would become "How does my response to Buber and Tillich illuminate my own assumptions about the nature of religious faith?" An advantage of this move, beyond making your analysis less general, is that it would help you to get perspective on your own position.

Another way of limiting your context is to consider how one author or recognizable point of view that you have encountered in the course might respond to a single statement from another author or point of view. If you used this strategy to respond to the topic "Does God exist?," you might arrive at a formulation such as "How would Martin Buber critique Paul Tillich's definition of God?" Although this topic appears to exclude personal response entirely, it in fact does not. Your opinion would necessarily enter because you would be actively formulating something that is not already evident in the reading (that is, how Buber might respond to Tillich).

Agree/Disagree

We offer here only a brief recap of this kind of topic, because it is discussed in both Chapter 1 (under "Habit: The Judgment Reflex") and Chapter 2 (under Reformulating Binaries). Assignments are frequently worded as "agree or disagree," but such wording may be misleading because you will rarely be asked for an unqualified agree or disagree opinion.

Creating opposing categories (binary oppositions) is fundamental to defining things. But binaries are also dangerous because they can invite *reductive thinking*—oversimplifying a subject by eliminating alternatives between the two extremes. In most cases, your best strategy in dealing with agree/disagree questions is to choose *neither* side. Instead, question the terms of the binary so as to arrive at a more complex and qualified position to write about. In place of choosing one side or the other, decide to what extent you agree and to what extent you disagree. You are still responsible for coming down more on one side than the other, but this need not mean that you must locate yourself in a starkly either/or position. The code phrase for accomplishing this shift is "*the extent to which*": "To what extent do you agree (or disagree)?"

Here is a brief review of these strategies:

Strategy 1: Locate a range of opposing categories.
Strategy 2: Analyze and define the opposing terms.
Strategy 3: Question the accuracy of the binary.
Strategy 4: Change "either/or" to "the extent to which" (or "to what extent?").

Applying these strategies will usually cause you to do one or more of the following:

1. Weight one side of your binary more heavily than the other, rather than seeing the issue as "all or nothing" (all of one and none of the other).

2. Discover that you have not adequately named the binary: another opposition would be more accurate.

3. Discover that the two terms of your binary are not really so separate and opposed after all, but actually part of one complex phenomenon or issue.

Comparison/Contrast

Although comparison/contrast is meant to invite analysis, it is too often treated as an end in itself. The fundamental reason for comparing and contrasting is that you can usually discover ideas about a subject much more easily when you are not viewing it in isolation. When executed mechanically, however, without the writer pressing to understand the significance of a similarity or difference, comparison/contrast can suffer from pointlessness. The telltale sign of this problem is the formulaic sentence beginning "Thus we see there are many similarities and differences between X and Y": "chaos" and "cream cheese" would fit this formula (both begin with the letter "c").

Comparison/contrast topics produce pointless essays if you allow them to turn into matching exercises—that is, if you match common features of two subjects but don't get beyond the equation stage (a, b, c = x, y, z). Writers fall into this trap when they have no larger question or issue to explore, and perhaps resolve this lack of point by making the comparison. If, for example, you were to pursue the comparison of the representations of the

Boston Tea Party in British and American history textbooks, you would begin by identifying similarities and differences. But simply presenting these and concluding that the two versions resemble and differ from each other in some ways would be pointless. You would need to press your comparisons with the "So What?" question (see Chapter 1) in order to give them interpretive weight.

Comparison/contrast leads to the more sophisticated task of synthesis. Synthesis involves more than two sources, often for the purpose of composing the opening frame of a research-based paper (known as the "literature review") that typically opens papers in the social sciences. For more on synthesis, see Chapter 8, "Conversing with Sources: Writing the Researched Paper." For advice on organizing comparison/contrast papers, see Chapter 10, "From Paragraphs to Papers: Forms and Formats Across the Curriculum."

Strategies for Making Comparison/Contrast More Analytical, Including DIFFERENCE WITHIN SIMILARITY

Strategy 1: Argue for the significance of a key comparison.
Rather than covering a range of comparisons, focus on a key comparison. Although narrowing the focus might seem to eliminate other important areas of consideration, in fact it usually allows you to incorporate at least some of these other areas in a more tightly connected, less list-like fashion. So, for example, a comparison of the burial rites of two cultures will probably reveal more about them than a much broader but more superficial list of cultural similarities and differences. In most cases, covering less is covering more.

You can determine which comparison is key by ranking. You are ranking whenever you designate one part of your topic as especially important or revealing. Suppose you are asked to compare General David Petraeus's strategy in the Afghanistan conflict with General Douglas MacArthur's strategy in World War II. As a first move, you could limit the comparison to some revealing parallel, such as the way each man dealt with the media, and then argue for its significance above other similarities or differences. You might, for instance, claim that in their treatment of the media we get an especially clear or telling vantage point on the two generals' strategies. Now you are on your way to an analytical point—for example, that because MacArthur was more effectively shielded from the media at a time when the media was a virtual instrument of propaganda, he could make choices that Petraeus might have wanted to make but could not.

Strategy 2: Use one side of the comparison to illuminate the other.
Usually it is not necessary to treat each part of the comparison equally. It is a common misconception that each side must be given equal space. In fact, the purpose of your comparison governs the amount of space you'll need to give to each part. Often, you will be using one side of the comparison primarily

to illuminate the other. For example, in a course on contemporary military policy, the ratio between the two parts would probably be roughly seventy percent on Petraeus to thirty percent on MacArthur, rather than fifty percent on each.

Strategy 3: Imagine how one side of your comparison might respond to the other. This strategy, a variant of the preceding one, is a particularly useful way of helping you to respond to comparison/contrast topics more purposefully. This strategy can be adapted to a wide variety of subjects. If you were asked to compare Sigmund Freud with one of his most important followers, Jacques Lacan, you would probably be better off focusing the broad question of how Lacan revises Freud by considering how and why he might critique the interpretation of a particular dream in Freud's *The Interpretation of Dreams*. Similarly, in the case of the Afghanistan example, you could ask yourself how MacArthur might have handled some key decision in dealing with Kabul, and why. Or you might consider how he would have critiqued Petraeus's decisions, and why.

Strategy 4: Focus on DIFFERENCE WITHIN SIMILARITY (or similarity despite difference). Too often, writers notice a fundamental similarity and stop there. Asked to compare two subjects, they typically collect several parallel examples and merely show how they are parallel. This practice leads to bland tallying of similarities without much analytical edge—a matching exercise. Ideas tend to arise when a writer moves beyond this basic demonstration and complicates (or qualifies) the similarity by also noting areas of difference and accounting for their significance.

The solution is to practice what we call "looking for DIFFERENCE WITHIN SIMILARITY" (see Figure 4.2).

1	Decide whether the similarities or differences are most obvious and easily explained.
2	Explain the most important similarity or difference by ASKING "SO WHAT?" Why is this similarity or difference significant?
3	Then focus your attention on the most important difference within the similarity or similarity despite the difference. You can expect this difference to be less obvious than the most important similarity, but therefore probably more revealing.

FIGURE 4.2
Looking for DIFFERENCE WITHIN SIMILARITY

The phrase "DIFFERENCE WITHIN SIMILARITY" is to remind you that once you have started your thinking by locating apparent similarities, you can usually refine that thinking by pursuing significant, though often less obvious, distinctions among the similar things.

In Irish studies, for example, scholars characteristically acknowledge the extent to which contemporary Irish culture is the product of colonization. To this extent, Irish culture shares certain traits with other former colonies in Africa, Asia, Latin America, and elsewhere. But instead of simply demonstrating how Irish culture fits the general pattern of colonialism, these scholars also isolate the ways that Ireland *does not fit* the model. They focus, for example, on how its close geographical proximity and racial similarity to England, its colonizer, have distinguished the problems it encounters today from those characteristic of the generalized model of colonialism. In effect, looking for DIFFERENCE WITHIN SIMILARITY has led them to locate and analyze the anomalies.

A corollary of the DIFFERENCE WITHIN SIMILARITY formula is similarity despite difference—that is, focusing on unexpected similarity rather than obvious difference. Consider, for example, two popular twenty-something TV sitcoms from different generations, *Friends* and *The Big Bang Theory*. At first inspection, these would appear to differ profoundly—one presents a heterosexual group living together, in which everyone is straight; the other centers on an essentially all-male group living together, in which sexual orientation is—in at least one case—ambiguous.

But how are the two shows similar despite these differences? Both offer the consoling prospect of a comfortable space between the teen years and the specter of adulthood, before the kind of separation that coupling off and having kids incurs. In other words, both suggest that adulthood can be comfortably forestalled by offering a group of friends who become family, regardless of male/female or gay/straight binaries.

Regardless of whether you begin by deciding that the similarities or the differences are most obvious, choosing to focus on less immediately noticeable differences or similarities will cause you to notice things that you otherwise might not have noticed. This is what comparison and contrast is designed to reveal. To sum up:

When A & B are obviously similar,
   look for unexpected difference.
When A & B are obviously different,
   look for unexpected similarity.

Definition

Definition becomes meaningful when it serves some larger purpose. You define "rhythm and blues" because it is essential to any further discussion of the evolution of rock and roll music, or because you need that definition in order to discuss the British Invasion spearheaded by groups such as the Beatles, the Rolling Stones, and the Yardbirds in the late 1960s, or because you cannot classify John Lennon or Mick Jagger or Eric Clapton without it.

Like comparison/contrast, definition can produce pointless essays if the writer gets no further than assembling information. Moreover, when you construct a summary of existing definitions with no clear sense of purpose, you tend to list definitions indiscriminately. As a result, you are likely to overlook conflicts among the various definitions and overemphasize their surface similarities. Definition is, in fact, a site at which there is contesting of authorities—different voices that seek to make their individual definitions triumph.

Strategies for Making Definition More Analytical

Strategy 1: Test the definition against evidence. One common form of definition asks you to apply a definition to a body of information. It is rare to find a perfect fit. Therefore, as a general rule, you should use the data to assess the accuracy and the limitations of the definition, rather than simply imposing it on your data and ignoring or playing down the ways in which it does not fit. Testing the definition against evidence will evolve your definition. The definition, in turn, will serve as a lens to better focus your thinking about the evidence.

Suppose you were asked to define capitalism in the context of third-world economies. You might profitably begin by matching some standard definition of capitalism with specific examples from one or two third-world economies, with the express purpose of detecting where the definition does *and does not* apply. In other words, you would respond to the definition topic by assaying the extent to which the definition provides a tool for making sense of the subject.

Strategy 2: Use a definition from one source to illuminate another. You should attempt to identify the points of view of the sources from which you take your definitions, rather than accepting them as uncontextualized answers. It is essential to identify the particular slant, because otherwise you will tend to overlook the conflicting elements among various definitions of a key term.

A paper on alcoholism, for example, will lose focus if you use every definition available. If, instead, you convert the definition into a comparison and contrast of competing definitions, you can more easily generate a point and purpose for your definition. By querying, for example, whether a given source's definition of alcoholism is moral, physiological, or psychological, you can more easily problematize the issue of definition.

Strategy 3: Problematize as well as synthesize the definition. To explore competing definitions of the same term requires you to attend to the difficulties of definition. In general, analysis achieves direction and purpose by locating and then exploring a problem. You can productively make a problem out of defining. This strategy, known as *problematizing*, locates and then explores the significance of the uncertainties and conflicts. It is always a smart move to problematize definitions, because this tactic reveals complexity that less careful thinkers might miss.

The definition of capitalism that you might take from Karl Marx, for example, will differ in its emphases from Adam Smith's. In this case, you would not only isolate the most important of these differences, but also try to account for the fact that Marx's villain is Smith's hero. Such an accounting would probably lead you to consider how the definition has been shaped by each writer's political philosophy, or by the culture in which each theory was composed.

Strategy 4: Shift from "what?" to "how?" and "why?" questions. It is no accident that we earlier offered the same strategy for making summary more analytical: analytical topics that require definition also depend on "why?" or "how?" questions, not "what?" questions (which tend simply to call for information).

If, for example, you sought to define the meaning of darkness in Joseph Conrad's *Heart of Darkness* and two other modern British novels, you would do better to ask why the writers find "darkness" such a fertile term, rather than simply to accumulate various examples of the term in the three novels. You might start by isolating the single best example from each work, preferably one that reveals important differences as well as similarities. Then, in analyzing how each writer uses the term, you could work toward some larger point that would unify the essay. You might show how the conflicts of definition within Conrad's metaphor evolve historically, get reshaped by female novelists, change after World War I, and so forth.

In sum, definition is a site of power, and when you are offering one, or analyzing someone else's, you should expect tension and complexity. Don't elide the tension and complexity: bring them out and analyze the strengths and limitations of competing definitions.

Assignments: Responding to Traditional Writing Assignments More Analytically

1. **Analyze the wording of an assignment.** Analyze the following topic for unstated questions:

   > In a well-written essay, evaluate the truth of the assertion that follows. Use evidence and examples from your reading or experience to make your argument convincing. "It is human nature to want patterns, standards, and a structure of behavior. A pattern to conform to is a kind of shelter."

   As we began to do with "Is feminism good for Judaism?" earlier, make a list of all the questions implicit in this topic. Which words, both in the directions given to students and in the quotation, itself, require attention? When you have compiled your list, write a paragraph or two in which you explain, as specifically as possible, what the question is asking writers to do and how a writer might go about fulfilling these tasks.

2. **Write two summaries of the same article or book chapter.** Make the first one consecutive (the so-called "coverage" model)—that is, try to cover the piece by essentially listing the key points as they appear. Limit yourself to a typed page. Then rewrite the summary, doing the following:

   - Rank the items in order of importance according to some principle that you designate, explaining your rationale.
   - Eliminate the last few items on the list or, at most, give each a single sentence.
   - Use the space you have saved to include more detail about the most important item or two.

   The second half of this assignment will probably require close to two pages.

3. **Look for significant difference or unexpected similarity.** Choose any item from the list below. After you've done the research necessary to locate material to read and analyze, list as many similarities and differences as you can: go for coverage. Then review your list and select the two or three most revealing similarities and the two or three most revealing differences. At this point, you are ready to write a few paragraphs in which you argue for the significance of a key difference or similarity. In so doing, try to focus on an *unexpected* similarity or difference—one that others might not initially notice.

   - Accounts of the same event from two different newspapers or magazines or textbooks.
   - Two albums (or even songs) by the same artist or group.
   - Two ads for the same kind of product, perhaps aimed at different target audiences.
   - The political campaigns of two opponents running for the same or similar office.
   - Courtship behavior as practiced by men and by women.
   - Two clothing styles emblematic of class or subgroup in your school, town, or workplace.

4. **Write a comparative definition.** Seek out different and potentially competing definitions of the same term or terms. Begin with a dictionary such as the *Oxford English Dictionary* (popularly known as the *OED*, available in most library reference rooms or online) that contains both historically based definitions tracking the term's evolution over time and etymological definitions that identify the linguistic origins of the term (its sources in older languages). Be sure to locate both the historical evolution and the etymology of the term or terms.

Then look up the term in one—or preferably several—specialized dictionaries. You can also ask your reference librarian for pertinent titles. Generally speaking, different disciplines generate their own specialized dictionaries.

Summarize key differences and similarities among the ways the dictionaries have defined your term or terms. Then write a comparative essay in which you argue for the significance of a key similarity or difference, or an unexpected one.

Here are some suggested terms: hysteria, ecstasy, enthusiasm, witchcraft, leisure, gossip, bachelor, spinster, romantic, instinct, punk, thug, pundit, dream, alcoholism, aristocracy, atom, ego, pornography, conservative, liberal, entropy, election, tariff. Some of these words are interesting to pair, such as ecstasy/enthusiasm or liberal/conservative or bachelor/spinster. Feel free to write on a pair, instead of on a single word.

CHAPTER 5

Thinking Like a Writer

Overview   This chapter offers various writing prompts aimed at helping you become more engaged with your own writing, including writing in forms other than the formal essay or paper, such as a writer's notebook (not the same thing as a diary or journal). The writing prompts in this chapter also make room for writing essays drawn from your own life experiences. The chapter argues that personal writing is not at odds with the kinds of thinking and writing that analysis requires, and is, in fact, exceptionally useful in teaching you how to use writing as a mode of inquiry. A goal throughout this book is to suggest ways of making classrooms and other group settings more genuinely collegial and collaborative. Toward that end, the chapter suggests alternatives to the usual ways of prompting revision and of working in groups with other writers, including, for example, writers' bootcamps, writing marathons, and a form of small-group peer review that relies on supportive description rather than critique.

Process and Product

The writing activities in this chapter aim to improve your fluency as a writer, your ability to get words down on the page. They also aim to help you become a more independent writer, one capable of finding things to write about on your own rather than always having to rely on other people's questions. As the chapter title suggests, writers have ways of thinking and of arriving at ideas that are the product of the time they spend writing.

This chapter is premised on the idea that we learn to write by writing. The more you engage in writing as an activity, the more you will discover about how you think, and about what you need to do in order to make good writing happen. Growing as a writer requires some guidelines, but it also requires a lot of room for experimentation. Writing is more than a way of packaging an already-completed piece of thinking so that other people can understand it. Writing is a way of asking yourself questions and seeing where these might lead.

As we said at the beginning of this book, learning to write well means learning to use writing in order to think well. The best way to acquire this skill is to write often and in a variety of forms, including the sort of informal writing that causes you to hear yourself thinking on the page. Though there are rules to follow in the finished products of your writing—various kinds of rules for different situations—there is no substitute for having the space to experiment in your writing with how you think. This is what this chapter will ask you to do.

A Review of Some Strategies from *Writing Analytically* for Making Writing Happen

In the first four chapters of this book, you learned a number of writing-based activities called heuristics. A heuristic is a tool of discovery, a method of using writing in order to notice more in whatever it is that you are studying. The book's heuristics are ways of making writing happen. All of them are grounded in two central pieces of advice for enhancing your skills as a thinker and writer: 1) slow down leaps to conclusions in order to spend more time with the data, which requires learning to dwell comfortably with uncertainty, and 2) go local rather than global, which requires training yourself to focus on details, on individual words and sentences, rather than constantly trying to generalize about a subject as a whole, especially if that generalization takes the form of critique.

These orientations are essential to the type of writing you will probably be asked to do in and after college, which is exploratory, inquiry-based writing. This kind of writing, as opposed to writing that tries to prove a point and persuade others to accept a particular point of view, is necessary in situations where there is more than one "right answer" or perhaps no right answer—just various ways of understanding a problem. Even when there seems to be a "right answer," inquiry-based writing looks at some feature of the subject where there is room for more than one way of understanding: the subject's history, for example, or the rhetoric with which the "answer" is typically promoted. In Chapter 1 of this book, as one of the Five Analytical Moves, we suggested that in addition to asking what something means, it is essential to ask what else it might mean. This is to say that it is better to keep reformulating possible "answers" than insisting on the merits of only one.

Here is a list of some of the first four chapters' heuristics, plus a preview of two that you will find in the first two chapters of Part Two.

PARAPHRASE x 3. Use close restatement as a way of clarifying meanings to yourself and your readers. Don't assume that the meanings of words are obvious and self-evident. (See Chapter 2, "Reading Analytically.")

DO THE METHOD. Read for significant patterns of repetition and contrast. Circle words that repeat in your own writing (a good revision method) and in your reading. Look for strands—kinds of words that repeat—and binaries. The shorthand version of this heuristic is: What repeats? What goes with what? What is opposed to what? And (for all of these questions) "So what?" (See Chapter 1, "The Five Analytical Moves.")

DO NOTICE & FOCUS. Ask yourself "What do I notice?" and spend some time on this before leaping to "What do I think?" (See Chapter 1.)

Do 10 on 1. Say more about especially resonant examples rather than making the same general point about a bunch of thinly analyzed examples. (See Chapter 6, "Reasoning from Evidence to Claims.")

Reformulate Binaries—repeatedly. Follow the steps for Reformulating Binaries. Carefully name, rename, and redefine until you really understand what is at stake. (See Chapter 2.)

Seek complicating evidence for any claim you make, and use this evidence to qualify and evolve your idea. Think of evidence as a way of testing and reshaping your ideas rather than something you use only to prove that you are right. (See Chapter 7, "Finding and Evolving a Thesis.")

Note: At the end of this chapter you will find a prompt for writing what is known as a *literacy narrative*. A literacy narrative is an account of how you came to think about writing in the ways that you do. You might wish to do this assignment now, rather than waiting until you have read the whole chapter. It will help you take stock of what you have been taught about writing over time, including practices that have worked well for you and those about which you have questions.

Making Writing Happen

"But the choice of becoming a writer is the choice to face some fears, including the fear of being a hollow person, a dull person with nothing to say."

—R. V. CASSILL

How should you go about making a piece of writing happen, especially if you are not yet sure what you want to say? The most important thing is to write early and often. Rather than waiting for an idea to strike, just start writing and see where it takes you. A finished piece of writing needs to have a carefully staked-out sense of direction, with clear path markers for readers. The kind of writing people do in order to get to that finished piece is more likely to move on unmarked trails.

Even in cases such as dissertations and reports in the natural or social sciences, where much depends on careful gathering and interpretation of data, writing usually could start sooner. When there is a particular format that a writing project must eventually conform to, writing can still be done in pieces—informally—as a way of discovering what it is that you wish to say and how to go about constructing your study.

A good practice is to write for fifteen minutes or so whenever the opportunity arises, preferably every day or at least every other day. Try writing at different times of day and in different places. If you always write at the desk where you do other kinds of work, you risk making writing feel more burdensome than it needs to be. If you always write at night, try writing first thing in the morning. If you always write inside, find a nicely located outdoor bench to sit on. Inspiration can thrive on routine, but experimenting with when and how you write can lead to fresh insights.

If you are feeling anxious about a writing assignment or have been putting it off, try taking a notebook along with you while you are doing a boring task, such as waiting some place for your laundry to dry. You've heard the expression that nature abhors a vacuum. The bored brain will look for something to focus on—and what might pop up is that writing problem of yours, just waiting for a little unpremeditated attention. There is a reason why the history of great ideas includes thoughts that seemed to come out of nowhere to someone sitting under a tree, taking a shower, or listening to a long and not particularly riveting speech. (Unfortunately, television shows and online browsing tend not to have the same effect.)

In order to improve as a writer, you need to find a way of making the writing your own, even when it is being called for by someone else, such as a teacher or employer. People sometimes say that they cannot write about a particular topic because they have no interest in it. One of the virtues of doing frequent, informal writing on a topic before trying to turn your writing into a paper is that writing tends to generate interest. Interest, this book has argued, is a product of writing, as opposed to a prerequisite. Using writing in order to cultivate your curiosity is a skill, one that can be learned.

Freewriting Revisited

We are revisiting freewriting in this chapter in order to provide you with more options for experimenting with this very productive writing practice. Freewriting was originally proposed by Peter Elbow as an antidote to the problem of trying to revise and edit too soon. It is also an excellent antidote to a writer's fear that they may have nothing to say. Because there is much less at stake in freewriting than in formal papers, freewriting gives writers an opportunity to take chances and to more comfortably explore what they think. Note: Freewriting is a learned skill. The more you do it, the better you will get at it. Give it time.

Freewriting is a staple of many writing classes, wherein you might be asked to write for a set period of time at the beginning of class—sometimes as often as every class, or at least once every couple of classes. Freewriting typically starts not with an idea or a position you wish to defend, but with some kind of starting point, perhaps just a single word or image. Once you begin writing, each sentence invites the question "Where might I go from here?" Sentences trigger other sentences. The act of writing produces ideas rather than just recording ideas you already have. And the act of writing causes you to recognize ideas that you didn't know you had.

The most important thing in freewriting is to write continuously without stopping. Don't re-read as you go. Don't edit or correct, though you can cross things out and write other words that seem to you to be better choices as you go along. Try to stay in touch in some way with your starting point, rather than allowing yourself to drift off into loosely connected subjects. If you find yourself stopping too often and getting stuck, start again. Whenever you feel stuck, describe something closely to see what ideas come.

It is important to keep writing throughout the allotted time, even if you think you have run out of things to say. You will be surprised at how much you can write in fifteen or twenty minutes if you don't allow yourself to stop prematurely. Sometimes your best ideas will come in the last five minutes of your freewriting session, after you have forced yourself to keep your pen or keyboard moving. Writing is a physical as well as a mental activity. There is something about pressing yourself to keep writing that triggers ideas.

A community-building practice in writing classes is for students to volunteer to read all or part of their freewrites out loud. This practice has the advantage of everyone getting to hear what others are thinking—not just the teacher (as is often the case with papers). Especially in portfolio-based courses, class members typically type up their freewrites, title and date them, and let these accumulate in an online or paper folder. These are then available as starting points for a more extended draft or a collection of revised drafts on the same or similar subject. Usually freewrites aren't assigned letter grades, though teachers sometimes comment on a set of them or use them in writing conferences with the goal of thinking collaboratively with the writer about which direction to pursue next.

TRY THIS 5.1: Freewriting on a Single Word or Phrase

Write the word "change" at the top of a piece of paper and start writing. You don't need to know in advance what you want to say. You don't need a thesis statement or an introduction or conclusion in your freewriting draft. You can make abrupt changes in direction as you write. Go where each sentence invites you to go next. If you start drifting too far off topic, go back to the word "change" and start again. Here are two useful alternatives to this assignment. Write some provocative first sentences and go on from there. Or write at least a half-dozen possible titles for an essay and pick one to write on.

Observation Exercises: The Value of Close Description

Descriptive writing is important to thinking like a writer. It helps you train yourself to be more observant and thus less likely to leap to conclusions or judgments where writers can easily get stranded. It is also a great antidote to writer's block.

Description is essential to good thinking because when we describe things we are offering our readers not just our convictions but the grounds of our convictions. Grounding your thinking in careful description has a way of opening things up for further exploration rather than shutting things down. Life becomes much more interesting when we stop asking ourselves what we think and believe but instead start considering how we came to think and believe as we do. Description is important, by the way, in all kinds of writing—argument, analysis, reports—and not just in short stories or novels. If you want to learn more about something, start not with a point of view but with a description.

TRY THIS 5.2: Three Descriptive Freewrites

Do at least three descriptive freewriting exercises over the course of a week. Then craft a short, descriptive essay of roughly four typed pages called "College Life," or some other title that suits you, depending on where you did your writing and what you focused on. Your goal is to let your descriptions call out in you some ideas about the setting you chose to write about. Make your readers see and hear and experience a place as you do.

Select a place to set yourself up and observe, preferably on more than one occasion and without announcing to others what you are up to. Go to the place. Settle in. Take notes. In this idea-gathering stage, just do some listing and freewriting. Plan to visit the same place on two other days and repeat your initial procedure.

For each day's writing session, you need simply to begin with specific physical details. Include mostly concrete words—words that appeal to your and your readers' senses. Avoid evaluative words that offer only judgments and no sense impressions (words like "pretty," "ugly," "scary," and so on, all of which are judgments). Also avoid intensifiers, such as "really," "very," and "incredibly," which tend to make writing sound artificially inflated and overstated.

Don't try to make the description an essay, at least not initially. Don't make interpretive statements. Don't comment on whatever it is you are looking at. Just capture it—reproduce it—in words. If you describe what you see in some detail, you will certainly write your way to ideas about yourself, about life, about the natural world.

TRY THIS 5.3: Hemingway's Five-Finger Exercise

The fiction writer Ernest Hemingway prescribed this exercise as a regular practice for people who wish to train themselves to be better writers. Hemingway, in a letter to a young writer, wrote, using deep-sea fishing as an example, that the writer should "remember back until you see exactly what the action was that gave you that emotion—whether it was the rising of the line from the water and the way it tightened like a fiddle string until drops started from it, or the way he smashed and threw water when he jumped. Remember what the noises were and what was said. Find what gave you the emotion, what the action was that gave you the excitement. Then write it down, making it clear so the reader will see it too and have the same feeling you had. That's a five-finger exercise" (Hemingway, "To the Maestro").

"Five-finger exercise" is an analogy with the scales and other exercises that people do when learning to play the piano. Writers need exercises, too—activities that will make particular ways of writing and thinking habitual. In this exercise, you trace a reaction, some attitude or feeling, back to its concrete causes and then give your readers only the concrete data—not an explanation of your attitude or feeling. Your goal in the exercise is to recreate the experience in a way that will cause your readers to feel and think as you did.

The primary aim of the five-finger exercise is to sharpen your powers of observation and make you more aware of how your thoughts and feelings are affected by what is going on around you. The exercise is also designed to habituate you to keeping your conclusions in touch with the data, the actual particulars of your daily experience that produced them.

Alternative Models of Revision: New Starts and the Back Burner

Students are sometimes led to believe that writers invariably produce an entire draft and then revise that draft into a finished essay. This sequence may happen some of the time, but it is not typical of what we know about how experienced writers draft and revise their writing. In school-writing, the revision process often comes in response to a teacher's or a classmate's comments, in which case the writer tries to "fix" the essay, rather than re-seeing it (which is what the word "re-vision" means). Rather than writing an entire draft and then writing a second draft that improves upon the first, most writers repeatedly make new starts, coming at their subjects in different ways, before trying to produce a finished essay. This is to say that the revision process for many writers is generated by spending more time in the drafting stage.

In Chapter 1, we cited writing theorist Peter Elbow's claim that inexperienced writers' problems owe mostly to their trying to draft and edit at the same time. This, Elbow argues, is like a sculptor trying to sculpt a particular shape before assembling enough clay. This is not a perfect analogy, of course. We are not just piling up an infinitely malleable lump of clay. Nevertheless, the sculpting analogy is useful for breaking writers out of the idea that every time they sit down to draft they should write to a formula, some prescribed set of standards. However tight an academic discipline's rules for writing may be (such as the report format in the natural and social sciences, which we discuss in Chapter 10), a writer in the early stages of thinking needs the necessary room to experiment.

The most important tactic is to write repeatedly about your topic, rather than trying to revise your first efforts into a finished essay. Writers will tell you that once they have activated an interest by writing, once they have become engaged in trying to figure something out, their brains go to work on the writing project, even when they are not writing. They put it on the back burner, so to speak. The back burner is the place on a stove that a cook slowly simmers stock to be used later in actual recipes. Writing often in an experimental, informal way about a topic will activate your brain's back burner. Although your brain's ability to suddenly present you with ideas and solutions to problems is not magic, it sometimes feels like magic. But the magic is the product of method, as opposed to chance.

Keep making new starts rather than trying to fix the starts you have already made. There will be time to polish your draft (or combination of drafts) later. This tactic will help you generate ideas, finding the best entry point into your subject. Surprise yourself. If you find yourself being too sure of your answers, put these aside and start again.

But, you might say, I don't have time to get my brain into gear in this way because I have deadlines to meet. Our response is that once you train yourself to trust writing and to experiment with it over time, you will learn how to adapt the process in order to get things done on tight schedules. It has been our experience, for example, that students who engage in freewriting of some kind at least a few times a week develop the ability to produce writing that leads quickly to actual papers, without as much preliminary note-taking and outlining. Time spent on repeated stabs at addressing the topic, as opposed to trying to write the paper in the order it will eventually be read, can in fact save you time and will result in your becoming a more efficient writer in the long run.

Closing Your Eyes as You Speak

In his essay, "Closing My Eyes as I Speak: An Argument for Ignoring Audience," Peter Elbow observes that when people are thinking, they often close their eyes as they speak—even when talking to other people. Why, he asks, do we do this? His answer is that we often need to converse with ourselves before we are ready to converse with others. With our eyes closed, we can turn off distractions that might cause us to lose our train of thought or close down our options too soon. While it is true that imagining the needs of an audience can help you decide on things that your writing needs to include, trying to start with the needs of others is not always the best way of finding and developing your own thinking on a subject.

It is also true that much of what we think of as thinking isn't just naturally a part of us, but has been acquired through reading and conversing with others. We absorb from the audiences we spend time around, including the academic audiences we learn to write for in college, ways of arriving at as opposed to just communicating ideas. And so we can never forget entirely about audience. But dwelling too early and too exclusively on satisfying the needs of an audience can prevent us from hearing ourselves think.

On the matter of temporarily suspending the concern with audience Elbow writes, "If we ignore audience while writing on a topic about which we are not expert or about which our thinking is still evolving, we are likely to produce exploratory writing that is unclear to anyone else—perhaps even inconsistent or a complete mess. Yet by doing this exploratory 'swamp work' in conditions of safety, we can often coax our thinking through a process of new discovery and development. In short, ignoring audience can lead to worse drafts but better revisions."

When Class Members Become Audience: What Did You Hear?

Later in this chapter, we suggest ways that writers can provide support for each other in small-group peer review and one-on-one conversations. At this point in the chapter, in the context of freewriting and occasionally writing for yourself before dwelling on the needs of an audience, we wish to review a simple listening exercise recommended in "Try This 2.4" in Chapter 2. In the exercise, listeners jot down key words, phrases, and sentences that seem to them to stand out in a piece of writing that a writer reads aloud to the group. After one or more writers have read their writing aloud, group members respond to the question, "What did you hear?" by taking turns reading aloud from their notes.

There are several advantages to this procedure. Most importantly, it lets the writer know what registered with listeners—what they noticed. The feedback is evidence that someone was listening and doing so in order to understand rather than criticize. The chorus of voices does not offer specific revision advice, and yet when writers repeatedly hear what others are hearing in their writing, they can use this information to evaluate the effectiveness of what they have written. Rather than worry about the possible responses of an unseen audience, or an audience consisting only of a teacher, the writer can benefit from the presence of an immediate audience, one whose members are inclined to be sympathetic because they are engaged in the same challenges. (For more on how to use active listening in writers' groups, see "Beyond Critique: Alternative Ways for Writers to Respond to Other Writers," later in the chapter.)

Writing on Computers vs. Writing on Paper

Writers tend to be more than a little divided on this subject, as is published research. Some writers do all their work on computers, especially if they have pressing deadlines to meet. Other writers swear by pen and paper—writing on, for example, yellow legal pads or in spiral-bound notebooks. There are advantages and disadvantages to both options.

We have had students who manage to capture their best ideas by jotting them down on their cell phones as the ideas occur to them. It is easy to capture things quickly if you are writing on a computer. It is also easier to read what you have written, since too often a potentially great idea turns out to be indecipherable scribble. But these potential advantages of writing on a screen can also be disadvantages.

Perhaps the most common problem with writing on a computer is that this practice can tend to lock you into a draft or a particular idea too soon. Words that come up on a screen look more like finished text than handwritten words in a notebook, and so, the problem of trying to draft and edit at the same time is more likely to arise, as is the likelihood that you will close off fruitful options too soon by prematurely hitting the delete button. And then there is what we might call the low-hanging fruit problem: the temptation to keep interrupting ourselves to chase links to other people's thinking (and any number of funny pet pictures) online.

An advantage of paper notebooks is that things look and feel more tentative. Bursts of inspiration can get jotted down in a notebook as these occur, with the writer feeling little pressure to turn the resulting words into something approaching finished text. A notebook can come to feel like a verbal sketch pad, encouraging writers to take repeated stabs at capturing something they've been thinking about.

It is, of course, easier to move pieces of writing around on a laptop, but this convenience can also present a problem. Unless you repeatedly save files under different file names, you are likely to lose the order in which things occurred to you. By contrast, the notebook will serve as a record of what you thought and wrote, and in what order. Being able to see the various trails your writing followed will cause you to see connections that you otherwise might not have noticed. Admittedly, it is harder to find things when you need to page through your notebook: the only search function is you, looking for that idea you know you had one day last week. But the informal character of notebook-writing—its way of easing the writer into making new starts, into repeatedly seeing things from different angles—is, for many writers, definitely worth the effort.

The choice of paper versus a computer also affects writers' efforts to collaborate with other writers. It is sometimes easier for two or more writers to converse about a printed draft than it is for them to share a Word file, even if members of the pair or group have a version of the file in front of them on their own computers. If a writer comes to our campus Writing Center, for example, with a draft on their laptop, conversation between writer and peer tutor often becomes more rather than less difficult. There is a tendency on the part of the writer to simply take things down on the laptop, which has a way of reducing rather than enhancing opportunities for conversation. And it is more difficult to see the piece of writing as a whole when viewing a computer file, especially when the writer is using the keyboard to rapidly scroll through pages.

Having said all this, we acknowledge that writing and reading on paper is tough on the environment and places serious demands on organizational skills. You should, however, try both methods of writing and experiment with which one works best in particular writing situations. If you are ready to start doing full-fledged drafts, as opposed to various kinds of freewriting, brainstorming, and idea collecting, you might be ready to work from a keyboard and see the results on a screen. But at earlier stages in the writing process, and also, perhaps, in trying to work through a difficult revision, taking pen to paper might be the better tactic.

On Keeping a Writer's Notebook: Things to Try

A writer's notebook is a repository of potentially useful and inspiring things a writer has come across in their daily life, including things gleaned from reading (see "Commonplace Book" in Chapter 2). A writer's notebook is a good place to collect things you have noticed that stimulate your curiosity and which might provide a starting point for a piece of writing. Many writers find a focus for their writing by brainstorming lists of working titles. Spend a day trying to come up with at least ten possible titles for something that you have to or wish to write and see where this practice takes you.

One goal of your writer's notebook is to teach yourself through repeated practice that you are capable of finding things to write about, rather than always having to rely on topics assigned to you by someone else. Regular writing in your notebook will also teach you ways of making a topic your own, even when it was not originally your idea of something to write about.

Although a writer's notebook could be kept in a computer file, writers often choose to write in an actual notebook. Whatever form you choose, think of the notebook as a book that you are writing for yourself, one that you can return to and reread in order to see what has attracted your attention over time. In writing courses wherein making various kinds of notebook entries is a regular assignment, students often "point" from their notebooks at the beginning of class as a way of initiating class discussion (See "Pointing" in Chapter 2.)

Collecting Possible Starting Points for Writing

Start training yourself to be on the lookout for things that might offer you a starting point for an essay. Once you begin doing this on a regular basis, you will be surprised at how often topics occur to you. Begin this practice by writing down, for a single day, as many things as you can that strike you as interesting and arouse your curiosity.

Write down things that you have overheard people saying, things that you have seen while going about your everyday activities, random facts that you encounter, words that rise in your mind for no particular reason but which keep occurring to you, newspaper headlines, and so on. Sometimes, for example, a news story that you come across can and should be filed away in your notebook—or carefully excerpted there—for the possible starting points for further thinking that it suggests.

There was, for example, a story in *The New York Times* recently about a woman who has for the past twenty years made her living playing the saw in the New York subway system and on the streets. She is now famous and is regularly asked to perform at various venues, including concert halls. The story tells how it occurred to this woman one day to try her hand at the saw. It tells us that she now has twenty-three retired saws hanging on her living room wall, and that her husband, a composer, has composed pieces for her to perform on the saw. The story tells us that the woman once had to pay a fine for carrying a concealed weapon, so that she now uses only saws from which the teeth have been removed.

How might a story like this prompt a piece of writing? For one thing, it reminds us that people make their livings in interesting, offbeat ways, so that one might seek out more stories of this sort. It also reminds us that some people are really good at perseverance and at seeing opportunities, when others of us might not be. How, you might ask, does this happen? What does it take to get oneself to try and to persist in pursuing offbeat things—unusual ways of doing things?

Here is another example of the kind of thing you might begin collecting in the "Starting Points" section of your writer's notebook. You might start thinking about memory—yours in particular, but also other people's memories, based on what they are willing to tell you about them. Think what happens, for example, when you have misplaced something. Let's say that you cannot find your cell phone or your keys. What happens in your mind? Some of us are methodical types and will try to retrieve the lost item by repeating to ourselves what we were doing and where we were, trying to relive these steps. Others of us find, and this is very common, that if we try not to get too excited about the problem but instead let it rest on our mind, a picture of the lost item in its present location will pop into our brain. It is as if your brain is tapping you on the shoulder—telling you where to look. How do you go about remembering things that you want to remember? How do you compare in this with other people you know?

Be a journalist in your notebook, and be a storyteller. Storytelling is one way that we come to think about the world. It is not the exclusive province of fiction writers, but of anyone who wants to become more observant and reflective about the world. You might, for example, start writing in your notebook for five minutes a day about things you saw on the way to work or to class that attracted your attention. These could be interestingly small things, such as how new plant growth looks in early spring, or some new trend in hats or shoes. Collecting such things in a more or less random way is useful, because it trains you to pay attention to what is around you. It also trains you that you don't have to wait for something special and potentially earth-shaking to come along in order to discover a starting point for a piece of writing.

It is worth noting that this kind of noticing goes on regularly in every academic discipline. Where do the ideas come from that scientists, sociologists, psychologists, musicians, historians, and others decide to pursue? These ideas are, of course, the product at least in part of a person's training in some particular discipline and its characteristic way of seeing things. But the process of taking the time to look around and notice things and write them down is much the same.

Collecting Words, Similes, and Metaphors: Not Just for Poets

A common denominator of writers is that they are interested in language. They tend to notice words and how people use them, and so become word collectors. They write down unusual words, overused words that they would like to see go away, forgotten words that they wish would come back, words that only people living in certain parts of the country use, words that have odd histories, words that have come into English from other languages, words that are currently trendy. There are whole books that writers have written on words, such as a recent one called *On the Ascent of the A-Word*.

As we noted in Chapter 2, words don't simply reflect the world we inhabit. Words create our sense of reality, but often in ways that have become so familiar that we fail to notice them. Similes and metaphors, for example, are everywhere in what we hear and read and speak. They say a lot about how we think. In their book, *More Than Cool Reason*, linguist and cognitive scientist, George Lakoff, and his colleague, Mark Turner, argue that metaphors structure our ways of understanding: they determine how we think, although we are often not aware of them doing so. The fact is that metaphors and similes are not merely decorative—a way of adding interest to an already-completed piece of thinking. They are instead an essential and pervasive part of shaping our responses to the world. A useful exercise for your writer's notebook is to start collecting similes and metaphors as you encounter these in your day-to-day life.

Similes and metaphors are both ways of thinking by analogy—comparing one thing with another thing with which there might initially seem to be little or no similarity. (See the section in Chapter 3 on the logic of metaphor.) In the case of similes, the comparison is explicitly stated: my love is like a red, red rose. In the case of metaphors, comparisons are implied. The poet Robert Frost once said that metaphors offer one of those rare occasions when it is okay to say one thing and mean another. A premise of this chapter and the book as a whole is that writing makes people more observant, more tuned in to the world—an expression which is, of course, a metaphor.

Because it is easier to notice similes, we recommend that you start by accumulating lists of similes in your writer's notebook and, when the opportunity arises, share your lists with other writers. When you start collecting similes, you will discover that many of these have become clichés, which means that the comparisons underlying many common expressions, which were once thought-provoking, have lost this potential through overuse. These expressions are nevertheless interesting to think about. People say, for example, cool as a cucumber or happy as a clam (what might be the implicit logic of this comparison?). In the next five minutes, write down in your notebook as many familiar similes as you can come up with.

Try reading the front page of a newspaper to find as many metaphors and similes as you can. A recent headline read that populist movements in

Europe had reached their "high-water point." The high-water point is the height, often commemorated on sign posts and plaques, that flood waters had reached before beginning to recede and return to their normal levels. What does this expression imply metaphorically about extreme political movements?

In a recent editorial, writer Maureen Dowd compared two current government leaders to a pair of giant balloons in the Macy's Thanksgiving Day parade. She described the balloons as careening into buildings, wreaking havoc along the way, despite the efforts of the many people who were hanging on to the balloons' cables to keep them from going adrift. The explicit comparison between two potentially out-of-control politicians and the giant balloons is a simile. The lively visual image it proposes may not be worth a thousand words, but it certainly makes its point.

Over time, comparative thinking of the sort we find in similes become embedded in familiar expressions such as "pull yourself up by your bootstraps" or "strike while the iron is hot." The comparative logic of the second expression is clear. Just as a metalworker or blacksmith needs to work a piece of metal while it is still hot enough to be malleable, a person hoping to get something done needs to make a move before the opportunity passes. The other expression seems to advocate for self-reliance with an implied analogy between pulling on a pair of boots and pulling oneself up in the world. The problem is that the expression's implied comparison advises something that is impossible. I can pull up my boots by pulling upwards on the straps on their sides; I am, however, unlikely to be able to pull myself up in this way, no matter how hard I try.

Metaphors intriguingly embody a culture's ideas and values. We say, for example, that people climb a career ladder. The ladder in this expression is a metaphor, although we are so familiar with the expression that we don't recognize its being so. The ladder metaphor causes us to think that our work lives, if successful, ought to involve steadily moving up, step by step, to higher positions. This may or may not match the reality of people's work lives, or even our values as a culture, but the metaphor nevertheless conditions our expectations.

Another familiar metaphor is that life is a journey, which implies constant movement with the expectation of arrival at some destination. This is quite different from saying that life is an open field, or, as the saying goes, life is a bowl of cherries (which few of us believe). When we are depressed, we say that we are down, which is also a metaphor. When we are happy we say that we are up or upbeat. Once you start thinking about it, these implicit comparisons (which is what metaphors are) are everywhere and are everywhere shaping the way we think. Collecting metaphors and similes and interesting words and expressions in your writer's notebook will train you both to become more observant and to recognize in common comparisons and expressions things worth analyzing in your writing. You can, by the way, find metaphors and similes in just about every subject area. Watch for these, because they define key ideas in, for example, a science, economics, or other course you might be taking.

"Three Minutes": An Ongoing, Essay-Writing Prompt

We have suggested keeping a writer's notebook and writing frequently in the form of freewriting as ways of developing your fluency and confidence as a writer. Another, somewhat more challenging method is to employ the practice suggested by the PEN/Faulkner Foundation for its annual dinner event in Washington, D.C. At the dinner, well-known writers each speak for three minutes on an agreed-upon topic, such as Beginnings, First Love, Obsession, Journeys, A Sense of Place, A Lesson, Confessions, Reunion, and Endings. The subtitle of the book in which many of these short pieces appear is *Life Lessons from America's Greatest Writers*. This format, when used as a repeated writing assignment, causes writers to produce a series of short essays—pieces of writing more finished than the usual freewrite or notebook entry, and yet short and informal enough to leave plenty of room for experimentation.

The prompt's suggested three minutes is only a suggestion, not an iron-clad limit on length. The prompt invites essays of five or six paragraphs—something short enough to allow as many as five to seven writers to read aloud in a single hour-long session. As the ongoing writing assignment for a few weeks of a writing course or even for an entire semester, the three-minute writing prompt casts writers in the role of fellow thinkers: essayists operating together in the way that journalists or some kinds of bloggers do. By the end of a semester of regular writing, members of the writing community would each have assembled a portfolio of short essays.

Writing the three-minute essay might start from deliberately broad prompts that invite writers to define their own approach to a topic. Writers could, for example, follow the example of the assignments for the annual PEN/Faulkner dinner, by agreeing to start from the same word or concept. Another productive option is for writers to produce their own short pieces on a topic suggested by something they've all read. This option could also offer the opportunity to learn by imitation, with writers producing essays that are in some way in the style and manner of another writer. (See "Reading as a Writer" later in this chapter.)

In our classes, students read their short essays aloud to each other in class or in small group meetings outside of class. While writers could read each other's short essays online, we much prefer the immediacy of response that comes with writers reading aloud to each other, and the greater guarantee of an audience of sympathetic listeners. Reading out loud to a room full of other writers has its challenges, but this practice tends to help writers feel more in control of their own writing than having to post their writing and read readers' comments online. Whatever form the sharing takes, the goal is for writers to write regularly for each other, finding their own starting points on some kind of shared topic.

TRY THIS 5.4: Three Minutes on Attention and Distraction

This prompt calls for a short, reflective (as opposed to argumentative) piece on something you have learned about attention and focus, or lack thereof, in both your own life and in contemporary culture. An entertaining and thought-provoking essay on this topic is Sam Anderson's "In Defense of Distraction," which you can locate online. If working from an essay like Anderson's, choose something in the essay, perhaps a single sentence, as your starting point. With or without a reading for context and inspiration, you would take your readers on a tour of memorable moments that taught you something about attention/distraction in an era where focus and attention are not easily come by. Try not to sermonize or lecture readers on their habits. Instead, do an open-minded, exploratory piece of thinking on something you have observed about sustaining attention in the face of ever-present distractions.

A Sample Three-Minute Essay

There is a mental illness called "hypergraphia." Hypergraphic people feel compelled to write. If denied access to pen and paper (or laptop or cell phone), such people have been known to try writing with their own blood. I am not hypergraphic and I do not know any hypergraphic people, at least I think I don't. I also distrust the category, though I find it interesting. Was novelist and Russian dissident, Aleksandr Solzhenitsyn just acting out a compulsion to write when he scribbled secretly on every available scrap of paper, having first committed the thoughts to memory, the texts that would become *The Gulag Archipelago*—a memoir about his enforced isolation in Siberia that would change the world? Whew.

Along with writer, Jonathan Franzen, I have faith in writing as a life-saving and sanity-saving human activity. The act of writing is, itself, premised on acts of faith—faith that our thoughts as we know them will be recognizable to other human beings, faith that we are not crazy.

In his essay, "My Father's Brain," Franzen discovers after his father's death from Alzheimer's disease a letter he had written but never sent to the author's 6-year-old nephew. In the letter, Franzen's father reaches out to the boy, but also records his fear that he will not be understood: "In looking at what I have written, I expect you will have difficulty to understand, but with a little luck, I may keep up with you." Interestingly, the letter doesn't say "you may keep up with me" but "I may keep up with you." Writing is a solitary act. This is so even when we are doing it in those circus rings of self-revelation, Facebook and Twitter. When we write, we imagine the response of our imagined listeners, but we cannot know for sure what they will think or even that they will hear us. In the moment of writing we are alone with our thoughts, even if we are writing in a crowded room. This is the larger subject of Franzen's book of essays called *How to Be Alone*. While author Sam Anderson in his essay "In Defense of Distraction" argues that it is becoming nearly impossible to be alone with one's thoughts in a digitally crazed world, Franzen shows us that we cannot truly know and understand what other people are thinking, despite our need to believe that we can. We can, however, hope to keep up with others.

Our predicament seems to be that we must distrust as illusion the belief that we know what others are thinking while at the same time not giving up on trying to know. It is this paradox that Franzen writes about so honestly and searchingly in his essay, "My Father's Brain." The secret of how to be alone, as Franzen presents it, is to bravely persist in and acknowledge our solitariness while at the same time trying to cross over into the consciousness of the other solitary beings around us. "You don't always know what I am thinking" rages the first line of one of my favorite Frank O'Hara poems. The poet then goes on to tell us.

Writing from Life: The Personal Essay

"A major problem in bad writing is typically not a matter of form—of attending to topic sentences and paragraph structure, etc. It is a failure of engagement, an essential falseness."

"Good writing of virtually all kinds recreates and shares a learning process. Much of what we respond to as good writing is the writer's relentless desire to know, to understand. How do we come to know a thing truly?"

—PATRICK HOY, "SHAPING EXPERIENCE, CREATING ESSAYS"

Writing from life, from the writer's personal experience, is sometimes seen as necessarily separate from the kind of analytical writing that students need to do in their academic courses. The unfortunate split between academic writing (which is virtually always analytical) and writing that we think of as "personal" comes, perhaps, from a fear that writing from personal experience might cause writers to ignore evidence and audience and reason, instead dwelling in a private world of feelings and ungrounded opinions. In fact, our experience has taught us that the more a writer tries to inhabit and make sense of their own experience, the more likely it is that the writer will learn how to stand back and find the necessary distance to treat personal experience as evidence.

All writing is, to varying degrees, personal because it is generated by an active intelligence, which is what we hear when we read someone else's writing. But, personal writing is also analytical, a genre which this book defines as a search for meaning and understanding. Good personal essays are not merely personal. They allow readers to share in the discovery process of another human being in ways that should also provoke the reader's own discoveries.

If writing does not somehow invite readers in to the writer's thought process and experience, readers can't be expected to care about it. The same goes for analytical writing: writers need to share their thought processes with readers, not just assert what they think.

You don't bring exactly the same set of skills to personal writing as you do to analysis, but the necessary skills are more similar than you might suppose. Learning to reconstruct and reflect on some feature of your own experience is exceptionally useful in teaching you how to find in a mass of potential evidence what you need in order to arrive at and evolve an idea. The effort you put into making larger sense of your life experiences, and your own willingness to avoid easy answers, are skills that transfer to many other kinds of writing.

Students sometimes assume that writing papers in college, perhaps especially lab reports or papers in the natural and social sciences, requires writers to be invisible—conspicuously absent from their own writing. Clearly the *ethos* of academic writing is not the same as that of most personal essays, but writers are present even in the most seemingly detached and impersonal academic writing. The question is not whether a writer is present, but what kind of presence (*ethos*) the writer has, enabled by the conventions of a chosen discourse community.

Personal writing comes in more than one variety and with more than one goal. In one kind of personal writing, memoir/autobiography, the writer stands behind but also in front of the camera, hoping to learn something about him or herself. In another kind, the personal essay, the writer stands behind the camera, directing the shots but without making the writer's self the subject of the piece. Rather than primarily serving the goal of self-understanding, the writer's experience offers a discernible vantage point for thinking about other people and the world. Both kinds of personal writing are enabling. Both are worth experimenting with as part of the project of becoming a smarter, more observant analytical writer. To a significant extent, writing of all kinds tells a story—the story of how we have come to understand something.

TRY THIS 5.5: Something You Know How to Do

Think of something you know how to do, perhaps more so than most other people. Describe this thing and how you learned to do it. What has this kind of knowing—and the stages you went through in order to acquire it—taught you? This topic, once you start writing about it, should lead you to ideas about how people go about learning to manage their lives and make sense of the world. Even some minor skill that you have developed over time could lead to interesting reflection. **Alternative Prompt:** Write about a problem (big or small) that you have been trying to solve, preferably repeatedly, over a period of time, and whatever progress you have made (or not) on trying to solve it.

TRY THIS 5.6: Writing the Self

Write a two-page descriptive piece about yourself that you would be willing to read out loud to others engaged in the same exercise. Offer a narrative of some revealing and representative moment—perhaps a kind of moment that tended to recur—in your life. Sometimes the most telling moments, those that play a significant role in how we come to be who we are, are subtle, small moments, rather than "big," life-changing experiences. Some of these small but significant moments are barely remembered until we start looking for them through writing. Thus, they engage readers in the writer's process of discovery, which is what good writing does. Your piece will necessarily be a blend of showing and telling, of description and more explicit analysis, but make sure not to substitute telling readers how you felt for re-creating the experience that made you feel as you did.

TRY THIS 5.7: Reconstruct and Reflect

Conjure up in your mind's eye an experience in your past that, when recalled in the present, makes you feel inspired or at least pleasantly nostalgic. Reconstruct the experience for readers so that they can experience it too—as you did. Refrain from commenting on the experience as you write your reconstruction, or at least keep commentary to a minimum. Use lots of concrete detail—tangible things readers can see and hear.

Then, ask yourself: What did I learn, both in that past experience and now, in the process of reliving it? What was it about the experience that caused me to arrive at the ideas that I did—in the past and now? Respond to these questions in a freewrite, or more than one freewrite, until you are confident that you have begun to do justice to your experience. Rigorously avoid clichéd ideas—overly familiar, un-thought-provoking statements that risk reducing your experience to a feel-good formula.

Make a list of possible essay ideas that your reconstructions and freewrites about them suggest. Your goal is an essay of five pages in which you share with readers both your experiences and your process of arriving at ideas to which the experiences have led. In your final draft, you will want to find ways to blend the reconstruction (re-enactment) of your experience with your reflections on it.

For your final draft, experiment with opening sentences that create some kind of low-key suspense for your readers. Here is an example: "I had walked along a rocky path to a flat spot on a hillside overlooking the ocean." A sentence like this makes readers want to know more. Why has the person taken this walk? Why is she in this place? What about the experience made it memorable? What will happen next? It is worth noting, by the way, that creating forward momentum of this kind for readers is not exclusively the province of short stories and novels.

TRY THIS 5.8: A Childhood Experience that Changed, Somehow, Your View of the World

Recreate a significant experience in your early life (big or small)—some kind of turning point. Aim for understatement and rely more on description—on reconstructing the experience so your readers can share it—than on telling them what you thought at the time. Be aware that this topic will cause you to inhabit two different places in time—in fact two different people: the person you were in the past, struggling to understand something, and the person you are now, who may well have a different point of view. You are not, by the way, being asked to write a confession or expose. You are being asked to share with your readers a learning experience and your process of discovery. This, by the way, is also what most good analytical writing does, on all manner of subjects—it shares the process by which you arrived at and evolved your understanding of something.

Reading Like a Writer: Text Marking and Listing

Arguably, the best way to improve as a writer is to become as attentive a reader as you can possibly be. Learn to write by studying other writers. Toward this end, you should always mark up the writing as you read. Rather than repeatedly underlining things that seem to you to be important, use circling, selective underlining, and margin notes. It is easier to see a pattern in your markings in this way, whereas constant highlighting and underlining remain undifferentiated. Your goal is to be able to look at the essay and see the words and ways of using words that you thought were chiefly responsible for the essay's meaning and effect. It is hard to retain understanding of a piece of writing without, in effect, mapping it for yourself. To a considerable extent, an unmarked text is an unread one, and one to which you cannot easily return. Here are some useful text-marking strategies for reading like a writer, that is, with an emphasis on how the writer does what they do as opposed to just what the writer has to say.

- Do The Method as you read by underlining or circling words that repeat, kinds of words that repeat, and words that are in opposition to other words (binaries). Be able to say which repetitions and strands and binaries you thought were the most important and interesting in the essay. (See Chapter 1.)

- Mark places in the essay where the writer's thinking progresses through a process of formulating and Reformulating Binaries. A primary value of locating binaries in a piece of writing is to find out what is at stake in it, what is at issue. Circle binaries as you notice them, and list them in your notes. How, and to what extent, does the writer go about defining and redefining the governing binaries? (See Chapter 2.)

- Mark in the essay what we call in Chapter 2 The Pitch, The Complaint, and The Moment. What is the complaint (the position the writer wishes to work against)? What counter argument (pitch) does the writer make? In what sentences are each of these most evident?

- Mark each occurrence of the essay's controlling idea (thesis) as it evolves (changes and develops) over the course of the essay. Which sentence would you pick as the essay's earliest statement of its thesis? What has happened to this idea by the time you get to the end of the essay? (See Chapter 7, "Finding and Evolving a Thesis.")

- Inquiry-based essays of the kind you are likely to study in college usually progress through a series of steps or discoveries, rather than being organized under a single claim. Mark sentences in the essay that you think were the writer's primary discoveries in writing the piece. Then write these sentences out in list form.

- Write the word "*ethos*" in the margins next to sentences that seem to you significant in creating the speaking character, or persona, the writer establishes in the piece. (See "*Ethos* and Analysis" in Chapter 1.)

- Mark what you think is a characteristic kind of sentence for this author—one of the author's "go-to" sentences. Circle or underline the parts of the sentence that are characteristic of its shape. (See Chapter 11, "Style: Choosing Words, Shaping Sentences.")

- A lot of thinking is conducted through analogies (comparisons)—by likening something that is difficult to name or understand with something more familiar. Be on the lookout for a writer's use of comparisons, which often take the form of metaphors and similes. Start marking these in the margins with the word "analogy" or "comparison." (See more on this in the section earlier in this chapter on collecting metaphors and similes in a writer's notebook.)

Beyond Critique: Alternative Ways for Writers to Respond to Other Writers

This section of the chapter is designed to help you work more productively with other writers, whether in a classroom setting or other kind of writers' group. Many if not all writing courses include some kind of peer review, wherein class members comment on each other's writing, either in small groups or in pairs. We will describe two methods of peer review: small group peer review and one-on-one peer review based on the writing center model of writers conversing with other writers.

The traditional workshop approach that has long been a mainstay in creative writing courses is usually prescriptive. The writer submits a piece to a small group or to a class as a whole, and the group makes suggestions, either orally, in writing, or both, on how the piece might be improved. This process may include description, but tends to be more oriented toward guiding the writer's revision process—moving the draft via explicit advice toward a finished product. A prescriptive approach usually offers evaluative commentary, suggesting to the writer someone else's idea of what is good, better, or not-so-good.

A descriptive approach instead offers writers an account of how their writing affects a reader and by what means. Rather than tell writers what to do, a descriptive response tells writers what their writing is already accomplishing, what effects their choices might have on readers. On the basis of this feedback, the writer often makes more pervasive changes than prescriptive feedback might prompt. This is so because description allows the writer to determine not only what got through to readers, but also what the writer might actually wish to accomplish in the piece.

Procedures for Description-Based, Small-Group Peer Review

The essential rule of this kind of small-group peer review is that the writer must not speak, either before, during or, in some cases, even after the group's consideration of the draft: no apologies, no explanations, no questions to readers, no disclaimers. This rule is usually hard for writers, and sometimes also for readers, to follow but it is very important to the success of this method. If writers speak to the group about their writing, group members will be less able to tell the writer what they thought was accomplished by the writing itself, because the group's response will necessarily be colored by the writer's comments. (The writing center model of peer review, which we discuss next, takes an opposite approach wherein the reader invites the writer to say what they especially want the reader to attend to.)

It is equally important that group members not ask the writer any questions, as this too will prevent them from providing the writer with a description of what they were able to determine from the writing itself, rather than the writer's explanation of it. As time allows, writers may ask and answer questions *after* the group has marked up and spoken about the writing, but not before.

It is also important that group members' text marking, and written and spoken comments, avoid dwelling on things that the writer might be doing wrong. When peer review takes place in a relatively early stage in the writing process, it is better for respondents to avoid marking errors, because error marking distracts the group from focusing on what the writer is trying to accomplish in the piece, *the thinking*.

The primary goal of this kind of peer review is for the writer to hear the soundtrack, so to speak, of what their writing has triggered in readers. To make these responses helpful to the writer, respondents should try to stick to "I" statements, as in "This is what I thought your writing was asking me to think," or "This is what I didn't understand." Insofar as group discussion focuses on revision suggestions, group members should try to explain what in the writing caused them to respond in a particular way.

Here is the procedure in outline form:

Group members read and annotate each writer's draft. Each member of a small group, usually consisting of four writers, brings copies of their draft for other members of the group. Typically, paper drafts work better than having group members read drafts on a laptop. Before discussion begins, group members read the writer's draft silently, using some version of a text-marking system in which each person does the following:

- circles key words;
- perhaps does THE METHOD on the draft (see Chapter 1), noticing what repeats, what goes with what, and especially what is opposed to what (binaries); and
- then writes, in a couple of sentences, what they thought the piece communicated, and what the writer's goals seemed to be.

When this process becomes habitual, group members should be able to read and annotate a draft in less than fifteen minutes (depending on the paper's length). If time allows, the writer may read their writing aloud before group members begin their text marking and descriptions.

Discussion. After group members have finished marking and describing what they have read, each member of the group shares what they thought were the most important words and sentences in the piece. Group members also read their summary sentences that describe what they thought the writing communicated and what it revealed about the writer's goals. Usually one person starts this process, after which each group member speaks in turn, one at a time. The point of this method is that group members should each offer their observations before the group starts responding to each other's observations or tries to arrive at some kind of consensus. During this process, the writer takes notes but continues to remain silent.

The writer is not obliged to see their writing in the way group members did, but they *are* obliged to take note of what was said and to consider how this feedback might affect future efforts, either on the current piece of writing or a subsequent one.

Q & A. After all group members have had a chance to speak, they return their annotated drafts to the writer. At this point, if time allows, the writer can ask the group questions and the group can ask the writer questions. It usually works better to postpone this kind of question and answer discussion until each writer's work has been read, annotated, and discussed.

Procedures for One-on-One Peer Review: The Writing Center Model

In writing centers, students meet individually with other students who come to the center to talk about their writing. This type of discussion can take place at any stage in the writer's process, including an early drafting stage. A typical session in a writing center lasts from thirty to forty-five minutes. Unlike the small-group peer review model, in the peer tutoring model the writer is in charge of their writing. The peer tutor learns by listening to and conversing with the writer how best to facilitate the writer's writing process. The goal of peer tutoring in writing is not just to improve a piece of writing, but to contribute to the writer becoming a better, more confident writer.

As in the small-group peer review model, the aim of the writing center approach is to enable writers to hear themselves and to figure out what they need to do next in their writing. The peer tutor tries to understand the paper in light of what the writer thought they were trying to do. The writer, presented with an actual reader rather than a judge, is given a chance to experience how another person has entered into and shared the writer's thinking. The difference is that in the writing center model, the writer is invited to explain to the tutor what the writer was trying to do and to summarize what they think the paper communicates.

Here in outline form are the procedures for the writing center model of peer review:

Step One: Agenda Setting. The writer tells the peer tutor what the writer wants to work on, what the assignment is that the writer is trying to address, and how far along the writer is in the writing process. Sometimes the writer has not yet done much writing and is at the brainstorming stage. Sometimes the writer may have a first or mostly finished draft or even one commented on by a teacher that the writer is trying to revise.

Step Two: Reading Aloud. The writer reads the writing out loud while the tutor listens and takes notes on what they hear. The tutor's goal is to understand the writing and to figure out what the writer is trying to accomplish. Sometimes the tutor reads the paper aloud for the writer to hear. There are advantages in the writer reading aloud, because then the writer stays more in control and can also hear things that may have gone unnoticed before. If the peer tutor reads, they usually try to avoid periodically stopping to, for example, point out problems. If the paper is long, the writer nominates a part of the paper that the writer particularly wants to work on.

Step Three: Conversation. After hearing the paper read aloud, the tutor may play back to the writer what the tutor heard, offering a description of the paper rather than a critique. This is similar to what goes on in the kind of description-based, small-group peer review we recommended earlier. The writer could choose to begin the conversation by offering the writer's thoughts in response to having read the paper read aloud. Tutors facilitate this process with questions like, "Now that you have heard the paper, what are some of the things you think you might want to do next?"

Step Four: More Conversation, Plus More Agenda-Setting. The conversation keeps going with the tutor and/or the writer taking notes.

The tutor tries to gauge when the writer is ready to set an agenda for what the writer will work on when the session has ended. Sometimes this agenda-setting stage includes time when the writer does some listing and freewriting in response to the conversation the writer and the tutor have had.

This is admittedly a quick sketch of a complex process—one based on trust and slow, patient, open interaction between a writer and a listener. But, on the basis of what we have provided, you could begin to experiment with working on your writing in tandem with another writer. In some writing classes, the peer tutor model is a regular part of class work wherein pairs of students work together on a question or problem, or share in-class writing that they have done. The pairs often report back to the class as a whole on what they learned by talking with each other. This is one of many ways that critique-oriented models of peer review can be turned into collaborative, invention-oriented thinking and writing.

A Word on Google Docs and Interactive Blogging

In some writing classes, students are required to edit and comment on each other's drafts online. Software that enables this kind of collaborative work is a boon to writers, especially writers engaged in various forms of group writing. In the world of work, writers frequently prepare written documents together. Having said this, we would point to a couple of potential problems and try to suggest solutions.

A potential problem is that it is easy in Google docs for readers to make changes to a writer's paper independent of the writer's input. Commenting on and "correcting" a writer's writing in this way precludes conversation, making the commenting process a one-way street—one fraught with risk, because many students have learned only to look for errors and weaknesses in each other's writing. An inexperienced commenter writing on another writer's draft can easily do more harm than good by, for example, substituting their own ideas for the writer's ideas. Telling a writer, especially in the early stages of writing, that, for example, the writer's thesis is wrong or the writer needs more examples, can have the effect of discouraging the writer from pursuing something that the writer was just beginning to understand. Interactive blogging of the sort where writers respond to a reading, and then others comment on or add to what the writer has written, can run the same risk.

There is, however, no reason why some of the description-oriented practices described above couldn't be adapted to online commenting. Writing is personal. It is difficult for all of us to show our writing to another person. If this sharing can be done in the context of conversation and a desire to understand another's goals, then there is a chance that the interaction will be productive.

The main rule would have to be that readers respond with description, as in "I think you are trying to accomplish X, and here is what I learned from your paper," as opposed to making changes and leading with critique.

Writing with Other Writers

The stereotypical image of a writer is a person sitting alone in a room, usually at a desk, often with only a dim light burning, perhaps the light of a computer screen. We are accustomed to thinking of writers as solitary people and writing as a solitary act. Many writers, of course, actually write in public places, surrounded by other people—journalists in busy newsrooms, for example, or the many writers that can be regularly found hunched over their laptops in coffee shops. And yet, the idea persists that writing requires us to be alone with our thoughts.

The two activities in this section of the chapter offer writing situations that allow writers to be alone with their thoughts while also in the supportive company of other writers.

Writing Marathons: Taking Writing on the Road

The idea of the writing marathon—a kind of group writing activity—was first articulated by Natalie Goldberg in her book *Writing Down the Bones* and then was adapted by Richard Louth for an organization called the National Writing Project. As in running marathons, writing marathons are endurance tests of sorts, except that the challenge is to keep writing rather than keep running. Writing marathons are usually directed by an experienced group leader who plans the itinerary for the group's writing project and keeps the activity moving. But, given some imagination and patience and good will on the part of participants, a group of writers could find ways of organizing a writing marathon on their own.

A writing marathon might last anywhere from an afternoon to an entire weekend or longer. Typically, participants agree to the amount of time they wish to spend writing and to a tentative itinerary. The itinerary might include, for example, a list of coffee shops and other sorts of public places, including museums or churches or parks or whatever places the group deems appropriate for their writing and where there is enough room for participants to sit down and write.

At each stop along the route, participants settle in and write for a set period of time, usually anywhere from twenty minutes to a half hour, though people could choose to write longer. At the end of each writing session, participants volunteer to read aloud from what they wrote. People are not required to read at every stop along the way. After each person reads, members of the group, rather than discussing what they heard, thank each person for reading. Then the group moves on to the next location, which is easier to do if this can be done on foot, although there are other possibilities, including public transportation. Group members have the opportunity to talk while in transit. Then the whole process repeats again at each place on the marathon's itinerary.

One premise of the writing marathon is that it is inspiring to be writing when surrounded by other people who are also writing. Another premise is the same one that is central to this chapter—that writing prompts more writing and that the more you write the more ideas you have for writing. In the ordinary way of things, you would be unlikely to do as much writing in one weekend, or even one day, as you might do if engaged in a writing marathon. It is an interesting experience to have.

Some writing marathons have themes or predetermined subjects. A group of writers interested in the environment, for example, might spend a week writing in a series of environmentally sensitive places, like parks and marshland (bird refuges, perhaps) in and around a city or a desert area threatened by drought or development. In New Orleans shortly after Hurricane Katrina, groups of writers, including schoolchildren, wrote in various locales around the city that had been affected by the storm. The result was a book. Writing marathons could go on in various places in and around a college campus or in a school. Writers studying the elderly or the changing state of consumer culture in America might go write in malls and other places that are in the process of being repurposed for other uses. A colleague of ours takes students for writing-intensive meals in various ethnic restaurants that can be found in our small, formerly industrial city—where writers can also go to the remains of a steel mill, parts of which are being turned into a museum.

Taking part in a writing marathon offers many rewards. One is the opportunity to find ways of carrying writing away from your desk and out into the world with other people.

Writers' Boot Camp

This way of writing with other writers started with writers struggling to find time outside of their other work and life commitments to make regular progress on a writing project, such as an article or a dissertation. The writers' boot camp provides a place where writers facing pressing deadlines can rely on each others' company not only to get writing done but to reduce the stress that deadlines cause. As the name "boot camp" suggests, writers join the group in order to ramp up the necessary energy and endurance to get something done, perhaps something that they have repeatedly put off which now demands their time.

Writers' boot camps are as varied as the writers who participate in them and the kinds of writing they do. At the authors' college, a small group of writers from various academic departments meet, usually on a weekend, and agree to spend the day writing. It helps to have access to a space where writers can go off to separate spaces to write and then convene periodically during the day to report on their progress over lunch or coffee. Because writers in this group activity are often engaged in very different sorts of projects, group members usually don't talk at length about their work, but they do talk about their goals for getting writing done and their progress in meeting those goals.

Two of our students, both of whom were writing senior theses, wrote regularly for long stretches of time at the same table at the back of the college dining hall. They engaged in a friendly competition based on which one could get the most written in each designated writing period. Turning the act of writing into something resembling an athletic competition is humorous. It is also, for many writers, comforting and productive.

There are usually only a few rules for participants to follow on their group writing days. These have to do with staying on task in the face of the many things that compete for a writer's attention. And so, writers typically relinquish their cell phones and other means of contacting people, including people online.

A good thing about boot camps is that they don't require much arranging. All you need is a group of writers seeking to carve out the space to get some writing done, and a place for the group to go where they can establish the environment they choose for accomplishing their goals. If you have been putting off, something—something you really need or want to get written—participating with other writers in a writers' boot camp might be the way to go.

How to Assess Your Own Writing: Some Rubrics for Self-Evaluation

An important goal for writers is to develop confidence in their ability to evaluate their own work. We believe that the most important standards of evaluation come from writers themselves, and that these standards can evolve more or less naturally as the result of writers sharing their work with other writers (and, of course, reading and analyzing examples of good writing). In classes at our college, faculty members often invite students to study pieces of writing together and evolve from these a set of rubrics. In this case, the process of deriving the rubrics from their own and others' writing is as important as figuring out how to follow them.

The practices we have promoted in this book require that class members *not* engage, collectively or individually, in negative criticism, especially in the early drafting stage or while responding to each other's work. Our emphasis is on having writers share their work with an audience of other writers, as opposed to imagining a potentially disapproving audience seeking to correct the writing rather than listen carefully to it.

This is not to say, however, that evaluative standards can't fuel (in a positive way) the writing process. If you know, for example, that not all ideas in a paragraph should be at the same level of generality, or that you must explain why something means what you say it means, then you train yourself to operate on these principles when drafting. They will become habitual.

A paradox of writing instruction is that, although it is clearly helpful to acquire principles on what makes for good writing, writers usually work best when they try not to become too preoccupied with guidelines when they are actually writing. When the time comes to revise, however, it helps to have some ideas in mind on what makes writing good and what tends to get in the way.

The two lists that follow are for evaluating your writing. If you can keep in mind a few things that typically go wrong, and a modest list of things to do and not do, you will know what to look for—and when to look.

Short List of Things That Go Wrong

- Writer plugs in quotations from readings as answers—leaving the quotes to speak for themselves.

- Writer assumes the meanings of words to be self-evident.

- Writer puts evidence next to claims without explaining how the writer derived the claim from the evidence.

- Writer reduces complex subject matter to a single, overly generally, usually unqualified claim that the writer repeatedly attaches to a set of examples (1 ON 10).

- Writer substitutes a familiar, pre-conceived point—usually some kind of culture cliché—for what is in a reading.

- Writer offers a general impression of a reading without reference to specific words and details.

- Writer offers judgments/evaluations of a reading rather than analyzing.

- Writer is locked into a format that produces listing rather than analyzing (e.g., five-paragraph form).

Some Do's and Don'ts of Good Writing

Here is another relatively short, revision-oriented list for the purpose of self-assessment.

Cut all clichéd expressions. It is essential to cut all expressions that have become familiar through repetition, even if these were originally pretty good. Clichés flip switches in readers' minds, causing them to turn off. Find a fresher way of saying the thing that the cliché once effectively communicated. If you have heard the expression before, cut it. This takes discipline and a tough-minded attitude toward your own work.

Cut clichéd ideas. Our culture, like all cultures, is awash in prefabricated, ready-made ideas—generic truisms (one size fits all) to which people more or less automatically and unthinkingly subscribe. Don't waste your readers' time by letting clichéd formulations do your thinking for you. While it may be true that there is nothing new under the sun (cliché), you can always find a new angle on whatever you are writing about and a lively way of getting your readers to really think about what you have to say.

Cut unnecessary detail and unnecessary assertions. How do you know if the detail or assertion is unnecessary? Test each one with the "So what?" question. What is the detail doing? What is it accomplishing for the reader and the writer?

Quote in order to analyze; don't leave quotes to speak for themselves. First you should know that some academic disciplines want you to quote from reading (English, history, most of the humanities), and some disciplines don't, preferring instead that you produce very compact paraphrases and summaries (psychology, sociology, the more social-science-oriented political science courses). Unless you are told otherwise in a course, it is important to quote significant language in order to enhance the precision and accuracy and depth of your thinking on the reading. Meanings are not easily detached from the words we use to express them. When you include a quote, be sure to introduce it and then say something about it afterwards, using careful restatement and going after implication. Don't leave the quote to speak for itself, and don't just plug quotes in as answers. Do something with them. Make them an occasion for thought.

Substitute telling detail for broad and bland generalizations. Be specific. Consider how the specificity of examples enhances the clarity of thought and the experience of reading. Details—concrete details!

Share your thought process with your readers. Tell your readers why you think as you do; explain how you reason from your evidence to your claims. Most people mess up by including evidence and claims but without saying much about why they think the evidence means what they say it does. Here is an example that we offered in Chapter 1: 1) the party was terrible; there was no alcohol, and 2) the party was terrible; there was lots of alcohol.

Make that first sentence count; start fast; no say-nothing introductions. Much of what writers do in their first-draft introductions is little more than throat-clearing. We say things like, "There are interesting similarities and differences between these two essays." This statement literally goes without saying because it is predictably and certainly true. Start instead with something more incisive and substantive. Start looking at the first sentences of things you read, pondering how they draw readers in. Look also at the first sentences of paragraphs. A solution is to let yourself write any old intro paragraph in order to get started. Just be sure to go back and rewrite it after you have finished your draft.

Focus on the words. Hear them. See what they cause you to see. Words, not just ideas, matter. Bring your focus down from general impressions and broad claims to particular words and particular sentences. To a significant extent, when you put something into different words, you change the meaning. As we emphasized in Chapter 2, paraphrasing—close restatement—is extremely useful—essential, really—to figuring out what things mean and starting to think about them in depth. Through paraphrase you are attending to words, taking them into account, rather than just generalizing about them.

Some Useful Mantras for Writers

Slow down: Look longer at your data before leaping to conclusions.
Rather than start with "What do I think?," ask "What do I notice?"
Describe, describe, describe!

Assignment: Thinking Like a Writer

Write a Literacy Narrative

A literacy narrative is an account of how you have become the writer that you are, including how you have developed the attitudes about writing that you now hold. One goal of a literacy narrative is to prompt you to become more aware of your habits of mind associated with the act of writing.

Literacy narratives serve a variety of purposes. Writing and the sharing of writing is inevitably personal. Making a space for writers to consider and possibly share their personal experiences with writing can ease the way for writers to start working together in, for example, peer-review groups or as an audience for each other's writing. Sometimes, rather than have people read each other's narratives, a teacher or other group leader may select sentences from the narratives—without identifying authors—and distribute these to the group, taking care that there is no pressure for the writers to identify themselves. The point of this exercise is not to invite response to individuals, but to have people see the range of ideas and experiences held by others in the group.

The literacy narrative assignment: Write an account of things you have been taught and/or learned on your own about writing. You might get started by using the following descriptive title as a prompt: "Me as a Writer." Who are you as a writer? How have you come to think about writing and behave as a writer in the ways that you now do? What were some of your most formative experiences with writing? What, for example, are some of the do's and don'ts about writing that you have come across in your education so far? To what extent have these rules and methods served you well (or not) and enhanced your confidence and skill as a writer?

You need not and most likely could not respond to every question. Your best bet is to pick one as your starting point and then move quickly to describing and bringing to life experiences—good, bad, ambiguous—that have had some impact on you as a writer.

UNIT 2

Writing the Analytical Paper

CHAPTER 6

Reasoning from Evidence to Claims

Overview   The chapter begins by addressing two common problems: claims without evidence (unsubstantiated claims) and evidence without claims (point-less evidence). The chapter then offers a brief summary of rules of argument and of the two most basic forms of arranging evidence and claims: deduction (moving from a general claim to specific evidence) and induction (moving from specific evidence to a more general claim).

Ultimately, we argue for the importance of saying more about less. The phrase we use for this idea is DOING 10 ON 1—making ten points and observations about a single example. The chapter ends with several templates—step-by-step procedures—for organizing papers.

In all disciplines, and in virtually any writing situation, it is important to support claims with evidence, to make your evidence lead to claims, and especially to be explicit about how you've arrived at the connection between your evidence and your claims.

Linking Evidence and Claims

The relationship between evidence and claims is rarely self-evident. The word *evident* comes from a Latin verb meaning "to see." To say that the truth of a statement is "self-evident" means that it does not need proving because its truth can be plainly seen by all. The thought connections that have occurred to you about what the evidence means will not automatically occur to others. Persuasive writing always makes the connections between evidence and claim overt (see Figure 6.1).

The first step in learning to explain the connection between your evidence and your claims is to remember that evidence rarely, if ever, can be left to speak for itself. When you leave evidence to speak for itself, you are

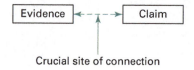

Crucial site of connection

FIGURE 6.1
Linking Evidence and Claims

assuming that it can be interpreted in only one way and that others will necessarily think as you do.

Writers who think that evidence speaks for itself generally do very little with it. Sometimes they will present it without making any overt claims, stating, for example, "There was no alcohol at the party," and expecting the reader to understand this statement as a sign of approval or disapproval. Alternatively, they may simply place the evidence next to a claim: "The party was terrible—there was no alcohol," or "The party was great—there was no alcohol." Juxtaposing the evidence with the claim (just putting them next to each other) leaves out the thinking that connects them, thereby implying that the logic of the connection is obvious. But even for readers prone to agreeing with a given claim, simply pointing to the evidence is rarely enough.

The Functions of Evidence

A common assumption about evidence is that it is "the stuff that proves I'm right." Although this way of thinking about evidence is not wrong, it is much too limited. Corroboration (proving the validity of a claim) is one function of evidence, not the only one.

It helps to remember that the word "*prove*" actually comes from a Latin verb meaning "to test." The noun form of prove, proof, has two meanings: (1) evidence sufficient to establish a thing as true or believable, and (2) the act of testing for truth or believability. When you operate on the basis of the first definition of proof alone, you are far more likely to seek out evidence that supports only your point of view, ignoring or dismissing other evidence that could lead to a different and possibly better idea.

The advantage to following the second definition of the word "proof"— in the sense of testing—is that you will be better able to negotiate among competing points of view. Doing so will predispose your readers to consider what you have to say, because you are offering them not only the thoughts a person has had, but also a person in the act of thinking. Writing well means sharing your thought process with your readers, telling them why you believe the evidence means what you say it does.

"Because I Say So": Unsubstantiated Claims

Problem: Making claims that lack supporting evidence.
Solution: Using concrete details to support and sharpen the claim.

Unsubstantiated claims occur when a writer concentrates only on conclusions, omitting the evidence that led to them. At the opposite extreme, pointless evidence results when a writer offers a mass of detail attached to an overly general claim. Both of these problems can be solved by offering readers the evidence that led to the claim and explaining how the evidence led there.

The word unsubstantiated means "without substance." An unsubstantiated claim is not necessarily false; it just offers none of the concrete "stuff" upon which the claim is based. When a writer makes an unsubstantiated claim, the writer has assumed that readers will believe it just because the writer put it out there. Perhaps more important, unsubstantiated claims deprive a writer of details. If you lack actual "stuff" to analyze, you tend to overstate your position and leave your readers wondering exactly what you mean.

You can see the problem of unsubstantiated assertions not only in papers but also in everyday conversation. It occurs when people get in the habit of leaping to conclusions—forming impressions so quickly and automatically that they have difficulty even recalling what triggered a particular response. Ask such people why they thought a new acquaintance is pretentious, and they will rephrase the generalization rather than offer the evidence that led to it: the person is pretentious because he puts on airs.

Simply rephrasing your generalizations rather than offering evidence starves your thinking; it also shuts out readers. If, for example, you defend your judgment that a person is pretentious by saying that he puts on airs, you have ruled on the matter and dismissed it. (You have also committed a logical flaw known as a circular argument; because "pretentious" and "putting on airs" mean virtually the same thing, using one in support of the other is arguing in a circle.) If, by contrast, you include the grounds upon which your judgment is based—that he uses words without regard to whether his listeners will understand or that he always wears a bow tie—you have at least given readers a glimpse of your evaluative criteria. Readers are far more likely to accept your views if you give them the chance to think with you about the evidence. The alternative—offering groundless assertions—is to expect them to take your word for it.

There is, of course, an element of risk in providing the details that have informed your judgment. You leave yourself open to attack if, for example, your readers wear bow ties. But this is an essential risk to take, for otherwise, you leave your readers wondering why you think as you do, or worse, unlikely to credit your point of view.

Most importantly, taking care to substantiate your claims will make you more inclined to think openly and carefully about your judgments. And precisely because what people have taken to be common knowledge ("women can't do math," for example, or "men don't talk about their feelings") so often turns out to be wrong, you should take care to avoid unsubstantiated claims.

Distinguishing Evidence from Claims

To check your drafts for unsubstantiated assertions, you first have to know how to recognize them. It is surprisingly difficult to separate facts from judgments, and data from interpretations of data. Writers who aren't practiced in this skill may believe that they are offering evidence when they are really offering only unsubstantiated claims. In your own reading and writing, pause once in a while to label the sentences of a paragraph as either evidence (E) or claims (C). What happens if we try to categorize the sentences of the following paragraph in this way?

The owners are ruining baseball in America. Although they claim they are losing money, they are really just being greedy. Some years ago, they even fired the commissioner, Fay Vincent, because he took the players' side. Baseball is a sport, not a business, and it is a sad fact that it is being threatened by greedy businessmen.

The first and last sentences of the paragraph are claims. They draw conclusions about as-yet unstated evidence that the writer will need to provide. The middle two sentences are harder to classify. If particular owners have said publicly that they are losing money, the existence of the owners' statements is a fact. But the writer moves from evidence to unsubstantiated claims when he suggests that the owners are lying about their financial situation and are doing so because of their greed. Similarly, it is a fact that Commissioner Fay Vincent was fired, but it is only an assertion that he was fired "because he took the players' side," an unsubstantiated claim. Although many of us might be inclined to accept some version of this claim as true, we should not be asked to accept the writer's opinion as self-evident truth. What is the evidence in support of the claim? What are the reasons for believing that the evidence means what the writer says it does?

The writer of the baseball paragraph, for example, offers as fact that the owners claim they are losing money. If he were to search harder, however, he would find that his statement of the owners' claim is not entirely accurate. The owners have not unanimously claimed that they are losing money; they have acknowledged that the problem has to do with poorer, "small-market" teams competing against richer, "large-market" teams. This more complicated version of the facts might at first be discouraging to the writer, because it reveals his original thesis ("greed") to be oversimplified. But as we have been saying, the function of evidence is not just to corroborate your claims; it should also help you to test and refine your ideas, and define your key terms more precisely.

TRY THIS 6.1: Distinguishing Evidence from Claims

Take an excerpt from your own writing, at least two paragraphs in length—perhaps from a paper you have already written, or a draft you are working on—and label every sentence that seems to function as either evidence (E) or claim (C). For sentences that appear to offer both, determine which parts of the sentence are evidence and which are claim, and then decide which one, E or C, predominates. What is the ratio of evidence to claims? This is also an instructive way of working with other writers.

Giving Evidence a Point: Making Details Speak

Problem: Presenting a mass of evidence without explaining how it relates to the claims.

Solution: Make details speak. Explain how evidence confirms and qualifies the claim.

To make your thinking visible to your readers, follow through on the implications of your evidence. You have to make the details speak, conveying to your readers why they mean what you say they mean.

The following example illustrates what happens when a writer leaves the evidence to speak for itself.

> Baseball is a sport, not a business, and it is a sad fact that it is being threatened by greedy businessmen. For example, Eli Jacobs, the previous owner of the Baltimore Orioles, sold the team to Peter Angelos for one hundred million dollars more than he had spent ten years earlier when he purchased it. Also, a new generation of baseball stadiums has been built in the last few decades—in Baltimore, Chicago, Arlington (Texas), Cleveland, San Francisco, Milwaukee, Houston, Philadelphia, Washington, and, most recently, in Miami. These parks are enormously expensive and include elaborate scoreboards and luxury boxes. The average baseball players, meanwhile, now earn more than a million dollars a year, and they all have agents to represent them. Zack Greinke, the ace of the Arizona Diamondbacks, has the richest average annual contract in the game: $34, 416, 666. Sure, he has an outstanding won-loss record for his career, but is any ballplayer worth that much money?

Unlike the previous example, which was virtually all claims, this paragraph, except for the opening claim and the closing question, is all evidence. The paragraph presents what we might call an "evidence sandwich": it encloses a series of facts between two claims. (The opening statement blames "greedy businessmen," presumably owners, and the closing statement appears to indict greedy, or at least overpaid, players.) Readers are left with two problems. First, the mismatch between the opening and concluding claims leaves it not altogether clear what the writer is saying that the evidence suggests. And second, he has not told readers why they should believe that the evidence means what he says it does. Instead, he leaves it to speak for itself.

If readers are to accept the writer's implicit claims—that the spending is too much and that it is ruining baseball—he will have to show how and why the evidence supports these conclusions. The rule that applies here is that evidence can almost always be interpreted in more than one way.

We might, for instance, formulate at least three conclusions from the evidence offered. We might decide that the writer believes baseball will be ruined by going broke, or that its spirit will be ruined by becoming too commercial. Worst of all, we might disagree with his claim and conclude that baseball is not really being ruined, because the evidence could be read as signs of health rather than decay. The profitable resale of the Orioles, the expensive, new ballparks (which, the writer neglects to mention, have drawn record crowds), and the skyrocketing salaries all could testify to the growing popularity, rather than the decline, of the sport.

How to Make Details Speak: A Brief Example The best way to begin making the details speak is to take the time to look at them, asking questions about what they imply.

1. Say explicitly what you take the details to mean.

2. State exactly how the evidence supports your claims.

3. Consider how the evidence complicates (qualifies) your claims.

The writer of the baseball paragraph leaves some of his claims and virtually all of his reasoning about the evidence implicit. What, for example, bothers him about the luxury-seating areas? Attempting to uncover his assumptions, we might speculate that he intends it to demonstrate how economic interests are taking baseball away from its traditional fans because the new seats cost more than the average person can afford. This interpretation could be used to support the writer's governing claim, but he would need to spell out the connection, to reason back to his own premises. He might say, for example, that baseball's time-honored role as the all-American sport—democratic and grass-roots—is being displaced by the tendency of baseball as a business to attract higher box office receipts and wealthier fans.

The writer could then make explicit what his whole paragraph implies: that baseball's image as a popular pastime in which all Americans can participate is being tarnished by players and owners alike, whose primary concern appears to be making money. In making his evidence speak in this way, the writer would be practicing step 3 above—using the evidence to complicate and refine his ideas. He would discover which specific aspect of baseball he thinks is being ruined, clarifying that the "greedy businessmen" to whom he refers include both owners and players.

Let's emphasize the final lesson gleaned from this example. When you focus on tightening the links between evidence and claim, the result is almost always a "smaller" claim than the one you set out to prove. This is what evidence characteristically does to a claim: it shrinks claim and restricts its scope. This process is known as "qualifying a claim."

Sometimes it is hard to give up on the large, general assertions that were your first responses to your subject. But your sacrifices in scope are exchanged for greater accuracy and validity. The sweeping claims you lose ("Greedy businessmen are ruining baseball") give way to less resounding—but also more informed, more incisive, and less judgmental—ideas ("Market pressures may not bring the end of baseball, but they are certainly changing the image and nature of the game").

More than Just "the Facts": What Counts as Evidence?

Thus far this chapter has concentrated on how to use evidence after you've assembled it. In many cases, though, a writer has to consider a more basic and often hidden question before collecting data: what counts as evidence?

This question raises two related concerns:

> *Relevance:* in what ways does the evidence bear on the claim or problem that you are addressing? Do the facts really apply in this particular case, and if so, how?
>
> *Framing assumptions:* in what ways is the evidence colored by the point of view that designated it as evidence? At what point does this coloring undercut the authority or reliability of the evidence?

To raise the issue of framing assumptions is not to imply that all evidence is merely subjective, somebody's impressionistic opinion. We are implying, however, that even the most apparently neutral evidence is the product of some way of seeing that qualifies the evidence as evidence in the first place. In some cases, this way of seeing is embedded in the established procedure of particular disciplines. In the natural sciences, for example, the data that go into the results section of a lab report or formal paper are the product of a highly controlled experimental procedure. As its name suggests, the section presents the results of seeing in a particular way.

The same kind of control is present in various quantitative operations in the social sciences, in which the evidence is usually framed in the language of statistics. And in somewhat less systematic—but nonetheless similar—ways, evidence in the humanities and in some projects in the social sciences is conditioned by methodological assumptions. A literature student cannot assume, for example, that a particular fate befalls a character in a story because of events in the author's life (it is a given of literary study that biography may inform, but does not explain, a work of art). Evidence is never just some free-floating, absolutely reliable, objective entity for the casual observer to sample at random. It is always a product of certain starting assumptions and procedures that readers must take into account.

In the following "Voices from Across the Curriculum," Professor of Political Science Jack Gambino suggests that it is always useful to try to figure out the methodological *how* behind the *what*, especially since methodology is always based in certain assumptions as opposed to others.

VOICES FROM ACROSS THE CURRICULUM

Questions of Relevance and Methodology: A Political Science Professor Speaks

What counts as evidence? I try to impress upon students that they need to substantiate their claims with evidence. Most have little trouble with this. However, when I tell them that evidence itself is dependent upon methodology—that it's not just a question of gathering "information," but also a question of how it was gathered—their eyes glaze over. Can we trust the source of information? What biases may exist in the way questions are posed in an opinion poll? Who counts as an authority on a subject? (No, Rush Limbaugh cannot be considered an authority on women's issues, or the environment, or, for that matter, anything else!) Is your evidence out-of-date?

(In politics, books on electoral behavior have a shelf life only up to the next election. After two years, they may have severe limitations.)

Methodological concerns also determine the relevance of evidence. Some models of, say, democratic participation define as irrelevant certain kinds of evidence that other models might view as crucial. For instance, a pluralist view of democracy, which emphasizes the dominant role of competitive elites, views the evidence of low voter turnout and citizen apathy as a minor concern. More participatory models, in contrast, interpret the same evidence as an indication of the crisis afflicting contemporary democratic practices.

In addition to this question of relevance, methodology makes explicit the game plan of research: How did the student conduct his or her research? Why did he or she consider some information more relevant than others? Are there any gaps in the information? Does the writer distinguish cases in which evidence strongly supports a claim from evidence that is suggestive or speculative?

Finally, students need to be aware of the possible ideological nature of evidence. For instance, Americans typically seek to explain such problems as poverty in individualistic terms, a view consistent with our liberal heritage, rather than in terms of class structure, as a Marxist would. Seeking the roots of poverty in individual behavior simply produces a particular kind of evidence different from that which would be produced if we began with the assumption that class structure plays a decisive influence in shaping individual behavior.

—JACK GAMBINO, PROFESSOR OF POLITICAL SCIENCE

The preferences of different disciplines for certain kinds of evidence notwithstanding, most professors share the conviction that the evidence you choose to present should not be one-sided. They also understand that the observation of and use of evidence is never completely neutral. Whatever kind of evidence you're using, the emphasis rests on how you use what you have: how you articulate what it means, and how carefully you link the evidence to your claims. It needs to be acknowledged, though, that the contingent nature of all evidence does not mean that we are free to dismiss it. Just because it is framed by a system or approach or (as Gambino uses the term) an ideology, evidence still carries significant authority with people who are reasonable and reasonably civic-minded. This needs to be said at a time when "fake news" is on the rise.

The Rules of Argument

Attempts to codify rules of argument—the reasoning process that connects evidence and claims—is part of a tradition of logic reaching back into antiquity. We will now take a brief excursion there to provide theoretical background about ways of reasoning with evidence and claims.

Philosophers have long quested for forms that might lend to human argument greater clarity and certainty such as is possible with formulas in math. As you will see, and as most philosophers readily admit, the reality of evaluating arguments in day-to-day life is necessarily a less tidy process than the rules of argument might make it seem. The kinds of certainty that are sometimes possible with formulas in math are not so easily available when using words to make claims about human experience. Nevertheless, the rules of argument offer a set of specific guidelines for discovering things that go right—and wrong—in the construction of an argument.

Probably the most common way of talking about logical argumentation dates back to Aristotle. This approach doesn't always have direct applications to generating the kinds of analytical writing described in this book, but knowing the methods that philosophers have devised for evaluating arguments can expand your ability to assess your own and others' reasoning about claims and evidence.

Syllogism and Enthymeme

At the heart of the Aristotelian model is the syllogism. There are a number of rules for evaluating the validity of a syllogism's conclusion. In this short section, we cannot offer enough of the details about argument analysis to equip you with the necessary skills. But we will give you enough detail so that you can understand the basic principles and methods of this way of thinking about argument.

The syllogism is divided into three parts or steps:

1. Major premise: a general proposition presumed to be true.

2. Minor premise: a subordinate proposition also presumed to be true.

3. Conclusion: a claim that follows logically from the two premises, if the argument has been properly framed.

Here is a frequently cited example of a syllogism:

All men are mortal (major premise).
Socrates is a man (minor premise).
Therefore, Socrates is mortal (conclusion).

A premise is a proposition (assumption) upon which an argument is based and from which a conclusion is drawn. The two premises in a syllogism offer reasons for believing the conclusion of the syllogism to be valid. If both premises have been stated in the proper form (both containing a shared term), then the conclusion must be valid.

An important thing to know about syllogisms is that they are only as true as the premises upon which they are based. It is not, however, the business of the syllogism to test the truth of the premises. Syllogisms can only demonstrate that the form of the argument is valid. As you will see, this word "valid" is a key term in argument evaluation, a term that does not mean the same thing as right or true.

If a writer follows the prescribed steps of the syllogism without violating any of the rules on proper wording and on the way the steps may be put together, then the conclusion arrived at in step 3 is valid. An argument evaluated in this way can be valid and still be false. For example:

All politicians are corrupt.
The mayor of Chicago is a politician.
Therefore, the mayor of Chicago is corrupt.

The problem here is not with the form of the syllogism, but with the fact that the major premise is untrue.

To make good use of syllogistic reasoning, you need to get into the habit of recasting arguments that you write, read, or hear into the proper syllogistic form. The way that most people articulate claims—often without even recognizing that they are making claims—is rarely, if ever, syllogistic. Claims, for example, if they are to be most easily assessed for validity, need to be recast so that they use forms of "to be" rather than other kinds of verbs (as in the Chicago example above).

Arguments as we encounter them in daily life are considerably less easy to evaluate. These real-life arguments typically appear in a form that philosophers call the "enthymeme." An enthymeme is an incomplete syllogism. One of its premises has been left unstated, usually because the person offering the argument takes the unstated assumption to be a given, something so obviously true that it doesn't even need to be made explicit.

Sample Enthymeme #1: Cats make better pets than dogs because cats are more independent.
Unstated Assumption: Independent animals make better pets.
Sample Enthymeme #2: Charter schools will improve the quality of education because they encourage competition.
Unstated Assumption: Competition improves the quality of education.

Recognizing and testing the accuracy of the unstated assumption is critical to evaluating any claim. This skill—uncovering unstated assumptions—is extremely useful in analyzing the claims you encounter in life and in your own writing.

Toulmin's Alternative Model of the Syllogism

The British philosopher Steven Toulmin offered a competing model of argument in his influential book, *The Uses of Argument* (1958). Toulmin's model was motivated by his belief that the philosophical tradition of formal logic, with its many rules for describing and evaluating the conduct of arguments, conflicts with the practice and idiom (ways of phrasing) of arguers. To radically simplify Toulmin's case, it is that the syllogism does not adequately account for what thinkers do when they try to frame and defend various claims. Toulmin describes the structure of argument in a way that he thought came closer to what actually happens in practice when we try to take a position.

The Toulmin model of argument renames and reorders the process of reasoning described in the Aristotelian syllogism as follows:

1. Data: the evidence appealed to in support of a claim; data respond to the question "What have you got to go on?"

2. Warrant: a general principle or reason used to connect the data with the claim; the warrant responds to the question "How did you get there?" (from the data to the claim).

3. Claim: a conclusion about the data (see Figure 6.2).

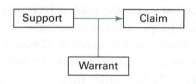

FIGURE 6.2

The Toulmin Model

Consider Figure 6.2 in terms of the chapter's opening discussion of linking evidence and claims. In the Toulmin model, the warrant is the link. It supplies the reasoning that explains why the evidence (support) leads to the conclusion (claim).

Let's look briefly at how this reasoning structure works in practice by looking at one of Toulmin's examples.

Data: Harry was born in Bermuda.

Warrant: The relevant statutes provide that people born in the colonies of British parents are entitled to British citizenship (reason for connecting data to claim).

Claim: So, presumably, Harry is a British citizen (conclusion).

We can now follow Toulmin a little further in his critique and revision of syllogistic ways of describing thinking. A syllogism, as you saw above in the Socrates example, is designed to reveal its soundness through the careful framing and arrangement of its terms:

All men are mortal. (All x's are y.)
Socrates is a man. (Socrates is an x.)
Therefore, Socrates is mortal. (Socrates is y.)

At what price, asks Toulmin, do we simplify our phrasing of complex situations in the world in order to gain this appearance of truth? In how many situations, he asks, can we say that "All x's are y"?

The strictness of the rules necessary for guaranteeing formal validity, Toulmin argues, leaves out the greater amount of uncertainty that is a part of reasoning about most questions, issues, and problems. Toulmin observes, using his own argument structure as a case in point, that as soon as an argument begins to add information in support of its premises, the complexity and inevitable tentativeness of the argument become apparent, rather than its evident truth.

Here is Toulmin's explanation of what must happen to the form of an argument when a person begins to add more supporting information, which Toulmin calls "backing." The backing for the warrant in the example above about the British citizenship of people born in Bermuda would inevitably involve mentioning "the relevant statutes"—acts of Parliament, statistical reports, and so forth—to prove its accuracy. The addition of such information, says Toulmin, would "prevent us from writing the argument so that its validity shall be manifest from its formal properties alone" (*The Uses of Argument*, 123).

To use an analogy, if the Aristotelian syllogism appears to offer us the promise of never mistaking the forest for the trees, Toulmin's revision of that model is to never let us forget that the forest is in fact made up of trees.

As a writer, you will naturally want some guidelines and workable methods for selecting evidence and linking it to claims. But don't expect to find a set of predetermined slots into which you can drop any piece of evidence and find the truth. Rather, analyses and arguments operate within the complex set of details and circumstances that are part of life as we live it. An argument depends not only on whether or not its premises follow logically, but also on the quality of the thinking that produces those premises in the first place and painstakingly tests their accuracy. This is the job of analysis.

Rogerian Argument and Practical Reasoning

Contemporary rhetoricians are less concerned about testing the adequacy of arguments than they are with making argument better serve the needs of people in everyday life and in the larger arena of public discourse. The view of argument offered throughout this book—for example, in the discussion of counterproductive habits of mind in Chapter 1—is aligned with the thinking of two such rhetoricians, Carl Rogers and Wayne Booth.

For these and other like-minded rhetoricians, the language of argument, which is often drawn from warfare, reflects its goal of gaining strategic advantage over others, who are considered as opponents. Booth and Rogers propose that the aim of argument should not be primarily to ensure certainty in order to defeat opponents, but to locate common ground.

Both Rogers and Booth emphasize the need to understand and accurately represent the positions of "opponents" in an argument rather than search for the best and quickest way to defeat them. "For Booth," as one scholar notes, "reasoning equates not just with rational thought but instead with inquiry, a term that more expansively describes the process all of us are daily engaged in to shape and make sense of the world—a process the ends of which are seldom certain or empirically measurable" (Zachary Dobbins, "Wayne Booth, Narrative, and the Rhetoric of Empathy"—a talk delivered at the 2010

Conference on College Composition and Communication). As Dobbins quotes from Booth's *Modern Dogma and the Rhetoric of Dissent,* "The supreme purpose of persuasion [. . .] should not be to talk someone else into a preconceived view; rather it must be to engage in mutual inquiry or exploration [. . .]." This goal is very much the norm in academic writing, where people try to put different points of view into conversation rather than set out to have one view defeat another.

Deduction and Induction: Two Ways of Linking Evidence and Claims

Next we will address how thinking moves in a piece of writing. The way evidence and claims are located creates different organizational shapes and sequences.

Anyone who looks seriously at the relationship between evidence and claims needs to know two key terms:

Induction: reasoning from particulars to the general.
Deduction: reasoning from the general to the particular.

Take a moment to study Figure 6.3. As a thought process, deduction reasons from a general principle to a particular case, in order to draw a conclusion about that case. It introduces this principle up front and then uses it to select and interpret evidence. For example, a deductive paper might state in its first paragraph that attitudes toward and rules governing sexuality in a given culture can be seen, at least in part, to have economic causes. The paper might then apply this principle, already assumed to be true, to the codes governing sexual behavior in several cultures or several kinds of sexual behavior in a single culture. The writer's aim would be to use their general principle as a means of explaining selected features of particular cases.

A good deductive argument is, however, more than a mechanical application or matching exercise of general claim and specific details that are explained by it. Deductive reasoning uses the evidence to draw out the implications—what logicians term *inferring the consequences*—of the claim. Particularly in the sciences, the deductive process aims at predicting one phenomenon from another. A scientist asks, in effect, "If x happens in a particular case, will it also happen in another similar case?"

The inductive thought process typically begins not with a general principle but with particular data for which it seeks to generate some explanatory principle. Whereas deduction moves by applying a generalization to particular cases, induction moves from the observation of individual cases to the formation of a general principle. Because all possible cases can obviously never be examined—every left-handed person, for example, if one wishes to theorize that left-handed people are better at spatial thinking than right-handers—the principle (or thesis) arrived at through inductive reasoning always remains open to doubt.

(A) Deduction

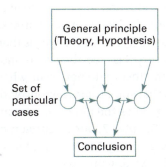

(B) Induction

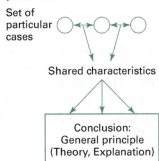

(C) Blend: Induction to Deduction

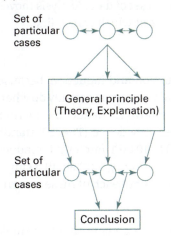

(D) Blend: Deduction to Induction

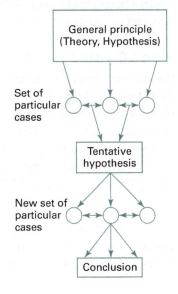

FIGURE 6.3

Deduction and Induction. Deduction (A) uses particular cases to exemplify general principles and analyze their implications. Induction (B) constructs general principles from the analysis of particular cases. In practice, analytical thinking and writing blend deduction and induction and start either with particular cases (C) or a general principle (D)

Nevertheless, the primary claim of an inductive paper is generally deemed credible if a writer can demonstrate that the theory is based on a reasonably sized sampling of representative instances. Obviously, a child who arrives at the claim that all orange food tastes bad on the basis of squash and carrots has not based that theory on an adequate sampling of available evidence.

Induction is a process aimed at forming theories about the meaning of things. The scientific method, for example, uses induction to evolve explanations for observed phenomenon such as the higher incidence of heart attacks among men than women. The proposed explanation (general principle) is then tested deductively according to the pattern: if theory X is true, then such-and-such should follow. If the results predicted by the theory do not occur when the theory is put to the test, the scientist knows that something is wrong with their induction. A deductive premise is only as good as the inductive reasoning that produced it in the first place. (See, in Chapter 7, our discussion of a student essay on the meaning of Velázquez's painting, *Las Meninas*, for an example of how inductive reasoning works in the writing process.)

As these examples show, in most cases induction and deduction operate in tandem (see Figure 6.3, C and D). The aim of analysis is usually to test (deductively) the validity of a hypothetical conclusion or to generate (inductively) a theory that might plausibly explain a given set of data. Analysis moves between the particular and the general, regardless of which comes first.

1 on 10 and 10 on 1

We use the terms 1 *on* 10 and 10 *on* 1 for deduction and induction, because these terms make it easy to visualize what in practice writers actually do when they use these thought processes. In 1 on 10, our term for deduction, a writer attaches the same claim (1) to a number of pieces of evidence. (The "10" stands for a series of examples, as shown in Figure 6.4.) In 10 on 1, our term for induction, the writer makes a series of observations (arbitrarily, "10") about a single example (the "1"; see Figure 6.5). We now will talk about each of these in turn.

DOING 1 ON 10

To get started on 1 on 10, you need, of course, a 1—a claim that you think usefully illuminates the pieces of evidence you are looking at. You can arrive at this claim by searching for patterns of repetition in the evidence

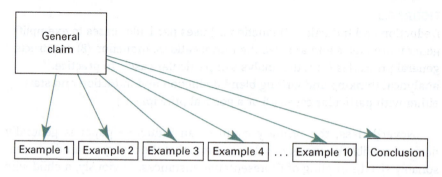

FIGURE 6.4

DOING 1 ON 10. 1 claim, 10 pieces of evidence (in which 10 stands arbitrarily for any number of examples)

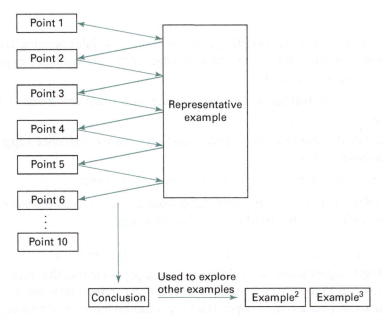

FIGURE 6.5

Doing 10 on 1. The pattern of 10 on 1 (in which 10 stands arbitrarily for any number of points) successively develops a series of points about a single representative example. Its analysis of evidence is in depth

(see THE METHOD in Chapter 1). The primary reason you are looking at a number of examples is to determine if there is sufficient evidence to make the claim. The pieces of evidence will in effect be united by the claim. If, for example, you discover that revolutionary movements at different historical moments and geographical locales produce similar kinds of violence, you would be able to demonstrate that there is a generalizable model for organizing and understanding the evidence—a model that provides a way of seeing a vast amount of information.

The search for a claim that enables the deductive way of seeing necessarily involves focusing on similarity rather than difference. If a writer reading the biblical book of Exodus focuses broadly on the difficulties of faith, she could formulate a principle that might be used deductively to reveal the unity in the book: that again and again the Israelites get into trouble whenever their faith in God falters.

Similarly, when scientists test a theory by seeing how well it explains certain phenomena, they are operating deductively. They use the theory—the "1"—to call attention to and explain what otherwise might have seemed entirely disconnected pieces of evidence. This is what is exciting about deduction at its best—it is revealing. It highlights a pattern in a body of evidence that, before the revelation of pattern, just seemed a collection of data.

Organizing Papers Using 1 on 10

1. Either start with a preexisting claim or generate a claim by using THE METHOD or NOTICE & FOCUS to find a revealing pattern or tendency in your evidence (see Chapter 1).

2. As you move through the evidence, look for data that corroborate your claim.

3. Formulate your reasons for saying that each piece of evidence supports the overarching claim.

4. Work out how the separate parts of your data connect.

5. Revise and enrich the implications of your claim (the 1) on the basis of the series of examples (the 10) you've presented.

A Potential Problem with 1 on 10: Mere Demonstration

The single biggest potential problem in 1 on 10 papers is that the form lends itself so easily to superficial thinking. This is true in part because when the time comes to compose a formal paper, it is very common for writers to panic, and abandon the wealth of data and ideas they have accumulated in the exploratory writing stage, telling themselves, "Now I better have my one idea and be able to prove to everybody that I'm right." Out goes careful attention to detail. Out goes any evidence that doesn't fit. Instead of analysis, they substitute the kind of paper we call a *demonstration*. That is, they cite evidence to prove that a generalization is generally true. The problem with the demonstration lies with its too-limited notions of what a thesis and evidence can do in a piece of analytical thinking.

The 1 on 10 demonstration, as opposed to a more productive deductive analysis, results from a mistaken assumption about the function of evidence: that it exists only to demonstrate the validity of (corroborate) a claim. Beyond corroborating claims, evidence should serve to test and develop them. A writer who makes a single and usually very general claim ("History repeats itself," "Exercise is good for you," and so forth) and then proceeds to affix it to ten examples is likely to produce a list, not a piece of developed thinking.

DOING 10 ON 1: Saying More About Less

The phrase "10 on 1" is the term the book uses to describe inductive ways of proceeding in a piece of writing. Rather than looking at the whole, you are looking in depth at a part that you think is representative of the whole. Note that 10 on 1 is a deliberate inversion of 1 on 10, so that the "1" now stands for a single, rich, and representative example, and the "10" stands for the various observations that you are able to make about it. To return to the Exodus example, a writer who wished to explore the dynamics of failed faith might make his "1" the episode of the golden calf in chapter 32: 1–35. He might isolate key repetitions and strands, and actively raise questions. Why, for example, does Moses burn the idol, grind it to powder, scatter it on water, and make the Israelites drink it?

Doing 10 on 1 will lead you to draw out as much meaning as possible from your best example—a case of narrowing the focus and then analyzing in depth. Eventually you will move from this key example to others that usefully extend and qualify your point, but first you need to let analysis of your representative example produce more thinking. In Exodus 35, for example, failed faith provokes anger (arguably, the key repetition in the chapter) and eventual bloodshed. Before a writer could see these three terms as a pattern in the text, he'd need to study other instances of failed faith in this book of the Bible.

The practice of Doing 10 on 1 remedies the major problem writers have when they do 1 on 10: simply attaching a host of examples to an obvious and overly general claim, with little or no analysis. Doing 10 on 1 requires writers to explore the evidence, not just generalize about it (see Figure 6.6).

1	Use The Method or Notice & Focus to find a revealing pattern or tendency in your evidence (See Chapter 1).
2	Select a representative example.
3	Do 10 on 1 to produce an in-depth analysis of your example.
4	Test your results in similar cases.

FIGURE 6.6
Organizing Papers Using 10 on 1

You can use 10 on 1 to accomplish various ends: locate the range of possible meanings your evidence suggests; make you less inclined to cling to your first claim; open the way for you to discover the complexity of your subject; and slow down the rush to generalization and thus help to ensure that when you arrive at a working thesis, it will be more specific and better able to account for your evidence.

A Potential Problem with 10 on 1: Not Demonstrating the Representativeness of Your Example

Focusing on your single best example has the advantage of economy, cutting to the heart of the subject, but it runs the risk that the example you select might not in fact be representative. You need to demonstrate its representativeness overtly. This means showing that your example is part of a larger pattern of similar evidence and not just an isolated instance. To establish that pattern it is useful to do 1 on 10—locating ten examples that share a trait—as a preliminary step and then select one of these for in-depth analysis.

In terms of logic, the problem of generalizing from too little and unrepresentative evidence is known as an unwarranted inductive leap. The writer leaps from one or two instances to a broad claim about an entire class or category. Just because you see an economics professor and a biology professor wearing corduroy jackets, for example, you would not want to leap to the conclusion that all professors wear corduroy jackets. Most of the time, unwarranted leaps result from making too large a claim and avoiding examples that might contradict it.

AP Images/Jeff Widener

FIGURE 6.7
Tiananmen Square, Beijing, China, 1989

Doing **10** on **1: A Brief Example (Tiananmen Square)** Note how the writer of the following discussion of the people's revolt in China in 1989 sets up his analysis. He first explains how his chosen example—a classic photograph (shown in Figure 6.7) from the media coverage of the event—illuminates his larger subject. The image is of a Chinese man in a white shirt who temporarily halted a line of tanks on their way to quell a demonstration in Tiananmen Square in Beijing.

> The tank image provided a miniature, simplified version of a larger, more complex revolution. The conflict between man and tank embodied the same tension found in the conflict between student demonstrators and the Peoples' Army. The man in the white shirt, like the students, displayed courage, defiance, and rebellious individuality in the face of power. Initially, the peaceful revolution succeeded: the state allowed the students to protest; likewise, the tank spared the man's life. Empowered, the students' demands for democracy grew louder. Likewise, the man boldly jumped

onto the tank and addressed the soldiers. The state's formerly unshakable dominance appeared weak next to the strength of the individual. However, the state asserted its power: the Peoples' Army marched into the square, and the tanks roared past the man into Beijing.

The image appeals to American ideology. The man in the white shirt personifies the strength of the American individual. His rugged courage draws on contemporary heroes such as Rambo. His defiant gestures resemble the demonstrations of Martin Luther King Jr. and his followers. American history predisposes us to identify strongly with the Chinese demonstrators: we have rebelled against the establishment, we have fought for freedom and democracy, and we have defended the rights of the individual. For example, The New York Times reported that President George [H. W.] Bush watched the tank incident on television and said, "I'm convinced that the forces of democracy are going to overcome these unfortunate events in Tiananmen Square." Bush represents the popular American perspective of the Chinese rebellion; we support the student demonstrators.

This analysis is a striking example of DOING 10 ON 1. In the first paragraph, the writer constructs a detailed analogy between the particular image and the larger subject of which it was a part. The analogy allows the writer not only to describe the event, but also interpret it. In the second paragraph, he develops his focus on the image as an image, a photographic representation tailor-made to appeal to American viewing audiences. Rather than generalizing about why Americans might find the image appealing, he establishes several explicit connections (does 10 on 1) between the details of the image and typical American heroes. By drawing out the implications of particular details, he manages to say more about the significance of the American response to the demonstrations in China than a broader survey of those events would have allowed.

TRY THIS 6.2: DOING 10 ON 1 with Newspaper Visuals

Search out photographs in the newspaper and do 10 on 1. Or alternatively, spend some time DOING 10 ON 1 on a comic strip. What perspectives emerge once you have restricted the focus? List details, along with multiple implications. Remember to ask not just What do I notice? but What else do I notice? And not just

What does it imply? but What else might it imply?

TRY THIS 6.3: DOING 10 ON 1 with a Reading

Take a piece of reading—a representative example—from something you are studying and do 10 on 1. Allow yourself to notice more and more about the evidence and make the details speak. A single, well-developed paragraph from something you are reading can be enough to practice on, especially because you are working on saying more about less, rather than less about more.

10 on 1 and Disciplinary Conventions

In some cases, the conventions of a discipline appear to discourage DOING 10 ON 1. The social sciences in particular tend to require a larger set of analogous examples to prove a hypothesis. Especially in certain kinds of research, the focus of inquiry rests on discerning broad statistical trends over a wide range of evidence. But some trends deserve more attention than others, and some statistics similarly merit more interpretation than others. The best writers learn to choose examples carefully—each one for a reason—and to concentrate on developing the most revealing ones in depth.

For instance, proving that tax laws are prejudiced in particularly subtle ways against unmarried people might require a number of analogous cases along with a statistical summary of the evidence. But even with a subject such as this, you could still concentrate on some examples more than others. Rather than moving through each example as a separate case, you could use your analyses of these primary examples as lenses for investigating other evidence.

Larger Organizational Schemes: Writing Papers Based on 1 on 10 and 10 on 1

The goal of this chapter has been to get you to think about all the choices you can make in arranging evidence and claims, and in clarifying the relation between the two. It's not surprising that the logical processes we've been discussing for moving between evidence and claims can be adapted into frameworks for organizing papers.

We're going to start with a negative example, a form with which many of you will be familiar, to show what can go wrong when a writer connects evidence and claims in too mechanical a fashion. We will then offer some templates (step-by-step roadmaps) that will show you how to arrange evidence and claims in a coherent fashion without sacrificing the necessary attention to detail and to careful qualification of ideas.

The Problem of Five-Paragraph Form: A Reductive Version of 1 on 10

As you've seen, some organizational schemes have the potential to resist careful thinking, as does 1 on 10, for example, when it is allowed to become a superficial demonstration. One version of this format is five-paragraph form, an organizational scheme that we criticized in Chapter 1 as a counterproductive habit of mind, an example of the slot-filler mentality.

Many of you will find the basic five-paragraph form familiar, as it is commonly taught in schools:

1. An introduction that ends with a thesis listing three points (the so-called tripartite or three-part thesis).

2. Three body paragraphs, each supporting one of the three points.

3. A conclusion beginning "Thus, we see" or "In conclusion" that essentially repeats the thesis statement as it was in paragraph one.

Here is an example in outline form:

> Introduction: The food in the school cafeteria is bad. It lacks variety, it is unhealthy, and it is always overcooked. In this essay, I will discuss these three characteristics.
> Paragraph 2: The first reason cafeteria food is bad is that there is no variety. (Plus one or two examples—no salad bar, mostly fried food, and so forth.)
> Paragraph 3: Another reason cafeteria food is bad is that it is not healthy. (Plus a few reasons—high cholesterol, too many hot dogs, too much sugar, and so forth.)
> Paragraph 4: In addition, the food is always overcooked. (Plus some examples—the vegetables are mushy, the "mystery" meat is tough to recognize, and so forth.)
> Conclusion: Thus, we see . . . (Plus a restatement of the introductory paragraph.)

Most high school students write dozens of themes using this basic formula. They are taught to use five-paragraph form because it seems to provide the greatest good—a certain, minimal clarity—for the greatest number of students. But the form does not promote logically tight and thoughtful writing. It is a meat grinder that can turn any content into sausages.

The two major problems it typically creates are easy to see.

1. *The introduction reduces the remainder of the essay to redundancy.* The first paragraph gives readers a list of what they're going to hear; the succeeding three paragraphs tell them the same thing again in more detail; and the conclusion repeats what they have just been told repeatedly. What is the primary cause of all this redundancy? As in the example above, an overly general thesis (cafeteria food is "bad") substitutes a list of predictable points for a complex statement of idea.

2. *The form arbitrarily divides content.* The format invites writers to list rather than analyze, plugging supporting examples into categories without examining them or how they are related. Isn't overcooked food unhealthy? Isn't a lack of variety also conceivably unhealthy? Why are there three points (or examples or reasons) instead of five or one? As is evident in the transitions ("first," "second," "in addition"), the form prompts the writer simply to append evidence to generalizations without saying anything about it.

The subject of the sample essay, on the other hand, is not as unpromising as the format makes it appear. It could easily be redirected along a more productive pathway. (If the food is bad, what are the underlying causes of the problem? Are students getting what they ask for? Is the problem one of cost? Why or why not?)

Now let's look briefly at the introductory paragraph from a student's essay on a more academic subject. Here we can see a remarkable feature of five-paragraph form—its capacity to produce the same kind of say-nothing prose on almost any subject.

> Throughout the film *The Tempest*, a version of Shakespeare's play *The Tempest*, there were a total of seven characters. These characters were Calibano, Alonso, Antonio, Aretha, Freddy, the doctor, and Dolores. Each character in the film represented a person in Shakespeare's play, but there were four people who were greatly similar to those in Shakespeare, and who played a role in symbolizing aspects of forgiveness, love, and power.

The final sentence of the paragraph reveals the writer's addiction to five-paragraph form. It signals that the writer will proceed in a purely mechanical and superficial way, producing a paragraph on forgiveness, a paragraph on love, a paragraph on power, and a conclusion stating again that the film's characters resemble Shakespeare's in these three aspects. The writer is so busy demonstrating that the characters are concerned with forgiveness, love, and power that she misses the opportunity to analyze the significance of her own observations.

Instead, readers are drawn wearily to a conclusion; they get no place except back where they began. Further, the demonstration mode prevents the writer from analyzing connections among the categories. She might consider, for example, how the play and the film differ in resolving the conflict between power and forgiveness (focusing on DIFFERENCE WITHIN SIMILARITY). Or she might complicate the relationship among her three points—for example, that the play only appears to be about love and forgiveness but is really about power.

These more analytical approaches lie concealed in the writer's introduction, but they never get discovered because the five-paragraph form militates against sustained analytical thinking. Its division of the subject into parts, which is only one part of analysis, has become an end unto itself.

Greek mythology offers a memorable way to think about the problem with five-paragraph form. On his way to Athens, the hero Theseus encounters a particularly surly host, Procrustes, who offers wayfarers a bed for the night, but with a catch: if they do not fit his bed exactly, he either stretches them or lops off their extremities until they do. This story has given us the word "procrustean," which the dictionary defines as "tending to produce conformity by violent or arbitrary means." Five-paragraph form is a procrustean formula that most students learn in high school. Although it has the advantage of providing a mechanical format that will give virtually any subject the appearance of order, it usually lops off a writer's ideas before they have the chance to form, or it stretches a single idea to the breaking point.

A complex idea is one that has many sides. To treat such an idea intelligently, writers need a form that will not require them to cut off all sides except the one that most easily fits the bed.

Rehabilitating Five-Paragraph Form

Here are two quick checks for whether five-paragraph form has closed down the thinking in your paper, in which case it needs rehabilitation:

1. Look at the paragraph openings. Do these read like a list, each beginning with an additive transition like "another" followed by a more or less exact repetition of your central point ("another example is . . . ," "yet another example is . . .")?

2. Compare the wording in the last statement of the paper's thesis (in the conclusion) with the first statement of it in the introduction. Is the wording at these two locations virtually the same?

If the answer is yes to these two questions, chances are great that you are listing, rather than analyzing, the evidence.

What can you do to remedy the situation? As we hope you can see, the problems that beset five-paragraph form have less to do with the form itself than with the underdeveloped thinking habits it allows and, perhaps, encourages. There is nothing inherently wrong with partitioning, dividing a paper into three or more parts or phases and connecting each deductively to some governing claim. There is also nothing wrong with a claim that becomes, in effect, a roadmap for the paper.

But to rehabilitate the form, you probably need to revamp the claim and restructure the way it connects with the evidence. The claim needs to do something: to lead readers to discover a meaning or see a pattern beyond the obvious in the data.

As for the evidence, don't just say repeatedly that each point or example or reason supports your thesis. Ask yourself, what has my thesis caused me to see in my evidence that might otherwise not be evident to readers? And what are the logical connections among the three parts or phases? (The next chapter will also suggest ways you might reshape and rephrase the thesis as you move it through the evidence.)

Outline for a Viable Version of Five-Paragraph Form

1. Write a half-page, typed, double-spaced paragraph in which you say what you think is the most interesting, revealing, or strange thing you've noticed about your subject. Conclude the paragraph by asking and answering an initial "So what?"—as in, where might this observation get us? How might we best understand it? Make sure this is not just a three-point list. This answer is a claim, your initial shot at a thesis.

2. Spend three body paragraphs, the three phases or parts of the middle of your paper, explaining what that claim has allowed you to notice in your data.

3. Make sure to explain the links among the three phases or parts. How does one lead to another? How do they differ despite their similarity, and "So what?"

4. End with an ultimate "So what?" How might the things you've noticed lead to a better understanding of the subject than would otherwise have been possible? What are the implications of your conclusion for further thinking on this or related subjects?

Pan, Track, and Zoom: "Directing" Your Paper

The language of filmmaking offers a useful way for understanding the different ways that a writer can focus evidence. The writer, like the director of a film, controls the focus through different kinds of shots—pan, track, and zoom. This analogy is particularly useful for locating 10 on 1 in the context of a larger paper. The zoom (a close-up shot) is equivalent to a writer DOING 10 ON 1. The zoom is then located in the context of two other kinds of shots—pans and tracks.

The pan: the camera pivots around a stable axis, giving the viewer the big picture. Using a pan, we see everything from a distance. Pans have a range of functions, one of which is to provide a context, some larger pattern, the "forest" within which the writer can also examine particular "trees." Pans in this usage establish the representativeness of the example the writer later examines in more detail, showing that it is not an isolated instance.

The track: the camera no longer stays in one place, but follows some sequence of action. For example, whereas a pan might survey a room full of guests at a cocktail party, a track would pick up a particular guest and follow along as she walks across the room, picks up a photograph, proceeds through the door, and throws the photo in a trash can. (The sequencing can also be achieved through a series of jump cuts, though the effect remains serial.) Analogously, some tracks by moving in on selected pieces of the larger picture and following them to make telling connections among them.

The zoom: the camera moves in even closer on a selected piece of the scene, allowing us to notice more of its details. (Technically, the camera's focal length is changed to enlarge the image.) For example, a zoom might focus in on the woman's hand as she crumples the photograph she's about to throw away, or on her face as she slams the lid on the trash can. A writer zooms in by giving us more detail on a particular part of the writer's evidence and making the details say more. The zoom is the shot that enables you to do 10 on 1.

Ultimately, pan, track, and zoom express a writer's authority—known in academic lingo as *agency*, the power to shape events. Many writers are not aware of their choices in how to present what they have to say; they don't realize that they can see things from different distances—close up, middle distance, far away—and that they can cover a lot of ground swiftly, or pause to linger over one small spot.

Pan, track, and zoom also have a lot to do with a writer's awareness of audience, and what that audience needs to know. Often, in the midst of the act of writing, you are tracking from one tree (or point) to the next in the forest, but you and your reader both can forget how you got there, where you've come from, and where you're bound.

At that point, suddenly panning on the forest, giving the reader the larger picture in one shot, can help reorient everyone. This need to reinforce the place of a particular part in terms of the larger whole (in film lingo, an establishing shot) is even more pronounced when a writer has been focused in close. After being asked to focus closely on a single issue or example, the reader needs to be brought back to the ongoing logical or narrative sequence (the what-comes-next) in order to stay on track. Just as in a film, the pan gives us a sense of the whole; the track gives us a sense of coherence and continuity; and the zoom gives us a privileged look at moments of greatest importance and interest, enabling us to consider the subject in more detail.

In a short paper (three to five pages), you might devote as much as 90 percent of your writing to exploring what one example (the "1"—your zoom) reveals about the larger subject. Even in a paper that uses several examples, however, as much as 50 percent might still be devoted to analysis of and generalization from a single case. The remaining portion of the paper would make connections with other examples, testing and applying the ideas you arrived at from your single case. In-depth analysis of your best example thus creates a center from which you can move in two directions: (1) toward generalizations about the larger subject, and (2) toward other examples, using your primary example as a tool of exploration.

A Template for Organizing Papers Using 10 on 1

Here is a template for writing papers using 10 on 1. It brings together much of the key terminology introduced in this chapter. Think of it not as a rigid format but as an outline for moving from one phase of your paper to the next. Unlike five-paragraph form, the template will give you room to think and to establish connections among your ideas.

1. In your introduction, start by noting (panning on) an interesting pattern or tendency you have found in your evidence. (As explained earlier in the chapter, you may find it useful to do 1 on 10 in order to discover the pattern.) Explain what attracted you to it—why you find it potentially significant and worth looking at. This paragraph would end with a tentative theory (working thesis) about what this pattern or tendency might reveal or accomplish.

2. Zoom in on your representative example, some smaller part of the larger pattern, and argue for its representativeness and usefulness in coming to a better understanding of your subject.

3. Do 10 on 1. Analyze your representative example, sharing with your readers your observations (what you notice) and your tentative conclusions (answers to the "So what?" question). Then use complicating evidence to refine your claims.

4a. In a short paper, you might at this point move to your conclusion, with its qualified, refined version of your thesis and brief commentary on what you've accomplished—that is, the ways in which your analysis has illuminated the larger subject.

4b. In a longer paper, you would begin "constellating"—organizing the essay by exploring and elaborating the connections among your representative examples analyzed via 10 on 1.

When you constellate evidence, you connect the dots, so to speak, as do the imaginary lines we draw between stars when creating a constellation in the night sky. We see the evidence coming together in a meaningful pattern.

In the language of the film analogy, you would move from your initial zoom to another zoom on a similar case, to see the extent to which the thesis you evolved with your representative example needed further adjusting to better reflect the nature of your subject as a whole. This last move is a primary topic of Chapter 7, "Finding and Evolving a Thesis."

Doing 10 on 1 to Find an Organizing Claim: A Student Paper

The essay below is an exploratory draft on a film, using a single scene to generate its thinking. As you read the essay, watch how the writer uses 10 on 1. Notice how the writer repeatedly tests her tentative conclusions against the evidence until she arrives at a plausible *working thesis* that might organize the next draft.

On the Edge: A Scene from *Good-bye Lenin*!

1. The movie shows us Alex and Lara's first date, which is to a sort of underground music club where the performers wear costumes made of plastic tubing and leather, and play loud hard-core rock music. At first, the musicians look surreal, as though they are part of a strange dream from which, at any moment, Alex will awake. The Western rock is real, though, as are the sci-fi costumes, and the scene moves forward to show Alex and Lara climbing a stairway out onto what looks like a fire escape and then through a window and into an apartment.

2. Here, Alex and Lara settle down into conversation. The young couple sits, hand in hand, and gazes together into the night sky; yet, as the camera pans away, we see that the apartment where the two have retreated is missing its façade. Inside, three walls are still decorated, complete with furniture, wallpaper, and even working lamps; yet, the two sit on the ledge of the fourth wall, which has crumbled away completely.

3. **["So what?":]** On the surface, I think the movie invites us to read this as a visual representation of the new lives Alex, Lara, and the other characters face now that the wall has fallen. As a Westerner, at first I read this scene as a representation of the new relationship between Lara and Alex. In other words, I imagined the movie's placement of the couple on the ledge of a domestic space as a representation of where their lives were going together—toward some shared domestic life, toward living together, toward becoming a family. I also thought this was a clever representation of the collapse of communism—this wall has also fallen down.

4. **[complicating evidence:]** I don't think, however, that the movie lets us entertain this one romanticized reading of the scene for long—the image is too frightening. As the camera pans away, we see that this isn't a new Westernized apartment; this is an East German flat decorated in much the same way as Alex's home was only months before. The image is alarming; the wall here has been ripped down, **["So what?":]** and we are forced to ask, did the fall of communism violently blow apart domestic and daily living of East German people?

5. The movie allows us this dichotomy and, I think, fights to sustain it. On one hand, Alex and Lara would not be on this date if the wall hadn't come down, and yet the scene is more than just another representation of East Germany torn between Communism and the new Westernization. **[working thesis:]** *The movie tries hard to remind us that the rapid Westernization of East Germany devastated while it liberated in other ways.* This scene uses space to represent Alex and Lara's (and East Germany's) dilemma: Alex and Lara gaze out at the night sky but only because the wall has been blown apart. The exposed apartment is uninhabitable and yet the lights still work, the pictures are still hung, and a young couple leans against one another inside.

Notice how the writer's DOING 10 ON 1 causes a main idea, a claim, to take shape. The writer would now evaluate this claim by asking herself how well it accounts for the things she has noticed. Review the Five Analytical Moves in Chapter 1 and the observational strategies included there. DOING 10 ON 1 uses these strategies repeatedly:

What do you notice? + Rank. Which observations seem the most significant, and why?
What repeats, what goes with what, what is opposed to what, and "So what?" (THE METHOD)

Rank by explaining which repetition, strand, or contrast (binary) you think is most significant and why. The answer to this question could become the 1 (a tentative theory) for organizing a paper.

TRY THIS 6.4: Marking Claims, Evidence, and Complications in a Draft
As a check on the range of concepts that this and the previous chapter have introduced, mark the student draft ("On the Edge: A Scene from *Good-bye Lenin!*") as follows:

- *Mark claims—assertions made about the evidence—with the letter C.* Claims are ideas that the evidence seems to support. An example of a claim is in paragraph 4: "I don't think, however, that the movie lets us entertain this one romanticized reading of the scene for long."

- *Underline evidence.* The evidence is the pool of primary material (data)—details from the film, rather than the writer's ideas about it. An example of evidence is in paragraph 2: "The young couple sits, hand in hand, and gazes together into the night sky; yet, as the camera pans away, we see that the apartment where the two have retreated is missing its façade." This piece of evidence is the 1 of the 10 on 1. In effect, the whole draft goes after the range of possible implications that may be inferred from the image of the young couple sitting at the edge of an apartment that is missing one of its walls, presumably a result of war damage.

- *Circle complications.* Complications can be found both in the evidence a writer cites and in the claims a writer makes about it. Complicating evidence is evidence that does not fit the claims the writer has been making. For example, in paragraph 4: "As the camera pans away, we see that this isn't a new Westernized apartment; this is an East German flat decorated in much the same way as Alex's home was only months before. The image is alarming; the wall here has been ripped down." This evidence causes the writer to reconsider an earlier claim from paragraph 3 that the scene is about the couple moving "toward some shared domestic life, toward living together, toward becoming a family."

Assignments: Reasoning from Evidence to Claims

1. **Locate and analyze enthymemes.** Gather a list of statements—claims that you either overhear, find yourself saying, or read. Treat these as enthymemes: reason back to and articulate the unstated assumption already accepted to be true upon which each claim depends. Here's an example: Standardized testing is a problem because it tends to control what teachers can teach.

2. **Do 10 on 1 on a scene from a film.** Write a 10 on 1 analysis on a single scene, or on a kind of scene, from a film, using the student paper on *Good-bye Lenin!* as a model. On the basis of this analysis, write a single-sentence claim that could become a thesis for a longer paper on this film.

3. **Revise a 1 on 10 paper using 10 on 1.** Locate a deductively organized paper you have written or have in draft. Choose the single example that you find most interesting in the paper, and do 10 on 1 on it to explore further its implications. This analysis should teach you more about your

subject, leading you to a revised thesis. Use this revised thesis as a lens to revise the entire essay.

4. **Study a feature piece from a magazine.** Write an analysis of an essay from a magazine that specializes in analytical journalism, such as *The New Yorker* or *The Atlantic Monthly*. Figure out the essay's organizational scheme by marking its claims and evidence and examining how the piece progresses among the various claims it makes. Describe this organizational pattern, noting for example how and when it moves inductively or deductively, and where it pauses to dwell in some detail (zoom) on a given piece of evidence.

5. **Write a paper following the template for organizing papers using 10 on 1.** Choose a topic for your paper from something you are studying that you are trying to think more carefully about: for instance, economic stimulus packages, government bailouts, intelligence tests, failed revolutions, successful fascist dictatorships. You might select a representative passage from a story or a representative story from a volume of stories by a single author. You might choose a representative passage of several pages or perhaps a chapter from a book in one of your other courses. Then write a short essay, following the template.

CHAPTER 7

Finding and Evolving a Thesis

Overview   This chapter is at the heart of what we have to say about essay writing, especially about the function of thesis statements. The chapter argues that, even in a final draft, a thesis develops through successive complications; it doesn't remain static, as people tend to believe. Even in cases such as the report format of the natural and social sciences, where the thesis itself cannot change, there is still development between the beginning of the paper and the end. The thesis in the sciences, usually called a "hypothesis," is tested in various ways in order to evaluate its adequacy.

Formulating a claim, seeking conflicting evidence, and then using these conflicts to revise the claim is a primary movement of mind in analytical writing. We describe this process in the chapter's primary heuristic, "Six Steps for Making a Thesis Evolve Through Successive Complications." Figure 7.1 offers a streamlined version of this process, which the chapter will demonstrate and define in more detail.

The chapter also offers advice on how to word thesis statements, and how to locate them in a piece of writing, including how to set up a thesis in an introductory paragraph and how to treat the thesis in a conclusion.

1	Formulate an idea about your subject, a working thesis.
2	See how far you can make this thesis go in accounting for evidence.
3	Locate evidence that is not adequately accounted for by the thesis.
4	Make explicit the apparent mismatch between the thesis and selected evidence, asking and answering "So what?"
5	Reshape your claim to accommodate the evidence that hasn't fit.
6	Repeat steps 2, 3, 4, and 5 multiple times as needed.

FIGURE 7.1

Six Steps for Making a Thesis Evolve Through Successive Complications

The Big Picture

Few elements of writing create more stress for writers than the prospect of formulating a thesis, and few topics in learning to write attract more unproductive advice than how to go about doing so.

It is something of a myth that all good writing must have a fully formed thesis statement at the end of paragraph one, which the writer will then go on to support. This is not to say that it is wrong to have a thesis statement at the end of paragraph one. Many—perhaps most—of your professors will expect to find a thesis in your first or second paragraph, although they may differ significantly in how they define what a thesis is. Some will encourage you to develop your ideas inductively (see Chapter 6), so that the fullest expression of the thesis doesn't appear until later in the essay.

Even writers who do offer a thesis statement at the end of paragraph one most likely did not start their thinking that way. A problem with trying to start your writing process with a thesis is that this move closes off the phase in which you do exploratory writing in order to arrive at ideas—usually more than one idea, and not an idea that can be tidily compressed into a single sentence at the end of an essay's first paragraph.

It is important to note that no one set of guidelines will serve you in all writing situations. You will need to observe the writing practices of the different disciplines you experience at college in order to determine how you are meant to go about setting up controlling ideas in your writing. You will also need to recognize that rules offered to students in what we might call "school writing" frequently don't match up with what most accomplished writers actually do, both in academic and nonacademic settings. This was a discovery we made in the earliest stages of writing this book—that the way thesis statements get articulated and evolved in the work of professional writers bears little similarity to what college writing courses sometimes require students to do.

If you desire to have the thesis become a more helpful element of your writing and your thinking, consider the following:

- Not all writing contexts are suitable for thesis-driven writing; most of the time we are not asked to confine our thinking to a single position, especially one that never changes over the course of a piece of writing.

- If your aim in writing is not just to communicate a single, unchanging claim but rather to explore a subject—to see what you can discover of interest—you need to delay the move to a thesis until fairly late in the paper-writing process.

- If at all possible, don't try to formulate a thesis before you begin analyzing (and writing about) the topic in depth by doing informal kinds of analytical writing (THE METHOD, NOTICE & FOCUS, PASSAGE-BASED FOCUSED FREEWRITING, and so on).

- There are important differences between an analytical thesis and an argumentative thesis. An analytical thesis is a governing idea that helps guide writers and keep them on task as they query a topic. An argumentative thesis generally seeks to prove an unchanging claim. Doing so can be a problem for inexperienced writers, who simply demonstrate the validity of the claim again and again rather than developing it. In that case, the argumentative thesis can lead to overstatement, cliché, and redundancy.

When the word "argument" is used in conversation, it most often means a disagreement. When people have an argument, they take different sides on an issue. Each person assumes the other person is wrong, and then offers as many reasons as possible in order to "win" the argument (or debate) by establishing that one position is obviously right, while an opposing position is obviously wrong. At its worst, this conception of argument drives much of what we see and hear in popular media.

But arguments are not *required* to be overstated and combative. In academic settings but also in popular writing for educated audiences, the norm is for writers to have respect for, or at least understand, others' thinking. Making an analytical argument means sharing one's thinking about an idea that seems to offer a reasonable (but probably not the only) way of thinking about a subject. Rather than aiming to defend the thesis by proving that you are right and others are wrong (and wrong-headed), this more exploratory, tentative, and dispassionate mode of argument seeks to be regarded as plausible, not obviously true (see the discussion of plausibility in Chapter 3, "Interpretation"). If your aim is not to polarize what "they" say from what you say—to elevate the pursuit of accuracy and truth(s) over the defeat of an opponent—then you need to expand your sense of what a thesis is and does. That is the aim of this chapter.

What a Good Thesis Is and Does

The thesis of an analytical paper is an idea about your subject, a theory that explains what some feature or features of your subject mean. A good thesis comes from carefully examining and questioning your subject in order to arrive at some point about its meaning and significance that would not have been immediately obvious to your readers. A weak thesis either makes no claim, or makes a claim that does not need proving, such as a statement of fact or an opinion with which virtually all of your readers would most likely agree before reading your paper (for example, "Exercise is good for you"). (See "Recognizing and Fixing Weak Thesis Statements" at the end of this chapter.)

Analytical writing typically begins with something puzzling that the writer wishes to better understand. Such writing often accounts for some dissonance, something that seems not to fit together, or it may locate previously unnoticed or inadequately addressed connections among elements of a subject, and then explain the significance of the connections. Good thesis statements enable exploration; they uncover questions where there seemed to be none. Weak thesis statements disable exploration by closing things down way too tightly at the outset.

The best way to learn about thesis statements is to look for them in published writing. You will find that the single-sentence thesis statement, usually occurring at the end of a paper's first paragraph, as prescribed in writing textbooks, is a rather rare specimen. It is most common in debate-style argument, wherein a writer has a proposition that the writer wants readers to either adopt or dismiss. The fact is that the governing idea of most analytical writing is too complex to be asserted as a single-sentence claim that could be understood at the beginning of the paper. In writing analytical arguments, the thesis is more likely to become evident in phases, guided by an opening claim sufficient to get the paper started. This claim is commonly known as the "working thesis." The kind of writing capable of prompting thinking on complex subjects where there is no single right answer usually includes more than one idea—perhaps a sequence of related ideas that *evolve* from one another and culminate in a conclusion.

Sometimes as much as a third of a paper will explore an idea that the rest of the paper will subsequently replace with a different though not necessarily opposing perspective. If you look closely, however, you will see the trail that lets readers follow a shift from one way of thinking to another. (See "Practice Tracking Thesis Statements in Finished Drafts," later in this chapter.)

A disabling assumption for students is that a writer must have a thesis before the writer begins writing. Good thesis statements are the product of writing, not its precursor. Worrying about having a thesis statement too early in the writing process will just about guarantee papers that support overly general and often obvious ideas. Arriving prematurely at claims blinds writers to complicating evidence and so deprives them of their best opportunities to arrive at better ideas.

WHAT A PRODUCTIVE THESIS DOES

Promotes thinking: leads you to arrive at ideas.

Reduces scope: separates useful evidence from the welter of details.

Provides direction: helps you decide what to talk about and what to talk about next.

WHAT A WEAK THESIS DOES

Addicts you too early to a too-large idea, so that you stop actually seeing the evidence in its real-life complexity or thinking about the idea itself.

Produces a demonstration rather than discovery of new ideas by making the same overly general point again and again about a range of evidence.

Includes too much possible data without helping you see what's most important to talk about.

Potential Problems with Thesis-Driven Writing

In an essay titled "Let's End Thesis Tyranny," author and professor Bruce Ballenger argues that thesis-driven writing, especially when thought of as supporting a single idea that the writer sets out to prove, is ill-suited to the kind of inquiry-based thinking that is the mainstay of academic writing. He notes, for example, that thesis-driven writing tends to limit students to ideas that are possible to prove. By contrast, inquiry-based writing most often operates in areas treating what he terms "complicated problems that might raise questions with multiple answers, none of them necessarily correct" (*The Chronicle of Higher Education*, July 17, 2013).

But these observations don't mean that you can do without a governing idea around which your thinking can cohere. Thesis statements give papers a sense of purpose and provide readers with something to follow. Without a governing idea to hold onto, readers can't be expected to understand why you are telling them what you are telling them. So, what to do? The answer lies in your better understanding the kinds of claims and ways of developing them that would allow you to foster inquiry and seek out rather than avoid complexity. Here are two suggestions for arriving at thesis statements that lead to exploration of ideas, as opposed to statements that reduce complex matters to oversimplified formulations:

- Focus on an area of your subject that is open to opposing viewpoints or multiple interpretations.

- Treat the thesis at which you arrive as a hypothesis to be tested, rather than an obvious truth.

Making a Thesis Evolve

A common misunderstanding about the thesis is that it must appear throughout the paper in essentially the same form—fixed and unchanging. In fact, it is only a weakly developed thesis that, like an inert (unreactive) material, neither makes anything happen nor undergoes any change itself. Think of the thesis as an agent of change. The thesis itself changes in an inductive essay. In a deductive essay, the thesis changes the way readers understand the range and implications of that claim.

Developing a Thesis Is More than Repeating an Idea

Weak thesis statements (poorly formulated and inadequately developed) are most easily detected by their repetitiveness and predictability. The writer says the same thing again and again, drawing the same overgeneralized conclusion from each piece of evidence ("So, once again we see that . . .").

Weak thesis statements tend to produce demonstrations. Demonstrations point at something—"See?"—and then are done with it. Demonstrations are not really interested in seeing into things—only at looking at them from a distance to confirm a point. The staple of the demonstration is the five-paragraph form, which we critiqued at some length in Chapter 6. The form predisposes the writer to begin with a big claim, such as "Environmentalism prevents economic growth," and then to offer a paragraph on each of three examples (say, statutes that protect endangered wildlife, inhibit drilling for oil, and levy excessive fines on violators). Then the big claim simply gets repeated in the conclusion.

At the least, such a thesis is inaccurate. It's too easy to find exceptions to the claim and to question what its key words actually mean. Mightn't environmentalism also promote economic growth by, say, promoting tourism? And is the meaning of economic growth self-evident? Couldn't a short-term economic boon be a long-term disaster, as might be the case for oil exploration in the polar regions?

In contrast, in nearly all good writing the thesis gains in complexity as well as precision and accuracy as the paper progresses. Developing a thesis, in other words, means making the paper's thinking evolve, pruning and shaping it in response to evidence.

In cases where the thesis itself cannot evolve—as, for example, in the report format of the natural and social sciences, where the initial hypothesis must be either confirmed or denied—there is still movement (conceptual development) between the beginning of the paper and the end, rather than the repeated assertion of one idea.

The Thesis as Camera Lens: The Reciprocal Relationship Between Thesis and Evidence

One function of the thesis is to provide the connective tissue, so to speak, that holds together a paper's three main parts—beginning, middle, and end. Periodic reminders of your paper's thesis, its central unifying idea, are essential for keeping both you and your readers on track. But how can you do that without simply repeating the idea? Insofar as the paper records the journey that your thinking has taken, it offers readers a developing idea, not just a repeating one.

In this context, a more useful way of envisioning how a thesis operates is to think of it as a camera lens. The advantage of this analogy (over that of connective tissue) is that it more accurately describes the relationship between the thesis and the subject it seeks to explain: while the lens affects how we see the subject (what evidence we select, what questions we ask about that evidence), the subject we are looking at affects how we adjust the lens.

The relationship between thesis and subject is, in other words, reciprocal. In good analytical writing—especially in the earlier, investigatory stages of writing and thinking—the thesis directs the writer's way of looking at evidence, while the analysis of evidence also directs and redirects (brings about revision of) the thesis. Even in a final draft, writers are usually adjusting—fine-tuning—their governing idea in response to their analysis of evidence.

The enemy of good analytical writing is the fuzzy lens—imprecisely worded thesis statements. Very broad thesis statements, made up of imprecise (fuzzy) terms, make bad camera lenses. They blur everything together, muddying important distinctions. If your lens is insufficiently sharp, you are not likely to see much in your evidence. If you say, for example, that education is costly, you will at least have some sense of direction, a means of moving forward in your paper, but the imprecise terms "education" and "costly" don't provide you with a focus clear enough to distinguish significant detail in your evidence. Without significant detail for you to analyze, you can't develop your thesis, either by showing readers what the thesis is good for (what it allows us to understand and explain) or by refining and clarifying its terms.

Induction and Deduction: Two Paths a Thesis May Take

In Chapter 6, we defined two ways that a piece of thinking can progress: inductively—from particular details to a general principle to which the details point, and deductively—from a general principle to details that it serves to explain. Chapter 6 presented as the mainstay of inductive thinking (in fact, of all good thinking) the practice we call 10 ON 1, making as many observations as possible (10) about a single representative example (1). We used the term 1 ON 10 for the deductive mode of progression wherein a writer attaches a single claim (1) to a number of examples (10). You will need to keep these terms—inductive and deductive, 10 ON 1 and 1 ON 10—in mind as we take you through this chapter's strategies for making a thesis evolve.

In inductively organized papers and in exploratory writing, the thesis changes as the paper progresses in order to more fully and accurately respond to evidence. Thus, the initial appearance of the thesis is usually fuzzier, less clearly worked out, than it is in the conclusion. This is because inductive writing repeatedly uses potentially conflicting evidence to bring the opening version of the thesis into better focus. In this kind of paper, you should suspect that a claim worded in the conclusion almost exactly as it was in the beginning has not adequately responded to evidence.

In deductively organized papers, the wording of the thesis statement does not change, or at least not very much, but what the thesis serves to reveal in the evidence becomes progressively more complex. In social science writing, for example, which typically follows the IMRAD (introduction, methods, results, discussion) format common to all the sciences, the evolution of the paper's thinking occurs in the concluding discussion section, where the writer theorizes the results. Here the writer does not just repeat the paper's opening claim (hypothesis). Even when the writer finds evidence to confirm the hypothesis, the writer uses the discussion section to develop a fuller understanding of what these results might mean. (For more on common formats in the sciences, see Chapter 10.)

In practice, good thinking is always a blend of induction and deduction. Claims lead to selection and analysis of evidence. Evidence leads to the reconsideration of the claims. Whether a paper is primarily inductive and the wording of its thesis actually changes as it encounters evidence, or is primarily deductive and the wording of the thesis does not change, the thesis functions as a lens that responds to evidence as the writing proceeds.

Making a Thesis Evolve: A Brief, Inductive Example

First, let's consider an inductive example. Keep in mind that evolving implies movement. As we have been suggesting, a thesis follows a path, recording the cognitive journey that a writer makes while bringing a claim to evidence. More often than not, when inexperienced writers face a situation in which evidence seems to be unclear or contradictory, they tend to make one of two unproductive moves: they either ignore the conflicting evidence, or they abandon the problem altogether and look for something more clear-cut to write about. Faced with evidence that complicates your thesis, the one thing not to do is run away.

The savvy writer will actively seek out complicating evidence, taking advantage of chances to bring out complications in order to make the thesis more fully responsive to evidence. Let's revisit a sample thesis from the discussion of Uncovering Assumptions in Chapter 2: "tax laws benefit the wealthy." If you were to seek out data that would complicate this overstated claim, you would soon encounter evidence that would press you to make some distinctions that the initial formulation of this claim leaves obscure. You would need, for example, to distinguish different sources of wealth and then determine whether all or just some wealthy taxpayers are benefited by tax laws.

Do people whose wealth comes primarily from investments benefit less (or more) than those whose wealth comes from high wages? Evidence might also lead you to consider whether tax laws, by benefiting the wealthy, also benefit other people indirectly. Both of these considerations would necessitate some reformulation of the thesis. By the end of the paper, the claim that tax laws benefit the wealthy would have evolved into a more carefully defined and qualified statement that would reflect the thinking you have done in your analysis of evidence. This, by and large, is what good concluding paragraphs do—they reflect back on and reformulate your paper's initial position in light of the thinking you have done about it (see Figure 7.2).

FIGURE 7.2

A strong thesis evolves as it confronts and assimilates evidence; the evolved thesis may expand or restrict the original claim. The process may need to be repeated a number of times.

But, you might ask, isn't this reformulating of the thesis something a writer does before writing the essay? Certainly, some of it is accomplished in the early exploratory writing and note-taking stage. But your finished paper will necessarily do more than list conclusions. Your revision process will have weeded out various false starts and dead ends that you may have wandered into on the way to your finished ideas, but the main routes of your movement from a tentative idea to a refined and substantiated theory should remain visible for readers to follow. To an extent, all good writing reenacts the chains of thought that led you to your conclusions, taking the readers along on a cleaned up version of the cognitive journey.

Making a Thesis Evolve: A Brief, Deductive Example

Now let's turn to a deductive example. A good deductive paper is best thought of as an experiment. In the experiment, the writer proposes a theory and then sees how far it is possible to go in getting the theory to satisfactorily explain whatever it is the writer has been observing. Evolution of the paper's thinking takes place when the writer tries to explain what happened when the theory met the evidence.

Let's take as an example a political science paper about people's responses to global warming. In political science papers, and more generally in social science writing, papers tend to begin with a broader theory from which the writer derives a hypothesis, a conjecture about what might happen, which the paper would then test.

We might speculate, for example, that people with more education would be more likely to use evidence to change, rather than to confirm, their views on global warming. This hypothesis might flow from the broader theory that educated people are less prone to dogmatism and thus are more capable of learning. The paper would then apply this hypothesis to evidence, usually statistical evidence, to see if it holds.

The aim of the paper would not be just to support or not support the hypothesis. A good deductive paper would also analyze results that only partially supported the hypothesis or complicated it. The paper might even conclude by analyzing why the evidence did not confirm the hypothesis.

Suppose the results of our study revealed the opposite of what our hypothesis predicted: educated people are less likely to change their views when confronted with evidence. To explain this result, our thinking would have to evolve. Was the result a measurement issue? Were we measuring "educated" wrong? Was the result a sampling issue (a methodological explanation)? Or what if our assumptions about the effects of education were too narrow? Might the educated be less likely to believe evidence because their education has trained them to be skeptical?

In virtually any good deductive study, the thinking will evolve somehow. Perhaps some secondary feature, something new, may emerge in the discussion as the primary feature. Perhaps the results will help us understand more fully why we obtained the results that we expected. Perhaps the study will suggest possibilities for future research.

For now, it is enough to emphasize that too many of us fail to recognize that a hypothesis is a speculation—a guess. The goal is not to have the answer before you begin, but to see where the results of testing the hypothesis might lead. This is where the hypothesis in a deductive paper causes new thinking to happen.

As these two examples illustrate, whether the thesis in a paper develops inductively, thus appearing in its fullest and most accurate form only at the end, or deductively, stated in full at the outset, the writer would not simply restate in the conclusion what the writer had proposed in the introduction. In both cases, the thinking would evolve.

The Evolving Thesis as Hypothesis and Conclusion in the Natural and Social Sciences

The natural and social sciences generally use a pair of terms, *hypothesis* and *conclusion,* in place of the single term *thesis.* Because writing in the sciences is patterned according to the scientific method, writers in disciplines such as biology and psychology must report how the original thesis (hypothesis) was tested against empirical evidence and then conclude on this basis whether or not the hypothesis was confirmed.

The scientific method is in sync with one of the chapter's main points, that something must happen to the thesis between the introduction and the conclusion. And as we have just demonstrated, although the hypothesis does not change (or evolve), the testing of it and subsequent interpretation of those results produce commentary on and, often, qualifications of the paper's central claim.

VOICES FROM ACROSS THE CURRICULUM

The Hypothesis in the Natural and Social Sciences: Three Professors Speak

The best papers are clear and up front about what their point is, then use evidence and argument to support and evaluate the thesis. I encourage students to have a sentence immediately following their discussion of the background on the subject that can be as explicit as: "In this paper I will argue that while research on toxic effects of methyl bromide provides troubling evidence for severe physiological effects, conclusive proof of a significant environmental hazard is lacking at this time."

I try to avoid the use of the term "hypothesis." I think it gives the false sense that scientists always start with an idea about how something works. Frequently, that is not the case. Some of the best science has actually come from observation. Darwin's work on finches is a classic example. His ideas about adaptation probably derived *from* the observation.

—BRUCE WIGHTMAN, PROFESSOR OF BIOLOGY

If the empirical evidence doesn't confirm your hypothesis, you rethink your hypothesis, but it's a complex issue. Researchers whose hypotheses are not confirmed in fact often question their *method* ("if I had more subjects" or "a better manipulation of the experimental group" or "a better test of intelligence," etc.) as much as their hypothesis. And that's often legitimate. Part of the challenge of psychological research is its reliance on a long array of assumptions. Failure to confirm a hypothesis could mean a problem in any of that long array of assumptions. So failure to confirm your hypothesis is often difficult to interpret.

—ALAN TJELTVEIT, PROFESSOR OF PSYCHOLOGY

Economists do make pretense to follow scientific methodology. Thus we are careful not to mix hypothesis and conclusion. I think it's important to distinguish between what is conjectured, the working hypothesis, and what ultimately emerges as a result of an examination of the evidence. Conclusions come only after some test has been passed.

—JAMES MARSHALL, PROFESSOR OF ECONOMICS

Evolving a Working Thesis in an Exploratory Draft: The Example of *Las Meninas*

Because the writing process is a way not just of recording but of discovering ideas, writers, especially in the early stages of drafting, often set out with one idea or direction in mind and then, in the process of writing, happen upon another, potentially better idea that only begins to emerge in the draft. That first idea, the so-called working thesis, is often a fairly general claim designed to get the writing started. Once you work with this thesis for a while, you will often begin to recognize other thoughts emerging, which lead to your evolving a markedly different thesis, or they may provide you with the means of extending your paper's original thesis well beyond the point you'd settled for initially.

Writers undertake this kind of conceptual revision—locating and defining the thesis—in different ways. Some writers rely on repeatedly revising while they work their way through a first draft (which, when finished, will be close to a final draft). Others move through the first draft without much revision and then comprehensively rethink and restructure it (sometimes two, three, or more times). Whatever mode of revision works best for you, the thinking processes we demonstrate here are central. They are the common denominators of the various stages of the drafting process.

Our means of demonstrating how writers use exploratory writing to locate and develop a workable thesis is to take you through the steps a student writer would follow in revising her initial draft on a painting, *Las Meninas* (Spanish for "the ladies in waiting") by the seventeenth-century painter Diego Velázquez. We are using a paper on a painting because all of the writer's data (the details of the painting) are on one page, allowing you to think with the writer as she develops her ideas.

As you read the draft, watch how the writer goes about developing the claim made at the end of her first paragraph—that, despite its complexity, the painting clearly reveals at least some of the painter's intentions (referred to elsewhere in the paper as what the painting is saying, what it suggests, or what the painter wants). We have underlined each appearance of potential thesis statements in the text of the paper. Using square brackets at the ends of paragraphs, we have described the writer's methods for arriving at ideas: Notice & Focus, The Method, Asking "So What?," and 10 on 1.

There are many good things about this student paper when considered as an exploratory draft. Studying it will help you train yourself to turn a more discriminating eye on your own works in progress, especially in that all-important early stage in which you are writing in order to discover ideas.

Velázquez's Intentions in *Las Meninas*

[1] Velázquez has been noted as being one of the best Spanish artists of all time. It seems that as Velázquez got older, his paintings became better. Toward the end of his life, he painted his masterpiece, *Las Meninas*. Out of all his works, *Las Meninas* is the only known self-portrait of Velázquez. There is much to be said about *Las Meninas*. The painting is very complex, but some of the intentions that Velázquez had in painting *Las Meninas* are very clear. **[The writer opens with background information and a broad working thesis (underlined).]**

[2] First, we must look at the painting as a whole. The question that must be answered is: who is in the painting? The people are all members of the Royal Court of the Spanish monarch Philip IV. In the center is the king's daughter, who eventually became Empress of Spain. Around her are her *meninas* or ladies-in-waiting. These *meninas* are all daughters of influential men. To the right of the *meninas* is a dwarf who is a servant, and the family dog who looks fierce but is easily tamed by the foot of a child. The more unique people in the painting are Velázquez, himself, who stands to the left in front of a large canvas; the king and queen, whose faces are captured in the obscure mirror; the man in the doorway; and the nun and man behind the *meninas*. To analyze this painting further, the relationship between characters must be understood. **[The writer describes the evidence and arrives at an operating assumption—focusing on the relationship among characters.]**

[3] Where is this scene occurring? Most likely it is in the palace. But why is there no visible furniture? Is it because Velázquez didn't want the viewers to become distracted from his true intentions? I believe it is to show that this is not just a painting of an actual event. This is an event out of his imagination. **[The writer begins pushing observations to tentative conclusions by Asking "So What?"]**

[4] Now, let us become better acquainted with the characters. The child in the center is the most visible. All the light is shining on her. Maybe Velázquez is suggesting that

FIGURE 7.3

Las Meninas, by Diego Velázquez, 1656. Approximately 10'5" × 9'. Museo del Prado, Madrid.

she is the next light for Spain and that even God has approved her by shining all the available light on her. Back in those days there was a belief in the divine right of kings, so this just might be what Velázquez is saying. **[The writer starts ranking evidence for importance and continues ASKING "SO WHAT?"; she arrives at a possible interpretation of the painter's intention.]**

[5] The next people of interest are the ones behind the *meninas*. The woman in the habit might be a nun and the man a priest.

[6] The king and queen are the next group of interesting people. They are in the mirror, which is to suggest they are present, but they are not as visible as they might be. Velázquez suggests that they are not always at the center where everyone would expect them to be. **[The writer continues using notice and focus plus ASKING**

"So What?"; in addition to looking for pattern in the painting's details, the writer has begun to notice evidence—the minimal presence of the king and queen in the painting—that could complicate her initial interpretation about the divine right of kings.]

[7] The last person and the most interesting is Velázquez. He dominates the painting along with the little girl. He takes up the whole left side along with his gigantic easel. But what is he painting? As I previously said, he might be painting the king and queen. But I also think he could be pretending to paint us, the viewers. The easel really gives this portrait an air of mystery because Velázquez knows that we, the viewers, want to know what he is painting. **[The writer starts Doing 10 on 1 with her selection of what she has selected as the most significant detail—the size and prominence of the painter.]**

[8] The appearance of Velázquez is also interesting. His eyes are focused outward here. They are not focused on what is going on around him. It is a steady stare. Also interesting is his confident stance. He was confident enough to place himself in the painting of the royal court. I think that Velázquez wants the king to give him the recognition he deserves by including him in the "family." And the symbol on his vest is the symbol given to a painter by the king to show that his status and brilliance have been appreciated by the monarch. It is unknown how it got there. It is unlikely that Velázquez put it there himself. That would be too outright, and Velázquez was the type to give his messages subtly. Some say that after Velázquez's death, King Philip IV himself painted it to finally give Velázquez the credit he deserved for being a loyal friend and servant. **[The writer continues Doing 10 on 1 and Asking "So What?" about the painter's appearance; this takes her to three tentative theses (underlined above).]**

[9] I believe that Velázquez was very ingenious by putting his thoughts and feelings into a painting. He didn't want to offend the king, who had done so much for him. It paid off for Velázquez because he did finally get what he wanted, even if it was after he died. **[The writer concludes and is now ready to redraft to tighten links between evidence and claims, formulate a better working thesis, and make this thesis evolve.]**

From Details to Ideas: Arriving at a Working Thesis in an Exploratory Draft

An exploratory draft uses writing as a means of arriving at or refining a working thesis that the next draft can more fully evolve. Most writers find that their best ideas emerge near the end of the exploratory draft, which is the case in this student draft (see the three claims underlined in paragraph 8).

The *Las Meninas* paper is a good exploratory draft. The writer has begun to interpret details and draw plausible conclusions from what she sees, rather than just describing the scene depicted on the canvas or responding loosely to it with her unanalyzed impressions. The move from description to analysis and interpretation begins when you select certain details in your evidence as more important than others and explain what they seem to you to suggest. The writer has done both of these things, and so has gotten to the point where she can begin methodically evolving her initial ideas into a perceptive analysis.

What is especially good about the draft is that it reveals the writer's willingness to push on from her first idea (reading the painting as an endorsement of the divine right of kings, expressed by the light shining on the princess) by seeking out complicating evidence. The process of revising for ideas begins in earnest when you start checking to make sure that the thesis you have formulated accounts for as much of the available evidence as possible and does not avoid evidence that might complicate or contradict it.

The writer's first idea (about divine right), for example, does not account for enough of the evidence and is undermined by evidence that clearly doesn't fit, such as the small size and decentering of the king and queen, and the large size and foregrounding of the painter himself. Rather than ignoring these troublesome details, the writer instead zooms in on them. She focuses on the painter's representation of himself and of his employers, the king and queen, as the 1 for Doing 10 on 1 (making a number of observations about a single representative piece of evidence and analyzing it in depth).

Six Steps for Finding and Evolving a Thesis in an Exploratory Draft

Getting the thesis to respond more fully to evidence, either by formulating a mostly new thesis and beginning again, or by modifying the existing thesis, is the primary activity of conceptual revision (as opposed to correcting and editing). Your aim here is not to go round and round forever, but to go back and forth between thesis and evidence, evidence and thesis, allowing each, in turn, to adjust how you see the other, until you find the best possible fit between the two. As we say in the section of this chapter on the thesis as camera lens, the thesis not only directs a writer's way of looking at evidence; the analysis of evidence should also direct and redirect—bring about revision of—the thesis.

As an overarching guideline, allow your thesis to run up against potentially conflicting evidence ("but what about this?") in order to build upon and revise your initial idea, extending the range of evidence it can accurately account for by clarifying and qualifying its key terms.

What follows is an expanded version of the six-step guide for evolving a thesis offered in Figure 7.1:

1. Formulate a working thesis or, in revision, locate multiple and possibly competing thesis statements in your draft.

2. Explain how the details you have focused on in the evidence lead to your working thesis.

3. Locate evidence that is not adequately accounted for by the working thesis and pursue the implications of that evidence by repeatedly Asking

"So What?" Explain how and why these pieces of evidence complicate the working thesis.

4. Use your analysis of the complicating evidence to reformulate the thesis. Share with readers your reasons for moving from your initial claim to this reformulation.

5. Test the adequacy of the evolved thesis by repeating steps two, three, and four until you are satisfied that the thesis statement accounts for your evidence as fully and accurately as possible. The best test of a thesis is to see how much of the relevant evidence it can reasonably account for.

6. Rewrite the draft into a more coherent and fuller analysis of evidence, while retaining for readers the "thesis trail"—the various steps that you went through along the way to formulating the thesis you ultimately chose.

Step 1: Formulate a working thesis or, in revision, locate multiple and possibly competing thesis statements in your draft.

Go through your draft and underline potential thesis statements (as we have done in the student's draft). View the presence of multiple, perhaps even competing theses as an opportunity rather than a problem. In an exploratory draft, a range of interpretations of evidence constitutes raw material, the records of your thinking that might be developed in a more finished draft.

In the *Las Meninas* paper no single idea emerges clearly as the thesis. Instead, the writer has arrived (in paragraph 8) at three related but not entirely compatible ideas:

"I think that Velázquez wants the king to . . ."

Thesis 1: give Velázquez "the recognition he deserves by including him in the 'family.'"

Thesis 2: "show that his [Velázquez's] status and brilliance [as an artist] have been appreciated."

Thesis 3: [give Velázquez] "the credit he deserved for being a loyal friend and servant."

These three ideas about the painter's intentions could be made to work together, but at present the writer is left with an uneasy fit among them. In order to resolve the tension among her possible thesis statements, the writer appears to have settled on *"I think that Velazquez wants the king to give him the recognition he deserves by including him in the family."* This idea follows logically from a number of the details the writer has focused on, so it is viable as a working thesis—the one that she will, in revision, test against potentially complicating evidence and evolve.

It helps that the writer has specified her *interpretive context*—the painter's intentions—because a writer's awareness of her interpretive context makes it much easier for her to decide which details to prioritize and what kind of questions to ask about them. A different interpretive context for the *Las Meninas* paper, such as the history of painting techniques or the social structure of seventeenth-century royal households, would have caused the writer to emphasize different details and arrive at different conclusions about their possible significance.

The success of analytical arguments often depends on a writer's ability to persuade readers of the appropriateness of her choice of interpretive context. And so it is important for writers to ask and answer the question "In what context might my subject best be understood and why?" (See Chapter 3 on interpretive context.)

It is okay, by the way, that the writer has not concerned herself prematurely with organization, introductions, or transitions. She has instead allowed her draft to move freely from idea to idea as these occurred to her. She might not have come up with the useful ideas in paragraph 8 had she pressed herself to commit to any one idea (the divine right of kings, for example) too soon.

Notice that this writer has prompted a sequence of thought by using the word *"interesting."* Repeated use of this word as a transition would not be adequate in a final draft because it encourages listing without explicit connections among claims or explanations of how each claim evolved into the next. In an exploratory draft, however, the word "interesting" keeps the writer's mind open to possibilities and allows her to try on various claims without worrying prematurely about whether her tentative claims are right or wrong.

Step 2: Explain how the details you have focused on in the evidence lead to your working thesis.

The writer of the *Las Meninas* paper has offered at least some evidence in support of her working thesis, "Velázquez wants the king to give him the recognition he deserves by including him in the family." She notes the symbol on the painter's vest, for example, which she says might have been added later by the king to show that the painter's "status and brilliance have been appreciated." She implies that the painter's "confident stance" and "steady stare" also support her thesis. Notice, however, that she has not spelled out her reasons for making this connection between her evidence and her claim.

Nor has she corroborated her claim about this evidence with other evidence that could lend more support to her idea. Interestingly, the potential thesis statements advanced in paragraph 8 are not connected with the rather provocative details she has noted in paragraphs 6 and 7: that "Velázquez dominates the painting along with the little girl," that he "takes up the whole left side along with his gigantic easel," and that "the king and queen are not as visible as they might be," suggesting that "they are not always at the center where everyone would expect them to be."

In revision, the writer would need to find more evidence in support of her claim and make the links between evidence and claims more explicit. She would also need to tackle the complicating evidence that she leaves dangling in paragraphs 6 and 7, which takes us to Step 3.

Step 3: Locate evidence that is not adequately accounted for by the working thesis and pursue the implications of that evidence by repeatedly Asking "So What?". Explain how and why these pieces of evidence complicate the working thesis.

This is a key step in evolving a thesis—pursuing the piece or pieces of evidence that do not clearly fit with the working thesis, explaining why they don't fit, and determining what their significance might actually be. For this purpose, the writer would need to zoom in on the details of her evidence that she describes in paragraphs six and seven and, Asking "So What?", about them.

- **So what** that there are size differences in the painting? What might large or small size mean?

- **So what** that the king and queen are small, but the painter, princess, and dwarf (another servant) are all large and fairly equal in size and/or prominence?

Proposed answer: Perhaps the king and queen have been reduced so that Velázquez can showcase their daughter, the princess.

Test of this answer: The size and location of the princess (center foreground) seem to support this answer, as does the princess being catered to by the ladies in waiting. But, if the painting is meant to showcase the princess, what is the point of the painter's having made himself so large?

Another possible answer: Perhaps the small size and lack of physical prominence of the king and queen are relatively unimportant, in which case what matters is that they are a presence, always overseeing events (an idea implied but not developed by the writer in paragraph six).

Test of this answer: Further support for this answer comes from the possibility that we are meant to see the king and queen as reflected in a mirror on the back wall of the painter's studio (an idea the writer mentions), in which case they would be standing in front of the scene depicted in the painting, literally overseeing events. There isn't much evidence against this answer, except, again, for the large size of the painter, and the trivializing implications of the king and queen's diminution, but these are significant exceptions.

Another possible answer: Perhaps the painter is demonstrating his own ability to make the king and queen any size—any level of importance—he chooses. The king and queen are among the smallest as well as the least visible figures in the painting. Whether they are being exhibited as an actual painting on the back wall of the painter's studio (a possibility the writer has not mentioned) or whether they appear as reflections in a small mirror on that back wall, they certainly lack stature in the painting in comparison with the painter, who is not only larger and more prominent than they are but also who, as the writer notes, "dominates the painting along with the little girl." The little girl is the princess herself and the supposed subject of the painting within the painting that Velázquez is working on.

Test: This answer about the painter demonstrating his control of the representation of the king and queen seems credible. It has the most evidence in its favor and the least evidence to contradict it. The writer would probably want to choose this idea and would need to reformulate her thesis to better accommodate it, which takes us to Step 4.

Step 4: Use your analysis of the complicating evidence to reformulate the thesis. Share with readers your reasons for moving from your initial claim to this reformulation.

On the basis of the writer's answers in Step 3, it would appear that rather than showcasing royal power, the painting showcases the painter's own power. This idea is not a clear fit with the writer's working thesis about the painter's intentions, that "Velazquez wants the king to give him the recognition he deserves by including him in the family." So, what should the writer do?

What she should not do is beat a hasty retreat from her working thesis. She should use the complicating evidence to qualify, rather than abandon, her initial idea, which did, after all, have some evidence in its favor. Good writing shares with readers the thinking process that carried the writer forward from one idea to the next.

The writer's evolved thesis would need to qualify the idea of the painter wishing to be recognized as a loyal servant and accepted as a member of the family (which are not entirely compatible ideas), because there is evidence in the painting suggesting a more assertive stance on the part of Velázquez about the importance of painters and their art.

The writer is now ready to pursue the next step in the revision process: looking actively for other features of the painting that might corroborate her theory. This takes us to step 5, the last step the writer would need to go through before composing a more polished draft.

Step 5: Test the adequacy of the evolved thesis by repeating steps two, three, and four until you are satisfied that the thesis statement accounts for your evidence as fully and accurately as possible. The best test of a thesis is to see how much of the relevant evidence it can reasonably account for.

The need to find additional corroboration is especially pressing for this writer because her new thesis formulation that the painting demonstrates the artist's power—not just his brilliance and desire for recognition—suggests an interpretation of the painting that would be unusual for an era in which most other court paintings flattered royal figures by portraying them as larger than life, powerful, and heroic.

It is unlikely that any thesis will explain all of the details in a subject, but a reasonable test of the value of one possible thesis over another is how much of the relevant evidence it can explain. So the writer would try to apply her new thesis formulation to details in the painting that have not yet received much attention, such as the painter's paralleling himself with the large dwarf on the other side of the painting.

This pairing of dwarf and painter might initially seem to spell trouble for the new thesis about the painter demonstrating his power to frame the way the monarchs are represented. If it was, in fact, the painter's intention to have his power recognized, why would he want to parallel himself—in size, placement, and facial expression—with a dwarf who is, presumably, a fairly low-level servant of the royal household, unlike the *meninas*, who are the daughters of aristocrats? So what that the dwarf is paralleled with the painter?

The writer might argue that the dwarf suggests a visual pun or riddle, demonstrating that in the painter's world the small can be made large (and vice versa, in the case of the king and queen). No longer "dwarfed" by his subordinate role as court painter, Velázquez stands tall. If this reading is correct, and if it is true, as the writer suggests, that Prince Philip later had the honorary cross added to Velázquez's vest, we might assume that the king either entirely missed or was able to appreciate the painter's wit.

Similarly, another of the writer's key observations—that the painter "plays" with viewers' expectations—fits with the thesis that the painting asks for recognition of the artist's power, not just his loyal service. In subverting viewers' expectations, both by decentering the monarchs and concealing what is on the easel, the painter again emphasizes his power, in this case, over the viewers (among whom might be the king and queen if their images on the back wall are mirror reflections of them standing, like us, in front of the painting). He is not bound by their expectations, and in fact appears to use those expectations to manipulate the viewers: he can make them wish to see something he has the power to withhold.

Step 6: Rewrite the draft into a more coherent and fuller analysis of evidence, while retaining for readers the "thesis trail"—the various steps that you went through along the way to formulating the thesis you ultimately choose.

It is tempting at the end of the exploratory writing process for the writer to simply eliminate all the ideas and analysis that did not support her final choice of thesis. Why should she include all six steps when she now knows the best version of the thesis?

Good analytical writing is collaborative. To a significant extent, it recreates for readers the thinking process that produced its conclusions. It shares with readers how a writer arrives at ideas, not just what the writer ultimately thinks. It takes readers along on a cognitive journey through the process of formulating and reformulating that results in a carefully qualified statement of ideas. Having made the trip, readers are more likely to appreciate the explanatory power of the most fully articulated statement of the thesis.

In a final draft, a writer can capture for readers the phases of thinking she went through by, for example, wording the thesis as a SEEMS TO BE ABOUT X, BUT COULD ALSO BE (OR IS "REALLY") ABOUT Y claim; see Chapter 3). This wording would allow the writer of the *Las Meninas* paper to share with readers the interesting shift she makes from the idea that the painting promotes the divine right of kings to the idea that it also endorses the power of the painter to cause people to see royalty in this light (a visual pun, as the light on the princess is actually produced by the painter's brush).

The writer could also set up a thesis that puts X in tension with Y, while granting some validity to both. In this case, X (the painter wanting to be recognized as a member of the family) would serve as back pressure to drive Y (the painter wanting to demonstrate, tongue-in-cheek, the power of painters).

In an inductively organized paper, you would begin with a working thesis somewhat closer to the final version of the thesis than was the case in the exploratory draft, but you would still take the readers along on your step-by-step journey to your conclusions. In a deductively organized paper, wherein the thesis must appear from the outset in something close to its full version, you would still be able to show your readers how your thinking evolved. The writer of the *Las Meninas* paper could do this by beginning with details that seem to obviously support the thesis (large size and prominence of the painter and his easel relative to the king and queen) and then move to details (such as the large dwarf) that readers would be less likely to connect with the thesis without her help.

Knowing When to Stop: How Much Revising Is Enough?

We emphasize before leaving this example that the version of the thesis we have just proposed is not necessarily the "right" answer. Looked at in a different context, the painting might have been explained primarily as a demonstration of the painter's mastery of the tools of his trade—light, for example, and perspective. But our proposed revision of the thesis for the *Las Meninas* paper meets two important criteria for evaluating thesis statements:

1. It unifies the observations the writer has made.

2. It is capable of accounting for a wide range of evidence.

The writer has followed through on her original desire to infer Velázquez's intentions in the painting. Whether or not Velázquez consciously intended to make his painting a tongue-in-cheek self-advertisement, there is clearly enough evidence to claim plausibly that the painting can be understood in this way.

How do you know when you've done enough reformulating of your thesis and arrived at the best possible idea about your evidence? Getting the thesis to account for as much of the relevant evidence as possible doesn't mean you need to discuss every detail of the subject. Writers must take care not to ignore important evidence, especially if it would alter their "case," but no analysis can address everything—nor should it. Your job as a writer is to select those features of your subject that seem most significant and to argue for their significance. An analysis says to readers, in effect, "These are the details that best reveal the nature and meaning of my subject, or at least the part of the subject that I am trying to address."

Practice Tracking Thesis Statements in Finished Drafts

Learning to write and think in the way that the six steps recommend will take time, practice, and patience—especially patience with yourself. As we hope our example of evolving a thesis in the student draft on *Las Meninas* has shown, good ideas don't come easily or naturally or magically, though sometimes it may feel that they do. Good ideas can be methodically courted, which is what the six steps teach you to do.

In addition to time and practice and patience, what you need are models of how good writers operate, how they move from evidence to idea and from initial formulations of ideas to better ones. Start looking for models on your own. When you find a smart piece of writing that you admire, look for its thesis and for the ways that the thesis evolves. Underline each occurrence of the thesis, taking care to note the places where the writer makes interesting shifts. Figure out what it was in the writer's evidence that caused these shifts. We call this exercise "tracking the thesis." Once you train yourself to become aware of thesis statements and how they develop, you will become more comfortable with writing your own thesis statements.

Tracking the Thesis in a Final Draft: The Example of *In Bruges*

We offer the following student paper as an example of how you might go about tracking the evolution of a thesis. As you will see, the writer repeatedly tests the paper's working hypothesis against evidence and arrives at an interestingly qualified version of his original claim. We have offered in square brackets brief comments on the development of the writer's thinking.

In Bruges: Finding Hope in the Presence of the Past, by James Patefield

In Bruges, a film by Academy-Award winning director, playwright, and Irishman Martin McDonagh, is obsessed with a sense of place. The city of Bruges, with its many old churches and old art (including a Bosch painting of the Last Judgment), seems to stand in the film for two starkly opposed ideas. One is that we can never escape our own histories—sequences of events that, once set in motion, can't and should not be stopped, and can't be changed. The other idea is that we can and must hold out for the possibility of change, for a future that past actions and rigid systems of value haven't already set in stone. Given the film's violence, dark comedy, and apocalyptic ending, it seems to offer only faint hope for change in the face of relentless cycles of determinism and fate. [**The writer puts two conflicting interpretations in tension with each other and posits a working thesis that there is only faint hope for change.**]

In the film, hitmen Ray and Ken have been sent by their boss Harry to hide out in the Belgian city of Bruges after a job has gone horribly wrong because Ray has accidentally killed a child. While in Bruges, Ray falls in love with Chloe, a Belgian drug dealer, on a film set. At the same time, Ken and Ray develop a strong bond while discussing Ray's suicidal feelings of guilt.

The story on some level is all about the fact that it takes place "in Bruges," a medieval city that embodies the presence of the past. The presence of the past is the idea that history is living and shaping the present—that it is not dead or absent but very much present and alive, actively controlling what people do. [**The writer begins to demonstrate that one side of the opposition gets considerable weight in the film.**] We can see that the past is alive in the many examples of tourists visiting the city's architecture and in the repeated discussions that Ken and Ray have about the tourist sites. As we also learn, Bruges is the crucial fairy-tale site of Harry's happy childhood. This is why it is the setting for the story in the first place: because Harry, who romanticizes the past, wants to give Ray one fairy-tale experience before ordering his death.

When we think about the film's point of view on Bruges, we find that Ken (and the cinematographer for the film) loves it while Ray hates it. This conflict defines the relationship between Ray and Ken that develops throughout the film, with Ray holding onto the present and Ken holding onto the past. The city and the relationship between the characters are intimately intertwined. [**Here the writer makes overt the two main characters' positions in the tension between closed past and future possibility.**]

It is crucial to know that Harry is set on killing Ray because Harry operates on a system of ethics and justice that operates on "honor." In this system, Ray can only pay for his sin of killing a child by dying himself. This comes into conflict with Ken and his system of justice/ethics when Ken refuses to kill Ray because he believes that Ray "has the capacity to change [and] do something decent with his life." Ken's system of ethics operates on an idea of choice, hope for personal change, and a future that is not already set in stone. In this way, it comes head to head with Harry's "honor" principles in the film. If we can read Ken as the most overtly religious character in the film, given his affinity for sightseeing Catholic churches and medieval Catholic art, we can then see Ken and Harry's conflict as one of a religious "spirit of the law" versus an honor-driven "letter of the law." (See 2 Corinthians 3:6.) [**Here the writer offers another version of the binary that is central to his interpretation.**]

Ray's guilt and the discussions it brings about in turn connect us back to Bruges as a symbolic location. Given that these churches are specifically identified as Catholic, we can link them back to a consistent theme of guilt, death, sin, and judgment. Churches are, after all, not tourist sites in the same way that something like the Empire State Building or the Statue of Liberty is. Churches imply a sense of pilgrimage for the characters—that they are going on a religious journey ending in enlightenment. The churches are refuges for Ken. They offer alternatives to a present that for Ken seems out of control and immoral.

When Ken receives orders from Harry to kill Ray, he is unwilling to obey, choosing instead to confront Harry. Harry in turn comes to Bruges to kill Ken for not killing Ray. The resulting showdown leads to Ken sacrificing his life to save Ray, Harry killing himself because of his own unyielding code of honor-driven ethics, and Ray being severely wounded as he is put onto oxygen in an ambulance, left with the hope of a new life and potential change.

In this conclusion, the film is fairly clear that Ken wins the ethics battle I've just laid out. Even though Ken dies, he does so by staying true to his code of ethics, in which preserving the potential for life and change is more important than rigid codes of honor. Harry's code of ethics also leads to his death but in a much more ironic way. When he is pursuing Ray in the final moments of the film, Harry accidentally kills Jimmy, a dwarf on the film set. When this happens, Harry thinks that he has killed a child in much the same way that Ray had in the opening scene, and he immediately kills himself, explaining "You've got to stick to your principles" before he blows his own head completely off.

This brings us to a way to interpret the ending of the film, which I think is actually quite hopeful in a situation without much hope. At the end of the film most of the main characters are dead, and Ray is being carried into an ambulance with three or four bullet wounds in his torso. One school of thought could say that the fact that the film ends with Ray's voiceover saying "I really hoped I wouldn't die" points to an interpretation that he dies and his ghost is narrating the story to us via voiceover. This interpretation seems a little bleak, however. After all, what good is Ken's sacrifice of his life if Ray dies almost immediately afterwards? **[Here the writer finds some evidence for his initial point that there is only faint hope in the film.]**

On this note, I would like to instead point to Ken's victory over Harry as a signpost for hope at the end of the film. If the film endorses Ken's viewpoint that Ray's undetermined future and possibility for change are worth dying for, the film must be holding out Ray's survival as a hopeful way of escaping the presence of the past.

In the last few moments of Ray's voiceover, as he's wheeled on a gurney towards the ambulance, he talks about how Bruges must be Hell. In this version of Hell, the past creates a vicious cycle in which we become trapped in our own histories, our own primal sins that we can never escape or gain forgiveness from. In *In Bruges*, however, Ray's primal sin of killing the child is ironically and finally reenacted by Harry, the person who is rendering justice for that very sin. **[The writer sees that Harry's choice to die by his own relentless code for what we see as a mistake starts to erode the film's support for the position that Harry represents.]**

Finally, it is significant that the last scene of *In Bruges* takes place on a film set—the film set of a Belgian dream sequence that describes and alludes to the Last Judgment, the end of time at which all humanity will be judged by God. This makes sense, given the references to the medieval painter Bosch and his painting, "The Last Judgment," which is showcased and discussed earlier in the film in relation to Ray's guilt and anxiety. The last judgment or final say of the film happens when the painting of *The Last Judgment* comes to life in the form of the film actors, who are dressed in costumes taken from Bosch's painting. [**Here the writer sees that the idea of final judgments is being presented quasi-comically as a fiction, something that takes place on a fantasy film set.**]

With all of this in mind, we come back to Ray's last line, "I really hoped I wouldn't die." This line remains unresolved by the film, in the sense that we almost expect Ray to say "And I didn't," or "But I did." The fact that this line remains unresolved makes its meaning open for interpretation and not predetermined, and thus a match for Ken's code of ethics. Lastly, even though Ray's line, "I really hoped I wouldn't die," ends on the word "die," it is more important that we look at the main verb of this sentence: "hope." This breakdown of the sentence is modeling on a smaller scale what the film is trying to say: that in the end, "hope" in the face of "dying" is all we can cling to and count on. In this way, we can view the ending of the film as offering hope for change and belief in potential—a breaking of old irreconcilable cycles of sin and punishment. This hope the film posits as necessary because without it we are held inescapably hostage to a cyclical repetition of our own histories and past deeds. [**The writer has arrived at an evolved version of his opening claim about hope, which he now sees as less faint than it had initially appeared.**] (Reprinted by permission of the author.)

Introductions, Conclusions, and the Thesis

Until you understand the expectations that introductions typically raise, it's difficult to know what kind of statement the thesis needs to be. Similarly, until you understand what a concluding paragraph does, you will have difficulty knowing what to do with your thesis in that final paragraph besides merely restating it.

Setting Up the Thesis: Two Tasks

Let's now get more specific about the thesis as a response to reader expectations created by the paper's introductory paragraph. These expectations are surprisingly uniform across the curriculum and in many kinds of writing—not just academic writing.

In setting up the thesis, the introduction accomplishes two tasks:

- It lays out something at stake—an issue, question, or problem to which the writer's thesis is a tentative answer or solution.

- It provides an interpretive context (see Chapter 3) that locates the thesis in relation to existing thinking.

In sum, the introduction tells readers why the idea that the paper is about to explore matters—why, in other words, a paper needs to be written about it. What typically goes wrong in introductions is that the writer offers a bunch of information, usually too much information, without focusing it in a way that would help a reader understand why the thesis is worth considering.

Here are the kinds of questions an introductory paragraph should answer in order to set up a thesis:

What is potentially interesting about what I have noticed, and why?

What am I seeing that other people perhaps have not seen or have not sufficiently acknowledged?

Why might what I have noticed matter in relation to the usual ways of thinking about my subject?

How might what I have noticed require a new way of thinking about my subject, or at least a revision, however slight, of the usual ways of thinking?

Making the Thesis Matter: Providing an Interpretive Context

In most courses there are a limited number of acceptable ways of broadly theorizing the material. For an interpretation to be acceptable, you usually need to locate it inside one of these contexts. In the case of Irish literature, for example, an interpretive context might be postcolonial theory on how writers negotiate the formation of new, national identities to replace their colonial inheritance. In a film history course, an interpretive context might be particular movements, such as neorealism, or the methods and concerns of a particular filmmaker (known as *auteur* theory). (See Chapter 3 for an extended discussion of interpretive contexts.)

This does not mean you won't be allowed to say what you think or to nominate new contexts in which to understand things. It means that in order to be heard and to make a contribution, you need to connect whatever you have to say with what people are talking about. In other words, thesis statements don't occur in a vacuum. For people to understand why your idea might matter, they need to see it in relation to the debates and questions that are currently energizing readers' interest in the topic.

Papers often begin by foregrounding something the writer has noticed that seems not to fit with what prevailing theories or discussion has led her to expect. In the sciences, for example, introductions begin by showing how some phenomenon or pattern of detail has not been accounted for in existing studies. The writer asks the question, how might this divergence from what was expected be explained?

Two especially useful strategies for setting up a thesis are Seems to Be About X and Difference within Similarity, (see Chapters 3 and 4, respectively). These strategies effectively set up tension in the thesis between competing ways of viewing your subject. (For more on this subject, see the upcoming section on establishing tension in the thesis statement.)

How Much of the Thesis Belongs in the Introduction?

Once you have created the opening frame that leads to your thesis, you have choices about how much of your thesis to state at the outset and in what form. These choices are determined in some cases by the standard practices of the various academic disciplines. In some disciplines, for example, the introduction must offer a complete statement of the guiding claim. This is often done overtly with a so-called *procedural statement* such as: "In this essay I will argue that . . ." This way of beginning is common not only in the natural and social sciences, but also in philosophy, art history, and in some other humanities disciplines. The procedural statement is sometimes followed by a roadmap that specifies the organization of the paper: "First A will be discussed, then B, . . . Such a detailed overview of a paper is not the norm, however, and is usually not necessary, especially in short essays.

To make your introduction sufficiently engaging and concrete, you should offer readers a brief preview of the details that led you to arrive at your thesis, or at least to the question that your thesis seeks to answer. Use these details to generate a theory, a *working hypothesis* about whatever you think is at stake in the material. As a general rule, assume that readers of your essay would need to know on page one, preferably by the end of your first paragraph or the beginning of the second, what your paper is attempting to resolve or negotiate. If you find yourself writing a page-long introductory paragraph to get to your initial statement of thesis, try settling for a simpler articulation of your central idea in its first appearance. Keep in mind that an introduction is not a conclusion. The opening claim is a hypothesis that the body of your paper will test. Your final assessment of the claim will appear in your paper's closing paragraphs.

In large, complex pieces of thinking (though sometimes even in short ones), the introductory paragraph may be used to set up the first phase of the paper's discussion without having to frame and forecast the whole paper. Especially in inductively organized (specific to general) essays, where a full and complexly qualified articulation of the thesis becomes evident in stages, you need an opening claim sufficient to launch the paper. Begin with your best version of the thesis, one that will be understandable to your readers without a lengthy preamble. Set up this working thesis as quickly and concretely as you can, avoiding generic (fits anything) comments, throat clearing, and overblown historical claims ("Since the beginning of time, humans have been fascinated by technology . . ."). Once established, the working thesis will supply a relatively stable point to which you can return periodically for updating and to keep your readers (and yourself) on track.

The Conclusion: Returning the Thesis to the Larger Conversation

The conclusion is in some ways the introduction in reverse. It begins with the more carefully qualified and evolved version of your thinking that the body of your paper has produced. It then locates the thesis in some kind of larger perspective.

The conclusion answers questions like this: What changes in people's ways of thinking might be needed? Where might we need to go next—i.e., what further work needs to be done? In the end, the conclusion returns the thesis to the ongoing conversation that people have been having about your subject and suggests why and how what you've said matters and where it might take us next.

VOICES FROM ACROSS THE CURRICULUM

Recognizing Your Thesis: A History Professor Speaks

The thesis usually is that point of departure from the surfaces of evidence to the underlying significance, or problems, a given set of sources reveal to the reader and writer. In most cases, the thesis is best positioned up front, so that the writer's audience has a sense of what lies ahead and why it is worth reading on. I say "usually" and "in most cases" because the hard and fast rule should not take precedence over the inspirational manner in which a thesis can be presented. But the inspiration is not to be sought after at the price of the thesis itself. It is my experience, in fact, that if inspiration strikes, one only realizes it after the fact.

Recognizing a thesis can be extremely difficult. It can often be a lot easier to talk "about" what one is writing, than to say succinctly what the thrust of one's discussion is. I sometimes ask students to draw a line at the end of a paper after they have finished it off, and then write one, at most two sentences, stating what they most want to tell their readers. My comment on that postscript frequently is: "Great statement of your thesis. Just move it up to your first paragraph."

—ELLEN POTEET, PROFESSOR OF HISTORY

How to Word Thesis Statements

The wording and syntax (sentence structure) of thesis statements have shaping force in the way a paper develops. Some thesis shapes are more effective than others. Here in condensed form is the advice offered in the upcoming discussion of thesis shapes:

- A productive thesis usually contains *tension*, the balance of this against that.
- Effective thesis statements often begin with a grammatically subordinate idea that will get outweighed by a more pressing claim: "Although X appears to account for Z, Y accounts for it better."
- A less effective thesis shape is the list.
- Active verbs and specific nouns produce strong thesis statements.

Put X in Tension with Y

One of the best and most common ways of bringing the thesis into focus is by pitting one possible point of view against another. Good ideas usually take place with the aid of some kind of *back pressure*, by which we mean that the idea takes shape by pushing against another way of seeing things. This is not to say that you set out your thesis as a way of overturning and completely refuting one idea in favor of another. In good thesis statements both ideas have some validity, but the forward momentum of the thesis comes from playing the preferred idea off the other one.

Notice the tension in the following two thesis statements, which results from the defining pressure of one idea against another potentially viable idea:

- It may not seem like it, but "Nice Pants" is as radical a campaign as the original Dockers series.

- If opponents of cosmetic surgery are too quick to dismiss those who claim great psychological benefits, proponents are far too willing to dismiss those who raise concerns. Cosmetic surgery might make individual people happier, but in the aggregate it makes life worse for everyone.

In the first thesis sentence, the primary idea is that the new advertising campaign for Dockers trousers is radical. The back pressure against which this idea takes shape is that this new campaign may not seem radical. The writer will demonstrate the truth of both claims, rather than overturning one and then championing the other.

The same can be said of the parts of the second thesis statement. One part of the thesis makes claims for the benefits of cosmetic surgery. The forward momentum of the thesis statement comes from the back pressure of this idea against the idea that cosmetic surgery will also make life worse for everyone. Notice that the thesis statement does not simply say, "Cosmetic surgery is bad." The writer's job will be to demonstrate that the potential harm of cosmetic surgery outweighs the benefits, but the benefits won't just be dismissed. Both ideas are to some extent true. Neither idea, in other words, is "a straw man"—the somewhat deceptive argumentative practice of setting up a dummy position solely because it is easy to knock down. A straw man does not strengthen a thesis statement because it fails to provide genuine back pressure.

TRY THIS 7.1: Spotting the Tension in Good Thesis Statements

Find the tension in each of the following thesis statements. Decide which of the ideas is primary—the one you think the writer plans to support. Then locate the claim or claims in the thesis against which this primary claim will take shape.

1. Emphasis on the self in the history of modern thought may be an exaggeration, but the consequences of this vision of a self set apart have surely been felt in every field of inquiry.

2. We may join with the modern builders in justifying the violence of means—the sculptor's hammer and chisel—by appealing to ends that

serve the greater good. Yet too often modern planners and engineers would justify the creative destruction of habitat as necessary for doubtful utopias.

3. The derogation of middlebrow, in short, has gone much too far. It's time to bring middlebrow out of its cultural closet, to hail its emollient properties, to trumpet its mending virtues. For middlebrow not only entertains, but also educates—pleasurably training us to appreciate high art.

Is It Okay to Phrase a Thesis as a Question?

The answer is yes and no. Phrasing a thesis as a question makes it more difficult for both the writer and the reader to be sure of the direction the paper will take, because a question doesn't make an overt claim. Questions, however, can clearly imply claims. And many writers, especially in the early, exploratory stages of drafting, will begin with a question.

As a general rule, use thesis questions cautiously, particularly in final drafts. While a thesis question often functions well to spark your thinking, it can allow you to evade the responsibility of making a claim. Especially in the drafting stage, a question posed overtly can provide focus, but only if you then answer it with what could become a first statement of thesis—a working thesis.

VOICES FROM ACROSS THE CURRICULUM

Getting Beyond the All-Purpose Thesis: A Dance Professor Speaks

Not so good thesis/question: "What were Humphrey's and Weidman's reasons behind the setting of *With My Red Fires*, and of what importance were the set and costume design to the piece as a whole?"

Good thesis: "While Graham and Wigman seem different, their ideas on inner expression (specifically subjectivism versus objectivism) and the incorporation of their respective countries' surge of nationalism bring them much closer than they appear."

What I like about the good thesis is that it moves beyond the standard "they are different, but alike" (which can be said about anything) to actually tell the reader what specific areas the paper will explore. I can also tell that the subject is narrow enough for a fairly thorough examination of one small slice of these two major choreographers' work rather than some overgeneralized treatment of these two historic figures.

—KAREN DEARBORN, PROFESSOR OF DANCE

Recognizing and Fixing Weak Thesis Statements

This closing section of the chapter provides a revision-oriented treatment of the five most common kinds of weak thesis statements. Typically, a weak thesis is an unproductive claim because it doesn't require further thinking or proof, as, for example, "An important part of one's college education is learning to better understand others' points of view" (a piece of conventional wisdom that most people would already accept as true, and thus not in need of arguing).

FIVE KINDS OF WEAK THESIS STATEMENTS

1. A thesis that makes no claim ("This paper examines the pros and cons of").

2. A thesis that is obviously true or a statement of fact ("Exercise is good for you").

3. A thesis that restates conventional wisdom ("Love conquers all").

4. A thesis that offers personal conviction as the basis for the claim ("Shopping malls are wonderful places").

5. A thesis that makes an overly broad claim ("Individualism is good").

Weak Thesis Type 1: The Thesis Makes No Claim

Problem Examples

> I'm going to write about Darwin's concerns with evolution in *The Origin of Species.*
> This paper addresses the characteristics of a good corporate manager.

Both problem examples name a subject and link it to the intention to write about it, but they don't make any claim about the subject. As a result, they direct neither the writer nor the reader toward some position or organizational plan. Even if the second example were rephrased as "This paper addresses why a good corporate manager needs to learn to delegate responsibility," the thesis would not adequately suggest why such a claim would need to be argued or defended. There is, in short, nothing at stake, no issue to be resolved.

Solution: Raise specific issues for the essay to explore.

Solution Examples

> Darwin's concern with survival of the fittest in *The Origin of Species* initially leads him to neglect a potentially conflicting aspect of his theory of evolution—survival as a matter of interdependence.
> The very trait that makes for an effective corporate manager—the drive to succeed—can also make the leader domineering and, therefore, ineffective.

Some disciplines expect writers to offer statements of method and/or intention in their papers' openings. Generally, however, these openings also make a claim: for example, "In this paper, I examine how Congressional Republicans undermined the attempts of the Democratic administration to legislate a fiscally responsible health care policy for the elderly," not "In this paper, I discuss America's treatment of the elderly."

Weak Thesis Type 2: The Thesis Is Obviously True or Is a Statement of Fact

Problem Example

> The jeans industry targets its advertisements to appeal to young adults.
> The flight from teaching to research and publishing in higher education is a controversial issue in the academic world. I will show different views and aspects concerning this problem.

A thesis needs to be an assertion with which it would be possible for readers to disagree.

In the second example, few readers would disagree with the fact that the issue is "controversial." In the second sentence of that example, the writer has begun to identify a point of view—that the flight from teaching is a problem—but her declaration that she will "show different views and aspects" is a broad statement of fact, not an idea. The phrasing of the claim is noncommittal and so broad that it prevents the writer from formulating a workable thesis.

> **Solution:** Find some avenue of inquiry—a question about the facts or an issue raised by them. Make an assertion with which it would be possible for readers to disagree.

Solution Examples

> By inventing new terms, such as "loose fit" and "relaxed fit," the jean industry has attempted to normalize, even glorify, its product for an older and fatter generation.
> The "flight from teaching" to research and publishing in higher education is a controversial issue in the academic world. As I will attempt to show, the controversy is based to a significant degree on a false assumption, that doing research necessarily leads teachers away from the classroom.

Weak Thesis Type 3: The Thesis Restates Conventional Wisdom

Problem Example

> "I was supposed to bring the coolers; you were supposed to bring the chips!" exclaimed ex-Beatle Ringo Starr, who appeared on TV commercials for Sun County Wine Coolers a number of years ago. By using rock music to sell a wide range of products, the advertising agencies, in league with corporate giants such as Pepsi, Michelob, and Ford, have corrupted the spirit of rock 'n' roll.

"Conventional wisdom" is a polite term for cultural cliché. Most clichés were fresh ideas once, but over time they have become trite, prefabricated forms of nonthinking. Faced with a phenomenon that requires a response, inexperienced writers sometimes resort to a small set of culturally approved "answers." Because conventional wisdom is so general and so commonly accepted, however, it doesn't teach anybody—including the writer—anything. Worse, because the cliché looks like an idea, it prevents the writer from engaging in a fresh exploration of their subject.

There is some truth in both of the preceding problem examples, but neither complicates its position. A thoughtful reader could, for example, respond to the advertising example by suggesting that rock 'n' roll was highly commercial long before it colonized the airwaves. The conventional wisdom that rock is somehow pure and honest while advertising is phony and exploitative invites the savvy writer to formulate a thesis that overturns these clichés. It could be argued that rock has actually improved advertising, not that ads have ruined rock—or, alternatively, that rock has shrewdly marketed idealism to gullible consumers. At the least, a writer committed to the original thesis would do better to examine what Ringo was selling—what he/wine coolers stand for in this particular case—than to discuss rock and advertising in such predictable terms.

> **Solution:** Seek to complicate—see more than one point of view on your subject. Avoid conventional wisdom unless you can qualify it or introduce a fresh perspective on it.

Solution Example

> While some might argue that the presence of rock 'n' roll soundtracks in TV commercials has corrupted rock's spirit, this point of view not only misrepresents the history of rock but also ignores the improvements that the music has brought to the quality of television advertising.

Weak Thesis Type 4: The Thesis Bases Its Claim on Personal Conviction

Problem Examples

> Sir Thomas More's *Utopia* proposes an unworkable set of solutions to society's problems because, like communist Russia, it suppresses individualism.
>
> Although I agree with Jeane Kirkpatrick's argument that environmentalists and business should work together to ensure the ecological future of the world, and that this cooperation is beneficial for both sides, the indisputable fact is that environmental considerations should always be a part of any decision that is made. Any individual, if he looks deeply enough into his soul, knows what is right and what is wrong. The environment should be protected because it is the right thing to do, not because someone is forcing you to do it.

Like conventional wisdom, personal likes and dislikes can lead inexperienced writers into knee-jerk reactions of approval or disapproval, often expressed in a moralistic tone. The writers of the preceding problem examples assume that their primary job is to judge their subjects, or testify to their worth, not to evaluate them analytically. They have taken personal opinions for self-evident truths. (See "Naturalizing Our Assumptions" in Chapter 1.)

The most blatant version of this tendency occurs in the second problem example, which asserts, "Any individual, if he looks deeply enough into his soul, knows what is right and what is wrong. The environment should be protected because it is the right thing to do." Translation (only slightly exaggerated): "Any individual who thinks about the subject will obviously agree with me because my feelings and convictions feel right to me and therefore they must be universally and self-evidently true." Testing an idea against your own feelings and experience is not an adequate means of establishing whether something is accurate or true.

> **Solution:** Try on other points of view honestly and dispassionately; treat your ideas as hypotheses to be tested rather than obvious truths. In the following solution examples, we have replaced opinions (in the form of self-evident truths) with ideas—theories about the meaning and significance of the subjects that are capable of being supported and qualified by evidence.

Solution Examples

> Sir Thomas More's *Utopia* treats individualism as a serious but remediable social problem. His radical treatment of what we might now call "socialization" attempts to redefine the meaning and origin of individual identity.
>
> Although I agree with Jeane Kirkpatrick's argument that environmentalists and business should work together to ensure the ecological future of the world, her argument undervalues the necessity of pressuring businesses to attend to environmental concerns that may not benefit them in the short run.

Weak Thesis Type 5: The Thesis Makes an Overly Broad Claim

Problem Examples

> Violent revolutions have had both positive and negative results for man.
> *Othello* is a play about love and jealousy.

Overly generalized theses avoid complexity and usually lead either to say-nothing theses or to reductive, either/or thinking. Similar to a thesis that makes no claim, theses with overly broad claims say nothing in particular about the subject at hand and so are not likely to guide a writer's thinking beyond the listing stage. One of the best ways to avoid drafting overly broad thesis statements is to sensitize yourself to the characteristic phrasing of such theses: "both positive and negative," "many similarities and differences," "both pros and cons." Virtually everything from meatloaf to taxes can be both positive and negative.

Solution: Convert broad categories and generic claims to more specific, more qualified assertions; find ways to bring out the complexity of your subject.

Solution Examples

> Although violent revolutions begin to redress long-standing inequities, they often do so at the cost of long-term economic dysfunction and the suffering that attends it.

> Although *Othello* appears to attack jealousy, it also supports the skepticism of the jealous characters over the naïveté of the lovers.

Assignment: Finding and Evolving a Thesis

Formulate and Evolve a Thesis on a Film, Painting, or Other Visual Image.

Using the model of *Las Meninas*, produce an interpretation of a film, painting, or other visual image of your choice.

Formulate a variety of possible statements about the film or painting, and then choose one to serve as a working thesis. These potential working theses might be in answer to the question "What is the film/painting about?" or "What does it 'say'?" Or you might begin by doing THE METHOD to uncover pattern of repetition or contrast you have observed and can then explain.

Obviously, this assignment could be adapted to other subjects—an essay, the coverage of a current event, and so on. Here are some specific suggestions:

- The contemporary appeal of a cartoon or other popular television character

- Differences in political rhetoric between Democrats and Republicans on the same issue

- The rhetoric of a popular print or television ad campaign for a familiar product, such as an insurance company, soft drink, or automobile

Next, follow the procedure for making the thesis evolve, using the six steps.

CHAPTER 8

Conversing with Sources: Writing the Researched Paper

Overview The idea of this chapter is that you should learn to put your sources in conversation with each other and with your own ideas, rather than just pointing to them as answers. The chapter's primary heuristic offers six strategies for analyzing sources.

The chapter also offers specific advice on how to integrate quotation and paraphrase into your writing and how to do in-text citation. The last section of the chapter shows you how to write an abstract and how to manage citation in the literature review that is the common opening section in formal papers in the sciences.

The Big Picture

If you want to think and speak intelligently about a subject, it's important to consult and interrogate multiple points of view. All knowledge is the product of learning communities, and in such communities you will encounter different points of view on a given topic. That goes for all topics, from the popular (sports, cooking, politics) to the rarefied (neurophysiology, econometrics). All knowledge has a history, and that's certainly true for scholarly topics, where a community of people have often been having a conversation for a long time.

Whenever you're engaged in writing on a subject, especially in an academic context, you're better off at some point making contact with the existing learning community. It's a great way to see the questions and the problems with which the learning community is grappling. You may take up one of these questions, or formulate your own, but in any case, if you do a little research, you will get a sense for the kinds of questions people ask and the ways that people comment on others' comments and questions—the scholarly etiquette. (The next chapter offers lots of advice on how to find and evaluate different kinds of sources.)

Especially if you're engaged in a sustained research project, your first goal is to apprehend the primary viewpoints that are evident inside a scholarly community. (See Chapter 9 on using specialized dictionaries as one way to identify these viewpoints.) Your ultimate goal in doing this kind of research, though, is to find a place for your own voice inside that community.

Using Sources Analytically

Integrating secondary sources into your writing is often a daunting task, because it requires you to negotiate with authorities who generally know more than you do about the subject at hand. Simply ignoring sources is a head-in-the-sand attitude, and besides you miss out on learning what people interested in your subject are talking about. But what role can you invent for yourself when the experts are talking? Just agreeing with a source is an abdication of your responsibility to present your thinking on the subject. But taking the opposite tack by disagreeing with an expert who has studied your subject and written books about it would appear to be a fool's game. What, then, are you to do?

This chapter attempts to answer that question. It lays out the primary trouble spots that arise when writers use secondary materials, and it suggests remedies—ways of using sources as points of departure for your own thinking, rather than using them as either "The Answer" or a straw man. We call this approach *conversing with sources*, a tactic that avoids the temptation to plug in sources as answers, seeing them instead as voices inviting you into a community of interpretation, discussion, and debate.

We use the terms *source* and *secondary source* interchangeably to designate ideas and information about your subject that you find in the work of other writers. Secondary sources allow you to gain a richer, more informed, and complex vantage point on your *primary sources*. Here's how primary and secondary sources can be distinguished: if you were writing a paper on the philosopher Nietzsche, his writing would be your primary source, and critical commentaries on his work would be your secondary sources. If, however, you were writing on the poet Yeats, who read and was influenced by Nietzsche, a work of Nietzsche's philosophy would become a secondary source on your primary source, Yeats's poetry. A scholarly article about Nietzsche's influence on Yeats would also be a secondary source.

Here are a few guidelines for using sources in analytical writing:

- Locate and highlight what is at stake in your source. Which of its points does the source find most important? What positions does it want to modify or refute, and why? (See The Pitch, The Complaint, and The Moment in Chapter 2.)

- Look for ways to develop, modify, or apply what a source has said, rather than simply agreeing or disagreeing with it.

- If you challenge a position found in a source, be sure to represent it fairly. First, give the source some credit by identifying assumptions you share with it. Then, isolate the part that you intend to complicate or dispute.

- Look for sources that address your subject from different perspectives. Avoid relying too heavily on any one source. Aim to synthesize these perspectives: what is the common ground? Alternatively, map out the different viewpoints as clearly as you can, so you and your reader can grasp the general landscape of writing on the subject.

- When your sources disagree, consider playing mediator. Instead of immediately agreeing with one or the other, clarify areas of agreement and disagreement among them.

- Distinguish clearly what a source has to say about the subject from what you are saying about the subject. Don't leave the reader to guess where the source's commentary stops and yours picks up.

"Source Anxiety" and What to Do About It

Typically, inexperienced writers either use sources as "answers"—they let the sources do too much of their thinking—or ignore them altogether as a way of avoiding losing their own ideas. Both approaches are understandable but inadequate.

Confronted with the seasoned views of experts in a discipline, you may well feel that there is nothing left for you to say because it has all been said before or, at least, it has been said by people who greatly outweigh you in reputation and experience. This anxiety explains why so many writers surrender to the role of conduit for the voices of the experts, providing little more than conjunctions between quotations. So why not avoid what other people have said? Won't this avoidance ensure that your ideas will be original and that, at the same time, you will be free from the danger of getting brainwashed by some expert?

The answer is no. If you don't consult what others have said, you run at least two risks: you will waste your time reinventing the wheel, and you will undermine your analysis (or at least leave it incomplete) by not considering information and ideas commonly discussed in the field. By remaining unaware of existing thinking, you choose, in effect, to stand outside of the conversation that others interested in the subject are having.

It is possible to find a *middle ground* between developing an idea that is entirely independent of what experts have written on a subject and producing a paper that does nothing but repeat other people's ideas. A little research—even if it's only an hour's browse in the relevant databases on your library's website—will virtually always raise the level of what you have to say above what it would have been if you had consulted only the information and opinions that you carry around in your head.

A good rule of thumb for coping with source anxiety is to formulate a tentative position on your topic before you consult secondary sources. In other words, give yourself time to do some preliminary thinking. Try writing informally about your topic, analyzing some piece of pertinent information already at your disposal. That way you will have your initial responses written down to weigh in relation to what others have said.

The Conversation Analogy

Now let's turn to the major problem in using sources—a writer leaving the experts cited to speak for themselves. In this situation, the writer characteristically makes a generalization in the writer's own words, juxtaposes it to a quotation or other reference from a secondary source, and assumes that the meaning of the reference will be self-evident. This practice not only leaves the connection between the writer's thinking and the source material unstated, but also substitutes mere repetition of someone else's viewpoint for a more active interpretation. The source has been allowed to have the final word, with the effect that it stops the discussion and the writer's thinking.

First and foremost, then, you need to *do something* with the reading. Clarify the meaning of the material you have quoted, paraphrased, or summarized, and explain its significance in light of your evolving thesis. If you have not formulated a thesis yet, try doing PASSAGE-BASED FOCUSED FREEWRITING on a key passage from the source. Don't let yourself simply take notes on what a source has to say: try to force yourself to write a paragraph or two recording your initial impressions about the source—what you notice, what you find most intriguing or dubious.

It follows that the first step in using sources effectively is to reject the assumption that sources provide final and complete answers. If they did, there would be no reason for others to continue writing on the subject. As in conversation, we raise ideas for others to respond to. Accepting that no source has the final word does not mean, however, that you should shift from unquestioning approval to the opposite pole and necessarily assume an antagonistic position toward all sources. Indeed, a habitually antagonistic response to others' ideas is just as likely to bring your conversation with your sources to a halt as is the habit of always assuming that the source must have the final word.

Most people would probably agree on the attributes of a really good conversation. There is room for agreement and disagreement, for give and take, among a variety of viewpoints. Generally, people don't deliberately misunderstand each other, but a significant amount of the discussion may go into clarifying one's own as well as others' positions. Such conversations construct a genuinely collaborative chain of thinking: Karl builds on what David has said, which induces Jill to respond to Karl's comment, and so forth.

There are, of course, obvious differences between conversing aloud with friends and conversing on paper with sources. As a writer, you need to construct the chain of thinking, orchestrate the exchange of views with and among your sources, and give the conversation direction. A good place to begin in using sources is to recognize that you need not respond to everything another writer says, nor do you need to come up with an entirely original point of view—one that completely revises or refutes the source. You are using sources analytically, for example, when you note that two experiments (or historical accounts, or the like) are similar but have different priorities, or that they ask similar questions in different ways. Building from this kind of observation, you can then analyze what these differences imply.

TWO METHODS FOR CONVERSING WITH SOURCES

- Choose one sentence from a secondary source and one from a primary source, and put these into conversation in a focused freewrite. What does each reveal about the other?

- Pick one sentence from one source (A) and one from another (B) to anchor a focused freewrite. How does A speak to B? How does B speak to A?

Remember: go local, not global. You will be better off if you bring together two representative moves or ideas from the sources rather than trying to compare a summary of one source with a summary of another. A useful phrase here is "points of contact": look for ways that an idea or observation in source A appears to intersect with one in source B. Then stage the conversation you imagine taking place between them.

Conversing with a Source: A Brief Example

Consider, for example, the following quotation, the opening sentences of the essay "Clichés" by Christopher Ricks, which is ostensibly a review of a reissued book on the subject:

> The only way to speak of a cliché is with a cliché. So even the best writers against clichés are awkwardly placed. When Eric Partridge amassed his *Dictionary of Clichés* in 1940 (1978 saw its fifth edition), his introduction had no choice but to use the usual clichés for clichés. Yet what, as a metaphor, could be more hackneyed than *hackneyed*, more outworn than *outworn*, more tattered than *tattered*? Is there any point left to—or in or on—saying of a cliché that its "original point has been blunted"? Hasn't this too become blunted? [Christopher Ricks, "Clichés," in *The State of the Language*, ed. Leonard Michaels and Christopher Ricks (Berkeley: University of California Press, 1980), p. 54.]

A writer would not want to cite this passage simply to illustrate that clichés are "bad"—uses of language that are to be avoided—or to suggest, as a dictionary might, that a cliché is a form of expression one might call "hackneyed" or "outworn" or "tattered," even though this information is clearly included in Ricks' sentences. Nor would a writer simply want to reiterate Ricks' leading claim, that "The only way to speak of a cliché is with a cliché," because Ricks has already said that.

Instead, you'd need to talk about how Ricks treats the topic—that he has uncovered a paradox, for example, in that first sentence. You might go on to say that his point of view provides a useful warning for those who wish to talk about clichés. And then you might make some inferences you could build on: that simply dismissing clichés on rhetorical grounds as unoriginal (hackneyed) does not add anything to our knowledge, and so perhaps it is time to rethink our usual response to clichés and see them afresh. In any case, as a rule of thumb, only include a quotation if you plan to say something about it.

Ways to Use a Source as a Point of Departure

There are many ways of approaching secondary sources, but they share a common goal: to use the source as a point of departure. In the next section of this chapter, we offer six new strategies for analyzing sources.

Here is a quick summary of strategies you've already encountered in this book that can help you make better use of sources:

- Make as many points as you can about a single representative passage from your source, and then branch out from this center to analyze other passages that "speak" to it in some way. (See "10 on 1" and "Pan, Track, and Zoom" in Chapter 6.)

- Use Notice & Focus to identify what you find most strange in the source (See Chapter 1.); this will help you cultivate your curiosity about the source and find the critical distance necessary to thinking about it.

- Use The Method to identify the most significant organizing contrast in the source (See Chapter 1.); this will help you see what the source itself is wrestling with, what is at stake in it.

- Apply an idea in the source to another subject. (See "Apply a Reading as a Lens" in Chapter 2.)

- Uncover the assumptions in the source, and then build upon the source's point of view, extending its implications. (See Uncovering Assumptions in Chapter 2.)

- Agree with most of what the source says, but take issue with one small part that you want to modify.

- Identify a contradiction in the source, and explore its implications, without necessarily arriving at a solution.

In using a source as a point of departure, you are in effect using it as a stimulus for having an idea. If you quote or paraphrase a source with the aim of conversing rather than allowing it to do your thinking for you, you will discover that sources can promote rather than stifle your ability to have ideas. Remember to think of sources not as answers but as voices inviting you into a community of interpretation, discussion, and debate.

Six Strategies for Analyzing Sources

Many people never get beyond like/dislike responses with secondary materials. If they agree with what a source says, they say it's "good," and they cut and paste the part they can use as an answer. If the source somehow disagrees with what they already believe, they say it's "bad," and they attack it or—along with readings they find "hard" or "boring"—discard it. As readers they have been conditioned to develop a point of view on a subject without first figuring out the conversation (the various points of view) that their subject attracts. They assume, in other words, that their subject probably has a single meaning—a gist—disclosed by experts, who mostly agree. These six strategies offer ways to avoid this trap:

Six Strategies for Analyzing Sources

Strategy 1: Make Your Sources Speak

Strategy 2: Attend Carefully to the Language of Your Sources by Quoting or Paraphrasing

Strategy 3: Supply Ongoing Analysis of Sources (Don't Wait Until the End)

Strategy 4: Use Your Sources to Ask Questions, Not Just to Provide Answers

Strategy 5: Put Your Sources into Conversation with One Another

Strategy 6: Find Your Own Role in the Conversation

Strategy 1: Make Your Sources Speak

Quote, paraphrase, or summarize *in order to* analyze—not *in place of* analyzing. Don't assume that either the meaning of the source material or your reason for including it is self-evident. Stop yourself from the habit of just stringing together quotations for which you provide little more than conjunctions. Instead, explain to your readers what the quotation or paraphrase or summary of the source means. What elements of it do you find interesting, revealing, or strange? Emphasize how those affect your evolving thesis.

In making a source speak, focus on articulating how the source has led to the conclusion you draw from it. Beware of simply putting a generalization and a quotation next to each other (juxtaposing them) without explaining the connection. Instead, fill the crucial site between claim and evidence with your thinking. Consider this problem in the following paragraph from a student's paper on political conservatism:

> Edmund Burke's philosophy evolved into contemporary American conservative ideology. There is an important distinction between philosophy and political ideology: philosophy is "the knowledge of general principles that explain facts and existences." Political ideology, on the other hand, is "an overarching conception of society, a stance that is reflected in numerous sectors of social life" (Edwards 22). Therefore, conservatism should be regarded as an ideology rather than a philosophy.

The final sentence offers the writer's conclusion—what the source information has led him to—but how did the source get him there? The writer's choice of the word "therefore" indicates to the reader that the idea following it is the result of a process of logical reasoning, but this reasoning has been omitted. Instead, the writer assumes that the reader will be able to connect the quotations with his conclusion. The writer needs to make the quotation speak by analyzing its key terms more closely.

By contrast, writer Emily Casey makes her sources speak. Focus on how she integrates analysis with quotation in this early paragraph from an essay comparing two rhetorical theorists:

> Bartholomae first discusses the process of student writing. He says in his first paragraph, "Every time a student sits down to write for us, he has to invent the university. [...] He has to learn to speak our language, to speak as we do, to try on the peculiar ways of knowing, selecting, evaluating, reporting, concluding, and arguing that define the discourse of our community" (Bartholomae 1). Students, then, have to take on that long list Bartholomae lays out: knowing, selecting, evaluating, reporting, concluding and arguing. It makes sense, then, that the students would have to pretend that they are capable of doing all six, as that seems rather a monumental task. Bartholomae recognizes that there is a good amount of pretending, but he argues that this appropriation, this taking, is necessary to gain access through the gates of the Academy. "I think that all writers, in order to write, must imagine for themselves the privilege of being 'insiders,'" he claims, saying that students must imagine themselves with the authority that a scholar might have, in order for them to have the confidence and clarity with which to properly utilize the right vocabulary, choosing the appropriate language with the skilled hands of a member of that elite society (Bartholomae 1).

We have underlined the places where the writer moves from quotation to implication. Initially, she focuses on a piece of the evidence—the "long list" that Bartholomae uses—as implying "the monumental task" facing inexperienced writers, of "pretending" they are fluent speakers of academic language. That necessity of pretending is the conclusion she draws about the implications of the quotation. She immediately follows with a second quotation from the essay, which she then paraphrases ("saying that") to draw a further implication: that Bartholomae recognizes and sympathizes with the challenges student writers face. Note that making a source speak involves both paraphrasing what the source says and moving beyond that to explore what its logic suggests.

Strategy 2: Attend Carefully to the Language of Your Sources by Quoting or Paraphrasing

Rather than generalizing broadly about ideas in your sources, spell out what you think is significant about their key words. In those disciplines in which it is permissible, *quote sources if the actual language that they use is important to your point.*

Generally, disciplines in the humanities expect you to quote as well as paraphrase, while in the social sciences, students are encouraged to paraphrase, not quote.

Quoting and paraphrasing have the benefit of helping writers to represent the views of their sources fairly and accurately. In situations in which quoting is not allowed—such as in the report format in the discipline of psychology—you still need to attend carefully to the meaning of key words in order to arrive at a summary or paraphrase that is not overly general. As we have argued in Chapter 2, paraphrasing provides an ideal way to begin interpreting, because the act of careful rephrasing usually illuminates attitudes and assumptions implicit in a text. It is almost impossible not to have ideas and not to see the questions when you start paraphrasing.

Quoting and paraphrasing are important because your analysis of a source will nearly always benefit from attention to the way the source represents its position. The content or information being conveyed by a source is always influenced by how it is presented. If you are going to quote *The Huffington Post* on conflicts in Syria, for example, you will be encountering not "the truth" about American involvement in this Middle Eastern nation but rather one particular representation of the situation—in this case, one crafted to meet or shape the expectations of mainstream popular culture. Similarly, if you quote Donald Trump on terrorism, what probably matters most is that the president chose particular words to represent—and promote—the government's position. It is not neutral information. The person speaking, and the kind of source in which the person's words appear, usually acquire added significance when you make note of these words rather than just summarizing them.

In sum, you should aim to:

- Quote, paraphrase, or summarize *in order to* analyze. Explain what you take the source to mean, showing the reasoning that has led to the conclusion you draw from it.

- Quote sparingly. You are usually better off centering your analysis on a few quotations, analyzing the key terms, and branching out to aspects of your subject that the quotations illuminate. (Remember, not all disciplines allow direct quotation.)

- Recognize the value of close paraphrasing. You will almost invariably begin to interpret a source once you start paraphrasing its key language.

- Acknowledge the rhetorical agenda of the quotation—that who says it in what context is a significant part of its meaning.

Strategy 3: Supply Ongoing Analysis of Sources (Don't Wait Until the End)

Unless disciplinary conventions dictate otherwise, analyze *as* you quote or paraphrase a source, rather than summarizing everything first and leaving your analysis for the end. A good conversation does not consist of long monologues alternating among the speakers. Participants exchange views, query, and modify what other speakers have said. Similarly, when you orchestrate conversations with and among your sources, you need to integrate your analysis into your presentation of them.

In supplying ongoing analysis, you are much more likely to explain how the information in the sources fits into your unfolding presentation, and your readers will be more likely to follow your train of thought and grasp the logic of your organization. You will also prevent yourself from using the sources simply as an answer. A good rule of thumb in this regard is to force yourself to ask and answer "So What?" at the ends of paragraphs. In laying out your analysis, however, take special care to distinguish your voice from the sources. (For discussion of integrating your own language with language from your sources, see "Integrating Quotations Into Your Paper," later in this chapter.)

In the following Voice from Across the Curriculum, psychology professor Alan Tjeltveit offers a tip about how members of his discipline orchestrate a number of sources on more than one topic.

VOICES FROM ACROSS THE CURRICULUM

Bringing Sources Together: A Psychology Professor Speaks

Avoid serial citation summaries; that is, rather than discussing what Author A found, then what Author B found, then what Author C found, and so forth, *integrate* material from all of your sources. For instance, if writing about the cause and treatment of a disorder, discuss what all authors say about cause, then what all authors say about treatment, and so forth, addressing any contradictions or tensions among authors.

—ALAN TJELTVEIT, PROFESSOR OF PSYCHOLOGY

Strategy 4: Use Your Sources to Ask Questions, Not Just Provide Answers

Use your selections from sources as a means of raising issues and questions. Avoid the temptation to plug in such selections as answers that require no further commentary or elaboration. You will no doubt find viewpoints you believe to be valid, but it is not enough to drop these answers from the source into your own writing at the appropriate spots. You need to *do* something with the reading, even with sources that seem to have said what you want to say.

As long as you consider only the source in isolation, you may not discover much to say about it. Once you begin considering it in other contexts and with other sources, you may begin to see aspects of your subject that your source does not adequately address. Having recognized that the source does not answer all questions, you should not conclude that the source is "wrong"—only that it is limited in some ways. Discovering such limitations is in fact advantageous, because it can lead you to identify a place from which to launch your own analysis.

In the next example, writer Kate O'Donoghue uses a source to stimulate her thinking. In a paper about the implied audience in the film *Gentlemen Prefer Blondes*, she analyzes the opening song, "Little Rock":

> Turin claims that the film's audience is "never given spectacle for its own sake— each instance of performance/seduction is grounded in a logical purpose. [. . .] This embedding acts as a justifying force, tempering the eroticism" of the performance (372). In other words, in this film, each "performance/seduction" *should* have a narrative purpose and *should not* be pure spectacle. How "Little Rock" differs from this formula must then be significant, as it is pure opening number—it is not grounded (at first) in narrative purpose, nor does it "temper" its supposed eroticism. In almost direct contrast to Turin's claim, the film's audience is thrown straight into the performance without even a hint as to who these characters are, nor why they are performing for us and/or the fictional audience.

Note that the writer's analysis begins by quoting and then paraphrasing the claim that the source has made (as indicated by beginning the next sentence with "in other words"). At the same time, her rewording brings out implications from the claim: the italicized terms suggest Turin's assumptions about what a film should do, and should not be. But perhaps most interestingly, in order to spur her own thinking she locates an instance (the opening production number, "Little Rock") in which the scholar's rules do *not* fit the "formula." The tension between the source and the evidence, in other words, raises questions that the writer will go on to answer in her essay. As readers, we are taken along on the cognitive journey that Kate is taking, and we are made privy both to what an expert thinks, which is interesting in itself, and to what Kate thinks as she attempts to puzzle out why the film uses the opening number as it does. This example also illustrates a widespread and extremely useful practice in analyzing quotations: the repetition of key words from the quotation in the discussion that follows it. This practice, which we call the use of "spot quotes," helps to anchor readers in the discussion, identifying for us the specific language that the writer is using as evidence in her interpretation of the quotation. In the example about "Little Rock," Kate O'Donoghue puts "performance/seduction" and "temper" in spot quotes both to clarify and emphasize key points.

In using sources to ask questions, it does not necessarily follow that your analysis will culminate in an answer to replace those offered by your sources. Often—in fact, far more often than many writers suspect—it is enough to discover issues or problems and raise them clearly. Phrasing explicitly the issues and questions that remain implicit in a source is an important part of what analytical writers do, especially with cases in which there is no solution, or at least none that can be presented in a relatively short paper. Here, for example, is how Marie Goldzung, writing about Stephen Greenblatt's concept of self-fashioning, concludes her essay:

It is not only the author whose role is complicated by New Historicism; the critic also is subject to some of the same qualifications and restrictions. According to Adam Begley, "it is the essence of the new-historicist project to uncover the moments at which works of art absorb and refashion social energy, an endless process of circulation and exchange" (39). In other words, the work is both affected by and affects the culture. But if this is so, how then can we decide which elements of culture (and text) are causes and which are effects? If we add the critic to this picture, the process does indeed appear endless. The New Historicists' relationship with their culture infuses itself into their assessment of the Renaissance, and this assessment may in turn become part of their own self-fashioning process, which will affect their interpretations, and so forth....

Notice that this writer incorporates the quotation into her own chain of thinking. By paraphrasing the quotation ("In other words"), she arrives at a question ("how then?") that follows as a logical consequence of accepting its position ("but if this is so"). Note, however, that she does not then label the quotation right or wrong. Instead, she tries to figure out to what position it might lead and to what possible problems.

By contrast, the writer of the following excerpt, from a paper comparing two films aimed at teenagers, settles for plugging in sources as answers and consequently does not pursue the questions implicit in her quotations:

In both films, the adults are one-dimensional caricatures, evil beings whose only goal in life is to make the kids' lives a living hell. In *Risky Business*, director Paul Brickman's solution to all of Joel's problems is to have him hire a prostitute and then turn his house into a whorehouse. Of course, as one critic observes, "the prostitutes who make themselves available to his pimply faced buddies are all centerfold beauties: elegant, svelte, benign and unquestionably healthy (after all, what does V.D. have to do with prostitutes?)" (Gould 41)—not exactly a realistic or legal solution. Allan Moyle, the director of *Pump Up the Volume*, provides an equally unrealistic solution to Mark's problem. According to David Denby, Moyle "offers self-expression as the cure to adolescent funk. Everyone should start his own radio station and talk about his feelings" (59). Like Brickman, Moyle offers solutions that are neither realistic nor legal.

This writer is having a hard time figuring out what to do with sources that offer well-phrased and seemingly accurate answers (such as "self-expression is the cure to adolescent funk"). She settles for the bland conclusion that films aimed at teenagers are not "realistic"—an observation that most readers would already recognize as true. But unlike the writer of the previous example, she does not ask herself, "If this is true, then what follows?" Some version of the "So What?" question might have led her to inquire how the illegality of the solutions is related to their unrealistic quality. So what, for example, that the main characters in both films are not marginalized as criminals and made to suffer for their illegal actions, but rather are celebrated as heroes? What different kinds of illegality do the two films apparently condone, and how might these be related to the different decades in which each film was produced? Rather than use her sources to think with, in order to clarify or complicate the issues, the writer has used them to confirm a fairly obvious generalization.

Strategy 5: Put Your Sources Into Conversation with One Another

Rather than limiting yourself to agreeing or disagreeing with your sources, aim for conversation with and among them. Although it is not wrong to agree or disagree with your sources, it is wrong to see these as your only possible moves. It is okay to summarize a position that you intend to challenge in a carefully qualified way. It is not okay to construct a "dummy" position specifically in order to knock it down (the practice sometimes known as a "straw man").

In any case, if you are citing a source in order to frame the discussion, the more reasonable move is both to agree *and* disagree with it. First, identify shared premises; give the source some credit. Then distinguish the part of what you have cited that you intend to develop or complicate or dispute. This method of proceeding is obviously less combative than the typically blunt straw man approach; it verges on conversation.

In the following passage from a student's paper on Darwin's theory of evolution, the student clearly recognizes that he needs to do more than summarize what Darwin says, but he seems not to know any way of conversing with his source other than indicating his agreement and disagreement with it.

> The struggle for existence also includes the dependence of one being on another being to survive. Darwin also believes that all organic beings tend to increase. I do not fully agree with Darwin's belief here. I cannot conceive of the fact of all beings increasing in number. Darwin goes on to explain that food, competition, climate, and the location of a certain species contribute to its survival and existence in nature. I believe that this statement is very valid and that it could be very easily understood through experimentation in nature.

This writer's use of the word "here" in his third sentence is revealing. He is tagging summaries of Darwin with what he seems to feel is an obligatory response—a polite shake or nod of the head: "I can't fully agree with you there, Darwin, but here I think you might have a point." The writer's tentative language lets us see how uncomfortable, even embarrassed, he feels about venturing these judgments on a subject that is too complex for this kind of response. It's as though the writer moves along, talking about Darwin's theory for a while, and then says to himself, "Time for a response," and lets a particular summary sentence trigger a yes/no switch. Having pressed that switch, which he does periodically, the writer resumes his summary, having registered—but not having analyzed—his own interjections. There is no reasoning in a chain from his own observations, just random insertions of unanalyzed agree/disagree responses.

Here, by contrast, is the introduction of an previously quoted essay by Marie Goldzung, which uses summary to frame the conversation that the writer is preparing to have with her source.

> In *Renaissance Thought: The Classic, Scholastic and Humanist Strains*, Paul Kristeller responds to two problems that he perceives in Renaissance scholarship. The first is the haze of cultural meaning surrounding the word "humanism": he seeks to clarify the word and its origins, as well as to explain the apparent lack of religious concern in humanism. Kristeller also reacts to the notion of humanism as an improvement upon medieval Aristotelian scholasticism.

Rather than leading with her own beliefs about the source, the writer emphasizes the issues and problems she believes are the main focus of Kristeller's book. Although the writer's position on her source is apparently neutral, she is not summarizing passively. In addition to making choices about what is especially significant in the source, she has also located it within the conversation that its author, Kristeller, was having with his own sources—the works of other scholars whose view of humanism he wants to revise ("Kristeller responds to two problems").

In more extended, research-based writing projects, an effective strategy is for the writer to offer a map of the scholarship. This move both helps readers get a broader view of the critical conversations that are going on, and establishes the grounds within which the writer will locate their particular contribution. Note how the writer of the following excerpt, in his paper, "Progressive Era Women and Public Sphere Involvement," offers such a map:

> Two distinctive groups of historians surface in the scholarship: those who think that the Progressive Era clearly and distinctively marked an overt revolution of sexuality and gender in the US (like Michael Katz and Kim England) and those who assert that the change in gendered and sexuality norms shifted in the attempt to fit into the new nation's industrial set up (like Eileen Boris, Catherine Cocks, Kathleen Cummings, and Julie Norkov). Both sides of this discussion attempt to explain the Progressive Era in gender normative terms and sound much more like gender historians than women's history historians (considering that explanations of both sides utilize interactions between men and women in political, social, and economic settings to highlight the change in gender norms in the US during this time).

The writer, Steven Poirier, establishes authority by demonstrating his conversancy with the big picture. He follows with an elaboration of both sides in the scholarly discussion, before moving on to locate his own voice in the discussion.

Perhaps the best way to break the habit of agreeing/disagreeing with sources is to try constructing the conversation that you think the author of one of your sources might have with the author of another. How might they recast each other's ideas, as opposed to merely agreeing or disagreeing with those ideas? Where might they find common ground? Let's return to the essay by Emily Casey, which we excerpted earlier in this chapter, for a demonstration of this approach. Notice how, as she establishes the conversation, her blend of summary, quotation, and analysis highlights issues and problems that she believes are central to that conversation. Although her position is apparently neutral, she is not summarizing passively or inertly.

> Elbow calls out writing teachers who believe that "students can get along without the private writing serious writers find so crucial—or even that students will *benefit* from keeping their audience in mind for the whole time" (Elbow 3). Here we see Elbow specifically advocating for what he calls "private writing," meaning writing for oneself, as opposed to "public writing," writing to the audience as Bartholomae would suggest doing. However, Bartholomae and the writing teachers that Elbow criticizes are not one in the same; Bartholomae finds fault, too, in writing solely for an audience—that is, he notes the problem that students are intimidated by writing for the discourse community. His solution is where he and Elbow disagree, as Bartholomae advocates for the complete immersion and understanding of the discourse before writing, while Elbow wants the writer to factor in the audience after the private writing that he finds so important. "After," Elbow says, "we have figured out our thinking in copious exploratory"—extremely intense detailed thought and analysis—"or draft writing . . . then we can follow the traditional rhetorical advice: think about audience and revise carefully to adjust our words and thoughts to our intended audience" (Elbow 3). Elbow finds power in a writer's own ability to untangle the argument of the discourse, while Bartholomae would rather the writer find power in the already established conventions.

Notice how carefully the writer moves among positions. Early in the excerpt she distinguishes the "private" Elbow from the "public" Bartholomae, but then qualifies that the latter theorist "finds fault too" with "writing solely for an audience." The cognitive move here is "similarity despite difference"— an analytical version of comparison and contrast discussed in Chapter 4. Does the student writer seem to prefer Elbow's confidence in the power of the writer's voice to Bartholomae's emphasis on learning and obeying the conventions of any given writing situation? Perhaps—but her primary focus remains on the common problem that both theorists tackle, of how college writers negotiate the struggle to locate themselves in academic writing. In so doing, she deftly orchestrates the points of disparity and accord between her sources. The next step, for her and for most writers, is to figure out where she stands in relation to these sources. The next strategy addresses this issue.

Strategy 6: Find Your Own Role in the Conversation

Even in cases in which you find a source's position entirely congenial, it is not enough simply to agree with it. You need to find something of your own to say about it.

In general, you have two options when you find yourself strongly in agreement with a source. You can (1) apply it in another context to qualify or expand its implications. Or you can (2) seek out other perspectives on the source in order to break the spell it has cast upon you. To break the spell means that you will necessarily become somewhat disillusioned but not that you will then need to dismiss everything you previously believed.

How, in the first option, do you take a source somewhere else? Rather than focusing solely on what you believe your source finds most important, locate a lesser point, not emphasized by the reading, that you find especially interesting and develop it further. This strategy will lead you to uncover new implications that depend upon your source but lie outside its own governing preoccupations. In the preceding humanism example, Marie Goldzung might apply Kristeller's claims about Renaissance Italy to new geographic (rather than theoretical) areas, such as Germany.

Or consider how Emily Casey takes the key ideas of Bartholomae and Elbow and applies them to a new context near the end of her paper:

> Both Bartholomae and Elbow want student writers to be comfortable with their audience, and they both want the writers to eventually get to the place where they are engaged with ease [. . .]. It is in this similarity that we are provided insight as to why their differences matter; all student writers must take on a discourse that they may not be comfortable with, so it is crucial that their professors know different methods or theories on how they may achieve that appropriation. This is even more crucial for the tutors-in-training, who need to be the liminal cross-over between student and professor, the ultimate appropriation, to know how to successfully balance the language of a specialized disciplinary discourse and the language the student will understand. The tutor, then, can determine in the moment whether the student should be thrust into the deep end of the discourse without being taught how to swim, or perhaps led to paddle around in the middle part, until he or she is ready to dive in alone.

This paper, written in a training course for writing tutors, moves at the end to consider the way that the advice Bartholomae and Elbow give college teachers might be applied to the particular needs of writing center tutors.

The second option for finding your role in the scholarly conversation—researching new perspectives on the source—can also lead to uncovering new implications. Your aim need not be simply to find a source that disagrees with the one that has convinced you and then switch your allegiance, because this move would perpetuate the problem from which you are trying to escape. Instead, you would use additional perspectives to gain some critical distance from your source. An ideal way of sampling possible critical approaches to a source is to consult book reviews on it published in scholarly journals. Once the original source is taken down from the pedestal through additional reading, there is a greater likelihood that you will see how to distinguish your views from those it offers.

Especially in the case of extensive research projects, you will have the opportunity to accumulate perspectives, leading you to an increasingly complex apprehension of the subject. The more familiar you become with the learning community, the more spaces you will see to develop a point of view. In the following example, taken from an upper-level history seminar, consider how Patrick C. Smith moves among perspectives as he focuses on the National Centennial Exhibition of 1876:

> Recent scholarly narratives about Reconstruction and the Gilded Age that followed, such as David Blight's seminal *Race and Reunion* and Eric Foner's *Reconstruction*, demonstrate a popular push for white reconciliation beginning with Johnson's presidency and continuing beyond Hayes's withdrawal of Union military forces from the South in 1877. At the expense of a semi-healed bond between white North and South, the disenfranchisement of African-Americans has continued into the 21st century; Blight frames this as the sacrifice of black justice for the sake of white reconciliation. Mitch Kachun has studied this phenomenon in play at the Centennial itself: while African-Americans struggled with their place in the national story, white Exhibition organizers excluded them from construction crews, fundraising, and participation in ceremonies.[1] While Blight, Foner, Kachun, and Silber have suggested that the Centennial's construction of Americanness was a consciously shaped effort to showcase the best of the nation's past and future, this paper is the first to examine what participation and representation in the Centennial meant to both African-Americans and white Southerners: the perspectives of both are key to understanding the Exhibition's relationship with the Civil War in the context of American history.

By bringing together two perspectives that he argues need to be understood in relation to each other, the writer finds his own role in the conversation. He first posits that the push for "white reconciliation" between the North and the South, which required the "disenfranchisement" of African Americans, is generally part of "the American story." He then moves to the specific historical instance of this story, "the Centennial itself." Next, he cites four different sources to validate that the story was "consciously shaped" in order to clear the space for his contribution: to focus on the reception of the Centennial by two important audiences, African Americans and Southern White people. In short, the writer has constructed a map of the scholarly conversation, both general and specific, to disclose the uncharted territory that his work will proceed to explore and map.

One final implication of this example might well be that if you can't find a perspective on a given source or topic, you probably haven't done enough research.

In the following Voice from Across the Curriculum, molecular biologist Bruce Wightman suggests the range of tasks he expects students to do when they engage a source—not only to supply ongoing analysis of it and to consider its contributions in light of other research—but also to locate themselves in relation to the questions their analysis of the source has led them to discover.

Engaging Sources in the Sciences: A Biology Professor Speaks

One of the problems with trying to *read* critical analyses of scientific work is that few scientists want to be in print criticizing their colleagues. That is, for political reasons scientists who write reviews are likely to soften their criticism or even avoid it entirely by reporting the findings of others simply and directly.

What I want from students in molecular biology is a critical analysis of the work they have researched. This can take several forms.

First, *analyze* what was done. What were the assumptions (hypotheses) going into the experiment? What was the logic of the experimental design? What were the results?

Second, *evaluate* the results and conclusions. How well do the results support the conclusions? What alternative interpretations are there? What additional experiments could be done to strengthen or refute the argument? This is hard, no doubt, but it is what you should be doing every time you read anything in science or otherwise.

Third, *synthesize* the results and interpretations of a given experiment in the context of the field. How does this study inform other studies? Even though practicing scientists are hesitant to do this in print, everyone does it informally in journal clubs held usually on a weekly basis in every lab all over the world.

—BRUCE WIGHTMAN, PROFESSOR OF BIOLOGY

Using Sources Analytically: An Example

In her article on thinking, "The Other You," which appeared in the journal *New Scientist*, writer Kate Douglas introduces sources in sequence, wherein each source offers a different researcher's angle on the same central question: how is the subconscious related to the conscious activities of the mind? Douglas discusses the implications of each source without choosing any one as "the answer":

- "Shadlin sees the subconscious and conscious as two parts of the same system, rather than two separate thought processors working in the same machine."

- "Others want to further subdivide conscious and subconscious thought and have come up with alternative descriptions to replace the old two-part model."

- "Peter Dayan [and colleagues] see the mind as comprising four systems."

- "Dayan says that our behavior is often driven by more than one of the four controllers."

At the end of this phase of the article, Douglas then states, "Importantly, the subconscious isn't the dumb cousin of the conscious, but rather a cousin with different skills" (Kate Douglas, "The Subconscious Mind: Your Unsung Hero," *New Scientist*, December 1–7, 2007, vol. 196, no. 2632, p. 45.).

As this example demonstrates, often in conversing with sources a writer is not staging conflicts or debates, but bringing together multiple points of view and offering a concluding synthesis. Those familiar with the popular journalist Malcolm Gladwell may recognize that he is fond of this method. In books such as *Blink*, Gladwell presents one piece of research, and in making inferences about it leads us to the next and often unexpectedly related piece of research. Part of the appeal of Gladwell's method is how he quilts together a range of disparate voices into one unfolding narrative. The thinking in a Gladwell piece is presented in the way he connects the parts, not in the way that he is critiquing them, finding shortcomings, or emphasizing the differences.

Integrating Quotations Into Your Paper

An enormous number of writers lose authority and readability because they have never learned how to correctly integrate quotations into their own writing. The following guidelines should help. (For more detail on different citation styles, see Chapter 9.) The primary rules of thumb here are that you should:

- Tell your readers in the text of your paper, not just in citations, when you are using someone else's words, ideas, or information; rewording someone else's idea doesn't make it your idea.

- Always attach a quotation to some of your own language; never let it stand as its own sentence in your text.

1. **Acknowledge sources in your text, not just in citations.** *When you incorporate material from a source, attribute it to the source explicitly in your text—not just in a citation.* In other words, when you introduce the material, *frame it with a phrase such as "according to Sprayberry" or "as Gruen argues."*

   Although it is not required, you are usually much better off making the attribution overtly, even if you have also cited the source within parentheses or with a footnote at the end of the last sentence quoted, paraphrased, or summarized. If a passage does not contain an attribution, your readers will not know that it comes from a source until they reach the citation at the end. Attributing up front clearly distinguishes what one source says from what another says and, perhaps more importantly, what your sources say from what you say. Useful verbs for introducing attributions include the following: notes, observes, argues, comments, writes, says, reports, suggests, and claims. Cite the author by last name only— "Gruen," not "William Gruen" or "Mr. Gruen." (In some cases, the first time you mention a source, you may use both the author's first and last name.)

2. **Splice quotations onto your own words.** *Always frame quotations with some of your own language; don't let them sit in your text as independent sentences with quotation marks around them.* You can normally satisfy this rule with an attributive phrase—commonly known as a "tag phrase"—that introduces the quotation.

> According to Paul McCartney, "All you need is love."

Note that the tag phrase takes a comma before the quote.

Alternatively you can splice quotations into your text with a setup: a statement followed by a colon.

> Patrick Henry's famous phrase is one of the first that American schoolchildren memorize: "Give me liberty, or give me death."

The colon, you should notice, usually comes at the end of an independent clause (that is, a subject plus verb that can stand alone), where a period normally goes. It would be incorrect to write

> Patrick Henry is known for: "Give me liberty, or give me death."

The rationale for this guideline on splicing in quotations is essentially the same as that for the previous one: if you are going to move to quotation, you first need to identify its author so that your readers will be able to put it in context quickly.

Spliced quotations frequently create problems in grammar or punctuation for writers. Whether you include an entire sentence (or passage) of quotation or just a few phrases, you need to take care to integrate them into the grammar of your own sentence.

One common mistaken assumption is that a comma should always precede a quotation, as in

> A spokesperson for the public defender's office demanded, "an immediate response from the mayor."

The sentence structure does not call for any punctuation after "demanded."

3. **Cite sources after quotations.** *Locate citations in parentheses after the quotation and before the final period.* The information about the source appears at the end of the sentence, with the final period following the closing parenthesis.

> A recent article on the best-selling albums in America claimed that "Ever since Elvis, it has been pop music's job to challenge the mores of the older generation" (Hornby 168).

Note that there is normally *no punctuation* at the end of the quotation, either before or after the closing quotation mark. A quotation that ends either in a question mark or an exclamation mark is an exception to this rule because the sign is an integral part of the quotation's meaning.

As Hamlet says to Rosencrantz and Guildenstern, "And yet to me what is this quintessence of dust?" (2.2.304–05).

See the section "How to Cite Sources" in Chapter 9 for the appropriate formats for in-text citations.

4. **Use ellipses to shorten quotations.** *Add an ellipsis to indicate that you have omitted some of the language from within the quotation.* Form ellipses by entering three dots (periods) with spaces in between them, or use four dots to indicate that the deletion continues to the end of the sentence (the last dot becomes the period). Suppose you wanted to shorten the following quotation from an article about Radiohead by Alex Ross:

> The album "OK Computer," with titles like "Paranoid Android," "Karma Police," and "Climbing Up the Walls," pictured the onslaught of the information age and a young person's panicky embrace of it (Ross 85).

Using ellipses, you can emphasize the source's claim by omitting the song titles from the sentence:

> The album "OK Computer". . . pictured the onslaught of the information age and a young person's panicky embrace of it (Ross 85).

In most cases, the gap between quoted passages should be short, and in any case, you should be careful to preserve the sense of the original. The standard joke about ellipses is pertinent here: A reviewer writes a savage review of a film, saying that it "will delight no one and appeal to the intelligence of invertebrates only, but not average viewers." An unethical advertiser cobbles together pieces of the review to say that the film "will delight. . . and appeal to the intelligence of. . . viewers."

5. **Use square brackets to alter or add information within a quotation.** Sometimes it is necessary to change the wording slightly inside a quotation to maintain fluency. Square brackets indicate that you are altering the original quotation. Brackets are also used when you insert explanatory information, such as a definition or example, within a quotation. Here are a few examples that alter the original quotations previously cited.

> According to one music critic, the cultural relevance of Radiohead is evident in "the album 'OK Computer'. . .[which] pictured the onslaught of the information age and a young person's panicky embrace of it" (Ross 85).

> Popular music has always "[challenged] the mores of the older generation," according to Nick Hornby (168).

Note that both examples respect the original sense of the quotation; they have changed the wording only to integrate the quotations gracefully within the writer's own sentence structure.

Preparing an Abstract

There is one more skill essential to research-based writing that we need to discuss: how to prepare an abstract. The aim of the nonevaluative summary of a source known as an abstract is to represent a source's arguments as fairly and accurately as possible, not to critique them. Learning how to compose an abstract according to the conventions of a given discipline is a necessary skill for academic researched writing. Because abstracts differ in format and length among disciplines, you should sample some in the reference section of your library or search the Internet for models to imitate. Some abstracts, such as those in *Dissertation Abstracts*, are very brief—less than 250 words. Others may run as long as two pages.

Despite disciplinary differences, abstracts by and large follow a generalizable format. The abstract should begin with a clear, specific explanation of the work's governing thesis (or argument). This opening paragraph should also define the work's purpose, and possibly include established positions that it tries to refine, qualify, or argue against. What kind of critical approach does it adopt? What are its aims? On what assumptions does it rest? Why did the author feel it necessary to write the work—that is, what does the author believe the work offers that other sources don't? What shortcomings or misrepresentations in other criticism does the work seek to correct? (For specifics on writing abstracts in the natural sciences, see Chapter 10, "From Paragraphs to Papers: Forms and Formats Across the Curriculum.")

You won't be able to produce detailed answers to all of these questions in your opening paragraph, but in trying to answer some of them in your note taking and drafting, you should find it easier to arrive at the kind of concise, substantive, and focused overview that the first paragraph of your abstract should provide. Also, be careful not to settle for bland, all-purpose generalities in this opening paragraph. And if you quote there, keep the selections short and remember that quotations don't speak for themselves.

In summary, your aim in the first paragraph of an abstract is to define the source's particular angle of vision and articulate its main point or points, including the definition of key terms used in its title or elsewhere in its argument.

Once you've set up this overview of the source's central position(s), you should devote a paragraph or so to the source's *organization* (how it divides its subject into parts) and its *method* (how it goes about substantiating its argument). What kind of secondary material does the source use? That is, how do its own bibliographic citations cue you to its school of thought, its point of view, its research traditions?

Your concluding paragraph should briefly recount some of the source's conclusions (as related to, but not necessarily the same as, its thesis). In what way does it culminate its argument? What kind of significance does it claim for its position? What final qualifications does it raise?

The following is a good example of an abstract:

Abstract of "William Carlos Williams," an essay

By Christopher MacGowan in *The Columbia History of American Poetry*, 1993 (395–418).

MacGowan's is a chronologically organized account of Williams' poetic career and of his relation to both modernism as an international movement and modernism as it affected the development of poetry in America. MacGowan is at some pains both to differentiate Williams from some features of modernism (such as the tendency of American writers to write as well as live away from their own cultural roots) and to link Williams to modernism. MacGowan argues, for example, that an essential feature of Williams's commitment as a poet was to "the local—to the clear presentation of what was under his nose and in front of his eyes" (385).

But he also takes care to remind us that Williams was in no way narrowly provincial, having studied in Europe as a young man (at Leipzig), having had a Spanish mother and an English father, having become friendly with the poets Ezra Pound and H. D. while getting his medical degree at the University of Pennsylvania, and having continued to meet important figures in the literary and art worlds by making frequent visits to New York and by traveling on more than one occasion to Europe (where Pound introduced him to W. B. Yeats, among others). Williams corresponded with Marianne Moore, he continued to write to Pound and to show Pound some of his work, and he wrote critical essays on the works of other modernists. MacGowan reminds us that Williams also translated Spanish works (ballads) and so was not out of contact with European influences.

Williams had a long publishing career—beginning in 1909 with a self-published volume called *Poems* and ending more than fifty years later with *Pictures from Brueghel* in 1962. What MacGowan emphasizes about this career is not only the consistently high quality of work, but also its great influence on other artists (he names those who actually corresponded with Williams and visited with him, including Charles Olson, Robert Creeley, Robert Lowell, Allen Ginsberg, and Denise Levertov). MacGowan observes that Williams defined himself "against" T. S. Eliot—the more rewarded and internationally recognized of the two poets, especially during their lifetimes— searching for "alternatives to the prevailing mode of a complex, highly allusive poetics," which Williams saw as Eliot's legacy (395). MacGowan depicts Williams as setting himself "against the international school of Eliot and Pound—Americans he felt wrote about rootlessness and searched an alien past because of their failure to write about and live within their own culture" (397).

What Does Plagiarism Do to the Conversation?

One noteworthy survey indicated that 53 percent of Who's Who High Schoolers thought that plagiarism was no big deal (Sally Cole and Elizabeth Kiss, "What Can We Do About Student Cheating?," *About Campus*, May–June 2000, p. 6). So why should institutions of higher learning care about it? Here are two great reasons:

- Plagiarism poisons the environment. Students who don't cheat are alienated by students who do and get away with it, and faculty can become distrustful of students and even disillusioned about teaching when constantly driven to track down students' sources. It is much easier, by the way, than most students think for faculty to recognize language and ideas that are not the student's own. Furthermore, search engines like the one provided by Turnitin.com have been generated in response to the Internet paper-mill boom.

- Plagiarism defeats the purpose of going to college, which is learning how to think. You can't learn to think by just copying others' ideas; you need to learn to trust your own intelligence. Students' panic about deadlines, and their misunderstandings about assignments sometimes spur plagiarism. It is a good bet that your professors would much rather take requests for help and give extra time on assignments than have to go through the anguish of confronting students about plagiarized work.

So, plagiarism gets in the way of trust, fairness, intellectual development, and, ultimately, the attitude toward learning that sets the tone for a college or university community.

Frequently Asked Questions (FAQS) about Plagiarism

Is it still plagiarism if I didn't intentionally copy someone else's work and present it as my own; as in, if I plagiarized it by accident?
Yes, it is still plagiarism. Colleges and universities put the burden of responsibility on students for knowing what plagiarism is and making the effort necessary to avoid it. Leaving out the quotation marks around someone else's words, or omitting the attribution after a summary of someone else's theory, may be just a mistake—a matter of inadequate documentation—but faculty can only judge what you turn in to them, not what you intended.

If I include a list of works consulted at the end of my paper, doesn't that cover it?
No. A works-cited list (bibliography) tells your readers what you read but leaves them in the dark about how and where this material has been used in your paper. Putting one or more references at the end of a paragraph containing source material is a version of the same problem. The solution is to cite the source at the point that you quote or paraphrase or summarize it. To be even clearer about what comes from where, also use what are called "in-text attributions." See the next FAQ.

What is the best way to help my readers distinguish between what my sources are saying and what I'm saying?

Be overt. Tell your readers in the text of your paper, not just in citations, when you are drawing on someone else's words, ideas, or information. Do this with in-text attributions—phrases like "According to X" or "As noted in X."

Are there some kinds of information that I do not need to document?
Yes. Common knowledge and facts you can find in almost any encyclopedia or basic reference text generally don't need to be documented (for example, John F. Kennedy became president of the United States in 1960). This distinction can get a little tricky because it is not always obvious what is and is not common knowledge. Often, you need to spend some time in a discipline before you discover what others take to be known to all. When in doubt, cite the source.

If I put the information from my sources into my own words, do I still need to include citations?
Yes. Sorry, but rewording someone else's idea doesn't make it your idea. Paraphrasing is a useful activity because it helps you to better understand what you are reading, but paraphrases and summaries have to be documented and carefully distinguished from ideas and information you are representing as your own.

If I don't actually know anything about the subject, is it okay to hand in a paper that is taken entirely from various sources?
It's okay if (1) you document the borrowings and (2) the assignment called for summary. Properly documented summarizing is better than plagiarizing, but most assignments call for something more. Often comparing and contrasting your sources begins to give you ideas so that you can have something to contribute. If you're really stumped, see your professor.

   You also reduce the risk of plagiarism if you consult sources after—not before—you have done some preliminary thinking on the subject. If you have become somewhat invested in your own thoughts on the matter, you will be able to use the sources in a more active way, in effect, making them part of a dialogue.

Is it plagiarism if I include things in my paper that I thought of with another student or a member of my family?
Most academic behavior codes, under the category called "collusion," allow for students' cooperative efforts only with the explicit consent of the instructor. The same rule goes for plagiarizing yourself—that is, for submitting the same paper in more than one class. If you have questions about what constitutes collusion in a particular class, be sure to ask your professor.

What about looking at secondary sources when my professor hasn't asked me to? Is this a form of cheating?

It can be a form of cheating if the intent of the assignment was to get you to develop a particular kind of thinking skill. In this case, looking at others' ideas may actually inhibit your learning process and leave you feeling that you couldn't possibly learn to arrive at ideas on your own.

Professors usually look favorably on students who are willing to take the time to do extra reading on a subject, but it is essential that, even in class discussion, you make it clear that you have consulted outside sources. To conceal that fact is to present others' ideas as your own. Even in class discussion, if you bring up an idea you picked up on the Internet or somewhere else, say so explicitly.

Assignments: Conversing with Sources: Writing the Researched Paper

1. **Make one source speak to another**. Choose two articles or book chapters by different authors on the same subject or by the same author at different points in the author's career. Let's call them Smith and Jones. Then ask yourself, what would Jones think if they read Smith, and vice versa. Locate a particular key passage from each author, and place them in conversation. Use the quotations to ground your reasoning: for example, because Smith says X, they would be likely to have this or that response to Jones when they say Y. Try this exercise in a variety of forms—a focused freewrite, a short essay. The overriding aim of the assignment is to give you practice in getting beyond merely reacting and generalizing, and, instead, participating in your sources' thinking.

   Keep in mind that your aim is not to arrive at your opinion of the sources, but to construct the conversation that you think the author of one of your sources might have with the author of another. How might they recast each other's ideas, as opposed to merely agreeing or disagreeing with those ideas? It's useful to confine yourself to thinking as impartially as you can about the ideas found in your two sources.

2. **Use PASSAGE-BASED FOCUSED FREEWRITING to converse with sources.** Select a passage from a secondary source that appears important to your evolving thinking about a subject you are studying, and do a PASSAGE-BASED FOCUSED FREEWRITING on it. You might choose the passage in answer to the question "What is the one passage in the source that I need to discuss, that poses a question or a problem or that seems in some way difficult to pin down, anomalous or even just unclear?" Copy the passage at the top of the page, and write without stopping for twenty minutes or more. As noted in the discussion of freewriting in Chapter 2, paraphrase key terms as you relentlessly ask "So what?" about the details.

3. **Use a source as a lens on another source.** Apply a brief passage from a secondary source to a brief passage from a primary source, using the passage from the secondary source as a lens. Choose the secondary source passage first—one that you find particularly interesting, revealing, or problematic. Then locate a corresponding passage from the primary source to which the sentence from the first passage can be connected in some way. Copy both passages at the top of the page, and then write for twenty minutes. Include paraphrases of key phrases in both—not just the primary text; your goal is to think about the two together and allow them to interact.

4. **Compose a research sequence.** The traditional sequence of steps for building a research paper—or for any writing that relies on secondary materials—is *summary, comparative analysis, and synthesis.* The following sequence of four exercises addresses the first two steps as discrete activities. (You might, of course, choose to do only some of these exercises.)

A. **Compose an informal prospectus.** Formulate your initial thinking on a subject before you do more research. Include what you already know about the topic, especially what you find interesting, particularly significant, or strange. This exercise helps deter you from being overwhelmed by and absorbed into the sources you later encounter.

B. **Conduct a "What's going on in the field?" search, and create a preliminary list of sources.** This exercise is ideal for helping you to find a topic or, if you already have one, to narrow it. The kinds of bibliographic materials you consult for this portion of the research project depend on the discipline within which you are writing. Whatever the discipline, start in the reference room of your library with specialized indexes (such as the *Social Sciences Index* or the *New York Times Index*), book review indexes, specialized encyclopedias and dictionaries, and bibliographies (print or online) that give you an overview of your subject or topic. If you have access to databases through your school or library, you should also search them. (See the section in Chapter 9 titled "Finding Quality on the Web.")

The "What's going on in the field?" search has two aims:

- To survey materials in order to identify trends—the kinds of issues and questions that others in the field are talking about (and, thus, find important)

- To compile a bibliography that includes a range of titles that interest you, that could be relevant to your prospective topic, and that seem to you representative of research trends associated with your subject (or topic).

You are not committed at this point to pursuing every source, but rather to reporting what is being talked about. You might also compose a list of key words (such as Library of Congress headings) that you have used in conducting your search. If you try this exercise, you will be surprised how much value there is in exploring indexes *just for titles*, to see the kinds of topics people are currently conversing about. And you will almost surely discover how *narrowly* focused most research is (which will get you away from global questions).

Append to your list of sources (a very preliminary bibliography) a few paragraphs of informal discussion of how the information you have encountered (the titles, summaries, abstracts, etc.) has affected your thinking and plans for your paper. These paragraphs might respond to the following questions:

i. In what ways has your "What's going on in the field?" search led you to narrow or shift direction in or focus your thinking about your subject?
ii. How might you use one or more of these sources in your paper?
iii. What has this phase of your research suggested you might need to look for next?

C. **Write an abstract of an article (or book chapter).** Use the procedure offered in the preceding section, "How to Prepare an Abstract." Aim for two pages in length. If other members of your class are working on the same or similar subjects, it is often very useful for everyone to share copies of their abstracts. Remember that your primary concern should lie with representing the argument and point of view of the source as fairly and accurately as possible.

Append to the end of the abstract a paragraph or two that addresses the question "How has this exercise affected your thinking about your topic?" Objectifying your own research process in this way helps move you away from the cut-and-paste–provide-only-the-transitions mode of writing research papers.

D. **Write a comparative summary of two reviews.** Most writers, before they invest the significant time and energy required to study a book-length source, take the much smaller amount of time and energy required to find out more about the book. Although you should always include in your final paper your own analytical summary of books you consult on your topic, it's extremely useful also to find out what experts in the field have to say about the source.

Select from your "What's going on in the field?" list one book-length source that you've discovered is vital to your subject or topic. As a general rule, if a number of your indexes, bibliographies, and the like refer you to the same book, it is a good bet that this source merits consultation.

Locate two book reviews of the book, and write a summary that compares them. Ideally, you should locate two reviews that diverge in their points of view or in what they choose to emphasize. Depending on the length and complexity of the reviews, your comparative summary should require two or three pages.

In most cases, you will find that reviews are less neutral in their points of view than are abstracts, but they always do more than simply judge. A good review, like a good abstract, should communicate the essential ideas contained in the source. It is the reviewer's aim also to locate the source in some larger context; for example, by comparing it to other works on the same subject and to the research tradition the book seeks to extend, modify, and so forth. Thus, your summary should try to encompass how the book contributes to the ongoing conversation on a given topic in the field.

Append to your comparative summary a paragraph or two answering the question "How has this exercise affected your thinking about your topic?"

Obviously, you could choose to do a comparative summary of two articles, two book chapters, and so forth, rather than of two book reviews. But in any event, if you use books in your research, you should always find a means of determining how they are received in the relevant discourse community.

The next step, if you were writing a research paper, would involve the task known as *synthesis*, in which you essentially write a comparative discussion that includes more than two sources. Many research papers start with an opening paragraph that synthesizes prevailing, perhaps competing, interpretations of the topic being addressed. Few good research papers consist only of such synthesis, however. Instead, writers use synthesis to frame their ideas and provide perspective on their own arguments; the synthesis provides a platform or foundation for their subsequent analysis.

It is probably worth adding that bad research papers fail to use synthesis as a point of departure. Instead, they line up their sources and agree or disagree with them. To inoculate you against this unfortunate reflex, review the section titled "Six Strategies for Analyzing Sources," especially "Strategy 6: Find Your Own Role in the Conversation."

CHAPTER 9

Finding, Evaluating, and Citing Sources

— BY KELLY CANNON, OUTREACH AND SCHOLARLY COMMUNICATION LIBRARIAN, MUHLENBERG COLLEGE

Overview   The chapter that follows was written by a reference librarian at our college, Kelly Cannon. It offers a wealth of insider's tips for making more productive use of your research time. The final section of the chapter explains the four documentation styles that are most common in academic writing: APA (American Psychological Association), CSE (Council of Science Editors), Chicago (University Press of Chicago), and MLA (Modern Language Association).

Three Rules of Thumb for Getting Started with Research

- *A half-hour spent with a reference librarian can save you half a day wandering randomly though the stacks selecting sources.*

- *Start your research in the present and work backward.* Usually the most current materials include bibliographical citations that can help you identify the most important sources in the past. Along the same lines, you are usually better off starting with journal articles rather than books because articles are more current.

- *Consistently evaluate the reliability of the source you select in order to detect its potential bias or agenda.* Evidence is always qualified by how it is framed. For example, *Newsweek* can be a useful source if you want evidence about popular understanding of a subject or issue. In this case, the fact that the material comes from *Newsweek* and thus represents a position aimed at a mainstream, nonacademic audience provides the central reason for citing it.

The challenge of doing research in the Information Age is that there is so much information available. How do you know which information is considered authoritative in a particular discipline and which isn't? How can you avoid wasting time with source materials that have been effectively refuted and replaced by subsequent thinking? A short answer to these questions is that you should start in the reference room of your library or with its electronic equivalent. Many if not all of the resources listed below are now available online through your college library website. Your reference librarian can advise you on availability.

Start with Scholarly Indexes, Abstracts, and Bibliographies

These reference sources can rapidly provide you with both a broad perspective on your subject and a summary of what particular sources contain. An **index** offers a list of titles directing you to scholarly journals, books, and chapters; often this list is sufficient to give you an idea of the kinds of topics about which writers in the field are conversing. **Compilations of abstracts** and **annotated bibliographies** provide more information— anywhere from a few sentences to a few pages that summarize each source. The goal of these resources is to provide a listing of quality titles in a given area, regardless of full text availability. Some records may contain full text; others will provide only a title, subject headings, and/or abstract. As such, in their online form, indexes, abstracts, and bibliographies tend to search only the title, abstract, and/or subject headings, rather than the full text. This can mean that results will be fewer but highly relevant to your search. This stands in sharp contrast to—many full text databases—that by default search the entire text, providing more abundant though at times less relevant search results.

Nearly every discipline has its own major index, one most consulted by scholars. Here are a few: *MLA* (literary criticism), *ERIC* (education), *PsycInfo* (psychology), *Historical Abstracts* (non-U.S. history), *Sociological Abstracts* (sociology), and *PubMed* (medicine).

When professors refer to bibliographic research, they probably mean research done with indexes. Again, these indexes are specific to particular subject areas. Their coverage is typically deep and scholarly. These are the indexes to consult when seeking the most scholarly information in your area of study. Although the full text is sometimes not included, the indexing provides information sufficient to track down the complete article.

These indexes are a great aid in evaluating the scholarly merit of a publication, as they usually eliminate any reference that isn't considered scholarly by the academy. For example, *MLA* only indexes literary criticism that appears in peer-reviewed journals and academically affiliated books. So, consider the publications that appear in these indexes to have the academic "seal of approval."

For more information on this crucial aspect of research, see the later sections in this chapter titled "Subscriber-Only Databases" and "Four Steps Toward Productive Research Across the Disciplines."

Specialized Dictionaries and Encyclopedias

Specialized dictionaries and encyclopedias are sometimes extraordinarily useful in sketching the general terrain for a subject, and they often include bibliographical leads as well. Here are some titles, ranging from the expected to the eccentric:

Dictionary of the History of Ideas
Dictionary of Literary Biography
Encyclopedia of American History
Encyclopedia of Bioethics
Encyclopedia of Crime and Justice
Concise Encyclopedia of Economics
Encyclopedia of Native American Religions
Encyclopedia of Philosophy
Encyclopedia of Psychology
The New Encyclopedia of Unbelief
Encyclopedia of World Art
Encyclopedic Dictionary of Mathematics
Macmillan Encyclopedia of Computers
Encyclopedia of Medical History
McGraw-Hill Encyclopedia of Science and Technology
New Grove Dictionary of Music and Musicians
Oxford English Dictionary

Most of these include book reviews. Book reviews across all disciplines can be found in multidisciplinary databases like *Academic Search Premier/ Complete*, *Project Muse*, and *JSTOR*.

Finding Your Sources: Articles and Books

The resources above will both provide you with an excellent overview of your topic and also direct you to authoritative books and journal articles. The next step is to find out how to access the full text of those books and articles online or in print form.

Your library's online catalog or discovery service will direct you to books in your local library. You may wish to take advantage of this time in the catalog/discovery service to run a keyword search on your topic. Watch the subject headings that appear at the bottom of catalog records. You can click on these subject headings to guide you to books highly relevant to your topic.

Don't be concerned if many of the books that have been recommended in specialized dictionaries, encyclopedias, and indexes don't appear in your library's collection. The reference librarian can direct you to *WorldCat* or your library's discovery service (which includes books from other libraries throughout North America and elsewhere), where you can request, on interlibrary loan, any book to be sent to you from another library for your perusal. This is a valuable service, as it makes available to you the research collections of large universities, all with the stroke of a key.

As for journal articles, you will need to find which articles are available in-house, online or in print, and which you will need to request by submitting an interlibrary loan request (in this case, unlike with books, you will receive a PDF or photocopy of the interlibrary loaned article to keep—no need to return it to the lending library). Your library's online catalog/discovery service will generally—though not always—provide you with a complete list of journals available, electronically or in print. Just title search on the journal name, not the article title, in order to locate the journal. Ask a reference librarian for assistance in locating journals. A librarian can also assist you in requesting on interlibrary loan any articles from journals your library does not have.

In the following Voices from Across the Curriculum, a business professor and a psychology professor offer useful tips for searching under more than one heading in order to find more information.

VOICES FROM ACROSS THE CURRICULUM

Finding Quality Sources: Two Professors Speak

A critical part of the bibliographic effort is to find a topic on which there are materials. Most topics can be researched. The key is to choose a flexible keyword/phrase and then try out different versions of it. For example, a bibliography on "women in management" might lead you to look up *women, females, business* (women in), business (females in), *gender in the workplace, sexism and the workplace, careers* (of men, of women, in business), *women and CEOs, women in management, affirmative action and women, women in corporations, female accountants,* and so forth. Be imaginative and flexible. A little bit of time with some of the indexes will provide you with a wealth of sources.

Here is a sampling of indexes heavily used in business research, for instance: *Wall Street Journal Online, New York Times Online,* and *Business Source Elite/Premier/Complete.*

—FREDERICK NORLING, PROFESSOR OF BUSINESS

Use quality psychological references. That is, use references that professional psychologists use and regard highly. *Psychology Today* is not a good reference; *Newsweek* and *Reader's Digest* are worse. APA journals, such as the *Journal of Abnormal Psychology,* on the other hand, are excellent.

In looking for reference material, be sure to search under several headings. For example, look under *depression, affective disorders,* and *mood disorders.* Books (e.g., *The Handbook of Affective Disorders*) are often very helpful, especially for giving a general overview of a topic. Books addressing a professional audience are generally preferable to those addressing a general, popular audience.

Finally, references should be reasonably current. In general, the newer, the better. For example, with rare exceptions (classic articles), articles from before 2000 are outdated and so should not be used.

—ALAN TJELTVEIT, PROFESSOR OF PSYCHOLOGY

Finding Quality on the Web

Imagine a megalibrary to which anyone has access any time of day or night, and to which anyone can contribute material—to inform, but perhaps more so to sell and to promote, no matter how questionable the cause or idea. So it is with the web. A general caveat to this "library of the Internet" might well be User Beware.

Take as an example the website *Martin Luther King Jr.: A True Historical Examination* (www.martinlutherking.org). This site appears prominently in any web search for information about Martin Luther King, Jr. The site is visually appealing, claiming to include "essays, speeches, sermons, and more." But who created the site? As it turns out, after a little digging (see Tips #1 and #2 later in the chapter), the site is sponsored by Stormfront, Inc. (stormfront.org), an organization out of West Palm Beach, Florida, serving "those courageous men and women fighting to preserve their White Western culture, ideals and freedom of speech." This author is concealed behind the work, a ghostwriter of sorts. While the site is at one's fingertips, identifying the author is a challenge, more so than in the world of print publishing where protocols such as author and publisher appearing on the same pages as the title are followed. For those websites with no visible author, no publishing house, no recognized journal title, no peer-review process, and no library selection process (the touchstones of scholarship in the print world), seemingly easy Internet research is now more problematic: the user must discern what is and is not authoritative information.

Understanding Domain Names

But how is the user to begin evaluating a web document? Fortunately, there are several clues to assist you through the Internet labyrinth. One clue is in the web address itself. For example, the *Internet Movie Database* has www.imdb.com as its web address (also known as a URL, or uniform resource locator). One clue lies at the very end of the URL, in what is known as the domain name, in this case the abbreviation ".com." Websites ending in .com are commercial, often with the purpose of marketing a product. Sites ending in .org generally signal nonprofits, but many have a veiled agenda, whether it is marketing or politics.

Like the .coms, .org addresses are sold on a first-come, first-served basis. (The organization that oversees the many vendors of .com and .org domain names is The Internet Corporation for Assigned Names and Numbers, or ICANN [www .icann.org/].)

On the other hand, .edu and .gov sites may indicate less bias, because they are ostensibly limited exclusively to educational and government institutions, and they are often the producers of bona fide research. In particular, .gov sites contain some of the best information on the Internet. This is in part because the U.S. government is required by an act of Congress to disseminate to the general public a large portion of its research. The U.S. government, floated as it is by tax dollars, provides the high-quality, free websites reminiscent of the precommercial Internet era. This means that government sites offer high-quality data, particularly of a statistical nature. Scholars in the areas of business, law, and the social sciences can benefit tremendously, without subscription fees, from a variety of government databases. Prime examples are the legislative site known as *Congress.gov* (www.congress.gov/) and data gathered at the website of the Census Bureau (www.census.gov).

Print Corollaries

A domain name can be misleading; it is simply one clue in the process of evaluation. Another clue is the correlation between a website and the print world. Many websites correlate with a print edition, such as the web version of *The Economist* (economist.com), offering some unique information as well as some identical to that offered in the print subscription. (Access to some web articles may be limited to subscribers.) Moreover, some websites are the equivalents of their print editions. For example, Johns Hopkins University Press now publishes its journals, known and respected for years by scholars, in both print and electronic formats, collectively known as *Project Muse* (muse.jhu.edu). Many college and university libraries subscribe to these Johns Hopkins journals electronically. In both cases—*The Economist* and *Project Muse*—the scholar can expect the electronic form of the publication to have undergone the same editorial rigor as the print publication.

Web-Published Gems

Building a reputation for high quality takes time. But the Internet has been around long enough now that some publications with no pre-web history have caught the attention of scholars who turn to these sites regularly for reliable commentary on a variety of subject areas.

These high-quality sites can best be found by tapping into scholarly web directories such as *Academic Index* (www.academicindex.net/), which work like mini search engines but are managed by humans who sift through the chaff, including in these directories only what they deem to be gems.

The student looking specifically for free, peer-reviewed journals original to the web can visit the highly specific *Directory of Open Access Journals* (www .doaj.org), which lists several hundred journals in a variety of subject areas. Many libraries have begun to link to these journals to promote their use by students and faculty.

Then there are the web treasures that compare to highbrow newspapers or magazines such as *The New Yorker*. Two celebrated examples are *Salon. com* (salon.com) and *Slate* (slate.com), both online journals. Once tapped into, these sites do a good job of recommending other high-quality websites. Scholars are beginning to cite from these web-based publications just as they would from any print publication of long-standing reputation.

An excellent site for links to all kinds of interesting articles from journals and high-level general interest magazine is *Arts and Letters Daily* (aldaily.com), sponsored by *The Chronicle of Higher Education*. You should also be aware of websites run by special interest organizations, such as *The Academy of American Poets* (poets.org), which offers bibliographic resources, interviews, reviews, and the like.

Wikipedia, Google, and Blogs

Three tools have in recent years dramatically altered the nature of web-based research. First and foremost, the search engine *Google*, through a proprietary search algorithm, has increased the relevance and value of search results. Relevance in *Google* is determined by text-matching techniques, while value is determined by a unique "PageRank" technology that places highest on the list those results that are most often linked to from other websites.

However, the determination of value is by no means foolproof. *Google*'s ranking of value assesses less a website's authoritativeness than its popular appeal. For example, a recent search on "Tijuana" yielded on its first page of results six tourism-oriented sites. These sites could be useful in any number of ways in a research paper (i.e., as primary resources reflecting popular perceptions of the locale). That they dominate the first page of results suggests *Google*'s algorithm of popularity over authoritativeness. This is not necessarily a bad thing, just something to be aware of. It is a little like picking a pebble off the ground. Its value is not inherent: responsibility rests with the user to discover its value. Finding information in *Google* is never the challenge. Discerning appropriateness and authoritativeness is the bigger task.

High on the list of most search results in *Google*—if not first—is *Wikipedia*. Is this an authoritative source? Certainly *Wikipedia* has revolutionized the way web pages are authored. The world is the author of every entry. That is the beauty and the hazard, and the secret to its broad scope and thus to its popularity. Anyone can write and edit in *Wikipedia*; in this way, it is infinitely democratic. All opinions count equally, for better or worse—while authority languishes. Consequently, *Wikipedia* is likely to contribute little to a scholarly research project. In fact, it could detract from an assertion of authority. In short, use

Wikipedia entries judiciously. Like any encyclopedia, *Wikipedia* will be viewed by the informed reader as introductory, not as the hallmark of thorough research.

Just as *Wikipedia* invites all of us to be writers, so too do blogs. But unlike *Wikipedia*, blogs typically reveal the identity or at least the assumed identity of the author, and are written by a closed group of people, often one individual. As such, over time the identity and politics of the author(s) show through. In the best tradition of the World Wide Web, blogs have extended the sphere of publication, inviting everyone to be published authors, possibly achieving popularity and authority on a topic—no matter how narrow—by being at the right place at the right time, with access to the right information written in a voice of confidence. Blogs invite outside comment, but lack the formal structure of a peer review. As such, use blogs sparingly in academic research, and be attentive to the credentials of the author(s) and the wider acceptance of a particular blog in the scholarly community.

Asking the Right Questions

In the end, it is up to the individual user to evaluate each website independently. Here are some critical questions to consider:

Question: Who is the author?
Response: Check the website's home page, probably near the bottom of the page.

Question: Is the author affiliated with any institution?
Response: Check the URL to see who sponsors the page.

Question: What are the author's credentials?
Response: Check Google Scholar (scholar.google.com) to see if this person is published in scholarly journals or books.

Question: Has the information been reviewed or peer-edited before posting?
Response: Probably not, unless the posting is part of a larger scholarly project; if so, the submission process for publication can be verified at the publication home page.

Question: Is the page part of a larger publication that may help to assess authoritativeness?
Response: Try the various links on the page to see if there is an access point to the home page of the publication. Or try the backspacing technique mentioned later in the chapter.

Question: Is the information documented properly?
Response: Check for footnotes or methodology.

Question: Is the information current?
Response: Check the "last update," usually printed at the bottom of the page.

Question: What is the purpose of the page?
Response: Examine content and marginalia.

Question: Does the website suit your purposes?

Response: Review what the purpose of your project is. Review your information needs: primary vs. secondary, academic vs. popular. And always consult with your instructor.

Subscriber-Only Databases

An organized and indexed collection of discrete pieces of information is called a *database*. The World Wide Web is full of databases, though they are often restricted to subscribers. Subscription fees can be prohibitive, but fortunately for the average researcher, most college and university libraries foot the bill. These databases are well known, and arguably contain the most thoroughly reviewed (i.e., scholarly) full text available on the web (inquire at your library to see if you have access to these databases):

> *Academic Search Premier/Complete* from EBSCO (www.ebscohost.com)
> *Academic OneFile* from Gale Cengage (www.cengage.com)
> *JSTOR* from ITHAKA (www.jstor.org)
> *Project Muse* from Johns Hopkins (muse.jhu.edu/)
> *ProQuest Central* from ProQuest (www.proquest.com)

Each of these databases contains its own proprietary search engine, allowing refinement of searches to a degree unmatched by search engines on the Internet at large. How does this refinement occur? For one, these databases are exclusive rather than inclusive, as the Internet is. More is not better in an information age. The fact that information is at your fingertips, and sometimes "in your face," can be a problem. Well-organized databases are shaped and limited by human hands and minds, covering only certain media types or subject areas.

Second, databases allow searching by subject heading, in addition to keyword searching. This means that a human has defined the main subject areas of each entry, consequently allowing the user much greater manipulation of the search. For example, if you enter the words "New York City" in a simple keyword search, you will retrieve everything that simply mentions New York City even once; the relevance will vary tremendously. On the other hand, if subject headings have been assigned, you can do a subject search on New York City and find only records that are devoted to your subject. This may sound trivial, but in the age of information overload, precision searching is a precious commodity.

The most specialized databases are those whose primary purpose is not to provide full text but to index all of the major journals, along with books and/or book chapters, in a discipline, regardless of where the full text to that journal can be found. These electronic indexes provide basic bibliographic information and sometimes an abstract (summary) of the article or book chapter. (See "Scholarly Indexes, Abstracts, and Bibliographies" earlier in the chapter.)

TRY THIS 9.1: Tuning in to Your Research Environment: Four Exercises

Every university and college is different, each with its own points of access to information. Following are some exercises to help you familiarize yourself with your own scholarly environment.

Exercise #1: Go to your library's reference desk and get a list of all the scholarly journal indexes (some may include full text) that are available electronically at your school. Then get a list of all online, full-text databases that are available to you.

Exercise #2: Contact your reference librarian to get a list of all the journals that the library subscribes to electronically. Then get a list of all journals that are available at your library, either in print or electronically, in your major area of study.

Exercise #3: Ask the reference librarian about web access in general for your major area of study. What tips can the library give you about doing electronic research at your academic institution? Are there any special databases, web search engines/directories, or indexes that you should consult in your research?

Exercise #4: Try out some or all of the full-text databases available on your campus, identified by a reference librarian. Now try the same searches in a scholarly index that doesn't search the full text, but instead searches title/abstract/subject headings only. What differences do you see in the quality and/or scope of the information?

Eight Tips for Locating and Evaluating Electronic Sources

Tip #1: Backspacing

"Backspacing" a URL can be an effective way to evaluate a website. It may reveal authorship or institutional affiliation. To do this, place the cursor at the end of the URL and then backspace to the last slash and press Enter. Continue backspacing to each preceding slash, examining each level as you go.

Tip #2: Using WHOIS

WHOIS (www.networksolutions.com/whois/index.jsp) is an Internet service that allows anyone to find out who's behind a website.

Tip #3: Beware of the ~ in a Web Address

Many educational institutions allow the creation of personal home pages by students and faculty. While the domain name remains .edu in these cases, the fact that they are personal means that pretty much anything can be posted, and thus you cannot assure academic quality.

Tip #4: Phrase Searching

Not finding relevant information? Trying using quotation marks around key phrases in your search string. For example, search in *Google* for this phrase, enclosed in quotation marks: "whose woods these are I think I know."

Tip #5: Title Searching

Still finding irrelevant information? Limit your search to the titles of web documents. A title search is an option in *Google* (advanced search) (www .google.com/advanced_search).

Tip #6: Wikipedia Talk Tab

Use *Wikipedia* to full advantage by clicking on the Talk tab located at the top of *Wikipedia* entries. The Talk tabs expose the often intense debates that rage behind the scenes on topics like marijuana, genocide, and Islam. The Talk tab is an excellent source for locating paper topics because it highlights ongoing sources of controversy—those areas worthy of additional writing and research. To find the most controversial topics at any given moment, visit *Wikipedia's* Controversial Issues page (en.wikipedia.org /wiki/ Wikipedia:List_of_controversial_issues).

Tip #7: Full Text from Library Databases

The widest selection of previously published full texts (newspapers, magazines, journals, book chapters) is available in library subscription databases. Inquire at your library to see if you have access to Academic Search Premier/ Complete, from EBSCO (www.ebscohost.com); Academic OneFile, from Gale Cengage (www.cengage.com.); JSTOR (www.jstor .org); Project Muse, from Johns Hopkins (muse.jhu.edu/); ProQuest Central, from ProQuest (www .proquest.com); or other full-text databases.

For the full text of books, try the Internet Archive and Open Library (www .archive.org/details/texts), pointing to the major digital text archives.

Tip #8: Archives of Older Published Periodicals

Full text for newspapers, magazines, and journals published prior to 1990 is difficult to find on the Internet. One subscription site that your library may offer is JSTOR (www.jstor.org), an archive of scholarly, full-text journal articles dating back in some cases into the late 1800s. LexisNexis Academic (academic .lexisnexis.com), also a subscription service, includes the full text of popular periodicals such as the *New York Times* as far back as 1980.

Two free sites offer the full text of eighteenth-and nineteenth-century periodicals from Great Britain and the United States, respectively: Internet Library of Early Journals (www.bodley.ox.ac.uk/ilej) and Nineteenth Century in Print (memory.loc.gov:8081/ammem/ndlpcoop/moahtml/snchome.html).

Use your library's interlibrary loan service to acquire articles from periodicals not freely available on the web. Electronic indexing (no full text) for older materials is readily available, back to as early as 1900, sometimes earlier. Inquire at your library.

Four Steps Toward Productive Research Across the Disciplines

The steps below include some of the sites most relied upon by academic librarians. For the subscription databases, you will need to inquire at your library for local availability.

Step 1: search at least one of these multidisciplinary library subscription databases; check your library's website for availability.

- *Academic Search Premier/Complete* (EBSCOhost) for journals
- *Academic Onefile* (Gale Cengage) for journals
- *JSTOR* for journals
- *Project Muse* for journals
- *ProQuest Central* for journals
- *WorldCat* (OCLC FirstSearch) for books, or use your library's discovery service

Step 2: search subject-specific databases. These too are mostly subscription databases; check your library's website for availability.

- Anthropology: *Anthropology Plus*
- Art: *Art Full Text*
- Biology: *ScienceDirect*
- Business: *ABI Inform, Business Source Elite/Premier, Business Insights Essentials, Dow Jones Factiva, LexisNexis Academic*
- Chemistry: *SciFinder Scholar, ScienceDirect*
- Communication: *Communication and Mass Media Complete*
- Computer Science: *ACM Digital Library, MathSciNet, ScienceDirect*
- Economics: *EconLit*
- Education: *ERIC* (free)
- Film Studies: *Communication & Mass Media Complete, Film & Television Literature Index, MLA*
- Geography/Geology: *GeoBase*
- History: *America: History and Life, Historical Abstracts*
- Language, Literature: *MLA, Literature Criticism Online*
- Law: *LexisNexis, Westlaw*
- Mathematics: *MathSciNet*

- Medicine: *PubMed* (free), *ScienceDirect*
- Music: *RILM Abstracts of Music Literature*
- Philosophy: *Philosopher's Index, PhilPapers*
- Physics: arXiv.org (free), *Physical Review Online Archive (PROLA), ScienceDirect*
- Political Science: *Columbia International Affairs Online (CIAO), ProQuest PAIS International, Worldwide Political Science Abstracts*
- Psychology: *PsycINFO*
- Religion: *ATLA Religion*
- Sociology: *Sociological Abstracts*

Step 3: visit these not-to-be-missed free websites and metasites that lead to a variety of materials relevant to a discipline:

- All subjects: *Google Scholar* scholar.google.com (books and journals)
- Anthropology: *Anthropological Index Online* aio.anthropology.org.uk /(journals), *Anthropology Resources on the Internet* www.aaanet.org /resources/
- Art: *Artcyclopedia* www.artcyclopedia.com (images and critical bibliographies)
- Biology: *BiologyBrowser* www.biologybrowser.org (gateway to digital archives of colleges and universities), *Agricola* agricola.nal.usda.gov (journals)
- Business: *EDGAR* www.sec.gov/edgar.shtml (company annual reports)
- Chemistry: *Chemdex* www.chemdex.org (chemical compounds), *Eric Weisstein's World of Chemistry* scienceworld.wolfram.com/chemistry (encyclopedia)
- Communication: *Television News Archive: Vanderbilt University* tvnews. vanderbilt.edu (index to television news)
- Computer Science: *CompInfo* www.compinfo-center.com (magazines and downloads)
- Economics: *Penn World Tables* www.rug.nl/research/ggdc/data/pwt/ (data sets)
- Education: *ERIC* eric.ed.gov/ (vast collection of research on education)
- Film Studies: *Film Studies Resources* www.lib.berkeley.edu/MRC/filmstudies /index.html (index to reviews and criticism)
- Geography/Geology: *U.S. Geological Survey* www.usgs.gov/pubprod/ (array of maps and other resources)
- History: *American Memory* memory.loc.gov/ammem/index.html (primary documents)

- Language, Literature: *Project Gutenberg* www.gutenberg.org/ (literary texts)
- Law: *FindLaw* www.findlaw.com (free legal information)
- Mathematics: *arXiv.org* arxiv.org/ (non-peer-reviewed but moderated scholarly e-print submissions), *Wolfram MathWorld* mathworld.wolfram.com/ (encyclopedia)
- Medicine: *BioMed Central* www.biomedcentral.com (journals)
- Music: *Petrucci Music Library* imslp.org/wiki/ (music scores)
- Philosophy: *Stanford Encyclopedia of Philosophy* plato.stanford.edu
- Physics: *arXiv.org* arxiv.org/ (non-peer-reviewed but moderated scholarly e-print submissions), *Eric Weisstein's World of Physics* scienceworld.wolfram.com/physics
- Political Science: Political Resources on the Net www.politicalresources.net/ *Congress.gov* www.congress.gov (U.S. government documents)
- Psychology: Psych Web www.psywww.com/ (gateway site)
- Religion: *Religion Online* www.religion-online.org/ (articles and book chapters), *Hartford Institute for Religion Research* hirr.hartsem.edu/ (surveys and statistics)
- Sociology: *CIA World Factbook* www.cia.gov/library/publications/the-world-factbook/ (demographic data)

Step 4: search the web using this selective search engine:

- *Academic Index* (www.academicindex.net)
- Use with discretion. Contains a moderate percentage of academic websites. Favors nonprofit over commercial sites.

The Four Documentation Styles: Similarities and Differences

The four most common styles of documentation are those established by:

- The American Psychological Association (APA)
- The Council of Science Editors (CSE)
- The University Press of Chicago
- The Modern Language Association (MLA).

Note: The University of North Carolina at Chapel Hill Libraries offers authoritative examples of basic citations of electronic and print resources in all four styles at guides.lib.unc.edu/citing-information/.

For citation examples not given at the University of North Carolina at Chapel Hill Libraries website, consult the various organizations' printed manuals—*Publication Manual of the American Psychological Association* (7th edition),

The Chicago Manual of Style (16th edition), *Scientific Style and Format: The CSE Manual for Authors, Editors, and Publishers* (8th edition), and the *MLA Handbook for Writers of Research Papers* (9th edition). It is important to use the most recent edition available of each of these manuals.

You have probably already discovered that some professors are more concerned than others that students obey the particulars of a given documentation style. Virtually all faculty across the curriculum agree, however, that *the most important rule for writers to follow in documenting sources is formal consistency.* That is, all of your in-text citations, or footnotes/endnotes, should follow the same format, and all of your end-of-text citations should follow the same format.

Once you begin doing most of your writing in a particular discipline, you may want to purchase or access on the Internet the more detailed style guide adhered to by that discipline. Because documentation styles differ not only from discipline to discipline but also even from journal to journal within a discipline, you should consult your professor about which documentation format they wish you to use in a given course.

The various styles differ in the specific ways that they organize the bibliographical information, but they also share some common characteristics.

1. They place an extended citation for each source, including the author, the title, the date, and the place of publication, at the end of the paper (though in Chicago this end-of-text list is optional when employing footnotes/endnotes: consult with your professor). These end-of-text citations are organized in a list, usually alphabetically.

2. All four styles distinguish among different kinds of sources—providing slightly differing formulas for citing books, articles, encyclopedias, government documents, interviews, and so forth.

3. They all ask for these basic pieces of information to be provided whenever they are known: author, title of larger work along with title of article or chapter as appropriate, date of publication, and publisher or institutional affiliation.

To briefly distinguish the styles:

- The APA style employs the author-date format of parenthetical in-text citation and predominates in the social sciences.
- The Chicago style, best known for its use of footnotes or endnotes, is employed in history, the fine arts, and some other humanities disciplines.
- The CSE (aka CBE) style, which employs alternately the citation-sequence system and the name-year system, is commonly used throughout the sciences, especially the natural sciences.
- The MLA style, which uses the author-page format of parenthetical in-text citation, prevails in the humanities disciplines of language, literature, film, and cultural studies.

Following are some basic examples of in-text and end-of-text citations in the four most commonly used styles, followed by a brief discussion of the rules that apply.

APA Style, 7th Edition

General note: Writers should use language free of bias to ensure fair treatment of groups and individuals. Avoid use of any language that demeans or discriminates, and strive to use accurate, inclusive language at all times. To do this, describe people and groups with an appropriate level of specificity and be sensitive to labels. See the APA website (apa.org) for more guidance and examples.

In-text citation: Studies of students' changing attitudes towards the small colleges that they attend suggest that their loyalty to the institution declines steadily over a four-year period, whereas their loyalty to individual professors or departments increases "markedly, by as much as twenty-five percent over the last two years" (Brown, 1994, p. 41).

For both books and articles, include the author's last name, followed by a comma and then the date of publication. If you are quoting or referring to a specific passage, include the page number as well, separated from the date by a comma and the abbreviation "p." (or "pp."), followed by a space.

If the author's name has been mentioned in the sentence, include only the date in the parentheses immediately following the author's name.

In-text citation: Brown (1994) documents the decline in students' institutional loyalty.

End-of-text book citation:
Frost, N. (2011). *Qualitative research methods in psychology: Combining core approaches.* Open University.

End-of-text webpage citation:
Stobbe, M. (2020, January 30). *U.S. reports first case of coronavirus being spread person-to-person.* HuffPost. https://www.huffpost.com/entry/coronavirus-person-to-person-spread-us_n_5e332007c5b69a19a4ac03c0

End-of-text journal article citation without a DOI, from most academic research databases or print version:
Miao, M., & Gan, Y. (2019). How does meaning in life predict proactive coping? The self-regulatory mechanism on emotion and cognition. *Journal of Personality, 87*(3), 579–592.

End-of-text citation of a journal article retrieved from a website or database, with a DOI:
Sutton, J., Harris, C., Keil, P., & Barnier, A. The psychology of memory, extended cognition, and socially distributed remembering. *Phenomenology and the Cognitive Sciences, 9*(4), 521–560. https://doi.org/10.1007/s11097-010-9182-y

The DOI is typically located on the first page of the electronic journal article, near the copyright notice. When a DOI is used in your citation, no other retrieval information is needed. Use this format for the DOI in references: https://doi.org/xxxx

If no DOI has been assigned to the journal content found on the web, provide the URL of the journal or article. If you retrieve an article from a library (subscription) database, in general it is not necessary to include the database information in the citation. Do not include retrieval dates unless the source material has changed over time.

APA style requires an alphabetical list of references (by author's last name, which keys the reference to the in-text citation). This list, titled "References," is located at the end of the paper on a separate page. Regarding manuscript form, the first line of each reference is not indented, but all subsequent lines are indented three spaces.

In alphabetizing the references list, place entries for a single author before entries that the person has coauthored, and arrange multiple entries by a single author by beginning with the earliest work. If there are two or more works by the same author in the same year, designate the first with an "a," the second a "b," and so forth, directly after the year. For articles by two or more authors, use commas to connect the authors, and precede the last one with a comma and an ampersand (&).

The APA style divides individual entries into the following parts: author (using initials only for first and middle names), year of publication (in parentheses), title, and publication data. Each part is separated by a period from the others. Note that only the first letter of the title and subtitle of books is capitalized (although proper nouns would be capitalized as necessary).

Journal citations differ from those for books in a number of small ways. The title of a journal article is neither italicized, underlined, or enclosed in quotation marks, and only the first word in the title and subtitle is capitalized. The name of the journal is italicized (or underlined), however, and the first word and all significant words are capitalized. Also, notice that the volume number (which is separated by a comma from the title of the journal) is italicized (or underlined) to distinguish it from the page reference. The issue number should follow in parentheses but without italics. Page numbers for the entire article are included, with no "p." or "pp.," and are separated by a comma from the preceding volume or issue number.

Chicago Style, 17th Edition

Footnote or endnote citation: The earliest groups to explore that part of the country spent much of their time finding out of the way places to "hide their families and cache their grain."[1]

The raised numeral indicates a footnote at the bottom of the page or an endnote at the conclusion of a chapter. Following is an example of what that note would look like, assuming this is the first note to have appeared in the paper and is thus listed as note number one:

Footnote/endnote book citation:

    1. Juanita Brooks, *The Mountain Meadows Massacre* (Norman: University of Oklahoma Press, 1991), 154.

Here are some examples of other types of notes, numbered consecutively as if each were appearing in the same paper, in this order:

Footnote/endnote journal article citation:

    2. Luis Alonso-Alvarez, "The Value of Water: The Origins and Expansion of Thermal Tourism in Spain, 1750–2010," *Journal of Tourism History* 4, no. 1 (April 2012): 15, https://doi.org/10.10801755182X.2012.671373.

A DOI unique identifying number is always preferred. Otherwise, use a stable URL.

Footnote/endnote citation of a journal article from an academic research database:

    3. John Walter, "The English People and the English Revolution Revisited," *History Workshop Journal* 61 (Spring 2006): 171, https://www.jstor.org/stable/25472843.

Footnote/endnote webpage citation:

    4. Baha'i International Community, "What Baha'is," *The Baha'i Faith*, last modified 2020, https://www.bahai.org/beliefs/.

The access date is used if a publication or modification date is not available.

In addition to footnotes/endnotes, the Chicago style recommends but does not require an alphabetical list of references (by author's last name). This list, titled "Bibliography," is located at the end of the paper on a separate page. Listed below are the same references employed above, formatted for the bibliography:

End-of-text book citation:

Brooks, Juanita. *The Mountain Meadows Massacre*. Norman: University of Oklahoma Press, 1991.

End-of-text journal article citation:

Alonso-Alvarez, Luis. "The Value of Water: The Origins and Expansion of Thermal Tourism in Spain, 1750–2010." *Journal of Tourism History* 4, no. 1 (April 2012): 15–34. https://doi.org/10.10801755182X.2012.671373.

End-of-text citation of a journal article from an academic research database:

Walter, John. "The English People and the English Revolution Revisited." *History Workshop Journal* 61 (Spring 2006): 171–182. https://www.jstor.org/stable/25472843.

End-of-text webpage citation:

Baha'i International Community. "What Baha'is Believe." *The Baha'i Faith*. Last modified 2020. https://www.bahai.org/beliefs/.

Each part of a bibiography entry is separated by a period from the others. Titles of book-length works are italicized. Journal citations differ slightly: article names go inside quotations, no punctuation follows the titles of journals, and a colon precedes the page numbers when pagination is known.

CSE Style Employing Name-Year (Author-Date) System, 8th Edition

In-text citation: Soap works as a cleaning agent because of the distinctiveness of each end of the soap molecule, their "opposing tendencies," that is (McMurry and others 2010, p 768).

For both books and articles, include the author's last name followed by the date of publication. For two authors, include the two last names (Smith and Jones 2013). For more than two authors, as in the case above, employ the phrase "and others." If you are quoting or referring to a specific passage, include the page number as well, separated from the date by a comma and the abbreviation "p" (or "pp") followed by a space. If the author's name has been mentioned in the sentence, include only the date in the parentheses, immediately following the author's name wherever it appears in the sentence.

In-text citation:
Romero (2008) reviews the transformation of scientific knowledge about the polymer.

End-of-text book citation:
McMurry J, Castellion ME, Ballantine DS. 2010. Fundamentals of general, organic, and biological chemistry. New York: Prentice Hall.

End-of-text journal article citation:
Healy R, Cerio R, Hollingsworth A, Bewley A. 2010. Acquired perforating dermatosis associated with pregnancy. Clin Exp Dermatol. 35(6): 621–623.

End-of-text website citation:
International Union for Conservation of Nature and Natural Resources. 2013. IUCN red list of threatened species. Gland, Switzerland and Cambridge, UK: IUCN; [accessed 2013 Aug 12]. http://www.iucnredlist.org/

End-of-text citation of journal article retrieved from a website:
Philippi TE, Dixon PM, Taylor BE. 1998. Detecting trends in species composition. Ecol Appl. [accessed 2013 Aug 12]; 8(2): 300–308. dx.doi.org/10.1890/1051-0761(1998)008[0300:DTISC]2.0.CO;2

End-of-text library (subscription) database journal article citation:
Kenny G, Yardley J, Brown C, Sigal R, Jay O. 2010. Heat stress in older individuals and patients with common chronic diseases. Can Med Assoc J. [accessed 2010 June 12]; 182(10): 1053–1060. In Health Source: Academic/Nursing Edition. http://search.ebscohost.com.library.muhlenberg.edu/login.aspx?direct=true&db=hch&AN=52226611&site=ehost-live&scope=site.

CSE style requires an alphabetical list of references (by author's last name, which keys the reference to the in-text citation). This list, titled "Cited References," is located at the end of the paper on a separate page. Regarding manuscript form, the first line of each reference is not indented, but all subsequent lines are indented three spaces.

In alphabetizing the references list, place entries for a single author before entries that the person has coauthored, and arrange multiple entries by a single author by beginning with the earliest work.

The CSE style divides individual entries into the following parts: author (using initials only for first and middle names), year of publication, title, and publication data. Each part is separated by a period from the others. Note that only the first letter of the title and subtitle of a book is capitalized (although proper nouns would be capitalized as necessary).

Journal citations differ from those for books in a number of small ways. The title of a journal article is neither italicized, or underlined, or enclosed in quotation marks, and only the first word in the article title and subtitle is capitalized. CSE style requires that journal titles be abbreviated in the standard manner used by science researchers, found at *ISI Journal Title Abbreviations* (www.efm.leeds .ac.uk/~mark/ISIabbr/). This is followed by a volume number and an issue number if available. Page numbers for the entire article are included, with no "p." or "pp.," and are separated by a colon from the preceding volume or issue number.

CSE Style Employing Citation Sequence System, 8th Edition

In-text citation: Soap works as a cleaning agent because of the distinctiveness of each end of the soap molecule, their "opposing tendencies," that is.[1]

Page numbers are generally not included in this system of CSE, but point to the source generally.

End-of-text book citation:
1. McMurry J, Castellion ME, Ballantine DS. Fundamentals of general, organic, and biological chemistry. New York: Prentice Hall; 2010.

End-of-text journal article citation:
2. Healy R, Cerio R, Hollingsworth A, Bewley A. Acquired perforating dermatosis associated with pregnancy. Clin Exp Dermatol. 2010;35(6):621–623.

End-of-text website citation:
3. International Union for Conservation of Nature and Natural Resources. IUCN red list of threatened species. Gland, Switzerland and Cambridge, UK: IUCN; 2013 [accessed 2013 Aug 12]. http://www.iucnredlist.org

End-of-text citation of journal article retrieved from a website:
4. Philippi TE, Dixon PM, Taylor BE. Detecting trends in species composition. Ecol Appl. 1998 [accessed 2013 Aug 12];8(2):300–308. dx.doi.org/10.1890 /1051-0761(1998)008[0300:DTISC]2.0.CO;2

End-of-text library (subscription) database journal article citation:
5. Kenny G, Yardley J, Brown C, Sigal R, Jay O. Heat stress in older individuals and patients with common chronic diseases. Can Med Assoc J . 2010 [accessed 2013 Jun 12];182(10):1053–1060. In Health Source: Academic/Nursing Edition. http://search.ebscohost.com.library.muhlenberg.edu/login.aspx?direct =true&db=hch&AN=52226611&site=ehost-live&scope=site.

In the CSE style, end-of-text citations appear in a list titled "Cited References" and correspond to the superscript numerals appearing in the text in the order of their introduction.

In CSE style, individual entries include the following parts: author (using initials only for first and middle names), title, and publication data. Each part is separated by a period from the others. Note that only the first letter of the title and subtitle of books is capitalized (although proper nouns would be capitalized as necessary).

Journal citations differ from those for books in a number of small ways. The title of a journal article is neither italicized (nor underlined) nor enclosed in quotation marks, and only the first word in the article title and subtitle is capitalized. CSE style requires that journal titles be abbreviated in the standard manner used by science researchers, found at ISI Journal Title Abbreviations www.efm.leeds.ac.uk/~mark/ISIabbr/. This is followed by a volume number and an issue number if available. Page numbers for the entire article are included, with no "p." or "pp.," and are separated by a colon from the preceding volume or issue number.

MLA Style, 9th Edition

In-text citation: The influence of Seamus Heaney on younger poets in Northern Ireland has been widely acknowledged, but Patrick Kavanagh's "plain-speaking, pastoral" influence on him is "less recognized" (Smith 74).

"(Smith 74)" indicates the author's last name and the page number on which the cited passage appears. If the author's name had been mentioned in the sentence—had the sentence begun "According to Smith"—you would include only the page number in the citation. If the author is not known, include the title or a shortened version of the title in place of an author's name. A page number is not required if there is no pagination in the referenced document. Note that there is no abbreviation for "page" and no intervening punctuation between name and page, and that the parentheses precede the period or other punctuation. If the sentence ends with a direct quotation, the parentheses come after the quotation marks but before the closing period. Also note that no punctuation occurs between the last word of the quotation ("recognized") and the closing quotation mark.

End-of-text book citation:
Shaikh, Fariha. *Nineteenth-Century Settler Emigration in British Literature and Art.* Edinburgh UP, 2018.

End-of-text journal article citation:

Belsey, Catherine. "The Death of the Reader." *Textual Practice,* vol. 23, no. 2, 2009, pp. 201–14.

End-of-text website citation:

Poetry Society of America. 2021, poetrysociety.org.

End-of-text citation of a journal article retrieved from a website:

Starshinova, Alentina V., et al. "Youth as Social Service Customers: The Case of Russia." *Social Work and Society International Online Journal,* vol. 19, no. 1, 2021, ejournals.bib.uni-wuppertal.de/index.php/sws/article/view/714.

End-of-text library (subscription) database journal article citation:

Arias, Judith H. "The Devil at Heaven's Door." *Hispanic Review,* vol. 61, no. 1, 1993, pp. 15–34. JSTOR, www.jstor.org/stable/473284.

MLA style stipulates an alphabetical list of references (by author's last name, which keys the reference to the in-text citation). This list is located at the end of the paper on a separate page and entitled "Works Cited."

Each entry in the Works Cited list is divided into three parts: author, title, and publication data. Each of these parts is separated by a period from the others. Titles of book-length works are italicized. Journal citations differ slightly: article names go inside quotations, and the journal title is italicized. Website titles are also italicized, as are database titles.

Guidelines for Finding, Evaluating, and Citing Sources

1. Examine bibliographies at the end of the articles and books you've already found. Remember that one quality source can, in its bibliography, point to many other resources.

2. Citing sources isn't just about acknowledging intellectual or informational debts; it's also a courtesy to your readers, directing them how to find out more about the subject cited.

3. Before you settle in with one author's book-length argument, use indexes, bibliographies, and other resources to achieve a broader view.

4. URLs with domain names ending in .edu and .gov usually offer more reliable choices than do the standard .com domain names.

5. When professors direct you to do bibliographic research, they usually are referring to research done with indexes; these are available in print, online, and CD-ROM formats.

6. In evaluating a website you don't know much about, try backspacing a URL to trace back to its authorship or institutional affiliation.

UNIT 3

Matters of Form

CHAPTER 10

From Paragraphs to Papers: Forms and Formats Across the Curriculum

Overview This chapter is about organization, about the various formats writers use to structure their ideas. You will learn the *why* as well as the *how* of the formats prescribed by particular academic disciplines in the humanities and in the natural and social sciences, such as English, political science, psychology, biology, and chemistry. The chapter argues that these formats are actually much more similar than their stylistic differences may lead you to believe. It also includes discussion of transitions and of typical paragraph shapes, including introductions and conclusions—the building blocks of writing in any discipline.

Overall, the chapter seeks to increase your **rhetorical awareness**, that is, your awareness of how an audience's attitudes and needs can affect the shape of your writing.

The Two Functions of Formats

We began this book by saying that learning to write well means learning to use writing in order to think well. Writing is not just a way of organizing thoughts; it is a way of making thoughts happen. This chapter asks you to consider the relationship between the forms of certain kinds of academic writing, such as the lab report, and the way these forms shape thinking. Once you train yourself to see the kind of thinking a format asks you to do, you will be able to adapt your writing process accordingly.

It's important to recognize that all organizational schemes are conventional—which is to say, they are agreed-upon protocols with social functions. They show you how to write in a way that will allow you to be heard by others in a particular discourse community—a group of people connected by shared ways of talking and thus of thinking. But it's also important to recognize that these protocols are not just containers for information; they are tools of invention.

TWO FUNCTIONS OF FORMATS: RHETORICAL AND HEURISTIC

- Rhetorical: formats make communication among members of a discipline easier and more efficient.

- Heuristic: formats offer writers a means of finding and exploring ideas.

Because formats offer a means not only of displaying thinking in a discipline, but also of shaping it, the format that a discipline requires (whether tacitly or overtly) conditions its members to think in particular ways. Learning to use the format that scientists use predisposes you to think like a scientist. Although knowing the required steps of a discipline's writing format won't write your papers for you, not knowing how writers in that discipline characteristically proceed can keep you from being read.

Academic disciplines differ in the extent to which they adhere to prescribed organizational schemes. In biology and psychology, for example, formal papers and reports generally follow an explicitly prescribed pattern of presentation. Some other disciplines are less uniform and less explicit about their reliance on formats, but writers in these fields—economics, for example, or history or English or religion—usually operate within fairly established forms as well.

The writing strategies and heuristics in this book are formats in the sense that most prescribe a series of steps. The emphasis of *Writing Analytically* rests more on the process of invention than it does on the organization of the finished paper, but, as we have been suggesting, the two are not really separate. The book's heuristics can be used as organizational models; they can also be adapted for use in the various disciplinary formats that college writing requires.

Using Formats Heuristically: An Example

To lose sight of the heuristic value of formats is to become preoccupied with formats merely as disciplinary etiquette. The solution to this problem is to find the spaces in a format that will allow it to work as a heuristic. Consider how you might go about using even a highly specified organizational scheme like the following.

1. State the problem.
2. Develop criteria of adequacy for a solution.
3. Explore at least two inadequate solutions.
4. Explicate the proposed solution.
5. Evaluate the proposed solution.
6. Reply to anticipated criticisms.

The best reason not to ignore any of the six steps in this problem/solution format is that the format does have a logic, although it leaves that logic unstated. The purpose of including at least two inadequate solutions (step 3), for example, is to protect the writer against moving to a conclusion too quickly on the basis of too little evidence. The requirements that the writer evaluate the solution and reply to criticisms (steps 5 and 6) press the writer toward complexity, preventing a one-sided and uncritical answer. In short, heuristic value in the format is there for a writer to use if not allowing a premature concern with matters of form to take precedence over thinking. It would be a mistake, in other words, to assume that one must move through the six steps consecutively; the writer would only need to arrange their thinking in that order when putting together the final product.

The Common Structure of Most Academic Writing

Differences in surface features—sentence style, word choice—tend to obscure the fact that a common underlying structure and set of aims unites most kinds of academic writing across the curriculum.

You can train yourself to start seeing this underlying structure by first recognizing that academic writing in all disciplines is **problem-oriented**, which is to say that academic writing typically starts by noting something that is missing from previous writing and research. As you will see, disciplines differ in how overtly writers may single out problems in other writers' thinking. And yet, in one way or another, most academic writing begins by locating something that needs to be done—something that calls for more research, for example—and saying why this new work might matter.

Science Format Compared with Other Kinds of Writing

Here is a quick overview of the organizational scheme prescribed in the natural sciences and for some kinds of papers in the social sciences, such as reports on research in psychology and political science. Although not all writing in these disciplines follows this format, most does—especially lab reports and articles based on the experimental method and quantitative research. The structure is commonly referred to as IMRAD:

I   introduction
M methods
R results
A and
D discussion

You can think of this format as two descriptions of the research (methods and results) framed by two sections (introduction and discussion) that locate it in the context of existing knowledge in the field. The introduction locates the new work in terms of what has already been done (which points to what still needs to be done). The discussion section considers how knowledge in the field might be changed by the addition of the new results. (See LabWrite Program sponsored by NSF at www.ncsu.edu/labwrite. Also see advice from the Council of Science Editors—CSE.)

The following Voice from Across the Curriculum offers a fuller definition of the parts of the report format used in the sciences, a format we will then restate in a way that makes the common denominators of this and other formats easier to recognize.

VOICES FROM ACROSS THE CURRICULUM

Writing in the Sciences: A Biochemistry Professor Speaks

The lab report as taught in college science courses teaches students to mimic the process of thinking required to write a scientific paper. The governing question of the lab report is, "To what extent is my data consistent with what I was supposed to get?"

The lab report, like most scientific writing, has four parts (five if you include the abstract):

Abstract
—The short synoptic version of essentially the entire paper: What you did, what you found, and how you did it.

Introduction/Purpose/Objective
—What you are trying to accomplish and why it is important.

Methods/Experimental Procedures
—The details of how you performed the experiments.

Results/Data
— Reporting of the data without commentary, often done with tables, graphs, and figures rather than text.
—Primarily summative and descriptive.

Discussion/Conclusions
— This is where the analysis happens. Cite the data, then make qualified, evidence-based claims from the data; draw implications.

In the written accounts of scientific experiments, some information is repeated across sections. This repetition is deliberate. No scientist reads a paper in order, and so every section must stand by itself.

—KERI COLABROY, PROFESSOR OF BIOCHEMISTRY

THE COMMON FORMAT OF ACADEMIC WRITING

The following restatement of the IMRAD format demonstrates how similar it is in its aims and methods to other kinds of academic writing. This format could be used to organize virtually any academic paper.

1. Begin with a problem, a question, or an uncertainty. Say why the new study might matter, why it needs doing. Offer a theory to be tested (working thesis/hypothesis).

2. Test the adequacy of the theory by conducting some kind of experimental procedure or other way of analyzing evidence.

3. Report resulting data—what was revealed by the experiment or other analytical method such as close reading of textual evidence or statistical analysis.

4. Interpret the results and draw conclusions about their significance. How might the results change current thinking and/or open the way to new questions and further study?

If you are just learning to write and think in an academic discipline, you cannot be expected to say in the opening paragraph the state of knowledge in the field on a particular question. Nor can you be expected to arrive at something that will alter thinking in a discipline—although sometimes this does, in fact, happen. Nevertheless, college writers and their teachers across the curriculum write with similar goals: *ask and answer a new question, offer alternatives to existing ideas or evidence, or provide a new perspective or better evidence on something already known.*

The observations in the following Voices from Across the Curriculum apply to much, but certainly not all, of the writing that goes on in the sciences. Writing in physics, for example, in which research is more theoretical, often takes a different form. There are other exceptions. Writing in psychology can appear in the form of the case study, rather than in reports on experiments.

VOICES FROM ACROSS THE CURRICULUM

How to Write—and Read—Scientific Formats: Two Professors Speak

Experimental Psychology uses a very rigid format. I explain to the students the functions of the different sections for the reader. Once students start to read journal articles themselves, the functions of the sections become clear. Readers do not always want to read or reread the whole article. If I want to replicate someone's research, I may read just the "Methods" section to get the technical details I need. I may read just the "Results" section to get a sense of the numerical results I might expect. On the other hand, I may not care about the details of how the experiment was run. I might just want to know if it worked, in which case I would read the first few sentences of the "Discussion" section. The format lets me know exactly where to find whatever I might be looking for, without having to read through the whole article.

—LAURA EDELMAN, PROFESSOR OF PSYCHOLOGY

In writing in the social sciences, there is a standard plot with three alternative endings. The "Introduction" (a standard section of APA style) sets forth the problem, which the "Methods" section promises to address. The "Results" section "factually" reports the outcome of the study, with the "Discussion" section interpreting the results. "The data" are given the starring role in determining which ending is discussed in the "Discussion" section: hypothesis confirmed, hypothesis rejected, or hard to say. (I would say "which ending the author chooses" versus "which ending is discussed," but the data are supposed to be determinative, and the role of the author/investigator neutral.) Analytical thinking comes in setting up the problem and making sense of the results in conjunction with existing literature on the subject.

—ALAN TJELTVEIT, PROFESSOR OF PSYCHOLOGY

Three Organizing Strategies

Let's move now to organization on a smaller scale, ways of arranging inside the common format of academic writing. Here are three organizational patterns that are useful in many kinds of writing. They have both rhetorical and idea-generating (heuristic) value.

Climactic Order: Saving the Best for Last

Climactic order arranges elements from least to most important. The idea is to build to your best points, rather than leading with them and thereby allowing the paper to trail off from your more minor, less interesting observations.

But what are your best points? A frequent mistake that writers commit in arranging their points climactically is to assume that the best point is the most obvious, the one with the most data attached to it and the one least likely to produce disagreement with readers. This assumption can lead you to give more space than you should to ideas that really don't need much development because they are already evident to most readers.

If you follow the principle of climactic order, you would begin with the most obvious and predictable points—and ones that, psychologically speaking, would get readers assenting—and then build to the more revealing and less obvious ones. So, for example, if the comparisons between film A and film B are fairly mundane, but the contrasts are really provocative, you'd get the comparisons out of the way first and build to the contrasts, exploiting DIFFERENCE WITHIN SIMILARITY (see Chapter 4). So, for example, if there are four important reasons for labeling genetically modified foods, consider placing the most compelling one last. If you were to put it first, you might draw your readers in quickly (a principle used by news stories) but then would risk losing them as your argument descended into less important points.

Comparison/Contrast: Two Formats

In Chapter 4, we discuss comparison as an invention strategy. We now want to address this subject from the perspective of organizing a paper. The first decision a writer has to make when arranging comparisons and contrasts is whether to address the two items being compared and contrasted in sequential blocks (A and then B) or point by point:

- Organize by subjects being compared (subject A and then subject B).
- Organize the comparison under a series of topics (Topic 1: A and B, Topic 2: A and B, etc.).

If you are comparing subject A with subject B, you might first make all the points you wish to make about A and then make points about B by explicitly referring back to A as you go. The advantage of this format is that it allows you to use comparing and contrasting to figure out what you wish to say as you are drafting.

The disadvantage of this "subject-A-then-subject-B" format is that it can easily lose focus. If you don't manage to keep the points you raise about each side of your comparison parallel, you may end up with a paper comprised of two loosely connected halves. The solution is to make your comparisons and contrasts in the second half of the paper connect explicitly with what you said in the first half. What you say about subject A, in other words, should set the subtopics and terms for discussion of subject B.

The alternative pattern of organization for comparisons and contrasts is to organize by topic—not A and then B, but A1 and B1, A2 and B2, A3 and B3, and so forth. That is, you talk about both A and B under a series of subtopics. If, for example, you were comparing two films, you might organize your work under such headings as directing, script, acting, special effects, and so forth. The advantage of this format is that it better focuses the comparisons, pressing you to use them to think with. The disadvantage is that organizing in this way is sometimes difficult to manage until you've already done quite a bit of thinking about the two items you're comparing.

Concessions and Refutations: Giving and Taking Away

In the language of argument, you *concede* whenever you acknowledge that a position at odds with your own does indeed have merit, even though you continue to believe that your position overall is the more reasonable one. When making a concession, a writer needs to represent this competing point of view as genuinely creditable—rather than only seemingly creditable—until laying out a means of opposing it. Another option is to argue against these views so as to *refute* their reasonableness. (For misuse of concessions and refutations, see "Straw man" under "A Brief Glossary of Common Logical Fallacies" in Chapter 3.)

As a rule of thumb, avoid making your readers wait too long before you either concede or refute a view that you can assume will already have occurred to them. If you delay too long, you may inadvertently suggest either that you are unaware of the competing view or that you are afraid to bring it up.

In the case of short, easily managed concessions and refutations, you can often house these within the first several paragraphs and, in this way, clear a space for the position you wish to promote. In the case of more complicated and potentially more threatening alternative arguments, you may need to express your own position clearly and convincingly first. But to avoid the rhetorical problem of appearing to ignore the threat, you will probably need to give it a nod, telling readers that you will return to a full discussion of it later, once you have laid out your own position in some detail.

The placement of arguments has much to do with their relative complexity. Reasonably straightforward and easily explained concessions and refutations can often all be grouped in one place, perhaps as early as the second or third paragraph of a paper. The approach to concession and refutation in more complex arguments does not allow for such grouping. For each part of your argument, you will probably need to concede and refute as necessary before moving to the next part of your argument and repeating the procedure.

TRY THIS 10.1: Locating Concessions and Refutations
Study the paragraph on gender inequality and language to answer the following questions: (1) What language functions as concession? (2) What language functions as refutation? (3) What part of the competing argument does the refutation still appear willing to concede? (4) How is the refutation that the writer offers different from the position to which he concedes?

Gender Inequality and Linguistic Bias

The more conservative side on this issue questions whether the elimination of generic pronouns can, in fact, change attitudes, and whether intentionally changing language is even possible. The reformist side believes that the elimination of generic pronouns is necessary for women's liberation from oppression and that reshaping the use of male pronouns as generic is both possible and effective. Although the answer to the debate over the direct link between a change in language and a change in society is not certain, it is certain that the attitudes and behaviors of societies are inseparable from language. Language conditions what we feel and think. The act of using "they" to refer to all people rather than the generic "he" will not automatically change collective attitudes toward women. These generic pronouns should be changed, however, because 1) the struggle itself increases awareness and discussion of the sexual inequalities in society, and subsequently, this awareness will transform attitudes and language, and 2) the power of linguistic usage has been mainly controlled by and reserved for men. Solely by participating in linguistic reform, women have begun to appropriate some of the power for themselves.

What Introductions Do: "Why What I'm Saying Matters"

Introductions and conclusions are sites of difficulty for many writers. It's a challenge to decide how to start—the power of first impressions is legendary—and a last impression is often *the* lasting one. In both locations, the beginning and the end, a piece of writing needs to do a lot of work. We've said earlier, when we presented the idea that there is a common structure underlying most academic writing that it is *problem-oriented*. This is generally the case, despite surface differences in various disciplinary contexts. The same goes, on a smaller scale, for introductions and conclusions. That is, we can generalize about what they need to do, what they seek to accomplish, and what risks they run regardless of the specific cosmetic features of a particular disciplinary format. Let's start with introductions.

Most kinds of academic writing begin by telling readers what the writer found interesting, worth pursuing, and why. The Latin roots of the word suggest that introductions bring the reader into a subject (*intro*, meaning "within," and *ducere*, meaning "to lead or bring"). The length varies, depending on the scope of the writing project. An introduction may take a paragraph, a few paragraphs, a few pages, a chapter, or even a book. In most academic writing, one or two paragraphs is a standard length.

The primary challenge in writing introductions lies in occupying the middle ground between saying too much too soon (overassertive prejudgment) and saying too little up front (avoidance of taking a position or posing a problem). The most important thing to do in the introductory paragraph of an analytical paper is to lay out a *genuine issue*, something that seems to be *at stake* in whatever it is you are studying.

Most effective introductions set up this issue as quickly and concretely as possible. The introduction should give your reader a quick sampling of some feature or features in your evidence that initially aroused your curiosity. As a rule, assume that readers of your essay will need to know on page one—preferably by the end of your first paragraph—what your paper is attempting to resolve or negotiate. Your introduction is saying: "Look at this, reader; it is worth thinking about, and here's why."

As we said in Chapter 7, in most academic disciplines (with some significant exceptions, such as philosophy) the first paragraph of a paper usually does not need to—and most often can't—offer your conclusion; it will take the body of your paper to accomplish that. The introduction should, however, provide a quick look at particular details that set up the issue. You can then use these details to generate a *theory*, a *working hypothesis*, about whatever it is you think is at stake in the material. The rest of the paper then tests and develops this theory. (See "Introductions, Conclusions, and the Thesis" in Chapter 7.)

In the sciences, the standard instructions for composing an introduction are worded somewhat differently, but with similar intent: to create a context by citing previous work relevant to your study; to show the need for new information by pointing to an uncertainty or problem in existing knowledge; and to say what you are trying to accomplish and why it is important.

We here repeat from Chapter 7 a list of kinds of questions that introductory paragraphs usually answer:

> What is potentially interesting about what I have noticed, and why?
> What am I seeing that other people perhaps have not seen or have not sufficiently acknowledged?
> Why might what I have noticed matter in relation to the usual ways of thinking about my subject?
> How might what I have noticed require a new way of thinking about my subject, or at least a revision, however slight, of the usual ways of thinking?

How Much to Introduce Up Front: Typical Problems

The danger is trying to turn the introduction into a miniature essay. Consider the three problems discussed next as symptoms of overcompression—

telltale signs that you need to reconceive, and probably reduce, your introduction.

Digression Digression results when you try to include too much background. If, for example, you plan to write about a recent innovation in video technology, you'll need to monitor the amount and kind of technical information you include in your opening paragraphs. You'll also want to avoid starting at a point that is too far away from your immediate concerns, as in "From the beginning of time humans have needed to communicate."

As a general rule in academic writing, don't assume that your readers know little or nothing about the subject. Instead, use the social potential of the introduction to negotiate with your audience, setting up your relationship with your readers and making clear what you are assuming they do and do not know.

Incoherence Incoherence results when you try to preview too much of your paper's conclusion in the introduction. Such introductions move in too many directions at once, usually because the writer is trying to conclude before going through the discussion that will make the conclusion comprehensible. The language you are compelled to use in such cases tends to be too dense, and the connections between the sentences tend to get left out, because there isn't enough room to include them. After having read the entire paper, your readers may be able to make sense of the introduction, but in that case, the introduction has not done its job.

The following introductory paragraph is incoherent, primarily because it tries to include too much. It neither adequately connects its ideas nor defines its terms.

> Twinship is a symbol in many religious traditions. The significance of twinship will be discussed and explored in the Native American, Japanese Shinto, and Christian religions. Twinship can be either in opposing or common forces in the form of deities or mortals. There are several forms of twinship that show duality of order versus chaos, good versus evil, and creation versus destruction. The significance of twinship is to set moral codes for society and to explain the inexplicable.

Prejudgment Prejudgment results when you appear to have already settled the question to be pursued in the rest of the paper. The problem here is logical. In the effort to preview your paper's conclusion at the outset, you risk appearing to assume something as true that your paper will, in fact, need to test. Opening in this way, in any event, can make the rest of the paper seem redundant. Even in the sciences, in which a concise statement of objectives, plan of attack, and hypothesis are usually required up front, separate "Results" and "Discussion" sections are reserved for the conclusion.

VOICES FROM ACROSS THE CURRICULUM

Avoiding Strong Claims in the Introduction: An Economics Professor Speaks

I advise students to be careful about how they set up tentative conclusions in the opening paragraph, because these can easily slide into a prejudging of the question at hand. I would be more comfortable with a clear statement of the prevailing views held by others. For example, a student could write on the question, "Was Franklin Delano Roosevelt a Keynesian?" What purpose would it serve in an opening paragraph to reveal without any supporting discussion that FDR was or was not a Keynesian?

What might be better would be to say that in the public mind FDR is regarded as the original big spender, that some people commonly associate New Deal policies with general conceptions of Keynesianism, but that there may be some surprises in store as that common notion is examined.

In sum, I would discourage students from making strong claims at or near the beginning of a paper. Let's see the evidence first. We should all have respect for the evidence. Strong assertions, bordering on conclusions, too early on are inappropriate.

—JAMES MARSHALL, PROFESSOR OF ECONOMICS

Some Good Ways to Begin a Paper

All of the following ways to begin a paper enable you to play an ace, establishing your authority with your readers, without having to play your whole hand. They offer a strong starting position, rather than a miniaturized version of the entire paper. Remember that the aim of the introduction is to answer the questions, Why does what I'm about to say matter? and What makes it especially interesting or revealing, and in what context? Here are a few methods of accomplishing this aim.

Challenge a Commonly Held View This move provides you with a framework against which to develop your ideas; it allows you to begin with some back pressure, which will help you to define your position. Because you are responding to a known point of view, you have a ready way of integrating context into your paper. As the economics professor notes of the FDR example, until we understand the prevailing view on FDR, it is pointless to start considering whether or not he was a Keynesian.

Begin with a Definition Beginning with a definition is a reliable way to introduce a topic, as long as that definition has some significance for the discussion to follow. If the definition doesn't do any conceptual work in the introduction, the definition gambit becomes a pointless cliché.

You are most likely to avoid cliché if you cite a source other than a standard dictionary for your definition. The reference collection of any academic library contains a range of discipline-specific lexicons that provide more precise and authoritative definitions than Webster ever could. A useful alternative is to quote a given author's definition of a key term because you want to make a point about the author's particular definition: for example, "Although the *Dictionary of Economics* defines Keynesianism as XYZ, Smith treats only X and Y (or substitutes A for Z, and so forth)." (See the discussion of definition topics in Chapter 4 for more on this subject.)

Lead with Your Second-Best Example Another versatile opening gambit, where disciplinary conventions allow, is to use your *second-best example* to set up the issue or question that you later develop in-depth with your best example. This move is especially useful in papers that proceed inductively on the strength of representative examples, an organizational pattern common in the humanities. As you are assembling evidence in the outlining and pre-writing stage, in many cases you will accumulate a number of examples that illustrate the same basic point. For example, several battles might illustrate a particular general's military strategy; several primaries might exemplify how a particular candidate tailors their speeches to appeal to the religious right; several scenes might show how a particular playwright romanticizes the working class; and so on.

Save the best example to receive the most analytical attention in your paper. If you were to present this example in the introduction, you would risk making the rest of the essay vaguely repetitive. A quick close-up of another example will strengthen your argument or interpretation. By using a different example to raise the issues, you suggest that the phenomenon exemplified is not an isolated case and that the major example you will eventually concentrate upon is, indeed, representative.

Exemplify the Topic with a Narrative The narrative opening, an occasional gambit in the humanities and social sciences, introduces a short, pertinent, and vivid story or anecdote that exemplifies a key aspect of a topic. Although generally not permissible in the formal reports assigned in the natural and social sciences, narrative openings turn up in virtually all other kinds of writing across the curriculum.

As the introduction funnels to its thesis, the readers receive a graphic sense of the issue that the writer will now develop nonnarratively. Nonnarrative treatment is necessary because by itself anecdotal evidence can be seen as merely personal. Storytelling is suggestive but usually does not constitute sufficient proof; it needs to be corroborated.

What Conclusions Do: The Final "So What?"

Like the introduction, the conclusion has a key social function: it escorts readers out of the paper, just as the introduction has escorted them in. The concluding paragraph presents the paper's final "So What?"

Conclusions always state the thesis in its most fully evolved form. (See "The Conclusion: Returning the Thesis to the Larger Conversation" in Chapter 7.) In addition, the conclusion usually makes all of the following moves:

- *It comes full circle.* That is, it creates a sense of closure by revisiting the way the paper began. Often, it returns to some key phrase from the context established in the introduction and updates it. To come full circle always involves more than just restatement; it amplifies or extends the original version.

- *It pursues implications.* That is, it reasons from the particular focus of the essay to broader issues, such as the study's practical consequences or applications, or future-oriented issues, such as avenues for further research. To unfold implications in this way is to broaden the view from the here and now of the paper by looking outward to the wider world and forward to the future.

- *It identifies limitations.* That is, it acknowledges restrictions of method or focus in the analysis, and qualifies the conclusion (and its implications) accordingly.

These moves are quite literally movements—they take the thinking in the essay, and the readers with it, both backward and forward. The backward thrust we call *culmination*; the forward thrust we call *send-off*.

When you culminate a paper, you bring together things that you have already said, establishing their connection and ascending to one final statement of your thinking. The word "culminate" is derived from the Latin "*columen*," meaning "top or summit." To culminate is to reach the highest point, and it implies a mountain (in this case, of information and analysis) that you have scaled.

The climactic effects of culmination provide the basis for the send-off. The send-off is both social and conceptual, a final opening outward of the topic that leads the reader out of the paper with something further to think about. Here the thinking moves beyond the close analysis of data that has occupied the body of the paper into a kind of speculation that the writer has earned the right to formulate.

Simply put, you culminate with the best statement of your big idea, and your send-off guides you and your reader out of the paper. The professors in the following Voices from Across the Curriculum suggest ways of ending on a note of expanded implication, bringing the paper's more focused analysis to a larger perspective.

Beyond Restatement: A Business and a Political Science Professor Speak

I tell my students that too many papers "just end," as if the last page or so were missing. I tell them the importance of ending a work. One could summarize main points, but I tell them this is not heavy lifting.

I believe the ending should be an expansion of possibilities, sort of like an introduction to some much larger "mental" paper out there. I sometimes encourage students to see the concluding section as an option to introduce ideas that can't be dealt with now. Sort of a "Having done this, I would want to explore boom, boom, boom if I were to continue further." Here the students can critique and recommend ("Having seen 'this,' one wonders 'that'").

—FREDERICK NORLING, PROFESSOR OF BUSINESS

The conclusion does not appear simply as a restatement of a thesis, but rather as an attempt to draw out its implications and significance (the "So What?"). This is what I usually try to impress upon students. For instance, if a student is writing on a particular proposal for party reform, I would expect the concluding paragraph to consider both the significance of the reform and its practicality.

I should note that professional papers often indicate the tentativeness of their conclusions by stressing the need for future research and indicating what these research needs might be. Although I haven't tried this, maybe it would be useful to have students conclude papers with a section entitled "For Further Consideration" in which they would indicate those things that they would have liked to have known but couldn't, given their time constraints, the availability of information, and lack of methodological sophistication. This would serve as a reminder of the tentativeness of conclusions and the need to revisit and revise arguments in the future (which, after all, is a good scholarly habit).

—JACK GAMBINO, PROFESSOR OF POLITICAL SCIENCE

Solving Typical Problems in Conclusions

The primary challenge in writing conclusions lies in finding a way to culminate your analysis without claiming either too little or too much. There are a number of fairly common problems to guard against if you are to avoid either of these two extremes.

Redundancy In Chapter 6, we lampooned an exaggerated example of the five-paragraph form for constructing its conclusion by stating "Thus, we see" and then repeating the introduction verbatim. The result is redundancy. It's a good idea to refer back to the opening, but it's a bad idea just to reinsert it mechanically. Instead, reevaluate what you said there in light of where you've ended up, repeating only key words or phrases from the introduction. This kind of selective repetition is a desirable way of achieving unity and will keep you from making one of two opposite mistakes—either repeating too much or bringing up a totally new point in the conclusion.

Raising a Totally New Point Raising a totally new point can distract or bewilder a reader. This problem often arises out of a writer's praiseworthy desire to avoid repetition. As a rule, you can guard against the problem by making sure that you have clearly expressed the conceptual link between your central conclusion and any implications you may draw. An implication is not a totally new point, but rather one that follows from the position you have been analyzing.

Similarly, although a capping judgment or send-off may appear for the first time in your concluding paragraph, it should have been anticipated by the body of your paper. Conclusions often indicate where you think you (or an interested reader) may need to go next, but you don't actually go there. In a paper on the economist Milton Friedman, for example, if you think that another economist offers a useful way of critiquing him, you probably should not introduce this person for the first time in your conclusion.

Overstatement Many writers are confused over how much they should claim in the conclusion. Out of the understandable (but mistaken) desire for a grand (rather than a modest and qualified) culmination, writers sometimes overstate the case. They assert more than their evidence has proven or even suggested.

Must a conclusion arrive at some comprehensive and final answer to the question that your paper has analyzed? Depending on the question and the disciplinary conventions, you may need to come down exclusively on one side or another. In a great many cases, however, the answers with which you conclude can be more moderate. Especially in the humanities, good analytical writing seeks to unfold successive layers of implication, so it's not reasonable for you to expect neat closure. In such cases, you are usually better off drawing the line at points of relative stability.

Anticlimax The end of the conclusion is a "charged" site because it gives the reader a last impression of your paper. If you end with a concession—an acknowledgment of a rival position at odds with your thesis—you risk leaving the reader unsettled and possibly confused. The term for this kind of letdown is "anticlimax." In most cases, you will flub the send-off if you depart the paper on an anticlimax.

There are many forms of anticlimax besides ending with a concession. If your conclusion peters out in a random list, an apparent afterthought, or a last-minute qualification of your claims, the effect is anticlimactic. And for many readers, if your final answer comes from quoting an authority in place of establishing your own, that, too, is an anticlimax.

A useful rule for the introduction is to play an ace but not your whole hand. In the context of this card-game analogy, it is similarly effective to save an ace for the conclusion. In most cases, this high card will provide an answer to some culminating "So What?" question—a last view of the implications or consequences of your analysis.

Introductions and Conclusions Across the Curriculum

Throughout the following discussion of disciplinary practices in introductions and conclusions, we quote first-hand advice from faculty colleagues at our college. You will notice differences in the guidelines that the various disciplines offer, but you will also see that the jobs introductions and conclusions do are actually quite similar across the curriculum.

Introductory Paragraphs in the Humanities

Here is a typical set of guidelines for writing introductory paragraphs in a humanities paper—in this case, a poetry analysis in an English course. Introductions are not the same across all disciplines in the humanities, but much in the following guidelines is representative.

An introduction is not a conclusion. You do not need to announce, in short form, your whole argument. In English papers, the introductory paragraph is an opening gambit. The thesis you state at the end of paragraph one should be an idea, not a statement of fact. For example, you might offer an idea about what you think is the most important difference and/or similarity between the poem you have chosen to analyze and another poem. This statement will get qualified and expanded and tested in the paper. You should not simply march the statement through the paper and prove that you are right.

The intro offers readers some piece of your evidence—some data from your poem: perhaps a binary that you see in both poems or some other tendency of the language in both that you found interesting and that you think is worth exploring. The reader should come away from your opening paragraph knowing concretely what you found interesting and worth pursuing and why.

Resist dumping a great lump of background into the intro. You should do some contextualizing in the opening but don't overdo it. Stay focused on the poem and what you notice about the kind of thinking it is inviting us to do.

Resist what is known as "freshman omniscience"—recognizable by sweeping claims and a grandiose tone . . . "Since the beginning of time poets have been . . ."

The last sentence of the paragraph should make some kind of claim—probably a comparative claim about the relation between your two poems. This claim should not take the form of the standard tripartite thesis typical of the 5-paragraph form essay. Rather than offering three points, each of which would then get a paragraph or two, you want to set up a sequence of thought in which you try on various ways of understanding the problem, issue, or question you have noticed about your subject.

Here are a couple of differences between science and humanities papers that are worth noting. In the sciences, it is considered inappropriate to name and especially to criticize pieces of research or their authors. Writers in the humanities, however, are much more likely to name names, to quote other studies, and to be explicit on where these studies seem to fall short. Papers in the humanities often begin with a compressed account of who said what, why they may have said it, and what in it needs revising.

Writers in the humanities quote and then paraphrase key statements, rather than summarizing and paraphrasing without the original language, as is the rule in psychology and some other science and social science writing. Because most writing in the humanities is grounded in textual analysis, humanities writers think it important to attend to the actual language of other people's writing. Words and their meanings are data to humanities writers. It is a habit of mind in the humanities to always share the actual evidence with readers—the language being paraphrased and cited—rather than asking readers to take the writer's word for it.

Using Procedural Openings: Introductions and Conclusions in the Social Sciences

In this section and the next one, we will be addressing issues that are not limited to social science writing but are most likely to be found there. In the interests of clear organization, some academic disciplines require students to include in the introduction an explanation of how the paper will proceed. Such a general statement of method and/or intention is known as a *procedural opening*. Among the disciplines in which you are most likely to find this format are philosophy, political science, and sociology. The danger of procedural openings is that the writer will avoid making a claim at all, just describing the general shape to come instead.

The statement of a paper's plan is not and cannot take the place of a thesis (an idea about the topic that the paper will explore and defend). Consider the deficiencies of the following procedural opening.

> In this paper I will first discuss the strong points and weak points in America's treatment of the elderly. Then I will compare this treatment with that in other industrial nations in the West. Finally, I will evaluate the various proposals for reform that have been advanced here and abroad.

This paragraph identifies the subject, but it neither addresses why the subject matters nor suggests the writer's approach. Nor does it provide background to the topic or suggest a hypothesis that the paper will pursue. In some kinds of essays, especially those that move (inductively) from specific observations to more general claims, there is little need for procedural openings, with their declaration of intention and method at the outset. As the following Voice from Across the Curriculum reveals, however, the introductory "road map" is a common strategy in some disciplines.

Using Procedural Openings: A Political Science Professor Speaks

I encourage students to provide a "road map" paragraph early in the paper, perhaps the second or third paragraph. (This is a common practice in professional journals.) The "road map" tells the reader the basic outline of the argument. Something like the following: "In the first part of my paper I will present a brief history of the issue. . . . This will be followed by an account of the current controversy. . . . Part III will spell out my alternative account and evidence. . . . I then conclude. . . ." I think such a paragraph becomes more necessary with longer papers.

—JACK GAMBINO, PROFESSOR OF POLITICAL SCIENCE

Putting an Issue or Question in Context

Rather than leaping immediately to the paper's issue, question, or problem, most effective introductions provide some broader context to indicate why the issue matters. Things don't just "mean" in the abstract; they mean in specific contexts.

In the following Voice from Across the Curriculum, Political Science Professor Jack Gambino notes the usefulness of anomalies for contextualizing papers in his discipline. The discovery of an anomaly, something that does not fit with conventional ways of thinking, can serve as a useful point of departure in a paper that goes on to revise an existing theory or opinion.

VOICES FROM ACROSS THE CURRICULUM

Providing an Introductory Context: A Political Science Professor Speaks

An introduction is not simply the statement of a thesis but also the place where the student needs to set a context, a framework that makes such a thesis statement interesting, timely, or in some other way important. It is common to see papers in political science begin by pointing out a discrepancy between conventional wisdom (what the pundits say) and recent political developments, between popular opinion and empirical evidence, or between theoretical frameworks and particular test cases. Papers, in other words, often begin by presenting *anomalies*.

I encourage students to write opening paragraphs that attempt to elucidate such anomalies by:

1. Stating the specific point of departure: are they taking issue with a bit of conventional wisdom? Popular opinions? A theoretical perspective? This provides the context in which a student can "frame" a problem, issue, and so forth.

2. Explaining why the wisdom/opinion/theory has become problematic or controversial by focusing on a particular issue, event, test case, or empirical evidence.

3. Formulating a brief statement of the tentative thesis/position to be pursued in the paper. This can take several forms, including the revising of conventional wisdom/

theory/opinion, discarding it in favor of alternative conceptions, or calling for redefinition of an issue and question.

—JACK GAMBINO, PROFESSOR OF POLITICAL SCIENCE

In the following Voice from Across the Curriculum, Political Science Professor Chris Borick explains effective and less effective ways of stating research questions and hypotheses in the introduction.

VOICES FROM ACROSS THE CURRICULUM

Framing Research Questions and Hypotheses: A Political Science Professor Speaks

Different fields within Political Science—legal writing, political theory, political policy, and behavior—prescribe different forms of writing. Political policy and political behavior papers adhere to a version of the format used in science writing. This format has six parts: statement of the research question, literature review (context), statement of hypothesis, measurement of variables, description of tests, and analysis of findings. The literature review describes the conversation that is going on in the field on the paper's topic. It explains what others know. The research question tells readers what the writer is trying to do. The hypothesis states a claim that is specific enough to test.

The research question sets up the hypothesis; it is the point from which everything flows. Consider the following two versions of a research question on capital punishment. 1) In this study I seek to examine the capital punishment laws used at the state level. 2) In this study I seek to explain why some states adopt capital punishment and others do not. The second version is clearly better. It gives much better direction.

The hypothesis needs to indicate some direction for the research. Although general in scope, it must be specific enough to test. Here again are two examples. Which do you think would make the better hypothesis? 1) The greater the percentage of college educated individuals in a state, the more likely that state will be to allow same sex marriage. 2) The more educated a society, the more liberal it will be.

—CHRIS BORICK, PROFESSOR OF POLITICAL SCIENCE

Writing Introductions in the Sciences

In the following Voices from Across the Curriculum, Biochemistry Professor Keri Colabroy and Psychology Professors Laura Edelman and Mark Sciutto address the challenges of introducing and contextualizing research in science writing.

VOICES FROM ACROSS THE CURRICULUM

Introductions in the Sciences: Three Professors Speak

In scientific papers, introductions serve two purposes:

1. To orient your readers to the scientific context of your work while showing them the inherent need for new (your) information to solve an *uncertainty* or *problem*,

something you or the community doesn't quite understand. (In *Writing Analytically*, the prompts "interesting, significant, or strange" focus writers on problems and areas of uncertainty.)

2. To state succinctly what the paper/study has accomplished and what that means for the big picture you outlined in point #1.

The introduction of a scientific paper is full of references to primary literature (other scientific papers). In most undergraduate science courses, students are not asked to write the introduction section. Instead, the professor provides a paraphrase of the question/problem that the experiment is meant to solve.

—KERI COLABROY, PROFESSOR OF BIOCHEMISTRY

The introduction is one of the hardest sections to write. In the introduction, students must summarize, analyze, and integrate the work of numerous other authors and use that to build their own argument.

The task is to read each article and *summarize* it in their own words. The key is to analyze rather than just repeat material from the articles so as to make clear the connections among them. (It is important to note that experimental psychologists almost never use direct quotes in their writing. Many of my students have been trained to use direct quotation for their other classes, and so I have to spend time explaining how to summarize without directly quoting or plagiarizing the work that they have read.)

Finally, in the introduction the students must show explicitly how the articles they have summarized lead to the hypothesis they have devised. Many times the students see the connection as implicitly obvious, but I require that they explicitly state the relationships between what they read and what they plan to do.

—LAURA EDELMAN, PROFESSOR OF PSYCHOLOGY

The format of the empirical paper in Psychology resembles an hour glass. It starts reasonably broad, narrows, and then broadens again to the larger perspective: "Now that we know this, where can we go with it? What are the implications?" The introduction is especially difficult to write because it must contextualize the new research by pulling together a lot of reading from a variety of sources. This part of the introduction, the literature review, answers the question, "What do we know?"

In order to efficiently locate the new study in the context of others' work on the subject, writers must **integrate** citations. Rather than summarize what Johnson found and then what Smith found and then what Moore found, the writer needs to bring these together into a more concise summary. All three studies might be summarized and cited in one paragraph or even a single sentence. As a rule of thumb, citations should include more than one source. Single citations don't allow enough integration.

—MARK SCIUTTO, PROFESSOR OF PSYCHOLOGY

Integration of Citations in a Literature Review: A Brief Example

Note that in the following paragraph from a 1999 article in *Personality and Social Psychology Bulletin* the citations (in parentheses) include more than one study:

> Self-presentational motives play a role in a variety of potentially dangerous health-related behaviors, including behaviors that lead to risk of HIV infection; accidental death and injury; and alcohol, tobacco, and drug use (Leary, Tchividjian, & Kraxberger, 1994; Martin, Leary, & Rejeski, in press). The desire to be perceived as a risk-taker, brave, or one of the crowd (or conversely, concerns about being viewed as overly cautious or neurotic) may lead people to take chances with their health to create the desired image. (Denscombe, 1993; Finney, 1978)

Introductions in Scientific Papers: A Brief Example

The following example comes from a set of excerpted introductions that Biochemistry Professor Keri Colabroy uses to teach her students how to write concise, focused sentences of two types: Type #1: sentences that orient readers to the scientific context of a new study while also showing the need for it, and Type #2: sentences that succinctly state what the paper or study has accomplished. The sentences come from a paper published in *Nature Chemical Biology* 2006.

> #1 Although the antitumor activity of these two compounds has been shown to involve binding to microtubules, the targets and modes of actions for many other bioactive cyanobacterial metabolites remain elusive.

Dr. Colabroy comments: *This is a great sentence. You can see the tension. Some activity has been shown, but there is still something we don't understand . . . and that is the problem this paper will solve.*

> #2 Here we examine the mode of action of apratoxin A using a number of approaches based on functional genomics, including mRNA expression analysis and genome-wise, arrayed cDNA overexpression. These and other studies suggest that apratoxin A acts in part by blocking the FGFR signaling pathway.

Dr. Colabroy comments: *The use of "here" focuses your attention on the action that immediately follows—"we examine." That is different from "we found" or "we propose," and it implies that the authors didn't really have a hypothesis going in. They were just trying to learn some stuff, and in the process, they came up with some "implications" from the data.*

Writing Conclusions in the Sciences: The Discussion Section

As is the case with introductions, the conclusions of reports written in the natural sciences and psychology are regulated by formalized disciplinary formats. Conclusions, for example, occur in a section entitled "Discussion." There the writer analyzes conclusions and qualifies them in relation to some larger experimental context, "the big picture."

First specific results are interpreted (but not restated), and then their implications and limitations are discussed. At the end, the writer should rephrase the original research question and discuss it in light of the results presented. It is at this point that alternative explanations may be considered and new questions may be posed.

In the following Voices from Across the Curriculum, a psychology professor and a biochemistry professor explain how the Discussion section of a scientific paper locates its conclusions in the context of other research—that which came before and that which will follow.

VOICES FROM ACROSS THE CURRICULUM

Writing Conclusions in the Sciences: Two Professors Speak

The conclusion occurs in a section labeled "Discussion" and, as specified by the *Publication Manual of the American Psychological Association*, is guided by the following questions:

What have I contributed here?
How has my study helped to resolve the original problem?
What conclusions and theoretical implications can I draw from my study?

In a broad sense, a research report should be seen as but one moment in a broader research tradition that *preceded* the study being written about and that will *continue after* this study is published. The conclusion should tie this particular study into both previous research considering implications for the theory guiding this study and (when applicable) practical implications of this study. One of the great challenges of writing a research report is thus to place this study within that broader research tradition. That's an analytical task.

—ALAN TJELTVEIT, PROFESSOR OF PSYCHOLOGY

The Discussion section is where the scientist finally gets to analyze the data. The previous two sections of a science paper—Methods and Results—report rather than analyze. The discussion section is not a summary; rather, the writer makes qualified claims and backs them up with evidence (data). Analysis of the data tells readers what the study found in the context of current knowledge in the field and the researcher's expectations. The discussion section completes the frame set up by the introduction by arguing for the significance of the study within its scientific context.

The paper's conclusions, which usually appear in the last paragraph of the Discussion, always look back and then forward—first back to previous research and then forward to remaining questions. The conclusion explains how questions have been answered and how knowledge in the field might be changed because of the new information.

—KERI COLABROY, PROFESSOR OF BIOCHEMISTRY

Conclusions in Scientific Papers: A Brief Example

The following example is from the discussion/conclusion section of a scientific paper.

As you read this sample Discussion/Conclusion section of a scientific paper, refer back to Dr. Colabroy's preceding comments.

> The rapid and sustained elevations in 2-AG induced by JZL 184 were accompanied by an array of CB1-dependent behavioral effects, including analgesia, hypomotility, and hypothermia. This collection of phenotypes qualitatively resembles those induced by direct CB1 agonists. Overall these data suggest that MAGL-regulated 2-AG pathways endogenously modulate several behavioral processes classically associated with the pharmacology of cannabinoids . . .
>
> In summary, we believe that the properties of JZL184 warrant inclusion of this compound among the growing arsenal of efficacious and selective pharmacological probes used to examine the endocannabinoid system. JZL184 could itself serve as a lead scaffold for the development of such dual inhibitors, given that at high concentrations this compound inhibited both MAGL and FAAH without affecting other brain serine hydrolases.

VOICES FROM ACROSS THE CURRICULUM

Ethos and Style in Scientific Writing: A Biochemistry Professor Speaks

Word choice in scientific papers—especially the choice of verbs—is important. Scientific writing never "proves," for example. It "implies" and "indicates." The science writer chooses verbs to make carefully qualified claims based on an accumulation of evidence.

Scientific writing is corporate, by which I mean that scientific writers speak to and about the community of other science writers. To name a particular scientist is considered pretentious. It is appropriate to point out inconsistencies in thinking as in, "a lot of work has been done here, but we still don't understand X." It is not considered appropriate to locate shortcomings in the work of particular scientists.

—KERI COLABROY, PROFESSOR OF BIOCHEMISTRY

The Idea of the Paragraph

Throughout this section of the chapter, we will focus on what are sometimes called "body" paragraphs, as opposed to the more special-function paragraphs that serve as the beginnings and ends of papers.

It is useful to think of any piece of writing as consisting of parts or blocks. The paragraph is a fundamental building block, bigger than the sentence, smaller than the section or paper. Paragraphs can be thought of by analogy with the paper. Like papers, paragraphs have parts: they make opening gambits, they put forward evidence and analyze it, and they arrive at a summarizing or culminating closure. They have, in short, a beginning, a middle, and an end. But unlike the paper, the paragraph does not stand alone as an independent entity. For a paragraph to be effective, readers need to be able to understand its role in unfolding the thinking of the paper as a whole.

The two primary characteristics of virtually all strong paragraphs are unity and development.

- **Unity:** all the sentences in the paragraph should be related to some central idea or focus. Normally, the sentence that serves this function in the paragraph is the topic sentence.

- **Development:** the sentences in a paragraph need to connect to each other in some way; a paragraph needs to go somewhere, to build. Normally, the sentences in a paragraph either offer a series of observations about the main idea or build one upon the next to offer a more sustained analysis of one element of the main idea.

Notice that we don't say here that a paragraph offers a claim plus examples and reasons. This model of the paragraph is true in some cases, but paragraphs typically do more than make simple claims and then back them up with one or more examples.

Once you begin paying attention to paragraphs, you will see that they are far less uniform in their shapes and procedures than you may have been taught to believe. The paragraph police will not haul you away for producing a paragraph that lacks a topic sentence, or places it at the end of the paragraph instead of the front, or contains several claims instead of one, or delays the substantiating evidence till later. Nonetheless, most of the paragraphs you encounter—and most that you should write—have unity and development. *They are about one thing, and they tell you why it is important.*

How Long?: Paragraphs, Readers, and Writers

Paragraphing is a kindness to your reader because it divides your thinking into manageable bites. If you find a paragraph growing longer than half a page—particularly if it is your opening or second paragraph—find a place to make a paragraph break. More frequent paragraphing provides readers with convenient resting points from which to relaunch themselves into your thinking. In addition, paragraph indentations allow readers to scan essays, searching for connecting words and important ideas.

Long paragraphs are daunting for both readers and writers. When writers try to do too much in a single paragraph, they often lose the focus and lose contact with the larger purpose or point that got them into the paragraph in the first place. Remember that old rule about one idea to a paragraph? Well, it's not a bad rule, though it isn't exactly right because sometimes you need more space than a single paragraph can provide to lay out a complicated phase of your analysis. In that case, just break wherever it seems reasonable to do so in order to keep your paragraphs from becoming ungainly. Two paragraphs can be about the same thing, the first half and then the second half. This paragraph, for example, might have been easier to process if we had broken it right before the question about that old rule.

A short paragraph will always provide emphasis, for which most readers will thank you.

Paragraphs are a relief not just for your readers: they also give the writer a break. When you draft, start a new paragraph whenever you feel yourself getting stuck: it's the promise of a fresh start. Paragraph breaks are like turning a corner to a new view, even when the thinking is continuous. They also force the writer to make transitions, overt connections among the parts of the writer's thinking, and to state or restate key ideas.

It can be extraordinarily useful to draft a paper in phases, as a series of paragraphs:

- Break up the larger interpretation or argument into more manageable pieces.

- Give yourself space to think in short sections that you can then sequence.

- Clean up your thinking in revision by dividing its sections or phases into paragraphs.

Paragraphs need to justify their existence. A good way to check if your paragraph is really advancing your claims is to see if you have asked and answered "So What?" at the end of it.

Linking the Sentences in Paragraphs: Minding the Gaps

It helps to think of the space between the period at the end of a sentence and the beginning of the next sentence as a gap that the reader has to cross. Start thinking in this way as you follow the train of thought in this paragraph and those that follow it. Keep asking yourself: what is the connection between each sentence and the one that follows it? What keeps the reader from falling out of the paper at the gaps between sentences, losing sight of the thought connections that make a paragraph more than just a collection of sentences?

In many paragraphs, the connections between and among sentences are made apparent by the repetition of **key words**. This idea of key words brings us back to a core principle of this book: that both writers and readers make meaning by locating significant patterns of repetition and contrast. What is the pattern of repeated words in the paragraph above this one, for example? Notice the repetition of the key word "gap," which goes with the idea of falling and which is in opposition to such words as "connection" and "train of thought." The other connecting feature of the paragraph comes with its repeated use of questions. The paragraph you are now reading gets its sense of purpose from the previous paragraph's questions. Here we start answering them.

Sometimes (but not always) the connecting logic that helps readers negotiate the gaps between sentences must be made explicit. So, for example, some sentences begin with the words, "So, for example." The function of this type of connection is illustration. Some other words that operate in this gap-bridging way are "thus," "furthermore," "in addition," "similarly," "in other words," and "on the contrary."

When the organizing principle of a paragraph is sufficiently evident, explicit transitional words are often not needed. If parallelism is the paragraph's organizing principle, for example, readers will be able to see the relationship among the paragraph's sentences without frequent repetition of connecting words. (For more on parallelism, see Chapter 11.)

What a Paragraph Does: The Paragraph as Movement of Mind

The key to understanding how to write paragraphs, as well as how to analyze what you read in them, is to focus on what the various sentences in a paragraph *do*. To follow what a paragraph does is to follow its succession of sentences as a movement of mind, an unfolding of consciousness on the page that conveys to readers the relationships among its various pieces of information.

The sentences in a paragraph have different jobs; there is a distribution of labor. To see this element of paragraphing, it is essential that you "look beyond content"—focus not just on what the sentences are saying, but on how they are functioning individually and together. In Chapter 6, "Reasoning from Evidence to Claims," we asked you to distinguish which sentences in a paragraph were evidence and which were claims, and to mark these with an E or a C. Those are two tasks that sentences in a paragraph can perform.

Let's look briefly now at three ways of thinking about the internal logic of paragraphs, focusing on the interrelationship among sentences.

Paragraph Structure #1: Topic Sentence, Restriction, Illustration

One model for thinking about paragraph structure comes from the rhetorician Alton Becker: topic sentence (T), restriction (R), and illustration (I). The topic sentence states a claim—an idea that the paragraph will develop in some way. Restriction limits the claim in some way. Illustration supplies examples in support of the claim.

The TRI model does not cover everything that goes on in various kinds of paragraphs, but it is a good way to start looking at paragraphs in order to begin thinking about what the sentences do. Here is an expanded list of jobs that sentences may do inside paragraphs:

WHAT SENTENCES DO INSIDE PARAGRAPHS

T = topic sentence → announces the main idea of the paragraph

R = restriction → qualifies, further defines, limits claims; happens at various points in the paragraph

P = paraphrasing → restates claims and evidence to analyze them

I = illustration → provides substantiating evidence

EXP = explains the illustrations → draws out meaning of evidence

Th = thesis restatement → offers versions of an evolving thesis

Tr = transitional wording → links sentences, connects ideas inside paragraph but also connects paragraph to what precedes and follows it

SW= Answers "So What?" → tells readers the purpose of the paragraph, why the writer bothered to tell them this

Let's look at a paragraph to see what its sentences are doing. We have labeled some of the sentences (in square brackets) according to our expanded version of Becker's marking scheme.

> **[T:]** Armin Schnider, a neurologist from the Cantonal University Hospital in Geneva, Switzerland, says that the vast majority of confabulations he has heard from his patients over the years relate directly to their earlier lives. **[I:]** One of his patients, a retired dentist, worried while in hospital that he was keeping his patients waiting. **[I:]** Another, an elderly woman, talked regularly about her baby in the present tense. **[EXP:]** Most of these patients had damage to the temporal lobes of the brain, particularly the memory regions of the hippocampus, so it seemed likely that they had somehow lost the ability to make new memories and were retrieving old ones instead. **[EXP:]** The intriguing thing was that they didn't realise these memories were old— they seemed convinced by their stories, and sometimes even acted on them. **[SW:]** So Schnider decided to study their memory in more detail. (Helen Phillips, "Everyday Fairytales," *New Scientist*, 7 October 2006)

TRY THIS 10.2: Label the Function of the Sentences in a Paragraph

One of the best ways to understand how paragraphs work—to apprehend them as tools of thought and to be able to deploy them to work for you—is to label the function of the sentences in a sample paragraph as we have just done. Try this with any healthy paragraph in anything you have written or read.

Paragraph Structure #2: Observation → Implication → Conclusion One of the models described in this book for the analytical movement of mind is as follows: *Observation → So WHAT? → implication → So WHAT?→ tentative conclusions.* This sequence goes beyond the simplest kind of paragraph development—idea + illustration—because it contains more of the writer's thinking on how they reason to the claim from evidence. Not all paragraphs in an analytical paper move in this way, but a significant number do. We reprint the following paragraph from Chapter 1, adding annotations about what the paragraph does.

> **[Paragraph opens with empirical observation:]** If you look closely at Camilo Vergara's photo of Fern Street, Camden, 1988, you'll notice a sign on the side of a dilapidated building that reads "Danger: Men Working - W. Hargrove Demolition."

> **[Implication:]** Perhaps that warning captures the ominous atmosphere of these very different kinds of photographic documents by Camilo Vergara and Edward Burtynsky: "Danger: Men Working." Watch out—human beings are at work! **[Topic sentence:]** But the work that is presented is not so much a building-up as it is a tearing-down— the work of demolition. **[Qualification of claim:]** Of course, demolition is often necessary in order to construct anew: old buildings are leveled for new projects, whether you are building a highway or bridge in an American city or a dam in the Chinese countryside.

[Paraphrasing—interpretive restatement:] You might call modernity itself, as so many have, a process of creative destruction, a term used variously to describe modern art, capitalism, and technological innovation. **[Topic sentence:]** The photographs in this exhibit, however, force us to pay attention to the "destructive" side of this modern equation. **[Writer asks "So WHAT?" and concludes:]** What both Burtynsky and Vergara do in their respective ways is to put up a warning sign—they question whether the reworking of our natural and social environment leads to a sustainable human future. **[Restatement]:** And they wonder whether the process of creative destruction may not have spun recklessly out of control, producing places that are neither habitable nor sustainable. **[Supporting observation:]** In fact, a common element connecting the two photographic versions is the near absence of people in the landscape. **[Observation:]** While we see the evidence of the transforming power of human production on the physical and social environment, neither Vergara's urban ruins nor Burtynsky's industrial sites actually show us "men working." **[Observation:]** Isolated figures peer suspiciously out back doors or pick through the rubble, but they appear out of place. **[Writer asks "So WHAT?" and concludes in reference to the paragraph's opening observation]:** It is this sense of displacement—of human beings alienated from the environments they themselves have created—that provides the most haunting aspect of the work of these two photographers. (Jack Gambino, "Demolition Zones: Contemporary Photography by Edward Burtynsky and Camilo Jose Vergara.")

Paragraph Structure #3: Coordinate and Subordinate Paragraphs Here is a third way of thinking about how paragraphs develop. In his influential essay, "A Generative Rhetoric of the Paragraph," Francis Christensen posits two kinds of paragraphs, coordinate and subordinate. In coordinate structures, all of the sentences following the topic sentence are equal in weight, or as he puts it, "all children of the same mother" (*Notes Toward a New Rhetoric*, 1967, p. 61).

Consider the following example of a coordinate paragraph, taken from earlier in this chapter. Most of the sentences relate back to the topic sentence in some way.

[T:] Paragraphs are a relief not just for your readers: they also give the writer a break.

1 When you draft, start a new paragraph whenever you feel yourself getting stuck: it's the promise of a fresh start.
1 Paragraph breaks are like turning a corner to a new view, even when the thinking is continuous.
1 They also force the writer to make transitions, overt connections among the parts of the writer's thinking, and to state or restate key ideas.
1 Paragraph indentations allow readers to scan essays, searching for connecting words and important ideas.

Christensen would call this paragraph coordinate because all of the sentences that come after the topic sentence (in his words) "develop or amplify" it. Each offers reasons for thinking that paragraphs are a relief not just for readers but also for writers.

In what Christensen identifies as subordinate structures, each sentence clarifies or comments on the one before it, as for example in this short sequence that he cites:

1 The process of learning is essential to our lives.
  2 All higher animals seek it deliberately.
    3 They are inquisitive and they experiment.
      4 An experiment is a sort of harmless trial run... (60).

Note how each sentence generates the one that follows it, rather than primarily relating back to the topic sentence. (The numbers indicate degrees of subordination, with 1 indicating a topic sentence.)

Here is another example of a subordinate paragraph to contemplate:

1 Another startling conclusion from the science of consciousness is that the intuitive feeling we have that there's another executive "I" that sits in a control room of our brain, scanning the screens of the senses and pushing the buttons of the muscles, is an illusion.
  2 Consciousness turns out to consist of a maelstrom of events distributed across the brain.
    3 These events compete for attention, and as one process outshouts the others, the brain rationalizes the outcome after the fact and concocts the impression that a single self was in charge all along. (Steven Pinker, "The Mystery of Consciousness," *Time*, January 19, 2007.)

It is less important to be able to accurately and precisely locate each sentence in a paragraph as coordinate or subordinate than it is to recognize that most paragraphs are a mix of these two thought patterns. In practice, as Christensen observes, most paragraphs combine coordinate and subordinate sequences, although one of the two structures often predominates.

You do not need to ponder these relationships each time you write a new sentence in a paragraph, but, when you find yourself getting stuck in your writing, you can help yourself move forward by thinking about which sentence in the paragraph is the actual generator (or jumping off point) for the next one.

TRY THIS 10.3: Identify the Structure of a Paragraph

Apply to the paragraph below the terms used in this section to describe what various sentences do. Look for coordinate versus subordinate structures, but more specifically, label the mental moves performed by individual sentences. We have numbered the sentences to make the paragraph easier to work with.

1. White might not have succeeded in completely ridding his life of modern civilization, but Strunk's manual in White's hands became a successful *primitivist* tract.

2. Perhaps that seems like an overstatement, but in fact what counts as primitivist is flexible, Marianna Torgovnick reminded us, entirely dependent on what bugs one about the modern.

3. The key feature of primitivism, Torgovnick offered, is defining the primitive in reaction to the present: "Is the present too majestic? Primitive life is not—it is a precapitalist utopia in which only use value, never exchange value, prevails. Is the present sexually repressed? Not primitive life—primitives live life whole, without fear of the body" (8).

4. For Strunk and White, modern life was verbose and obscure, so primitive life must be brief, direct, and clear.

5. New things are bad things, new words the worst of all.

6. The words *offputting* and *ongoing* appear in the third and subsequent editions of *The Elements of Style* as "newfound adjectives, to be avoided because they are inexact and clumsy" (*Third Edition* 54).

7. The suffix *oriented* is lambasted as "a clumsy, pretentious device, much in vogue" (*Third Edition* 55).

8. *The Elements of Style* thus had become, over a period of nearly unprecedented technological progress, the perfect complement to the manual typewriter—a deliberate rejection of "books with permissive steering and automatic transitions" that made our lives easier but rendered our prose impotent and our character lax (xvi).

9. For impotence and laxity, *The Elements of Style* offers a program of stylistic and moral restitution, word by word.

(Catherine Prendergast, "The Fighting Style: Reading the Unabomber's Strunk and White," *College English*, Volume 72, No 1, September 2009.)

The Shaping Force of Transitions

This entire chapter has been concerned with how the parts of various kinds of writing, particularly academic projects, are structured. This final section addresses the crucial role that transitions play. It's crucial because the linkage between where you've been and where you're going is usually a point in your writing at which thinking is taking place. This is especially the case in the evolving rather than the static model of thesis development, in which the writer continually *updates* the thesis as it moves through evidence.

Here are the key points to keep in mind:

- Thinking tends to occur at points of transition.
- A good transition articulates a paper's logical links—how each phase of the paper leads to the next.
- Too many additive transitions ("also," "another example of ") produce papers that list, an overly loose form of organization.

It is useful to think of transitions as *directional indicators*, especially at the beginnings of paragraphs but also within them. "And," for example, is a plus sign. It indicates that the writer will add something, continuing in the same direction. The words "but," "yet," "nevertheless," and "however" are among the many transitional words that alert readers to changes in the direction of the writer's thinking. They might indicate the introduction of a qualification, or a potentially contradictory piece of evidence, or an alternative point of view.

Some additive transitions do more work than "also" or "another." The word "moreover" is an additive transition, but it adds emphasis to the added point. The transitional sequence "not only . . . but also" restates and then adds information in a way that clarifies what has gone before.

Too many additive transitions can pose a problem for your writing. A list is a slack form of organization, one that fails to identify how this is related to that. Although transitional wording such as "another example of" or "also" at the beginning of paragraphs does tell readers that a related point or example will follow, it does not specify that relationship beyond piling on another "and." Essentially, these words just list.

If you find yourself relying on "another" and "also" at points of transition, force yourself to substitute other transitional wording that indicates more precisely the nature of the relationship with what has gone before in the paper. Language such as "similarly" and "by contrast" can sometimes serve this purpose. Often, some restatement is called for to keep your reader on track—brief repetition is not necessarily redundant. A good transition reaches backward, telling where you've been, as the grounds for making a subsequent move forward.

The first step toward improving your use of transitions (and thereby the organization of your writing) is to become conscious of them. If you notice that you are beginning successive paragraphs with "Another reason," for example, you can probably conclude that you are listing rather than developing your ideas. If you notice a number of sentences that start with the vague referent "This," you probably need to name the thing "This" refers to.

Think of transitions as echoes in the service of continuity. If you study the transitions in a piece, you will usually find that they echo either the language or the ideas of something that precedes them as they point to what is ahead.

TRY THIS 10.4: Tracking Transitions

Track the transitions in a piece of writing. Take a few pages of something you are reading (such as a short article) and circle or underline all the transitions, figuring out how they function as directional indicators. Remember to check not only the beginnings of paragraphs but within them. Then survey your markings. What do you notice now about the shape of the piece? This exercise is also useful for expanding your vocabulary of transitional words to use in your own writing.

Assignments: From Paragraphs to Papers: Forms and Formats Across the Curriculum

1. **Infer the format of a published article.** Often, the format governing the organization of a published piece is not immediately evident. That is, it is not subdivided according to conventional disciplinary categories that are obeyed by all members of a given discourse community. Especially if you are studying a discipline in which the writing does not follow an explicitly prescribed format, such as history, literature, or economics, you may find it illuminating to examine representative articles or essays in that discipline, looking for an implicit format. You can usually discern some underlying pattern of organization—the formal conventions, the rules that are being followed—even when these are not highlighted.

   The following assignment works well whether you tackle it individually or in a group. It can lead to a paper, an oral report, or both. First, assemble several articles from the same or a similar kind of journal or magazine. "Journal" is the name given to publications aimed at specialized, usually scholarly, audiences, as opposed to general or popular audiences. *Time, Newsweek,* and *The New Yorker* are called "magazines" rather than "journals" because they are aimed at a broader general audience. *Shakespeare Quarterly* is a journal; *Psychology Today* is a magazine.

   Having found at least three journal or magazine articles, study them in order to focus on the following question: *Insofar as there appears to be a format that articles in this journal adhere to, what are its parts?*

   How, for example, does an article in this journal or magazine typically begin and end? Does there seem to be a relatively uniform place in which these articles include opposing arguments? You will, in other words, be analyzing the articles inductively (reasoning from particular details to general principles). Begin with the product and reason backward to the skeleton beneath the skin.

   If you choose to work with a magazine rather than single articles, you should narrow your focus. You might focus on *Time* cover stories, or on *The New Yorker*'s "Talk of the Town" or another such recurring feature. Even gossip columns and letters of advice to the lovelorn in teen magazines adhere to certain visible, though not explicitly marked, formats.

Write up your results. Cite language from at least two articles in support of your claims about the implicit format.

2. **Analyze introductions**. One of the best ways to learn about introductions is to gather some sample introductory paragraphs and, working on your own or in a small group, figure out how each one works, what it accomplishes.

Here are some questions you might pose:

- Why does the writer start in this way—what is accomplished?

- What kind of relationship does this opening establish with the audience, and to what ends?

- How does the writer let readers know why the writing they are about to read is called for, useful, and necessary?

- Where and by what logic does the introduction funnel?

3. **Compare and contrast introductions and audiences**. Compare and contrast introductory paragraphs from a popular magazine with those from an academic journal aimed at a specialized audience. Select one of each and analyze them to determine what each author assumes the audience knows. Where in each paragraph are these assumptions most evident? If you write out your analysis, it should probably take about a page, but this exercise can also be done productively with others in a small group.

4. **Analyze conclusions**. Find examples of concluding paragraphs from published writing. First, compare the conclusion with the introduction, looking for the way the conclusion comes full circle. Which elements of the introduction are repeated to accomplish this? Then look for the statement of the essay's thesis in its final, culminating form. Finally, locate the send-off by finding implications and limitations that the writer has noted as part of their final "So what?" Based on your findings, write a few paragraphs in which you describe the writer's approach to conclusions.

At this point, you will be ready to repeat this exercise with some of your own work. Only this time, rather than describing the writer's approach, write an improved version of one of your conclusions based on what you learned from your analysis.

CHAPTER 11

Style: Choosing Words, Shaping Sentences

Overview This chapter on style seeks to make you more conscious of the kinds of words and sentences you use and to expand your range of options. In the book's final chapter, we will move from stylistic questions—a matter of choice—to common grammatical errors, which are a matter of correct versus incorrect forms. In this chapter, we'll be asking you to think rhetorically; that is, in terms of appropriate choices for particular contexts rather than right versus wrong.

A writer who is practiced at different ways of putting sentences together is a writer in touch with the key concept of sentence style—that there is a powerful link between the shape of a sentence and the shape of a thought. A sentence is the shape that thought takes. In order to enhance your awareness of sentence shapes, start analyzing sentences as you read. Keep an eye out for sentences you think are good rather than looking for things that are wrong, as school grammar exercises too often ask you to do. The chapter will provide you with the vocabulary and observation skills you need in order to figure out what makes a sentence good and what causes it to create the effects that it does.

Seeing Style as Inseparable From Meaning

Broadly defined, *style* refers to all of a writer's decisions in selecting, arranging, and expressing what they have to say. Getting the style right is not as simple as proofreading your paper in the late stages of drafting, looking for errors in grammar and punctuation. Whereas proofreading occupies the relatively comfortable linguistic world of simple right and wrong, stylistic considerations take place in the more exploratory terrain of making choices among more and less effective ways of formulating and communicating your meaning.

Many people mistakenly assume that style is separate from meaning. From this perspective, paying close attention to style seems finicky, or worse, cynical—a way of dressing up the content to sell it to readers or listeners. The problem with this view is that it subscribes to what we earlier referred to as *the transparent theory of language.* This theory tries to locate meaning outside of language. It suggests that we somehow see *through* words to meaning and can then address that meaning without addressing the words that embody it. In the transparent theory of language, words are merely pointers to get to meanings that exist somewhere underneath or beyond them.

Yet style is not a mask you don or a way of icing the cake. Attending to style is more like sculpting. As a sculptor uses a chisel to "bring out" a shape from a block of walnut or marble, a writer uses style to bring out the shape of the conceptual connections in a draft of an essay. This bringing out demands a certain detachment from your own language. It requires that you become aware of your words as words and of your sentences as sentences. You have to look *at* them—as opposed to *through* them.

If stylistic considerations are not merely cosmetic, then it follows that rethinking the way you have said something can lead you to rethink the substance of what you have said. The decisions you make about how to phrase your meaning inevitably exert a powerful influence on the meaning you make.

Is style a function of character and personality? Is it, in short, personal, and thus something to be preserved in the face of would-be meddlers carrying style manuals and grammar guides? Well, as you might guess at this point in the book, the answer is yes and no. We all need to find our own ways of using words so that they don't succumb to the mind-numbing environment of verbal cliché in which we dwell. Through becoming more self-conscious about style we more easily recognize that it is not inborn. Staying locked into one way of writing because that is "your style" is as limiting as remaining locked into only one way of thinking. Studying and imitating other people's sentences will not erase your style, but rather, extend its range.

About Prescriptive Style Manuals: A Word of Warning

The key idea of this chapter is that there are not necessarily right and wrong choices when it comes to sentence style but better and best choices for particular situations. The from-the-hip plain style of a memo or a set of operating instructions for your lawn mower are very likely not the best style choices for a good-bye letter to a best friend, a diplomatic talk on a sensitive political situation, or an analysis of guitar styles in contemporary jazz. Rather than relying on a single set of rules for distinguishing good style from bad, a writer needs to be thinking about how the writer's words and arrangement of words are suited to the subject matter and audience.

You may have been taught some or all of the following: that you should always avoid the first-person "I" in academic writing, steer clear of jargon, and never start a sentence with *and* or *but*. There are occasions when these rules apply, but there are also many occasions when they don't. Such rules are matters of usage—socially determined conventions—rather than hard-and-fast rules of grammar. All writing is *contextual*. The primary rule is that you should adapt your style to the demands of different rhetorical situations.

Although style manuals and handbooks can be very useful when they illuminate the range of choices a writer has and the implications of those choices, most style manuals value one style and tone over others and tend to present this style as self-evidently good and right. Despite Strunk & White's rule (in their famous book, *The Elements of Style*), three words are not better than six in every rhetorical situation. And, their edict against it notwithstanding, passive voice has its place, its own special advantages; active voice is not always better. The key to growing as a stylist is learning to see the choices.

In his essay, "Style and Good Style," philosophy professor Monroe Beardsley takes this point one step further. He writes: "Many charming, clever, and memorable things have been said about style—most of which turn out to be highly misleading when subjected to analysis"(4). Changes in style, says Beardsley, always produce changes in meaning: "If the teacher advises a change of words, or of word order, he is recommending a different meaning" (13). ["Style and Good Style" from *Reflections on High School English: NDEA Institute Lectures 1965*, ed. Gary Tate, University of Tulsa 1966 as reprinted in *Contemporary Essays on Style* by Glen A. Love and Michael Payne, Scott, Foresman and Company 1969]

Here is one of the examples Beardsley offers in response to the common stylistic advice that writers should replace forms of "to be" with active verbs. He cites as an example from Strunk and White the suggestion that the sentence "There were a great number of dead leaves lying on the ground" be replaced with the sentence "Dead leaves covered the ground." Of this suggested change Beardsley observes, "But isn't that a difference in meaning? For one thing, there are more leaves in the second sentence. The second one says that the ground was covered; the first one only speaks of a great number. Stylistic advice is a rather odd sort of thing if it consists in telling students to pile up the leaves in their descriptions" (6).

Sentence Logic: Seeing How the Parts of a Sentence Are Related

Every sentence is composed of moveable parts. To understand your stylistic options fully, you will want to become an adept arranger and rearranger of those parts. You need to learn to see these parts and understand the different relationships they can have to each other. Initially this takes conscious effort—a fair bit of effort. Eventually you will assimilate this knowledge so that it starts to kick in whenever you sit down to write.

Only a small amount of specialized vocabulary is needed to describe and discuss sentence shapes:

—clause (independent and dependent)
—subject and predicate

—coordination and subordination
—conjunctions (coordinating and subordinating)
—parallelism

(See "Glossary of Grammatical Terms" at the end of Chapter 12.)

You will need this vocabulary in order to better define what you see, but, even before you are in control of the necessary language, you can begin to evolve your understanding of sentences by just trying to describe what you see. Teach yourself to look at sentences and say, "What do I notice?" How are the parts of the sentence laid out? How does the sentence begin and end? What, if anything, repeats in it—what words and patterns of language?

Finding the Spine of a Sentence: Subjects and Predicates

It is helpful to think of sentences as having spines to which various limbs (modifiers—additional information) can be attached. We will talk first about the spine and then about the ways that writers can build things onto it in various places.

—The spine of a sentence is its main **subject/verb combination**.
—The primary subject/verb combination of a sentence is called the **main clause**.
—A **clause** is a group of words containing both a subject and a predicate.

Finding the main clause is the first step in understanding how a writer has put a sentence together. Look for the key words of the sentence's subject (a noun or noun phrase) and the key words of its predicate (a verb or verb phrase). The **subject** is a noun, noun phrase, or pronoun that serves as the actor of the sentence, the doer of the action that the sentence describes or the thing that has been affected by it. In the following sentence, the subject is "Congress":

Congress passed the bill.

"Congress" does the action that the second part of the sentence, the predicate, names. In the sentence "Bob was hurt," Bob is the subject. Bob has been affected.

Always start your analysis of sentences by finding what is called the "simple subject," the noun, noun phrase, or pronoun that serves as the sentence subject. In the following examples, we have boldfaced the nouns that are the subjects of the sentences' main clauses.

Despite objections from local preservationists, the **building** was destroyed.
A **statue** stands at the center of town.

In both examples there is more than one noun, but in each case only one of these nouns is the thing that acts (**statue** stands) or is acted upon (**building** was destroyed). "At the center of town" is a prepositional phrase naming where the statue stands. The nouns "objections" and "preservationists" are part of a phrase that modifies the action in the main clause, and so neither of those nouns acts as the sentence's subject.

The **predicate** is the action part of the sentence. It contains a verb or verb phrase that describes some kind of action or that links the subject to a word or words that characterize it. In the sample sentences above, "was destroyed" and "stands at the center of town" are the predicates. To keep your sense of the sentence's spine as clear as possible, look for the predicate's verb or verb phrase. Here are two examples. We have boldfaced the verbs or verb phrases that are the key terms of each sentence's predicate.

I **have seen** a ship into haven fall.
The book **was** full of highly detailed drawings.

By the way, if this matter of finding subjects and predicates sounds too simple to require discussion, we can only remark that even our best students sometimes have a hard time finding the main clause of a sentence. As you read further in this chapter, you will come to understand why this is so. More complicated sentence structures have multiple clauses and often a number of separate pieces of modifying information. In order to really see these structures, your ability to see a sentence's primary subject/verb combinations is critical. Your skill with sentences (and with punctuating them accurately) will grow rapidly if you make it a habit to always locate the main clause before going on to other considerations. If you think it is easy and obvious in every case to spot the predicate and its primary verb or verb phrase, consider the following sentence. Which of the sentence's two verbs (both boldfaced) serves as the predicate?

These **are** the times that **try** men's souls.

"These" in the sentence is a demonstrative pronoun. It functions as the subject of the sentence, so the primary verb in the main clause is "are." The word "that" is a relative pronoun that attaches a restrictive dependent clause—"that try men's souls"—to the main clause. The dependent clause is restrictive because it specifies a particular kind of time. This second clause in the sentence functions as an adjective because it modifies the noun, *times*. Soon you will start making a habit of noting the different kinds of connecting words that link the parts of a sentence together. But first you have to become adept at seeing the primary subject/verb combination or combinations that serve as the sentence's spine.

Kinds of Verbs: Transitive, Intransitive, and Linking

When you focus on the spine of a sentence, its main clause, you will notice that there are different kinds of predicates. Sentences often take the form commonly abbreviated as SVO (subject-verb-object). The predicate of such sentences consists of a verb or verb phrase describing an action, and a noun that names the thing receiving the action. Look at these sentences:

The boy kicked the ball
The teacher gave the student a book.

In the first example, "boy" is the subject, "kicked" is the verb, and "ball" is the **direct object.** The verb in this sentence is transitive: it requires an object. The second example is a slightly more complicated construction that includes both an **indirect object** and a direct object. Here, "teacher" is the subject, "gave" is the verb, "student" is the indirect object, and "book" is the direct object.

A verb that takes an object is called **transitive,** from the word "trans," meaning across. Transitive verbs carry action across the sentence from the subject to the object that functions as the recipient of that action. When a verb in a sentence has no object—as in the sentences "He laughed out loud" or "He spoke quickly"—it is called **intransitive.**

A third type, the **linking verb,** links the sentence subject to a word after the verb that in some way describes the subject. The most common linking verbs are forms of "to be": is, are, was, were, and so on. In the sentence, "My Great Pyrenees dog is white," the verb links the subject to what is called a **complement** or, in this case, a **predicate adjective**—an adjective describing the color of my dog. In the sentence, "The ambassador was gracious," the simple subject (primary noun) of the sentence is "ambassador," the verb is "was," and the predicate adjective is "gracious."

Verbals: Verb Forms that Function as Other Parts of Speech

The task of finding a sentence's main clause can be made more difficult by the presence of words that look like—but don't actually function as—verbs. These words, called **verbals**, come in three different forms: present participles (-ing), past participles (-ed), and infinitives (to).

A verbal (verb-like word) ending in "ing" that acts as a noun is called a **gerund.**

Dancing is easy.
To judge is easy; suspending judgment is the more difficult task.

In the first sentence, dancing is a gerund that serves as the sentence subject. In the second sentence, the infinitive "to judge" acts as a noun as does the gerund phrase "suspending judgment."

Verbals can appear as the object of a preposition, as in "The dog could always find time for fetching the ball," or as the object of a verb: "The committee wanted to understand their responsibilities." Verbals can function as adjectives: "Worried that I had somehow hurt her feelings, I stayed away from my friend." "Referring angrily to the school dress code, the principal asked him to leave." The point of recognizing verbals is to avoid confusing them with verbs. The subject and verb of the main clause in the previous sentence is "point," and the verb is "is." The other verb-like words in the sentence—"recognizing" "confusing" and "to avoid"—are verbals.

Sentence Combining: Coordination

We have been looking at sentences containing only one main clause. Such sentences are called **simple sentences**, not because their ideas are simple, but because all of the sentence's information is added onto a single subject/verb combination. A writer may use many words in a sentence and still keep it simple, provided that the writer does not add any more clauses. In the following simple sentence, we have boldfaced the one main clause; everything else in the sentence modifies one of the words in this main clause.

Just before midnight, **Lesley**, one of the party guests, **gulped down her champagne** with a flourish, having promised herself to never again be unprepared when the clock struck.

The spine of a sentence may, however, include more than one clause. When two or more clauses (each containing a subject plus a predicate) are linked in the same sentence by what is called a **coordinating conjunction** or by a **semicolon**, the resulting sentence is referred to as a **compound sentence**. We have italicized each of the clauses in the following compound sentences, and we have boldfaced the coordinating conjunctions that connect the clauses.

The *house of representatives favored the bill*, **and** *the governor did not*.
The *house of representatives passed the bill*, **but** *the governor refused to sign it*.

Notice that a **comma** comes before the coordinating conjunction in each case. The comma tells the reader that a **new** clause is coming. *The primary rule of comma placement is that commas are there to help the reader easily find the sentence's main clause or clauses.* (We will have to say more about this a little further on in the chapter when we discuss what the different punctuation marks do, which we will ask you to think of in terms of the signals they send to readers.)

These two compound sentences are not, of course, identical in structure. In the first sentence, the word **"and"** indicates that another clause is simply being added to the sentence. The word "and" functions like a plus sign. It is, therefore, a rather imprecise kind of conjunction (joining element). The word **"but"** in the second sentence indicates the relationship between the two clauses more precisely. It indicates that the two clauses stand in opposition to each other. The word "but" says that the relation between the two clauses is one of contrast.

The fastest way to see the shape of coordinate structures—compound sentences—is to look for the conjunctions that serve as the glue, the connectors between the clauses. Coordinating conjunctions connect grammatically equal elements in a sentence.

The professor chose the first-year students **but** not the sophomores.
Speak up, **and** you will be heard.

In the first example, the conjunction connects two direct objects. In the second, it connects two independent clauses.

Coordinating conjunctions: *and, for, nor, but, or, yet, so*

Style fact: Ideas located in coordinate clauses tend to be seen by readers as equal in importance because the coordinate clauses are equal grammatically, although, as we will soon discuss, the order of clauses has an impact on which one is perceived by the reader as having the most weight.

Two other types of connecting words, **conjunctive adverbs** and **correlative conjunctions**, link grammatically equal clauses in a sentence. Conjunctive adverbs, like coordinating conjunctions, connect independent clauses and indicate the relation between them. Correlative conjunctions do the same job; they come in pairs.

Common Conjunctive adverbs: *however, therefore, thus, moreover, then, furthermore, finally, nevertheless, similarly, accordingly, consequently, subsequently, otherwise, still, hence, also, besides, now, specifically, conversely*

Conjunctive adverbs serving to connect independent clauses in a sentence should be preceded by a semicolon, the purpose of which is to make it clear which of the two clauses the conjunctive adverb describes.

Scientists observe things very closely; however, they still can make mistakes.
Boys will be boys; nevertheless, they can choose behaviors not described by
this too-popular cliché.

Correlative conjunctions: *either/or, neither/nor, not only/but also, whether/or, both/and*

Correlative conjunctions are especially useful for defining terms. They tend to play one phrase or clause against another:

She was <u>neither</u> angry <u>nor</u> sad.
The cause of the recession was <u>not only</u> greed, <u>but also</u> lack of effective
legislation.

There used to be a rule, by the way, that writers should not start sentences with coordinating conjunctions or conjunctive adverbs. This rule most likely owed to the fact that these conjunctions typically operate inside sentences. This did not need to mean, however, that these handy words couldn't be used at the beginning of sentences, where they would also indicate a relationship between clauses. In conservative writing environments, you may still be expected to avoid starting sentences with the various kinds of coordinating conjunctions. A quick look, however, at a reputable magazine or newspaper will reveal that writers commonly start sentences with words like "and," "but," and "however." Because these words so efficiently indicate certain kinds of relationships among clauses, they have proved too handy to be ruled out as sentence openers.

Compound Predicates: A common problem in seeing the shape of compound sentences (and thus in punctuating them in a way that sends the right signals to readers) is to confuse compound sentences with sentences containing **compound predicates**. Both of the following sentences contain compound predicates. Notice that in each case there is only one sentence subject, while the predicate contains two verbs. We have boldfaced the verbs in each predicate and italicized the conjoining word, "and."

> The governor **criticized** the bill *and* **refused** to sign it.
> The house of representatives **resented** the governor's resistance *and* **said** so.

If you learned sentence diagramming in school, you will have discovered how useful this practice can be for revealing the relationship among the various parts of a sentence. There are not many rules to sentence diagramming. It is just a way to help you visualize the shape of sentences. Here is what sentence diagramming reveals about the shape of a sentence with a compound predicate:

> The governor **criticized the bill**
>   and
>   **refused** to sign it.

Both verbs in the sentence (boldfaced) refer back to the same sentence subject. So, rather than being a compound sentence—one that has two or more independent clauses—the sentence has a compound predicate.

Notice that it would send readers the wrong message if a writer were to put a comma in front of the word "and." A comma in that position would lead readers to expect another clause (subject/verb combination) rather than just another verb that refers back to the same subject. The comma would make the sentence illogical by, in effect, separating the second verb from its subject. If, however, you were to add the word "he" to the compound predicate above, you would convert the simple sentence with a compound predicate into a compound sentence—a sentence with two independent clauses:

> The <u>governor</u> criticized the bill, and <u>he</u> refused to sign it.

Sentence Combining: Subordination

When children learn to speak, they tend to put each piece of information into a separate sentence: "I fell down. My mother was there. She made me feel better." As the child grows older, she starts to combine related thoughts into more complex syntactical units, such as compound sentences: "I fell down, and my mother was there, and she made me feel better." These sentences read rather like a leaky faucet. Drip, drip, drip. Each thought unit gets equal weight. There is not much happening to cause one idea to stand out as more important or more interesting than another. Eventually, as the child becomes more proficient with language, she will write sentences that better indicate the relationship among her ideas and that allow some ideas to stand out as more important—more emphatic—than others:

After I fell down, my mother appeared and made me feel better.

This sentence contains one independent clause preceded by a dependent clause indicating the time, roughly, when mother appeared. This first idea has been subordinated—in a dependent clause—to the one that follows in the independent clause, which has a compound predicate (two verbs that both have the same subject: mother).

A **dependent clause** cannot stand alone as a sentence, while an **independent clause** can. It is from this sense of elements of a sentence depending on other elements that we derive our analogy for sentence shapes—spine plus limbs (or scaffold plus words and phrases that hang on the scaffold). An **independent clause** is a group of words that contains both a subject and a predicate and that can stand alone as a sentence. This definition becomes clearer if you consider the literal meaning of the words independent and dependent.

The word "depend" means literally "to hang from." A dependent clause hangs from and thus relies on an independent clause. Sentences containing both independent and dependent clauses are called **complex sentences.** They are called complex not because they are more difficult to read or to write, but because they contain different kinds of clauses and because the relationship among these clauses is explicitly specified.

Style fact: At this point in our discussion, it is worth saying that sentences become complicated not because the writer doesn't know how to say things more simply (though this is sometimes true) but because complex sentences are one of the shapes that complex thinking takes. The governing idea of this chapter is that a sentence is the shape that thought takes. A piece of thinking that provides careful specification of the way that ideas relate to each other will require a sentence structure that states these relationships explicitly.

In a complex sentence, clauses are not equally important grammatically. This inequality is marked by the use of **subordinating conjunctions**, which specify the subordinate status of some clauses in relation to others. The word "subordinate" means literally "arranged under" or "ordered under." Another useful word for describing sentences with subordinate elements is **hypotactic**, which means "arranged under." If you have had a hypodermic injection (under the skin), you are familiar with the prefix "hypo" for *under*. Coordinate structures are sometimes called **paratactic**, a word meaning "arranged next to each other."

The strength of complex sentences is that they specifically name the kind of relationship among clauses, and they present the information in some clauses (the main or independent clause or clauses) as more central, more important than the information in others. Below are two examples of complex sentences. In each case we have boldfaced the subordinating conjunction and italicized the independent clause upon which the dependent clause depends. Notice in these sentences that if you were to delete the subordinating conjunction, and add a comma plus a coordinating conjunction between the clauses, you would convert the complex to a compound sentence.

Although the vote was unanimous, *people continued to complain.*
Because the poverty level of the country had risen, *its citizens began to emigrate.*

In the dependent clause that opens the second sentence, the subject is "poverty level," and the predicate is "had risen." If you were to delete the subordinating conjunction at the beginning of either sentence, but leave the comma in between the two clauses, you would have created what is known as a **comma splice**—two independent clauses spliced together with a comma when another form of punctuation, such as a period or a semicolon, is called for. If you were to remove instead the second clause in each sentence—the independent clause upon which the subordinate clause depends—you would be left with what is known as a **sentence fragment**: a group of words that can't stand alone as a sentence but which is punctuated as a sentence. (For more on comma splices and sentence fragments, see Chapter 12.)

In sum, writers create complex (subordinated) sentences when it is important to specify the type of relationship and the relative importance of one idea to the main idea to which it is attached. The following list of common subordinating conjunctions allows you to see the kinds of relationships that these words assert between the dependent (subordinate) clause and the independent clause it modifies.

Some subordinate conjunctions: *Although, if, after, before, because, since, until, when, while, where, unless, even though, whether, though, as, in order that, whereas, provided that, just as*

Style fact: Ideas located in subordinate clauses tend to be seen by readers as less important than ideas located in independent clauses. As we shall see, however, in the section below called "Emphasis and the Order of Clauses," the perceived importance of an idea in a subordinate clause also depends on where it is located in a sentence.

TRY THIS 11.1: Identify Clauses and Conjunctions
Examine a piece of writing for the way it constructs and connects clauses. Start by finding the sentences' independent clause or clauses. Do this by underlining the main subject/verb combinations. Next, circle all conjunctions—coordinate, subordinate, conjunctive adverbs, and correlatives. What do you notice about the way that the writer puts sentences together? How is the writer's style related to the kind of thinking they are doing in the piece?

Seeing the Shape of Sentences: Why Commas Matter

Consider the following sentence in which a needed comma has been left out.

After eating the couple left the restaurant.

From this example you can infer the primary role commas play in a sentence. *Commas cause readers to distinguish the main clause or clauses of a sentence from various kinds of modifiers.* Once a comma is in place after the introductory prepositional phrase at the beginning of the sentence above, readers can easily see the shape of the sentence because the comma makes the sentence spine (main clause) stand out. No one has eaten the couple. They have gone home from the restaurant unharmed.

Commas allow writers to add modifying information at various places in a sentence without causing readers to lose track of the thinking in the main clause. Consider, for example, how information might be added to the following rather silly clause—and where commas would have to be located in order for readers to keep this clause in sight.

The cat was happy.

Let's say we wish to add some modifying information to this sentence, such as "despite not having enough for breakfast." There are three places (slots) in sentences where this modifying phrase might be added. In each sample sentence below, we have underlined the main clause and italicized the modifying information.

beginning: *Despite not having enough for breakfast,* the cat was happy.
middle: The cat, *despite not having enough for breakfast,* was happy.
end: The cat was happy, *despite not having enough for breakfast.*

These "slots" for adding information at the beginning, middle, and end are generally separated from the main clause by commas. *The commas are there to help the reader easily find and recognize the main clause.*

The first example, with the modifying phrase at the beginning, doesn't absolutely need a comma; we won't misread the sentence without it, though the comma does help clarify matters. And what if we raise the level of complexity by adding more modifiers to a more complicated idea?

modifying phrase at beginning: *Although both candidates claimed to be running clean races and blamed the other for the mudslinging,* the campaign was ugly.
modifying phrase at middle: The campaign, *although both candidates claimed to be running clean races and blamed the other for the mudslinging,* was ugly.
modifying phrase at end: The campaign was ugly, *although both candidates claimed to be running clean races and blamed the other for the mudslinging.*

TRY THIS 11.2: Find and Explain Commas in a Piece of Writing
Circle all of the commas in a page of an essay. Figure out why each one is there. What modifying elements do the commas allow us to see as separate from the main clause or clauses?

Commas With Restrictive and Nonrestrictive Modifiers: That vs. Which Because commas cause readers to distinguish a sentence's main clause or clauses from modifying information, it is important that commas not be placed in ways that send the wrong message about what are and aren't essential parts of the main clause. Consider the following sentences.

> People who live in glass houses should not throw stones.
> My sister, who lives in a glass house, has a stone collection.
> The tower that stands in the center of campus fell down.
> The tower, which had been slowly crumbling, fell down.

Why does the second sentence in each of these pairs require a pair of commas, while the first sentences do not? To answer this question, find the main clause in each sentence. Notice that in the second sentence of each pair you could take out the information enclosed in commas and the sentence would still make sense. The commas act, in effect, like **parentheses**. They close off a qualifying idea (something that can be referred to as a parenthetical element) that adds information to the sentence, but which is not essential to the meaning of the main clause.

> My sister has a stone collection.
> The tower fell down.

The sentence "People who live in glass houses should not throw stones" refers not just to people in general but to particular people, those who live in glass houses. Putting commas around "who live in glass houses" would cause readers to misunderstand the main clause. Similarly, in the sentence "The tower that stands in the center of campus fell down," the sentence refers not just to any tower, but to a particular tower, the one in the center of campus.

Modifying information that is essential to a clause's meaning is called **restrictive** because it restricts the meaning of the sentence subject. Information that is not essential to the meaning of the main clause—does not limit it—is called **nonrestrictive**. If you can take out words without changing the meaning of the sentence, those words are nonrestrictive. If you can't take out the words without changing the meaning of the sentence, the words are restrictive.

Nonrestrictive elements in a sentence require commas to close them off from the main clause, thus making the main clause easier to see. Restrictive elements do not get commas because they are part of the main clause. As we will discuss further in our discussion of **relative clauses** and **relative pronouns**, restrictive information in a sentence calls for **that** and no commas.

Nonrestrictive information is identified as such through the use of commas plus the relative pronoun **which**.

> The lights **that** shine in my window keep me awake at night.
> The lights, **which** are rarely turned off, keep me awake.

What Punctuation Marks Say: A Quick-Hit Guide

1. The **period** [.] marks the end of a sentence. Make sure it is preceded by an independent clause, that is, a subject plus verb that can stand alone. The period says to a reader, "This is the end of this particular statement. I'm a mark of closure."

   > Lennon rules.

2. As noted in the section above on why commas matter, the **comma** [,] separates the main (independent) clause from dependent elements that modify the main clause. It also separates two main clauses joined by a conjunction—known as a **compound sentence**. Information that is not central to the main clause is set off in a pair of commas, a comma sandwich. The comma does *not* signify a pause. The comma says to the reader, "Here is where the main clause begins (or ends)," or "Here is a break in the main clause."

   In the case of compound sentences (containing two or more independent clauses), the comma says "Here is where one main clause ends, and after the conjunction that follows me, another main clause begins."

   > Lennon rules, and McCartney is cute.
   > Lennon rules, although McCartney is arguably more tuneful.

3. The **semicolon** [;] separates two independent clauses not joined by a conjunction. Secondarily, the semicolon can separate two independent clauses joined by a conjunction if either of the clauses already contains commas. In either case, the semicolon both shows a close relationship between the two independent clauses that it connects and distinguishes where one ends and the other begins.

   The semicolon says to the reader, "What precedes and what follows me are conceptually close but grammatically independent and thus equal statements."

   > Lennon's lyrics show deep sympathy for the legions of "Nowhere Men" who inhabit the "Strawberry Fields" of their imaginations; McCartney's lyrics, on the other hand, are more upbeat, forever bidding "Good Day, Sunshine" to the world at large and "Michelle" in particular.

4. The **colon** [:] marks the end of a setup for something coming next. It provides a frame, pointing beyond itself, like a spotlight. The colon is quite dramatic, and unlike the semicolon, it links what precedes and follows it formally and tightly rather than loosely and associatively.

It usually operates with dramatic force. It can frame a list to follow, separate cause and effect, or divide a brief claim from a more expanded version of the claim. The language on at least one side of the colon must be an independent clause, though both sides can be.

The colon says to the reader, "Concentrate on what follows me for a more detailed explanation of what preceded me" or "What follows me is logically bound with what preceded me."

> *Rubber Soul* marked a change in The Beatles' songwriting: the sentimentality of earlier efforts gave way to a new complexity, both in the range of their subjects and the sophistication of their poetic devices.
> Nowhere is this change more evident than in a sequence of songs near the album's end: "I'm Looking Through You," "In My Life," "Wait," and "If I Needed Someone."

5. The **dash** [—] provides an informal alternative to the colon for adding information to a sentence. Its effect is sudden, of the moment—what springs up impulsively to disrupt and extend in some new way the ongoing train of thought. A **pair of dashes** provides an invaluable resource to writers for inserting information within a sentence. In this usage, the rule is that the sentence must read coherently if the inserted information is left out. (To type a dash, type two hyphens with no space between, before, or after. This distinguishes the dash from a hyphen [-], which is the mark used for connecting two words into one.)

The dash says to the reader, "This too!" or, in the case of a pair of them, "Remember the thought in the beginning of this sentence because we're jumping to something else before we come back to finish that thought."

> For all their loveliness, the songs on *Rubber Soul* are not without menace— "I'd rather see you dead little girl than to see you with another man."
> In addition to the usual lead, rhythm, and bass guitar ensemble, *Rubber Soul* introduced new instruments—notably, the harpsichord interlude in "In My Life," the sitar spiraling through "Norwegian Wood"—that had not previously been heard in rock 'n roll.

Emphasis and the Order of Clauses: The Importance of What Comes Last

Here are two ways of arranging the same sentence. Notice what happens to emphasis when we change the order of the clauses.

> The government has battled the opposition party for more than 30 years, though peace talks are now underway.
> Although peace talks are now underway, the government has battled the opposition party for more than 30 years.

Which sentence holds out the most hope for the success of the peace talks?

Style fact: Climactic order is a fact of sentence style. Sentences will seem to build up to and emphasize whatever comes last. This fact takes precedence over another fact of sentence style—that ideas placed in independent as opposed to dependent (subordinate) clauses tend to get more emphasis. In the first sentence above, the idea in the subordinate clause gets more emphasis than the one in the main clause simply because it comes last. Here is another example.

> The history of Indochina is marked by colonial exploitation as well as international cooperation.
>
> The history of Indochina, although marked by colonial exploitation, testifies to the possibility of international cooperation.

The emphasis at the end of the second sentence is made even more pronounced because the information about colonial exploitation is located in a subordinate clause that interrupts the main clause. As we will demonstrate soon in our discussion of **periodic vs. cumulative sentences**, creating **grammatical tension** by delaying closure—in this case, by putting information between the subject and the verb of the main clause—adds powerfully to emphasis.

Experiment with these stylistic principles. See what happens if you try moving the information you wish to emphasize to the end of your sentences. You will find that this tactic also improves the coherence of your writing because the placement of key ideas at the ends of sentences will press you to bridge from those ideas to whatever happens in the subsequent sentence. Also experiment with what you put into dependent as opposed to independent clauses. Try locating information in between the subject and verb of your main clause so as to exaggerate the emphasis naturally bestowed by climactic order.

TRY THIS 11.3: Order Clauses in a Sentence for Emphasis

Try some sentence combining in which you experiment with the effect of locating key information at the end of the sentence. Below are three ideas stated in separate sentences. Combine these into a single sentence. What happens to emphasis—to the meaning of the sentence—if you put the information about the time of year or the location of the proposal at the end of the sentence? Under what circumstances might a writer want to do this?

> I asked her/him/them to marry me.
> It was October.
> We were in a shop on Tremont Street.

Embedding Modifiers: Relative Clauses, Words, and Phrases

Other than coordination and subordination, there are a number of other ways that a writer can go about connecting information to the spine of a sentence. In order to understand these easily, you need to think about the different roles that modifiers can play in a sentence. A **modifier** is a word or a phrase or a clause that elaborates on an element in the sentence by describing it, limiting it somehow, or adding additional information. Consider the modifiers that we have boldfaced in each of the following sentences.

My **white** dog is huge.
My house, **which is painted yellow**, is cheerful.
The sun rose **slowly**.
I took the job **in 1987**.

In the first two examples above, the boldfaced modifiers—a single word in the first sentence, and a relative clause in the second—operate as adjectives. **Adjectives** modify nouns or pronouns. This relationship among sentence parts is easy to see in these simple sentences because the modifiers and the words they modify are so close together. The modifier in the third sentence functions as an adverb, because it modifies an action ("rose"). **Adverbs**, usually recognizable by their –ly ending, modify verbs, adjectives, or other adverbs. In the fourth sentence, the prepositional phrase "in 1987" also operates as an adverb because it modifies the verb "took." It answers the question, "when did you take the job?" Prepositional phrases are the most common modifiers.

The pair of sentences below include modifiers that take the form of relative clauses—because they relate to other words in the sentence.

The college chose students **who appreciated diversity.**
The things **[that] we come to miss the most** are things **[that] we once took for granted.**

The **relative clause** "who appreciated diversity" modifies the word "students," and so it is an **adjective clause**. The word "who" is a **relative pronoun**; "who appreciated diversity" is a clause because it has a subject (the pronoun "who") and a predicate ("appreciated diversity"). The clause is dependent because it cannot stand alone; it relates to and depends on the word in the main clause that it modifies. The sentence with the two longer relative clauses contains the relative pronoun "that," which you encountered earlier in our discussion of punctuating restrictive and nonrestrictive clauses. Both of these clauses also function as adjectives because they both modify nouns—"students" and "things." When the noun referred to is a person, use the relative pronoun "who" or "whom." When the noun is not a person, use "that" or "which."

Modifiers enhance a writer's stylistic choices. Writers have a lot of choices about where to place them in a sentence. Modifiers also present writers with choices about emphasis—whether, for example, an idea should be embedded in a sentence as a modifying word, clause, or phrase, or whether it should stand alone as a sentence.

We have already looked at clauses functioning as adverbs, since this is what subordinate clauses do. **Adverb clauses** modify some action in the sentence. If you look back at our list of subordinating conjunctions, you will see that they tell when, why, where, or how an action took place.

When the lights came on, the skating rink filled up.
Now that the waiting was over, the team came onto the field.

Relative pronouns: *who, whom, which, that,* (and sometimes *where* or *when*)
Demonstrative pronouns: *this, that, these, those*

Demonstrative pronouns function as adjectives because they point to nouns, as in "This is my favorite time of the year." They can also substitute for nouns ("This is my house").

Academic writing and, in fact, most forms of writing beyond elemental description, require writers to load various kinds of information into one sentence, a process known as **embedding**. At its worst, embedding produces overloaded, unwieldy sentences wherein readers and emphasis get lost. The opposite extreme—one idea to a sentence—produces disjointed writing in which sentences start to sound, as we said earlier, like the drip, drip, drip of a leaky faucet, each drop equal in importance and nothing standing out as what the writer especially wants the reader to pay attention to. In most good writing, each individual sentence does a fair bit of work. *The trick is to learn how to embed information in sentences in a way that doesn't drag the sentence to the ground like an overloaded branch.*

Appositives and **absolutes** offer another way of embedding information in a sentence and thus keeping your emphasis where you want it. An appositive comes immediately after a noun or noun phrase and renames it. The following two sentences can be combined into one by using an appositive.

Sean was a key member of the cast.
He is an able musician.
Revision: Sean, **an able musician**, was a key member of the cast.

Absolutes act like appositives, but, rather than echoing a single noun or noun phrase, the absolute phrase modifies the sentence as a whole.

He found the beach especially beautiful, **its blowing sand and broken shells always evocative, occasionally haunting.**

Periodic and Cumulative Styles: Two Ways of Locating Closure

The shape of a sentence governs the way it delivers information. The order of clauses, especially the placement of the main clause, affects what the sentence means. There are two common sentence shapes defined by the location of their main clauses; these are known as **periodic** and **cumulative** sentences. The periodic sentence is built on suspense and delay: it puts maximum emphasis on the way the sentence ends. The cumulative sentence aims for upfront impact; there is no suspense, but rather, the rolling momentum of an extended follow-through.

The Periodic Sentence: Delay Closure to Achieve Emphasis

The main clause in a periodic sentence builds to a climax that is not completed until the end. Often, a piece of the main clause (such as the subject) is located early in the sentence, as in the following example:

> The **way** that beverage companies market health—"No Preservatives," "No Artificial Colors," "All Natural," "Real Brewed"—**is** often, because the product also contains a high percentage of sugar or fructose, **misleading**.

We have boldfaced the spine of the main clause to clarify how various modifiers interrupt it. The effect is suspenseful: not until the final word does the sentence consummate its fundamental idea and achieve grammatical closure. Pieces of the main clause are spread out across the sentence.

Another version of the periodic sentence locates the entire main clause at the end, after introductory modifiers.

> Using labels that market health—such as "No Preservatives," "No Artificial Colors," "All Natural," and "Real Brewed"—while producing drinks that contain a high percentage of sugar or fructose, **beverage companies are misleading.**

Style fact: As previously discussed, the end of a sentence normally receives emphasis. When you use a periodic construction, the pressure on the end intensifies because the sentence waits until the end to complete its grammatical sense. In both of the preceding examples, the sentences "snap shut." They string readers along, delaying *grammatical closure*—the point at which the sentences can stand alone independently—until they arrive at climactic ends.

Periodic sentences are also known as *climactic sentences*. Periodic sentences can be arranged so as to produce different levels of grammatical tension—high, middle, and low. The longer the reader has to wait in order to arrive at sentence closure, the higher the grammatical tension.

You should be aware of one risk that accompanies periodic constructions. If the delay lasts too long because there are too many "interrupters" before the main clause gets completed, your readers may forget the subject being predicated. To illustrate, let's add more subordinated material to one of the preceding examples.

> The way that beverage companies market health—"No Preservatives," "No Artificial Colors," "All Natural," "Real Brewed"—is often, because the product also contains a high percentage of sugar or fructose, not just what New Agers would probably term "immoral" and "misleading" but what a government agency such as the Food and Drug Administration should find illegal.

Arguably, the additions (the "not just" and "but" clauses after "fructose") push the sentence into incoherence. The main clause has been stretched past the breaking point. If readers don't get lost in such a sentence, they are at least likely to get irritated and wish the writer would finally get to the point.

Nonetheless, with a little care, periodic sentences can be extraordinarily useful in locating emphasis. If you are revising and want to underscore some point, try letting the sentence snap shut upon it. Often the periodic potential will already be present in the draft, and stylistic editing can bring it out more forcefully. Note how minor the revisions are in the following example:

> **Draft:** The novelist Virginia Woolf suffered from acute anxieties for most of her life. She had several breakdowns and finally committed suicide on the eve of World War II.
>
> **Revision:** Suffering from acute anxieties for most of her life, the novelist Virginia **Woolf** not only **had** several **breakdowns but**, finally, on the eve of World War II, **committed suicide** as well.

This revision has made two primary changes. It has combined two short sentences into a longer sentence, and it has made the sentence periodic by stringing out the main clause. What is the effect of this revision? Stylistically speaking, the revision radiates a greater sense of its writer's authority. The information has been arranged for us. After the opening dependent clause ("Suffering…"), the subject of the main clause ("Woolf") is introduced, and the predicate is protracted in a *not only/but also* parallelism. The interrupters that follow "had several breakdowns" ("finally, on the eve of World War II") increase the suspense, before the sentence snaps shut with "committed suicide."

In general, when you construct a periodic sentence with care, you can give readers the sense that you are in control of your material. You do not seem to be writing off the top of your head, but rather from a position of greater detachment, rationally composing your meaning.

The Cumulative Sentence: Start Fast to Build Momentum

The cumulative sentence is in many respects the opposite of the periodic. Rather than delaying the main clause or its final piece, the cumulative sentence begins by presenting the independent clause as a foundation and then *accumulates* a number of modifications and qualifications. As the following examples illustrate, the independent clause provides quick grammatical closure, freeing the rest of the sentence to amplify and develop the main idea:

> **Robert F. Kennedy was assassinated** by Sirhan B. Sirhan, a twenty-four-year-old Palestinian immigrant, prone to occultism and unsophisticated left-wing politics and sociopathically devoted to leaving his mark in history, even if as a notorious figure.
>
> **There are two piano concerti** composed solely for the left hand, one by Serge Prokofiev and one by Maurice Ravel, and both commissioned by Paul Wittgenstein, a concert pianist (and the brother of the famous philosopher Ludwig Wittgenstein) who had lost his right hand in combat during World War I.

Anchored by the main clause, a cumulative sentence moves serially through one thing and another thing and the next thing, close to the associative manner in which people think. To an extent, then, cumulative sentences can convey more immediacy and a more conversational tone than can other sentence shapes. Look at the following example:

> **The film version of *Lady Chatterley's Lover* changed D. H. Lawrence's famous novel** a lot, omitting the heroine's adolescent experience in Germany, making her husband much older than she, leaving out her father and sister, including a lot more lovemaking, and virtually eliminating all of the philosophizing about sex and marriage.

Here, we get the impression of a mind in the act of thinking. Using the generalization of changes in the film as a base, the sentence then appends a series of parallel participial phrases ("omitting," "making," "leaving," "including," "eliminating") that moves forward associatively, gathering a range of information and laying out possibilities. Cumulative sentences perform this outlining and prospecting function very effectively. On the other hand, if we were to add four or five more changes to the sentence, readers would likely find it tedious, or worse, directionless. As with periodic sentences, overloading the shape can short-circuit its desired effect.

If you consciously practice using periodic and cumulative constructions, you will be surprised how quickly you can learn to produce their respective effects in your own writing. You will also discover that both of these sentence shapes are already present in your prose in some undiscovered and thus unrefined way. It is often simply a case of bringing out what is already there. Try including at least one of each in the next paper you write.

TRY THIS 11.4: Write Periodic and Cumulative Sentences

Compose a simple sentence on any subject—a sentence with one main clause. Then construct two variations expanding it, one periodic and one cumulative. Here, as a model, is an example using the core sentence "James Joyce was a gifted singer."

Periodic: Although known primarily as one of the greatest novelists of the twentieth century, James Joyce, the son of a local political functionary who loved to tip a few too many at the pub, was also a gifted—and prizewinning—singer.

Cumulative: James Joyce was a gifted singer, having listened at his father's knee to the ballads sung in pubs, having won an all-Ireland prize in his early teens, and having possessed a miraculous ear for the inflections of common speech that was to serve him throughout the career for which he is justly famous, that of a novelist.

Can't think of a core sentence? Okay, here are two:

> Why do airlines show such mediocre films?
> Every senator is a millionaire.

Symmetry and Sense: Balance, Antithesis, and Parallelism

Long and grammatically complicated sentences achieve clarity and emphasis primarily through various kinds of repetition. A writer can repeat similar words and phrases at the beginning of sentences (a device called **anaphora**), and the writer can accumulate a series of parallel clauses or phrases of the same or similar length (**isocolon**).

Style fact: Symmetry makes sentences easier to follow, whether the sentence shape is one that balances similar ideas or one that sets them up in contrast to each other (**antithesis**).

Parallel Structure: Put Parallel Information into Parallel Form

One of the most important and useful devices for shaping sentences is **parallel structure** or, as it is also known, **parallelism**. Parallelism is a form of symmetry: it involves placing sentence elements that correspond in some way into the same (that is, parallel) grammatical form. Consider the following examples, in which the parallel items are boldfaced or italicized:

> The three kinds of partners in a law firm who receive money from a case are popularly known as **finders, binders**, and **grinders**.
> The Beatles acknowledged their musical debts **to** American rhythm and blues, **to** English music hall ballads and ditties, and later **to** classical Indian ragas.
> There was **no way that** the President **could gain** the support of party regulars *without alienating* the Congress, and **no way that** he **could appeal** to the electorate at large *without alienating* both of these groups.
> In the entertainment industry, the money that **goes out** to hire *film stars* or *sports stars* **comes back** in increased ticket sales and video or television rights.

As these examples illustrate, at the core of parallelism lies repetition—of a word, a phrase, or a grammatical structure. Parallelism uses repetition to organize and emphasize certain elements in a sentence, so that readers can perceive more clearly the shape of your thought. In the Beatles example, each of the prepositional phrases beginning with *to* contains a musical debt. In the President example, the repetition of the phrase **no way that** emphasizes his entrapment.

Parallelism has the added advantage of economy: each of the musical debts or presidential problems might have had its own sentence, but in that case the prose would have been wordier and the relationships among the parallel items more obscure. Along with this economy come balance and emphasis. The trio of rhyming words (finders, binders, and grinders) that concludes the law-firm example gives each item equal weight; in the entertainment-industry example, "comes back" answers "goes out" in a way that accentuates their symmetry.

It is important to avoid what is known as *faulty parallelism*, which occurs when the items that are parallel in content are not placed in the same grammatical form.

> **Faulty: To study** hard for four years and then **getting** ignored once they enter the job market is a hard thing for many recent college graduates to accept.
>
> **Revised: To study** hard for four years and then **to get** ignored once they enter the job market is a hard thing for many recent college graduates to accept.

TRY THIS 11.5: Correct Errors in Parallelism

Rewrite the following examples of faulty parallelism using correct parallel structure:

1. The problems with fast food restaurants include the way workers are exploited, eating transfatty acids, and that the food can damage your liver.

2. Venus Williams likes to play tennis and also designing clothes.

3. In the 1960s, the use of drugs and being a hippie were ways for some people to let society know their political views and that they were alienated from the mainstream.

Two Powerful Forms of Parallelism: Antithesis and Chiasmus

One particularly useful form of balance that parallel structure accommodates is known as **antithesis** (from the Greek word for "opposition"), a conjoining of contrasting ideas. Here, the pattern sets one thing against another thing, as in the following example:

> Where bravura failed to settle the negotiations, tact and patience succeeded.

"Failed" is balanced antithetically against "succeeded," as "bravura" against "tact and patience." Antithesis commonly takes the form of "if not x, at least y" or "not x, but y."

Another specialized form of parallelism known as **chiasmus** is a rhetorical pattern that organizes elements in an ABBA structure. The most famous chiasmus known to most Americans comes from a speech by John F. Kennedy:

> Ask not what your country can do for you; ask what you can do for your country.

Note how this form also uses antithesis—the JFK example moves from "ask not" to "ask"—which is why it is known as a form of inverted parallelism, the second half of the expression balanced against the first, with the parts reversed. You can more easily remember the term chiasmus once you realize that it derives from the Greek letter *chi*, meaning X, as that is the shape of the AB → BA structure. Here is another memorable example of chiasmus from Matthew 19:30:

But many that are **first** shall be **last**; and the **last** shall be **first.**

As you write, and especially as you revise for style, search for opportunities to place sentence elements in parallel structure. Remember that parallelism can occur with clauses and phrases, especially prepositional phrases. Often, the parallels will be hidden in the sentences of your draft, but they can be brought out with a minimum of labor. After you've acquired the habit of casting your thinking in parallel structures, they will rapidly become a staple of your stylistic repertoire, making your prose more graceful, clear, and logically connected.

"Official Style"

Richard Lanham, in his influential style guide, *Revising Prose*, coined the term "Official Style" for the kinds of sentences he thought were steadily draining the life out of English prose style. For such sentences—the product of bureaucrats—Lanham prescribed his paramedic method, which calls for finding the action in sentences rather than allowing them to sink under the weight of nouns and strings of prepositions. For Lanham, perhaps the primary characteristic of Official Style is its reliance on forms of "to be," with the resulting conversion of verbs into nouns. In his paramedic method, Lanham instructs writers to mark all of the prepositions, identify the forms of *to be*, and find the action buried in the sentence and make it into an active verb. As you will see, avoiding Official Style is a matter not only of syntax, but also of concise and effective word choice.

Finding the Action in a Sentence: "To Be" Or Not "To Be"

Verbs energize a sentence. They actively connect the parts of the sentence with each other, as opposed to less active forms of connection such as relative pronouns (clauses beginning with "that" or "which") and prepositions. In a sentence of the subject–verb–direct object pattern, the verb—known as a *transitive verb*—functions as a kind of engine, driving the subject into the predicate, as in the following examples.

> John F. Kennedy effectively **manipulated** his image in the media.
> Thomas Jefferson **embraced** the idea of America as a country of yeoman farmers.

By contrast, "is" and other forms of the verb "to be" provide an equals sign between the subject and the predicate but otherwise tell us nothing about the relationship between them. "To be" is an *intransitive verb*; it cannot take a direct object. Compare the two preceding transitive examples with the following versions of the same sentences using forms of the verb "to be."

> John F. Kennedy **was** effective at the manipulation of his image in the media.
> Thomas Jefferson's idea **was** for America to be a country of yeoman farmers.

Rather than making things happen through an active transitive verb, these sentences let everything just hang around in a state of being. In the first version, Kennedy did something—*manipulated* his image—but in the second he just is (or *was*), and the energy of the original verb has been siphoned into an abstract noun, "manipulation." The revised Jefferson example suffers from a similar lack of momentum compared with the original version: the syntax doesn't help the sentence get anywhere.

Certain situations, however, dictate the use of forms of "to be." For definitions in particular, the equals sign that an "is" provides works well. For instance:

> Organic gardening *is* a method of growing crops without using synthetic fertilizers or pesticides.

As with choosing between active and passive voices, the decision to use "to be" should be just that—a conscious decision on your part.

If you can train yourself to eliminate every unnecessary use of "to be" in a draft, you will make your prose more lively and direct. In most cases, you will find the verb that you need to substitute for "is" lurking somewhere in the sentence in some other grammatical form. In the preceding sentence about Kennedy, "manipulate" is implicit in "manipulation." In Table 11.1, each of the examples in the left-hand column uses a form of "to be" for its verb (italicized) and contains a potentially strong active verb lurking in the sentence in some other form (boldfaced). These "lurkers" have been converted into active verbs (italicized) in the revisions in the right-hand column.

Clearly, the examples in the left-hand column have problems in addition to their reliance on forms of "to be." Notably, they are vague and wordy.

TABLE 11.1
Static and Active Verbs

Action Hidden in Nouns and "To Be" Verbs	Action Emphasized in Verbs
The **cost** of the book *is* ten dollars.	The book *costs* ten dollars.
The **acknowledgment** of the fact *is* increasingly widespread that television *is* a **replacement** for reading in American culture.	People increasingly *acknowledge* that television *has replaced* reading in American culture.
A computer *is* ostensibly a **labor-saving** device—until the hard drive *is* the victim of a **crash**.	A computer ostensibly *saves* labor—until the hard drive *crashes*.
In the **laying** of a flagstone patio, the important preliminary steps to remember *are* the **excavating** and the **leveling** of the area and then the **filling** of it with a fine grade of gravel.	To *lay* a flagstone patio, first *excavate* and *level* the area and then *fill* it with a fine grade of gravel.

TRY THIS 11.6: Find Active Verbs in Your Sentences

Take a paper you've written and circle the sentences that rely on forms of "to be." Then, examine the other words in these sentences, looking for "lurkers." Rewrite the sentences, converting the lurkers into vigorous verbs. You will probably discover many lurkers, and your revisions will acquire more energy and directness.

Active and Passive Voice: Emphasizing the Doer or the Action

In the **active voice**, the grammatical subject acts; in the **passive voice**, the subject is acted upon. Here are two examples.

> **Active:** Adam Smith wrote *The Wealth of Nations* in 1776.
> **Passive:** *The Wealth of Nations was* written by Adam Smith in 1776.

The two sentences convey identical information, but the emphasis differs—the first focuses on the author, the second on the book.

As the examples illustrate, using the passive normally results in a longer sentence than using the active. If we consider how to convert the passive into the active, you can see why. In the passive, the verb requires a form of "to be" plus a past participle. (For more on participles, see the "Glossary of Grammatical Terms" in Chapter 12.) In this case, the active verb "wrote" becomes the passive verb "was written," the grammatical subject ("Smith") becomes the object of the preposition "by," and the direct object (*The Wealth of Nations*) becomes the grammatical subject.

Now consider the activity described in the two versions of this example: a man wrote a book. The active example captures what happened in life most clearly: the grammatical subject ("Smith") performs the action, and the direct object (*The Wealth of Nations*) receives it, just as in life. By contrast, the passive example alters the close link between the syntax and the event: the object of the action in life (the book, *The Wealth of Nations*) has become the grammatical subject, whereas the doer in life (the man, "Smith") has become the grammatical object of a prepositional phrase.

Note, too, that the passive would allow us to omit "Smith" altogether: "*The Wealth of Nations* was written in 1776." A reader who desired to know more and was not aware of the author would not appreciate this sentence. More troubling, the passive can also be used to conceal the doer of an action—not "I made a mistake" (active) but rather "A mistake has been made" (passive).

Style fact: In sum, there are three reasons for avoiding the passive voice when you can: (1) it's longer, (2) its grammatical relationships can misrepresent what happened in life, and (3) it can omit the performer responsible for the action.

Style fact: On the other hand, sometimes there are good reasons for using the passive. If you want to emphasize the object or recipient of the action rather than the performer, the passive will do that: "*The Wealth of Nations* was written in 1776 by Adam Smith" places initial stress on the book. The passive is also preferable when the doer remains unknown: "The president has been shot!" is probably a better sentence than "Some unknown assailant has shot the president!"

Especially in the natural sciences, the use of the passive voice is a standard practice. There are sound reasons for this disciplinary convention: science tends to focus on what happens to something in a given experiment, rather than on the person performing the experiment. Compare the following sentences:

Passive: Separation of the protein was achieved by using an electrophoretic gel.
Active: The researcher used an electrophoretic gel to separate the protein.

If you opted for the active version, the emphasis would rest, illogically, on the agent of the action (the researcher) rather than on what happened and how (electrophoretic separation of the protein).

On balance, "consider" is the operative term when you choose between passive and active as you revise the syntax of your drafts. Recognize that you do have choices—in emphasis, in relative directness, and in economy. All things being equal and disciplinary conventions permitting, the active is usually the better choice.

TRY THIS 11.7: Analyze the Effect of Passive Voice

In the paragraph below, taken from the Declaration of Independence, please do the following:

— Circle the verb in each clause. Identify which clauses exhibit passive construction.
— Convert each sentence in passive voice to active voice.
— Explain how the meaning of the passive voice sentences change when rewritten in active voice.

We hold these truths to be self-evident, that all men are created equal, that they	1
are endowed by their Creator with certain unalienable Rights, that among these are	2
Life, Liberty and the pursuit of Happiness. That to secure these rights, Governments	3
are instituted among Men, deriving their just powers from the consent of the governed,	4
That whenever any Form of Government becomes destructive of these ends, it is the	5
Right of the People to alter or to abolish it, and to institute new Government, laying its	6
foundation on such principles and organizing its powers in such form, as to them shall	7
seem most likely to effect their Safety and Happiness.	8

TRY THIS 11.8: Write Passive and Active Voice Sentences

Identify all of the sentences that use the passive voice in one of your papers. Then, rewrite these sentences, converting passive into active wherever appropriate. Finally, count the total number of words, the total number of prepositions, and the average sentence length (words per sentence) in each version. What do you discover?

For more practice, here's another exercise. Compose a paragraph of at least half a page in which you use only the passive voice and verbs of being, followed by a paragraph in which you use only the active voice. Then, rewrite the first paragraph using only active voice, if possible, and rewrite the second paragraph using only passive voice and verbs of being as much as possible. How do the paragraphs differ in shape, length, and coherence?

Expletives: Beginning with "It Is" or "There Is"

Sentences that begin with openers like "It is" or "There is" are known as *expletive* constructions. The term *expletive* comes from a Latin word that means "serving to fill out." Most of the time, you can streamline your prose by getting rid of expletive constructions. Consider how expletives function in the following examples:

There are several prototypes for the artificial heart.

It is obvious that the American West exerted a profound influence on the photography of Ansel Adams.

Compare these with versions that simply eliminate the expletives.

The artificial heart has several prototypes.

The American West exerted a profound influence on the photography of Ansel Adams.

Expletives such as the "It is obvious that" opening cause the grammar of the sentence to subordinate its real emphasis.

In some cases, though, an expletive can provide useful emphasis, as in the following example: "There are three primary reasons that you should avoid litigation." Although this sentence grammatically subordinates its primary content (avoiding litigation), the expletive provides a useful frame for what is to follow.

In an excellent book, *Rhetorical Grammar* (Pearson, 2012), Martha Kolln and Loretta Gray make the case for using what they term "the there-transformation" as a strategy for adding emphasis. They do so by focusing on what they call "the rhythm pattern" of the sentence. Compare "There's a stranger standing on the porch," where the accent falls on "stranger," with "The stranger stands on the porch," where the accent—and thus the emphasis—falls on "porch."

Concrete vs. Evaluative Adjectives and Intensifiers: What's Bad About "Good" and "Bad"

Good. Pretty. Boring. Negative. Positive. All of these words are **evaluative adjectives**. They offer judgments without any supporting data. *Green* and *small* and *bright* are examples of **concrete (descriptive) adjectives**. They give us something specific to think with. Broad evaluative terms such as *good* and *bad* can seduce you into stopping your thinking while it is still too general and ill-defined—a matter discussed at length in "The Judgment Reflex" section of Chapter 1. If you train yourself to select more precise words whenever you encounter *good* and *bad* in your drafts, not only will your prose become clearer, but also the search for new words will start you thinking again, sharpening your ideas.

If, for example, you find yourself writing a sentence such as "The subcommittee made a bad decision," ask yourself why you called it a bad decision. A revision to "The subcommittee made a shortsighted decision" indicates what in fact is bad about the decision and sets you up to discuss why the decision was myopic, further developing the idea.

Be aware that often evaluative terms are disguised as neutrally descriptive ones—*natural*, for instance, and *realistic*. Realistic according to whom, and defined by what criteria? Something is natural according to a given idea about nature—an assumption—and the same goes for *moral*. The meaning of these terms depends on the context in which they are being used, and by whom they are being used. These are not terms that mean separately from a particular context or ideology—that is, an assumed hierarchy of value.

Many words fall somewhere between being evaluative and concrete. The word "complicated," for example, is concrete in that it means "having more than one side (complex)," but complicated or complex can be evaluative depending on context. In some circles, a complicated idea is thought to be insufficiently straightforward. In academic circles, wherein accuracy is valued more highly than ease of expression, complicated ideas are good.

Another type of word prone to adding evaluation without data is the kind of adverb called an **intensifier**—really, truly, actually, very, entirely, and so on. These words add little—except an overstated tone—to writing. It is usually (though not always) best to eliminate them.

Concrete and Abstract Diction

At its best, effective analytical prose uses both concrete and abstract words. Simply defined, concrete diction brings things to life by offering readers words that play on their senses. *Telephone, eggshell, crystalline, azure, striped, kneel, flare,* and *burp* are examples of concrete diction. You need concrete language whenever you are describing what happens or what something looks like—in a laboratory experiment, in a military action, in a painting or film sequence. The language of evidence consists of concrete diction. It allows us to see for ourselves the basis of a person's convictions in the stuff of lived experience.

By contrast, abstract diction refers to words that designate concepts and categories. *Virility, ideology, love, definitive, desultory, conscientious, classify,* and *ameliorate* are examples of abstract diction. So are *democracy, fascism, benevolence,* and *sentimentality*. Abstract words give us the language of ideas. We cannot do without abstract terms, and yet writing made up only of such words loses contact with experience, with the world that we can apprehend through our senses.

The line between abstract and concrete is not always as clear as these examples may suggest. You may recall the ladder of abstraction that we

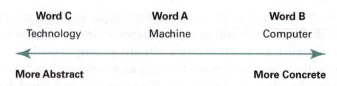

FIGURE 11.1
Abstract-Concrete Continuum

discussed in the section titled "Generalizing" in Chapter 1. There, we proposed that abstract and concrete are not hard-and-fast categories so much as a continuum, a sliding scale. In Figure 11.1, you would say that Word A (machine) is more abstract than Word B (computer) but more concrete than Word C (technology).

Concrete and abstract diction need each other. Concrete diction illustrates and anchors the generalizations that abstract diction expresses. Notice the concrete language used to define the abstraction *provinciality* in this example:

> There is no cure for **provinciality** like traveling abroad. In America, the waiter who fails to bring the check promptly at the end of the meal we rightly convict for not being watchful. But in England, after waiting interminably for the check and becoming increasingly irate, we learn that only an ill-mannered waiter would bring it without being asked. We have been rude, not he.

In the following example, the abstract terms *causality, fiction,* and *conjunction* are integrated with concrete diction in the second sentence:

> According to the philosopher David Hume, **causality** is a kind of **fiction** that we ascribe to what he called "the constant **conjunction** of observed events." If a person gets hit in the eye and a black semicircle develops underneath it, that does not necessarily mean the blow caused the black eye.

A style that omits concrete language can leave readers lost in a fog of abstraction that only tangible details can illuminate. Concrete language helps readers see what you mean, much in the way that examples help them understand your ideas. Without the shaping power of abstract diction, however, concrete evocation can leave you with a list of graphic but ultimately pointless facts. The best writing integrates concrete and abstract diction, the language of showing and the language of telling.

Latinate Diction

One of the best ways to sensitize yourself to the difference between abstract and concrete diction is to understand that many abstract words are examples of what is known as Latinate diction. This term describes words in English that derive from Latin roots, words with such endings as –*tion*, –*ive*, –*ity*, –*ate*, and –*ent*. (Such words are designated by an L in the etymological section of dictionary definitions.) Taken to an extreme, Latinate diction can leave your meaning vague and your readers confused. This is not because there is something dubious about words that come into English from Latin. A large percentage of English words have Latin or Greek roots, words like *pentagon* (Greek for five sides), *anarchy* (Latin for without order), and *automobile* (Latin for self-moving).

The problem with Latinate diction lies in the way it is sometimes used. Latin endings such as *–tion* make it too easy for writers to construct sentences made up of a high percentage of vague nouns, as in the following example:

> The examination of different perspectives on the representations of socio-political anarchy in media coverage of revolutions can be revelatory of the invisible biases that afflict television news.

This sentence actually makes sense, but the demands it makes on readers will surely drive off most of them before they have gotten through it. Reducing the amount of Latinate diction can make it more readable:

> Because we tend to believe what we see, the political biases that afflict television news coverage of revolutions are largely invisible. We can begin to see these biases when we focus on how the medium reports events, studying the kinds of footage used, for example, or finding facts from other sources that the news has left out.

Although the preceding revision retains many Latinate words, it provides a ballast of concrete, sensory details that allows readers to follow the idea. It's fine to use Latinate diction; just don't make it the sole staple of your verbal diet.

Etymology: Finding a Word's Physical History

In choosing the right shade of meaning, you will get a sharper sense for the word by knowing its etymological history—the word or words from which it evolved. In the preceding example, *aggressive* derives from the Latin *aggressus*, meaning "to go to or approach"; and *aggressus* is itself a combination of *ad*, a prefix expressing motion, and *gradus*, meaning "a step." An aggressive person, then, is "coming at you." *Assertive*, on the other hand, comes from the Latin *asserere*, combining *ad*, meaning "to or toward," with *serere*, meaning "join or bind together." An assertive person is "coming to build or put things together"—certainly not to threaten.

The best dictionary for pursuing word histories, by the way, is the *Oxford English Dictionary*, commonly known as the *OED*. Available in every library reference collection and usually online at colleges and universities as well, it provides examples of how words have been used over time.

TRY THIS 11.9: Tracing Word Histories

Look up one of the following pairs of words in the *Oxford English Dictionary*. Write down the etymology of each word in the pair, and then, in a paragraph for each, summarize the words' linguistic histories—how their meanings have evolved across time. (The OED's examples of how the word has been used over time will be helpful here.)

    ordinal/ordinary
    explicate/implicate
    tenacious/stubborn
    induce/conducive
    enthusiasm/ecstasy
    adhere/inhere
    monarchy/oligarchy
    overt/covert

"Right" and "Wrong" Words: Shades of Meaning

The nineteenth-century English statesman Benjamin Disraeli once differentiated between *misfortune* and *calamity* in a sentence describing his political rival William Gladstone: "If Mr. Gladstone fell into the Thames, it would be a misfortune; but if someone dragged him out, it would be a calamity." Misfortune and calamity might mean the same thing to some people, but in fact the two words allow a careful writer to discriminate fine shades of meaning.

One of the best ways to pay attention to words as words is to practice making subtle distinctions among related words. The "right" word contributes accuracy and precision to your meaning. The "wrong" word, it follows, is inaccurate or imprecise. The most reliable guide to choosing the right word and avoiding the wrong word is a dictionary that includes not only concise definitions but also the origin of words (their *etymology*). A dicey alternative is a thesaurus (a dictionary of synonyms, now included in most word-processing software). A thesaurus can offer you a host of choices, but you run a fairly high risk of choosing an inappropriate word because the thesaurus lists words as synonyms that really have different shades of meaning and connotation.

Many of the most common diction errors happen because the writer has not learned the difference between similar terms that actually have different meanings. A common error of this kind is use of the word "notorious" when what the writer means to say is "famous." A *notorious* figure is widely but unfavorably known, whereas a *famous* person is usually recognized for accomplishments that are praiseworthy. Referring to a famous person as notorious—a rather comic error—could be an embarrassing mistake.

A slightly less severe version of getting the wrong word occurs when a writer uses a word with a shade of meaning that is inappropriate or inaccurate in a particular context. Take, for example, the words *assertive* and *aggressive*. Often used interchangeably, they don't really mean the same thing—and the difference matters. Loosely defined, both terms mean forceful. But assertive suggests being bold and self-confident, whereas aggressive suggests being eager to attack. In most cases, you compliment the person you call assertive but raise doubts about the person you call aggressive.

One particularly charged context in which shades of meaning matter involves the potentially sexist implications of using one term for women and another for men. If, for example, in describing a woman and a man up for the same job, the employer were to refer to the woman as *aggressive* but the man as *assertive*, his diction would deservedly be considered sexist. It would reveal that what is perceived as poised and a sign of leadership potential in a man is construed as unseemly belligerence in a woman. The sexism enters when word choice suggests that what is assertive in a man is aggressive in a woman.

Tone

Tone is the *implied attitude* of a piece of language toward its subject and audience. Whenever you revise for style, your choices in syntax and diction affect the tone. There are no hard-and-fast rules to govern matters of tone, and your control of it depends on your sensitivity to the particular context—your understanding of your own intentions and your readers' expectations.

Let's consider, for example, the tonal implications of the warning signs in the subways of London as compared with New York.

> **London:** Leaning out of the window may cause harm.
> **New York:** Do not lean out of the window.

Initially, you may find the English injunction laughably indirect and verbose in comparison with the shoot-from-the-hip clarity of the American sign. But that is to ignore the very thing we are calling *style*. The American version appeals to authority, commanding readers what not to do without telling them why. The English version, by contrast, appeals to logic; it is more collegial toward its readers and assumes they are rational beings rather than children prone to misbehave.

In revising for tone, ask yourself if the attitude suggested by your language is appropriate to the aim of your message and to your audience. Your goal is to keep the tone *consistent* with your rhetorical intentions. The following paragraph, from a college catalogue, offers a classic mismatch between the overtly stated aim and the tonal implications:

> The student affairs staff believes that the college years provide a growth and development process for students. Students need to learn about themselves and others and to learn how to relate to individuals and groups of individuals with vastly different backgrounds, interests, attitudes and values. Not only is the tolerance of differences expected, but also an appreciation and a celebration of these differences must be an outcome of the student's experience. In addition, the student must progress toward self-reliance and independence tempered by a concern for the social order.

The explicit content of this passage—*what it says*—concerns tolerance. The professed point of view is student-friendly, asserting that the college exists to allow students "to learn about themselves and others" and to support the individual in accord with the "appreciation… of… differences." But note that the implicit tone—*how* the passage goes about saying *what* it says—is condescending and intolerant. Look at the verbs. An imperious authority lectures students about what they "*need* to learn," that tolerance is "*expected,*" that "celebration… *must* be an outcome," and that "the student *must* progress" along these lines. Presumably, the paragraph does not intend to adopt this high-handed manner, but its deafness to tone subverts its desired meaning.

TRY THIS 11.10: Analyze Prose with Questionable Tone

Using the example from the college catalogue as a model, locate and bring to class examples of tonal inconsistency or inappropriateness that you encounter in your daily life. If you have difficulty finding examples, try memos from those in authority at your school or workplace, which often contain excruciating examples of officialese. Write down one of your passages, and underneath it compose a paragraph of analysis in which you single out particular words and phrases and explain how the tone is inappropriate. Then, rewrite the passage to remedy the problem.

TRY THIS 11.11: Analyze Effective Tone

Find an example of tone that you think is just about perfect for the message and audience. Write it down, and under it discuss why it succeeds. Be as specific as you can about how the passage functions stylistically. Talk about particular phrasings, and the match between what is being said and how it is said. Factor into your discussion the relationship between levels of style in the example and its presumed audience.

Bias-Free Language

These recommendations aim to help writers treat language related to identity (race/ethnicity, religion, gender, sexual orientation, ability, age, and economic and social status) with sensitivity and to avoid bias.

Make Sure Identity Terms Used Are Relevant

- Make sure any specifications of identity are relevant to the context, to avoid "othering" certain people: Don't specify *woman doctor*, for example, unless that is crucial to the point.

Aim for Gender Neutrality

- Replace gender-specific terms with gender-neutral ones; for example, *man* for "humans" (man-made) with *human* (human-made). Make sure professions are expressed in gender-neutral terms.

- MLA suggests *Latinx* and other gender-neutral terms to refer to people of unknown genders or mixed-gender groups.

Be Specific

- Be specific as possible when referring to groups of people (e.g., use a tribe name instead of *Native American*) and, if possible, use the person's/group's preferred term.
- Do not use generalizations about groups, to avoid stereotyping.

Show Respect via Terms Used and Their Capitalization and Styling

- Use person-first language (a person with autism) or identity-first language (an autistic person) in keeping with the preferences of the individuals or groups referred to, if known.
- If the dictionary gives an identity term in both capitalized and lower-cased forms, pick one form and stick with it, following the preferences of the community, if known (Black, Deaf).
- Don't put identity terms in quotation marks or italics even when the term is not yet in the dictionary.

Avoid Pronouns That Exclude

- Although *he or she, his or her,* etc., are attempts to be inclusive, these phrases foreground gender and present it as a binary. Better solutions are to recast the sentence with plural subjects and pronouns or without pronouns.
- *They* or other pronouns (*hir*) should be used if known to be preferred by a person written about.
- Singular *they* can now also be used to refer to people in general (Each student… their…) or to a specific person whose gender is not known or relevant.
- Avoid writing that assumes, for example, through first-person plurals (our society), that the audience shares your identity, beliefs, etc.

Avoid Judgments

- Avoid descriptions like *suffers from, victim of,* and *afflicted with.* Similarly, avoid phrases like *wheelchair bound/confined to a wheelchair.*

Check the Dictionary

- Check the dictionary if you're not sure about how appropriate a term is, and make sure the dictionary is recent!
- If you can't change an offensive term in a source text, revise the term in the discussion about the text.

The Politics of Language

Style has political and ethical implications. A little over a half century ago, in his famous essay "Politics and the English Language," George Orwell warned of the "invasion of one's mind by ready-made phrases… [which] can only be prevented if one is constantly on guard against them." The worst modern writing, he declared, "consists in gumming together long strips of words which have already been set in order by someone else, making the results presentable by sheer humbug." It was Orwell who characterized what has come to be called the "Official Style" in terms of euphemism—calling a spade a certain garden implement. Orwell was also concerned with the substitution of abstract for concrete language for the purpose of what he called "the defense of the indefensible." His example was referring to attacks on a country's people as relocation of unreliable elements.

Insofar as style is an expression of the writer's self, Orwell implies, (1) we are under attack from broad cultural clichés and sentimental nostrums that do our thinking for us, and (2) it is thus a matter of personal integrity and civic responsibility to ask ourselves a series of questions about the sentences that we write. As Orwell puts it: What am I trying to say? What words will express it? What image or idiom will make it clearer? Is this image fresh enough to have an effect? Could I put it more shortly? Have I said anything that is avoidably ugly?

Words matter. They matter in how we name things, in how we phrase meanings—and also in how we are shaped by the words we read and hear in the media. Words don't simply reflect a neutral world that is out there in some objective way that we can universally agree upon. Words don't reflect—they constitute; they call the world into being. They call us into being when we write them.

In a previous example we noted, for example, that the decision to call a woman "aggressive" as opposed to "assertive" matters. There are examples all around you of language creating rather than merely reflecting reality. Start looking for these on the front page of your newspaper, in political speeches, in advertising, even in everyday conversation. Does it matter, for instance, that there are no equivalents to the words "spinster" or "whore" for men? Does it change things to refer to a bombing mission as a "containment effort" or, by way of contrast, to call an enthusiastic person "a fanatic"?

Ethos, Audience, and Levels of Style

Style can be thought of as occupying various levels depending on whether it is formal or informal, personal or impersonal, though most styles blend these extremes. It is best to think of levels of style in terms of *ethos*, the character of the speaker that your style creates, and the kind of relationship with and attitude toward your audience that your style suggests. Some rhetoricians classify levels of style in terms of a writer positioning himself or herself *above, below,* or *at the same level* as the reader. When analyzing a writer's style, try looking for sentences that reveal the writer's rhetorical choices—those that reveal the kind of relationship the writer wishes to establish with readers in order to engage their support: expert and authoritative (above), companionable (at the same level as readers—at least some of the time), or below (aware that readers may have some advantage in terms of knowledge or attitude).

Transparent vs. Opaque Styles: Knowing When to Be Visible

In his insightful book on style, *Analyzing Prose*, Richard Lanham speaks of two kinds of style—transparent and opaque. Usually, "opaque" is a negative word for describing a writer's style, suggesting that it is unduly dense and hard to understand, something through which light cannot pass. Lanham, however, uses the word in a different sense. He observes that some styles try to come off as transparent, by which he means that the style does its best not to be noticed. Opaque styles, on the other hand, like opaque rather than transparent surfaces, call attention to themselves. They are meant to be seen. Opaque styles, unlike transparent ones, do not create the illusion that the writer has disappeared into the fabric of their prose. Instead, opaque styles make the writer and their stylistic choices visible and relatively prominent. Style is an explicit component of what the writer has come to say.

These terms are especially useful for understanding how a writer is meant to position himself or herself in the style prescriptions of different academic disciplines. Nowhere are misunderstandings across the disciplines more pronounced. Writers in the humanities and in some social sciences are allowed, in fact even expected, to be present in their prose. Readers are meant to know that a human being is writing to them. In the natural and some of the social sciences, writers are expected to pull the strings but remain more or less invisible. In these disciplines, style is not meant to call attention to itself—though for outsiders the style of science writing is anything but transparent. When a science writer criticizes the writing of a student from the humanities as "flowery" (decorative), the science writer is saying that the student's style is calling too much attention to itself. It is opaque.

The Person Question: When and When Not to Use "I"

The matter of transparent versus opaque styles is especially evident in a writer's choice of writing in first person rather than third person. Most analytical prose is more precise and straightforward for the reader in the third person. When you cut "I am convinced that" or "In my opinion" from the beginning of a claim, what you lose in personal conviction you gain in concision and directness by keeping the focus on the main idea in a main clause. Most academic analysis focuses on the subject matter rather than on you as you respond to it. If you use the third person, you keep the attention where it belongs.

> **First person:** I believe Heraclitus is an underrated philosopher.
> **Third person:** Heraclitus is an underrated philosopher.

Although using the first-person "I" can throw the emphasis on the wrong place in a sentence, you might consider using the first person in the drafting stage if you are having trouble bringing your own point of view to the forefront. In this situation, the "I" becomes a strategy for loosening up and saying what you really think about a subject rather than adopting conventional and faceless positions.

The argument for using the first and second person ("you") is that "I" and "you" are personal and engage readers. Finding opportunities to do some kind of personal writing is important because it can help inexperienced writers to find the voice and kind of engagement they need in order to energize whatever kind of writing they are asked to do. And, contrary to the general rule, some professors actually prefer the first-person pronoun in particular contexts, as noted in the following Voices from Across the Curriculum. As a general rule, however, in the formal products of most academic writing, especially in the sciences and social sciences, you should avoid personal pronouns.

It is not necessarily the case that the third person is therefore impersonal. Just as film directors put their stamps on films by the way they organize the images, move among camera viewpoints, and orchestrate the sound tracks, so writers, even when writing in the third person, have a wide variety of resources at their disposal for making the writing more personal and accessible for their audiences.

Proceed with caution with the second person, direct address. Using "you" is a fairly assertive gesture. Readers could easily be annoyed, for example, by a paper about advertising that states, "When you read about a sale at the mall, you know it's hard to resist." Most readers resent a writer airily making assumptions about them or telling them what to do. Some rhetorical situations, however, call for the use of "you." Textbooks, for example, use "you" frequently because it creates a more direct relationship between authors and readers. Yet, even in appropriate situations, directly addressing readers as "you" may alienate them by ascribing to them attitudes and needs they may not have.

VOICES FROM ACROSS THE CURRICULUM

Using the First-Person "I": Two Professors Speak

The biggest stylistic problem is that students tend to be too personal or colloquial in their writing, using phrases such as the following: "Scientists all agree," "I find it amazing that," "The thing that I find most interesting." Students are urged to present data and existing information in their own words, but in an objective way. My preference in writing is to use the active voice in the past tense. I feel this is the most direct and least wordy approach: "I asked this," "I found out that," "These data show."

—RICHARD NIESENBAUM, PROFESSOR OF BIOLOGY

Avoid phrases like "The author believes (or will discuss)." Except in the paper's abstract, "I believe (or will discuss)" is okay, and often best.

—ALAN TJELTVEIT, PROFESSOR OF PSYCHOLOGY

In the following Voice from Across the Curriculum, Professor of Biochemistry Keri Colabroy shares the basic style guidelines that she provides to her science majors.

VOICES FROM ACROSS THE CURRICULUM

Sentence Style in Science Writing: A Biochemistry Professor Speaks

The voice, ethos, and tone of science writing is typically quite muted. Active verbs appear, but the style goes out of its way to not call attention to itself, and especially not to the writer. This muted quality is, in fact, true of most academic writing, but it is markedly so in the sciences.

Subjects (the "actor" is absent)

- Passive voice

  Correct: The gel was run. (*Not*: I ran the gel.)

  Better: The protein migrated at a molecular weight of... (data first, not procedure)

- Pronouns—it's safer to avoid them

Verbs (qualify, qualify, qualify...)

- Do: demonstrate, indicate, suggest, construct, deliver, observe
- Don't: show, prove, make

Sentences

- Don't say in two sentences what you can say with one (embedding).
- Subordinate and coordinate.

Words

- Data are plural.
- When making observations, use academic, not conversational, language.
- Choose words for precision and tone (qualify your verbs, not your adjectives).

—KERI COLABROY, PROFESSOR OF BIOCHEMISTRY

Formal vs. Colloquial Styles

Imagine that you call your friend on the phone, and a voice you don't recognize answers. You ask to speak with your friend, and the voice responds, "With whom have I the pleasure of speaking?" By contrast, what if the voice instead responds, "Who's this?" What information do these two versions of the question convey, beyond the obvious request for your name?

The first response—"With whom have I the pleasure of speaking?"—tells you that the speaker is formal and polite. He is also probably fastidiously well educated: he not only knows the difference between "who" and "whom," but also obeys the etiquette that outlaws ending a sentence with a preposition ("Whom have I the pleasure of speaking *with*?"). The very formality of the utterance, however, might lead you to label the speaker pretentious. His assumption that conversing with you is a "pleasure" suggests empty flattery.

On the other hand, the second version—"Who's this?"—while also grammatically correct, is less formal. It is more direct and also terse to a fault; the speaker does not seem particularly interested in treating you politely.

The two hypothetical responses represent two different levels of style. Formal English obeys the basic conventions of standard written prose, and most academic writing is fairly formal. An informal style—one that is more conversational—can have severe limitations in an academic setting. The syntax and vocabulary of written prose aren't the same as those of speech, and so attempts to import the language of speech into academic writing can result in your communicating less meaning with less precision. Let's look at one brief example:

> Internecine quarrels within the corporation destroyed morale and sent the value of the stock plummeting.

The phrase "internecine quarrels" may strike some readers as a pretentious display of formal language, but consider how difficult it is to communicate this concept economically in more colloquial (casual, conversational) terms. "Fights that go on between people related to each other" is awkward; "brother against brother" is sexist and a cliché; and "mutually destructive disputes" is acceptable but long-winded and less precise.

It is arguably a part of our national culture to value the simple and the direct as being more genuine and democratic than the sophisticated, which is supposedly more aristocratic and pretentious. This "plain-speaking" style, however, can hinder your ability to develop and communicate your ideas. In the case of *internecine*, the more formal diction choice actually communicates more, and more effectively, than the less formal equivalents.

The Problem of Inflated Diction

The flip side of overly colloquial (informal and conversational) word choice is the problem of writers choosing words that are several steps further up the abstraction scale than they need to be, such as using the phrase "linguistic option" when you mean "word choice." Inflated diction usually results from one of two related causes. The first of these comes from the laudable goal of college students trying to acclimate to all of the new vocabulary they need to learn in order to speak the languages of the various academic disciplines. Academic disciplines are discourse communities—groups of people connected by a shared way of speaking. While trying to learn these new language sets, students understandably have trouble knowing when to choose a familiar word and when to reach for a more rarified term. Probably it is better to make some mistakes trying to gain control of the new vocabularies than to not try them at all.

The other cause of inflated diction is insecurity, which causes the writer to cloak ideas in words larger and more abstract than called for by the writing situation in order to assuage the writer's fear of sounding stupid. This is understandable, but also avoidable. When in doubt, choose the more familiar and less polysyllabic word, except in cases where a specialized vocabulary or an unusually high level of formality are called for.

Jargon: When to Use Insider Language

Many people assume that all jargon—the specialized vocabulary of a particular group—is bad: pretentious language designed to make most readers feel inferior. Many writing textbooks attack jargon in similar terms, calling it either polysyllabic balderdash or a specialized, gatekeeping language designed by an in-group to keep others out.

Yet, in many academic contexts, jargon is downright essential. It is conceptual shorthand, a technical vocabulary that allows the members of a group (or a discipline) to converse with one another more clearly and efficiently. Certain words that may seem odd to outsiders in fact function as connective tissue for a way of thought shared by insiders.

The following sentence, for example, although full of botanical jargon, is also admirably cogent:

> In angiosperm reproduction, if the number of pollen grains deposited on the stigma exceeds the number of ovules in the ovary, then pollen tubes may compete for access to ovules, which results in fertilization by the fastest growing pollen tubes.

We would label this use of jargon acceptable because it is written, clearly, by insiders *for* fellow insiders. It might not be acceptable language for an article intended for readers who are not botanists, or at least not scientists.

The problem with jargon comes when this insiders' language is directed at outsiders as well. The language of contracts offers a prime example of such jargon at work:

> The Author hereby indemnifies and agrees to hold the Publisher, its licensees, and any seller of the Work harmless from any liability, damage, cost, and expense, including reasonable attorney's fees and costs of settlement, for or in connection with any claim, action, or proceeding inconsistent with the Author's warranties or representations herein, or based upon or arising out of any contribution of the Author to the Work.

Run for the lawyer! What does it mean to "hold the Publisher . . . harmless"? To what do "the Author's warranties or representations" refer? What exactly is the author being asked to do here—release the publisher from all possible lawsuits that the author might bring? A lawyer might reasonably argue that contract language, designed to communicate clearly and concisely to other lawyers, is not meant to be understood by the layperson. Such documents are written by lawyers for other lawyers—although non-lawyers are asked to sign them. At what point do insiders need to aim at language that the outsiders affected by it might understand? A lawyer's translation for the layperson would not, necessarily, mean the same thing as the language of the contract, but it is the language of the contract by which the layperson will be bound.

As the botanical and legal examples suggest, the line between acceptable and obfuscating jargon is complicated. Because most academic writing is addressed to insiders, students studying a particular area need to learn its jargon. By demonstrating that you can "talk the talk," you validate your authority to pronounce an opinion on matters in the discipline. But it is also important for writers to recognize when insider-language needs to be defined or replaced with more generally known terms.

Style Analysis: A Summary of Things to Look For

This chapter has presented terms and techniques for experimenting with sentence styles and word choice. Equipped with these, you might profitably begin to read and listen for style more self-consciously. Find models. When a style appeals to you, figure out what makes it work. Copy sentences you like. Try imitating them.

Most people simply don't pay attention to words. They use words as if their sounds were inaudible, their shapes were invisible, and their meanings were single and self-evident. One goal of this chapter has been to interest you in words themselves—as things with particular qualities, complex histories, and varied shades of meaning.

Start your practice by finding a piece of writing that you think is interesting for style. Or find two pieces to analyze, so that you can use comparison and contrast to help you notice things. Mark up your chosen passages. Put a single line under sentence subjects, and two lines under the verb in independent clauses. Start by finding the main clause or clauses in each sentence. Then circle all conjunctions—coordinating, conjunctive, correlative, subordinating, relative. You might want to use different colors in order to better see the balance of coordinate to subordinate structures in the piece. Also circle all commas, dashes, semicolons, and colons.

Your goal is to be able to see the shapes of sentences: where the main clauses are in each sentence, how often a clause is interrupted or predication is in some way delayed, where modifying information has been added onto the main clause or clauses and in what form. Are the sentences primarily compound or complex?

How does the writer like to start sentences? How do they typically end? Does the writer use a mostly periodic or a cumulative style or some combination of the two? Is there a lot of parallelism in the piece? Where is this most noticeable? Does the writer tend toward short or long sentences and clauses? How much variety of sentence types do you find? Where do short sentences occur? Why might the writer have used short sentences where they did?

Try to find the writer's **"go-to" sentence shapes**—the ones the writer seems fond of. When you have done all of this observation, try to explain why, given the subject matter, the writer might have been attracted to certain kinds of sentence shapes. What, in other words, seems to you to be the relation between form and content—*what* the sentences say and *how* they go about saying it?

Assignments: Style: Choosing Words, Shaping Sentences

1. **Compare the style of two writers**. Analyze the style—the syntax and the diction—of two writers doing a similar kind of writing; for example, two sportswriters, two rock music reviewers, or two presidents. Study first the similarities. What style characteristics does this type of writing seem to invite? Then study the differences. How is one writer recognizable through their style? The American Rhetoric website is a wonderful place to go hunting.

2. **Analyze your own style.** Assemble some pieces you have written, preferably of a similar type, and study them for style. Do you have some favorite stylistic moves? What sentence shapes (simple, compound, complex, highly parallel, periodic, or cumulative) dominate in your writing? What verbs? Do you use forms of "to be" a lot? What is the balance of abstract to concrete words?

3. **Find go-to sentences.** Whether we recognize it or not, most of us have a "go-to" sentence—the sentence shape we repeatedly go to as we write and talk. If a person's "go-to" sentence takes the form "Although _____, the fact is that _____," we might see that person as inclined to qualify their thoughts ("Although") and disinclined to immediately impose their ideas on others ("the fact that" comes in the second half of the sentence, where it gets a lot of emphasis but is also delayed and qualified by the sentence's opening observation).

   First, select one sentence in something you've been reading that you think is typical of that writer's way of putting sentences together. Describe that sentence shape and speculate about what it accomplishes and how it reveals the writer's characteristic mode of thinking in some way.

   Then, find a "go-to" sentence of your own in something that you've written. What does this structure reveal to you about how you think? Look for repeated conjunctions or subordinators, such as "x; however, y" or "although x, nevertheless, y," or "not only x, but also y."

4. **Analyze the Gettysburg Address.** For many people, Lincoln's Gettysburg Address is one of the best examples of the careful matching of style to situation. Delivered after a long talk by a previous speaker at the dedication of a Civil War battlefield on a rainy day, the speech, composed by Abraham Lincoln (some say on the back of an envelope), is a masterpiece of style. Analyze its sentence structure, such as its use of parallelism, antithesis, and other kinds of repetition. Which features of Lincoln's style

seem most important in creating the overall effect of the piece? Or do this with any popular journalist you read regularly and who you think has an especially effective style. Or look for another inspirational speech and see if such occasional writing has anything in common. (You can download and print the Gettysburg Address from many websites.)

5. **Do a full-fledged stylistic revision of a paper.** As you revise, try to accomplish each of the following:

   a. Sharpen the diction.

   b. Blend concrete and abstract diction.

   c. Experiment with the order of and relation among subordinate and coordinate clauses. Locate points that you wish to emphasize at the end of sentences.

   d. Choose more knowingly between active and passive voice.

   e. Cut the fat, especially by eliminating unnecessary "to be" constructions.

   f. Vary sentence length and shape.

   g. Use parallelism.

   h. Experiment with periodic and cumulative sentences.

   i. Fine-tune the tone.

CHAPTER 12

Nine Basic Writing Errors (BWEs) and How to Fix Them

Overview   The chapter shows writers how to recognize and correct the nine basic writing errors most likely to disrupt reader understanding. The chapter also includes discussion of the difference between grammatical errors and matters of usage. The chapter argues that, in many cases, errors are not just the product of carelessness but of the writer's ways of thinking about sentences. Until writers can uncover the logic of some of the errors they regularly make, they have a hard time fixing these errors or even finding them in their drafts.

The Concept of Basic Writing Errors (BWEs)

Error correction can be overwhelming. You get a paper back, and it's a sea of red ink. Fortunately, if you look more closely, you'll often find that you haven't made hundreds of mistakes—you've made only a few, but over and over in various forms. Rhetorician Mina Shaughnessy addressed this phenomenon in her book *Errors & Expectations* by creating the category she called "basic writing errors," or BWEs. Shaughnessy argues that, in order to improve your writing for style and correctness, you need to do two things:

- Look for a *pattern of error,* which will require you to understand your own logic in the mistakes you typically make.

- Recognize that not all errors are created equal, which means that you need to *address errors in some order of importance*—beginning with those most likely to interfere with your readers' understanding.

This chapter reflects Shaughnessy's view. It does not cover *all* of the rules of grammar, punctuation, diction, and usage—such as where to place the comma or period when you close a quotation, or whether or not to write out numerals. Instead, it emphasizes the errors that are potentially the most damaging to the clarity of your writing and to your credibility with readers. We have arranged the error types in a hierarchy, moving in descending order of severity (from most to least problematic).

As in our discussion of style in Chapter 11, the key premises of this chapter are that a sentence is made up of moveable parts, and that sentences disclose the relationships among those parts. Keep these premises in mind, and you will see what the errors have in common.

Nine Basic Writing Errors

For each basic writing error listed below, the chapter offers a definition with examples and then talks you through how to fix it—with a "Test Yourself" section to help you apply what you have learned. At the end of the chapter, a brief Glossary of Grammatical Terms defines and illustrates many of the key terms used in this chapter and the previous one (on style). Use the Glossary to look up any terms mentioned in our explanations that you don't understand, such as independent clause, subordinating conjunction, participle, etc. For more comprehensive explanation of such terms as these, in the context of sentence types, see Chapter 11. There is also an appendix that provides solutions to the chapter's various "Test Yourself" exercises.

- Sentence fragments
- Comma splices and fused (run-on) sentences
- Errors in subject–verb agreement
- Shifts in sentence structure (faulty predication)
- Errors in pronoun reference
- Misplaced modifiers and dangling participles
- Errors in using possessive apostrophes
- Comma errors
- Spelling/diction errors that interfere with meaning.

Advice on Proofreading

- Have a separate proofreading phase at the end of your composing process in which you attend only to grammar and punctuation.

- Look at each sentence as a discrete unit. If you have trouble doing this— if you get caught up in the flow of your thinking—try proofreading the paper backward. Start with the last sentence, then the next-to-last, and move all the way from back to front.

- Circle each punctuation mark, and ask yourself why it is there. In this way, you will be more likely to find commas where there should be periods.

- Read your paper out loud with a pencil in hand. Writers are much more likely to notice errors when they hear them. (Many of the BWEs typically make sentences difficult to follow and difficult to read out loud.)

BWE 1: Sentence Fragments

The most basic writing error, a **sentence fragment**, is a group of words punctuated like a complete sentence but lacking the necessary structure: it is only part of a sentence. Typically, a sentence fragment occurs when the group of words in question (1) lacks a subject, (2) lacks a predicate, or (3) is a subordinate (or dependent) clause.

To fix a sentence fragment, either turn it into an independent clause by providing whatever is missing—a subject or a predicate—or attach it to an independent clause on which it can depend.

Noun Clause (No Predicate) as a Fragment

A world where imagination takes over and sorrow is left behind.

This fragment is not a sentence but rather a noun clause—a sentence subject with no predicate. The fragment lacks a verb that would assert something about the subject. (The verbs *takes over* and *is left* are in a dependent clause created by the subordinating conjunction *where*. See the section "Sentence Combining: Subordination" in Chapter 11 and the glossary at the end of this chapter for more information.)

Corrections

A world **arose** where imagination takes over and sorrow is left behind.
   [new verb matched to "a world"]
She entered a world where imagination takes over and sorrow is left behind.
   [new subject and verb added]

The first correction adds a new verb ("arose"). The second introduces a new subject and verb, converting the fragment into the direct object of "she entered."

Verbal as a Fragment

Falling into debt for the fourth consecutive year.

"Falling" in the preceding fragment is not a verb. Depending on the correction, "falling" is either a verbal or part of a verb phrase. See the entry on verbals in the glossary at the end of this chapter.

Corrections

The company was falling into debt for the fourth consecutive year.
   [subject and helping verb added]
Falling into debt for the fourth consecutive year **led the company to consider relocating**. *[new predicate added]*
Falling into debt for the fourth consecutive year, **the company considered relocating**.
   [new subject and verb added]

In the first correction, the addition of a subject and the helping verb "was" converts the fragment into a sentence. The second correction turns the fragment into a gerund phrase functioning as the subject of a new sentence. The third correction converts the fragment into a participial phrase attached to a new independent clause. (See the Glossary of Grammatical Terms for definitions of gerund and participle.)

Subordinate Clause as a Fragment

> I had an appointment for 11:00 and was still waiting at 11:30. Although I did get to see the dean before lunch.

"Although" is a subordinating conjunction that calls for completion. Like "if," "when," "because," "whereas," and other subordinating conjunctions (see the Glossary of Grammatical Terms), "although" *always* makes the clause that it introduces dependent.

Correction

> I had an appointment for 11:00 and was still waiting at 11:30, **although** I did get to see the dean before lunch. *[fragment attached to preceding sentence]*

As the correction demonstrates, the remedy lies in attaching the fragment to an independent clause on which it can depend (or, alternatively, making the fragment into a sentence by dropping the conjunction).

Sometimes writers use sentence fragments deliberately, usually for rhythm and emphasis or to create a conversational tone. In less formal contexts, they are generally permissible, but you run the risk that the fragment will not be perceived as intentional. In formal writing assignments, it is safer to avoid intentional fragments.

Test Yourself 12.1: Fragments

There are fragments in each of the following three examples, probably the result of their proximity to legitimate sentences. What's the problem in each case, and how would you fix it? (See the Appendix following this chapter for answers to the Test Yourself exercises.)

1. Like many other anthropologists, Margaret Mead studied non-Western cultures in such works as *Coming of Age in Samoa*. And influenced theories of childhood development in America.

2. The catastrophe resulted from an engineering flaw. Because the bridge lacked sufficient support.

3. In the 1840s the potato famine decimated Ireland. It being a country with poor soil and antiquated methods of agriculture.

Using Dashes and Colons to Correct Fragments

Beyond what the punctuation guide in Chapter 11 offers, the virtues of the dash and colon as ways to correct sentence fragments deserve brief mention. One way to correct a fragment is to replace the period with a dash: "The campaign required commitment. Not just money." becomes "The campaign required commitment—not just money." The dash offers you one way of attaching a phrase or dependent clause to a sentence without having to construct another independent clause. In short, it is succinct. (Compare the correction that uses the dash with another possible correction: "The campaign required commitment. It also required money.") Moreover, with the air of sudden interruption that the dash conveys, it can capture the informality and immediacy that the intentional fragment offers a writer.

Be wary of overusing the dash as the slightly more presentable cousin of the intentional fragment. The energy it carries can clash with the decorum of formal writing contexts; for some readers, its staccato effect quickly becomes too much of a good thing.

One alternative to this usage of the dash is the colon. It can substitute because it also can be followed by a phrase, list, or clause. It must be preceded by an independent clause. And like the dash, it carries dramatic force because it abruptly halts the flow of the sentence.

The colon, however, does not convey informality. In place of a slapdash effect, it trains a light on what is to follow it. Hence, as in this sentence you are reading, it is especially appropriate for setting up certain kinds of information: explanations, lists, or results.

BWE 2: Comma Splices and Fused (or Run-On) Sentences

A comma splice consists of two independent clauses connected ("spliced") with a comma; a fused (also known as a run-on) sentence combines two such clauses with no conjunction or punctuation. The solutions for both comma splices and fused sentences are the same.

1. Place a conjunction (such as "and" or "because") between the clauses.

2. Place a semicolon between the clauses.

3. Make the clauses into separate sentences.

These solutions solve the same logical problem: they clarify the boundaries of the independent clauses for your readers.

Comma Splice

He disliked discipline, he avoided anything demanding.

Correction

Because he disliked discipline, he avoided anything demanding. *[subordinating conjunction added]*

Comma Splice

Today most TV programs are violent, almost every program is about cops and detectives.

Correction

> Today most TV programs are violent; almost every program is about cops and
> detectives. *[semicolon replaces comma]*

Because the two independent clauses in the first example contain ideas
that are closely connected logically, the most effective of the three comma-
splice solutions is to add a subordinating conjunction ("because") to the first
of the two clauses, making it depend on the second. For the same reason—
close conceptual connection—the best solution for the next comma splice is
to substitute a semicolon for the comma. The semicolon signals that the two
independent clauses are closely linked in meaning. In general, you can use a
semicolon where you could also use a period.

Cures for the Perpetual Comma Splicer

The comma splice is remarkably common, even among fairly sophisticated
writers. It indicates two things: (1) the writer is not distinguishing between
independent and dependent clauses and (2) the writer is operating on the so-
called "pause theory" of punctuation. All of the clauses in our two preceding
examples are independent. As written, each of these should be punctuated not
with a comma but rather with a period or a semicolon. Instead, the perpetual
comma splicer, as usual, acts on the "pause theory": because the ideas in the
independent clauses are closely connected, the writer hesitates to separate
them with a period. And so the writer inserts what they take to be a shorter
pause—the comma.

But a comma is not a "breath" mark; it provides readers with specific
grammatical information, in each of these cases mistakenly suggesting there
is only one independent clause separated by the comma from modifying
information. In the corrections, by contrast, the semicolon sends the appropriate signal to the reader: the message that it is joining two associated but
independent statements. Adding a coordinating conjunction such as "and"
would also be grammatically correct, though possibly awkward. (See the
discussion of independent clauses and comma rules in Chapter 11.)

Fused (or Run-on) Sentence

> The Indo-European language family includes many groups most languages in Europe
> belong to it.

Correction

> The Indo-European language family includes many groups. Most languages in Europe
> belong to it. *[period inserted after first independent clause]*

You could also fix this fused sentence with a comma plus the coordinating conjunction "and." Alternatively, you might condense the whole into a
single independent clause.

> Most languages in Europe belong to the Indo-European language family.

Note: the term "run-on" misleads many people into believing that any long sentence is a run-on. While such rambling sentences may be inelegant, they are not incorrect just because they are lengthy.

Comma Splices with Conjunctive Adverbs

Quantitative methods of data collection show broad trends, however, they ignore specific cases.

Sociobiology poses a threat to traditional ethics, for example, it asserts that human behavior is genetically motivated by the "selfish gene" to perpetuate itself.

Corrections

Quantitative methods of data collection show broad trends; however, they ignore specific cases. *[semicolon replaces comma before "however"]*

Sociobiology poses a threat to traditional ethics; for example, it asserts that human behavior is genetically motivated by the "selfish gene" to perpetuate itself. *[semicolon replaces comma before "for example"]*

Both examples contain one of the most common forms of comma splices. Both are compound sentences; that is, they contain two independent clauses. Normally, connecting the clauses with a comma and a conjunction would be correct: for example, "Most hawks hunt alone, but osprey hunt in pairs." In the preceding two comma splices, however, the independent clauses are joined by transitional expressions known as conjunctive adverbs. (See the "Glossary of Grammatical Terms" at the end of this chapter and the discussion of conjunctive adverbs in Chapter 11.) When a conjunctive adverb is used to link two independent clauses, it *always* requires a semicolon. This punctuation allows readers to see which of the two independent clauses the conjunctive adverb modifies. By contrast, when a coordinating conjunction links the two clauses of a compound sentence, it is *always* preceded by a comma.

In most cases, depending on the sense of the sentence, the semicolon precedes the conjunctive adverb and clarifies the division between the two clauses. There are exceptions to this general rule, though, as in the following sentence:

The lazy boy did finally read a **book, however,** it was the least he could do.

Here, "however" is a part of the first independent clause and qualifies its claim. The sentence thus suggests the boy was not totally lazy because he did get around to reading a book. Note how the meaning changes when "however" becomes the introductory word for the second independent clause.

The lazy boy did finally read a **book; however,** it was the least he could do.

Here, the restricting force of "however" suggests that reading the book was not much of an accomplishment.

What makes each of the following sentences a comma splice? Determine the best way to fix each one and why, and then make the correction.

1. "Virtual reality" is a buzzword, so is "hyperspace."

2. Many popular cures for cancer have been discredited, nevertheless, many people continue to buy them.

3. Elvis Presley's home, Graceland, attracts many musicians as a kind of shrine, even Paul Simon has been there.

4. She didn't play well with others, she sat on the bench and watched.

BWE 3: Errors in Subject–Verb Agreement

The subject and the verb must agree in number, a singular subject taking a singular verb and a plural subject taking a plural verb. Errors in subject–verb agreement usually occur when a writer misidentifies the subject or verb of a clause.

Agreement Problem: Plural Subject, Singular Verb

Various kinds of vandalism has been rapidly increasing.

Correction

Various kinds of vandalism **have** been rapidly increasing. *[verb made plural to match "kinds"]*

When you isolate the grammatical subject ("kinds") and the verb ("has") of the original sentence, you can tell that they do not agree. Although "vandalism" might seem to be the subject because it is closest to the verb, it is actually the object of the preposition "of." Most agreement problems arise from mistaking the object of a preposition for the actual subject of a sentence. If you habitually make this mistake, you can begin to remedy it by familiarizing yourself with the most common prepositions. (The Glossary of Grammatical Terms contains a list of these terms.)

Agreement Problem: Singular Subject, Plural Verb

Another aspect of territoriality that differentiates humans from animals are their possession of ideas and objects.

Correction

Another aspect of territoriality that differentiates humans from animals **is** their possession of ideas and objects. *[verb made singular to match subject "aspect"]*

The subject of the sentence is "aspect." The two plural nouns ("humans" and "animals") probably encourage the mistake of using a plural verb ("are"), but the word "humans" is part of the "that" clause modifying "aspect," and "animals" is the object of the preposition "from."

Agreement Problem: "Each" Must Take Singular Verb

> The Republican and the Democrat both believe in doing what's best for America, but each believe that the other doesn't understand what's best.

Correction

> The Republican and the Democrat both believe in doing what's best for America, but each **believes** that the other doesn't understand what's best. *[verb made singular to agree with subject "each"]*

The word "each" is *always* singular, so the verb ("believes") must be singular as well. The presence of a plural subject and verb in the sentence's first independent clause ("The Republican and the Democrat both believe") has probably encouraged the error.

Test Yourself 12.3: Subject–Verb Agreement

Diagnose and correct the error in the following example:

The controversies surrounding the placement of Arthur Ashe's statue in Richmond was difficult for the various factions to resolve.

A Note on Dialects and Standard Written English

Some people have trouble recognizing and fixing certain errors because they are not errors in their discourse communities. Different cultures inside the larger culture of English-language speakers use different syntactical forms. This fact has given rise to the phrase "Standard Written English," which designates one particular version of English as the norm. People whose language practices constitute a dialect, for example, are told they must acquire the other dialect—Standard Written English.

The concept of Standard Written English has been controversial. Critics argue that the concept enforces the language practices of privileged groups and discriminates against the practices of less powerful groups in the culture. The best-known instance of this discrimination appears in the matter of subject–verb agreement among some African Americans who leave off the verb ending -s in the third person singular present tense.

Standard Written English:	He walks to town. (singular)
	They walk to town. (plural)
Dialect:	He walk to town. (singular)
	They walk to town. (plural)

Speakers of the dialect do not differentiate singular from plural verb forms with a terminal "-s" in the present tense (only), as in Standard Written English.

If you look up the term "African American Vernacular English," you can study the debate about whether or not this particular "error" is descended from syntactical patterns in African languages. Like all ethical debates, this one is not easily resolved. In practical terms, however, you should be aware that these two ways of handling subject-verb agreement are recognized by linguists not in terms of right versus wrong but rather in terms of dialect difference.

A *dialect* is a version of a language characteristic of a region or culture and is sometimes unintelligible to outsiders. The problem for speakers of a dialect that differs from the norm is that they can't always rely on the ear—on what sounds right—when they are editing according to the rules of Standard Written English. Such speakers need, in effect, to learn to speak more than one dialect so that they can edit according to the rules of Standard Written English in situations in which this would be expected. This adaptation often requires adding a separate proofreading stage for specific errors, like subject-verb agreement, rather than relying on what sounds right.

BWE 4: Shifts in Sentence Structure (Faulty Predication)

This error involves an illogical mismatch between subject and predicate. If you continually run afoul of faulty predication, you should practice isolating the grammatical subjects and verbs of sentences. See "Finding the Spine of a Sentence" in Chapter 11.

Faulty Predication

In 1887, the release of more information became available.

Correction

In 1887, more **information** became available **for release**. *[new subject]*

It was the "information," not the "release," that "became available." The correction relocates "information" from its position as object of the preposition "of" to the subject position in the sentence; it also moves "release" into a prepositional phrase.

Faulty Predication

The busing controversy was intended to rectify the inequality of educational opportunities.

Correction

Busing was intended to rectify the inequality of educational opportunities. *[new subject formulated to match verb]*

The *controversy* wasn't intended to rectify, but busing was.

Test Yourself 12.4: Faulty Predication

Identify and correct the faulty predication in this example:

The topic of learning disabilities is difficult to identify accurately.

BWE 5: Errors in Pronoun Reference

There are at least three forms of this problem. All of them involve a lack of clarity about whom or what a pronoun (a word that substitutes for a noun) refers to. The surest way to avoid difficulties is to make certain the pronoun relates back unambiguously to a specific word to which it refers, known as the antecedent. In the sentence "Nowadays appliances don't last as long as they once did," the noun "appliances" is the antecedent of the pronoun "they."

Pronoun-Antecedent Agreement

In most cases, a pronoun should agree in number and gender with the noun or noun phrase to which it refers. An exception to this rule concerns the gender neutral use of "they" to refer to a singular subject. See the discussion titled "Gender-Neutral 'They' and Pronoun Usage" located below at the end of the section on plural pronouns with singular antecedents.

Pronoun Error: Plural Pronoun with Singular Antecedent

> It can be dangerous if a child, after watching TV, decides to practice what we saw.

Corrections

> It can be dangerous if **children**, after watching TV, **decide** to practice what **they** saw.
> *[antecedent (and verb) made plural to agree with plural pronoun.]*

> It can be dangerous if a child, after watching TV, decides to practice what **they** saw.
> *[singular pronouns substituted to match singular antecedent "child"]*

The error occurs because "child" is singular, but the pronoun referring to it, "we," is plural. The first correction makes both plural; the second makes both singular with the use of the singular "they." You might also observe in the first word of the example—the impersonal "it"—an exception to the rule that pronouns must have antecedents.

Test Yourself 12.5: Pronoun–Antecedent Agreement

What is wrong with the following sentence, and how would you fix it?

Every dog has its day, but all too often when that day happens, they can be found barking up the wrong tree.

Gender-Neutral "They" and Pronoun Usage

There have been various efforts over the past several decades to eliminate sexism in pronoun reference caused by using the pronoun "he" to refer to all people. In most circles, the following correction of a previous example would be considered sexist.

> It can be dangerous if a child, after watching TV, decides to practice what **he** saw.

Though the writer of such a sentence may intend "he" to function as a gender-neutral impersonal pronoun, it in fact excludes girls on the basis of gender. Implicitly, it also conveys sexual stereotypes (for example, that only boys are violent, or perhaps stupid enough to confuse TV with reality).

An agreed upon solution to the problem of sexism as well as the issue of language and gender identity in pronoun usage has traditionally been to put things into the plural form because plural pronouns ("we," "you," "they") don't indicate gender. (See the use of "children" in the first correction of the pronoun–antecedent agreement example.) Alternatively, accepted practice has been to use the phrase "he or she." Because some readers find this phrase and its variant "s/he" to be awkward, an alternative remedy lies in rewriting the sentence to avoid pronouns altogether, as in the following revision.

> It can be dangerous if a child, after watching TV, decides to practice some violent activity portrayed on the screen.

In recent years, the use of the plural gender-neutral pronoun "they" to refer to a singular antecedent has been widely adopted (including by major publications such as *The Washington Post, The New York Times*, and *The Economist*). The MLA and APA have also approved the use of the singular *they* when referring to people who use *they* as a pronoun or when referring to people whose gender is unknown or not relevant to the context. So for example you might expect to see a sentence like the following considered as correct:

> The author, Terry Smith, said that they would not be attending the rally because their mother was ill.

The first rule of pronoun usage, you'll recall, has been that pronouns should agree in number with their antecedents. To violate that rule in the name of gender neutrality runs the risk of inviting confusion, but for many users of the language, it is an absolutely necessary risk to run. For a range of interesting commentaries from wordsmiths of various political orientations, Google "gender-neutral they" and see what you find.

Pronoun Error: Ambiguous Reference

A pronoun should have only one possible antecedent. The possibility of two or more confuses relationships within the sentence.

> Children like comedians because they have a sense of humor.

Corrections

> Because children have a sense of humor, **they** like comedians. *[subordinate "because" clause placed first, and relationship between noun "children" and pronoun "they" tightened]*

> Children like comedians because **comedians** have a sense of humor. [pronoun eliminated and replaced by repetition of noun]

Does "they" in the original example refer to "children" or "comedians"? The rule in such cases of ambiguity is that the pronoun refers to the nearest possible antecedent, so here "comedians" possess the sense of humor, regardless of what the writer may intend. As the corrections demonstrate, either reordering the sentence or repeating the noun can remove the ambiguity.

Test Yourself 12.6: Ambiguous Reference

As you proofread, it's a good idea to target your pronouns to make sure they cannot conceivably refer to more than one noun. What's wrong with the following sentences?

1. Alexander the Great's father, Philip of Macedon, died when he was twenty-six.

2. The committee could not look into the problem because it was too involved.

Pronoun Error: Broad Reference

Broad reference occurs when a pronoun refers loosely to a number of ideas expressed in preceding clauses or sentences. It causes confusion because the reader cannot be sure which of the ideas the pronoun refers to.

> As a number of scholars have noted, Sigmund Freud and Karl Marx offered competing but also at times complementary critiques of the dehumanizing tendencies of Western capitalist society. We see this in Christopher Lasch's analysis of conspicuous consumption in *The Culture of Narcissism*.

Correction

> As a number of scholars have noted, Sigmund Freud and Karl Marx offered competing but also at times complementary critiques of the dehumanizing tendencies of Western capitalist society. We see **this complementary view** in Christopher Lasch's analysis of conspicuous consumption in *The Culture of Narcissism*. [broad "this" clarified by addition of noun phrase]

The word "this" in the second sentence of the uncorrected example could refer to the fact that "a number of scholars have noted" the relationship between Freud and Marx, to the competition between Freud's and Marx's critiques of capitalism, or to the complementary nature of the two men's critiques.

Beware "this" as a pronoun: it's the most common source of broad reference. The remedy is generally to avoid using the word as a pronoun. Instead, include the noun that the word "this" refers to, in effect converting "this" into an adjective: "this complementary view," as in the correction or, alternatively, "this competition" or "this scholarly perspective."

Test Yourself 12.7: Broad Reference

Locate the errors in the following examples and provide a remedy for each.

1. The new ordinance restricted rental housing, and the township developed an alternative plan. This was a topic of considerable discussion.

2. The public radio station tweeted the Declaration of Independence on July 4, which was greeted by a barrage of anxious comments. People didn't know what to make of this.

BWE 6: Misplaced Modifiers and Dangling Participles

Modifiers are words or groups of words used to qualify, limit, intensify, or explain some other element in a sentence. A misplaced modifier is a word or phrase that appears to modify the wrong word or words.

Misplaced Modifier: Modifier Appears to Modify Wrong Word

> At the age of three he caught a fish with a broken arm.

Correction

> At the age of three **the boy with a broken arm** caught a fish. *[noun replaces pronoun; prepositional phrase revised and relocated]*

The original sentence mistakenly implies that the fish had a broken arm. Modification errors often occur in sentences with one or more prepositional phrases, as in this case.

Misplaced Modifier: Modifier Appears to Modify Wrong Word

> According to legend, General George Washington crossed the Delaware and celebrated Christmas in a small boat.

Correction

> According to legend, General George Washington crossed the Delaware **in a small boat** and **then** celebrated Christmas **on shore**. *[prepositional phrase relocated; modifiers added to second verb]*

Generally, you can avoid misplacing a modifier by keeping it as close as possible to what it modifies. Thus, the second correction removes the implication that Washington celebrated Christmas in a small boat. When you cannot relocate the modifier, separate it from the rest of the sentence with a comma to prevent readers from connecting it to the nearest noun.

A dangling participle creates a particular kind of problem in modification: the noun or pronoun that the writer intends the participial phrase to modify is not actually present in the sentence. Thus, we have the name dangling participle: the participle has been left dangling because the word or phrase it is meant to modify is not there.

Dangling Participle: Subject That Participle Modifies Does Not Appear in the Sentence

> After debating the issue of tax credits for the elderly, the bill passed in a close vote.

Correction

> After debating the issue of tax credits for the elderly, **the Senate passed the bill** in a close vote. *[appropriate noun added for participle to modify]*

The bill did not debate the issue, as the original example implies. As the correction demonstrates, fixing a dangling participle involves tightening the link between the activity implied by the participle ("debating") and the entity performing that activity ("the Senate").

Test Yourself 12.8: Modification Errors

Find the modification errors in the following examples and correct them.

1. After eating their sandwiches, the steamboat left the dock.

2. The social workers saw an elderly woman on a bus with a cane standing up.

3. Crossing the street, a car hit the pedestrian.

BWE 7: Errors in Using Possessive Apostrophes

Adding 's to most singular nouns will make them show possession, for example, the plant's roots, the accountant's ledger. You can add the apostrophe alone, without the "s," for example, to make plural nouns that already end with "s" show possession: the flowers' fragrances or the ships' berths (although you may also add an additional "s").

Apostrophe Error

The loyal opposition scorned the committees decisions.

Corrections

The loyal opposition scorned the committee's decisions.

The loyal opposition scorned the committees' decisions. *[possessive apostrophe added]*

The first correction assumes there was one committee; the second assumes there were two or more.

Apostrophe Error

The advisory board swiftly transacted it's business.

Correction

The advisory board swiftly transacted **its** business. *[apostrophe dropped]*

Unlike possessive nouns, possessive pronouns ("my," "your," "yours," "her," "hers," "his," "its," "our," "ours," "their," "theirs") *never* take an apostrophe.

Test Yourself 12.9: Possessive Apostrophes

Find and correct any errors in the following sentence:

The womens movement has been misunderstood by many of its detractors.

BWE 8: Comma Errors

As with other rules of punctuation and grammar, the many that pertain to comma usage share an underlying aim: to clarify the relationships among the parts of a sentence. Commas separate the parts of a sentence grammatically. One of their primary uses, then, is to help your readers distinguish the main clause from dependent elements such as subordinate clauses and long prepositional phrases. (See also "Why Commas Matter" in Chapter 11.) They do not signify a pause, as was discussed in BWE 2.

Comma Error: Comma Missing After Introductory Phrase

> After eating the couple went home.

Correction

> After eating, the couple went home. *[comma added before independent clause]*

The comma after "eating" is needed to keep the main clause "visible" or separate; it marks the point at which the prepositional phrase ends and the independent clause begins. Without this separation, readers would be invited to contemplate cannibalism as they move across the sentence.

Comma Error: Comma Missing After Introductory Phrase

> In the absence of rhetoric study teachers and students lack a vocabulary for talking about their prose.

Correction

> In the absence of rhetoric study, teachers and students lack a vocabulary for talking about their prose. *[comma added to separate prepositional phrase from main clause]*

Without the comma, readers would have to read the sentence twice to find out where the prepositional phrase ends—with "study"—to figure out where the main clause begins.

Comma Error: Two Commas Needed Around Parenthetical Element

> Dog owners, despite their many objections will have to obey the new law.

Correction

> Dog owners, despite their many objections, will have to obey the new law.
> *[single comma converted to a pair of commas]*

A comma is needed after "objections" to isolate the phrase in the middle of the sentence ("despite their many objections") from the main clause. The phrase needs to be set off with commas because it contains additional information not essential to the meaning of what it modifies. (Dog owners must obey the law whether they object or not.) Phrases and clauses that function in this way are called *nonrestrictive*.

A Note on Restrictive versus Nonrestrictive Elements

As we noted in Chapter 11, the test of nonrestrictive phrases and clauses is to see if they can be omitted without substantially changing the message that a sentence conveys ("Dog owners will have to obey the new law," for example). Nonrestrictive elements always take two commas—a comma "sandwich"—to set them off. Using only one comma illogically separates the sentence's subject ("dog owners") from its predicate ("will have to obey"). This problem is easier to see in a shorter sentence. You wouldn't, for example, write "I, fell down." As a rule, commas virtually never separate the subject from the verb of a sentence. If you add information to a sentence enclosed in a pair of commas, you have no longer illogically separated the subject from the predicate. For example, "I, lost in my thoughts, fell down."

Comma Error: Two Commas Needed Around Parenthetical Element

Most people regardless of age like to spend money.

Correction

Most people, regardless of age, like to spend money. *[comma sandwich added]*

Here, commas enclose the nonrestrictive elements; you could omit this information without significantly affecting the sense. Such is not the case in the following two examples.

Comma Error: Restrictive Elements Should Not Be Enclosed Within Commas

People, who live in glass houses, should not throw stones.
Please return the library book, that I left on the table.

Corrections

People who live in glass houses should not throw stones. *[commas omitted]*
Please return the library book that I left on the table. *[comma omitted]*

As we noted with the same example in Chapter 11, it is incorrect to place commas around "who live in glass houses" if the sentence subject is actually "people who live in glass houses" and not just people in general. It is also incorrect to place a comma before "that I left on the table." Each of these is a *restrictive clause*; that is, each contains information that is an essential part of what it modifies.

In the first sentence, for example, the word "who" is defined by restricting it to "people" in the category of glass-house dwellers. Similarly, in the second example the "that" clause contributes an essential meaning to "book"; the sentence is referring to not just any book but to a particular one, the one "on the table."

So, remember the general rule: if the information in a phrase or clause can be omitted—if it is nonessential and therefore nonrestrictive—it needs to be separated by commas from the rest of the sentence. Moreover, note that nonrestrictive clauses are generally introduced by the word "which," so a "which" clause interpolated into a sentence takes a comma sandwich. ("The dinner, which I bought for $20, made me sick.") By contrast, a restrictive clause is introduced by the word "that" and takes no commas.

Test Yourself 12.10: Comma Errors

Consider the following examples as a pair. Punctuate them as necessary, and then briefly articulate how the meanings of the two sentences differ.

1. The book which I had read a few years ago contained a lot of outdated data.

2. The book that I had read a few years ago contained a lot of outdated data.

BWE 9: Spelling/Diction Errors That Interfere with Meaning

Misspellings are always a problem in a final draft, insofar as they undermine your authority by inviting readers to perceive you as careless (at best). If you make a habit of using the spellchecker of a word processor, you will take care of most misspellings; however, the problems a spellchecker won't catch are the ones that can often hurt you most. These are actually diction errors—incorrect word choices in which you have confused one word with another that it closely resembles. In such cases, you have spelled the word correctly, but it's the wrong word. Because it means something other than what you've intended, you end up misleading your readers.

The best way to avoid this problem is to memorize the differences between pairs of words commonly confused with each other but that have distinct meanings. The following examples illustrate a few of the most common and serious of these errors. Most handbooks contain a glossary of usage that *cites* more of these *sites* of confusion.

Spelling/Diction Error: "It's" versus "Its"

Although you can't tell a book by its' cover, its fairly easy to get the general idea from the introduction.

Correction

Although you can't tell a book by **its** cover, **it's** fairly easy to get the general idea from the introduction. *[apostrophe dropped from possessive and added to contraction]*

"It's" is a contraction for "it is." "Its" is a possessive pronoun meaning "belonging to it." If you confuse the two, it's likely that your sentence will mislead its readers.

Spelling/Diction Error: "Their" versus "There" versus "They're"

Their are ways of learning about the cuisine of northern India besides going their to watch the master chefs and learn there secrets—assuming their willing to share them.

Correction

There are ways of learning about the cuisine of northern India besides going **there** to watch the master chefs and learn **their** secrets—assuming **they're** willing to share them. *[expletive "there," adverb "there," possessive pronoun "their," and contraction "they're" inserted appropriately]*

"There" as an adverb normally refers to a place; "there" can also be used as an expletive to introduce a clause, as in the first usage of the correction. "Their" is a possessive pronoun meaning "belonging to them." "They're" is a contraction for "they are." (See Chapter 11 for a discussion of expletives.)

Spelling/Diction Error: "Then" versus "Than"

If a person would rather break a law then obey it, than the person must be willing to face the consequences.

Correction

If a person would rather break a law **than** obey it, **then** the person must be willing to face the consequences. *[comparative "than" distinguished from temporal "then"]*

"Than" is a conjunction used with a comparison, for example, "rather X than Y." "Then" is an adverb used to indicate what comes next in relation to time, for example, "first X, then Y."

Spelling/Diction Error: "Effect" vs. "Affect"

It is simply the case that BWEs adversely effect the way that readers judge what a writer has to say. It follows that writers who include lots of BWEs in their prose may not have calculated the disastrous affects of these mistakes.

Correction

It is simply the case that BWEs adversely **affect** the way that readers judge what a writer has to say. It follows that writers who include lots of BWEs in their prose may not have calculated the disastrous **effects** of these mistakes. *[verb "affect" and noun "effects" inserted appropriately]*

In their most common usages, "affect" is a verb meaning "to influence," and "effect" is a noun meaning "the result of an action or cause." The confusion of "affect" and "effect" is enlarged by the fact that both words have secondary meanings: the verb "to effect" means "to cause or bring about"; the noun "affect" is used in psychology to mean "emotion or feeling." Thus, if you confuse these two words, you will inadvertently make a meaning radically different from the one you intend.

Test Yourself 12.11: Spelling/Diction Errors

Make corrections as necessary in the following paragraph.

Its not sufficiently acknowledged that the behavior of public officials is not just an ethical issue but one that effects the sale of newspapers and commercial bytes in television news. When public officials don't do what their supposed to do, than their sure to face the affects of public opinion—if they get caught—because there are dollars to be made. Its that simple: money more then morality is calling the tune in the way that the press treats it's superstars.

Correctness vs. Usage: Grammar Rules and Social Convention

Grammar is a volatile subject. Grammatical errors evoke not just disapproval but anger in some people. Why? Well, clearly correct grammar matters. Readers should not have to struggle to figure out where your sentences begin and end, or what goes with what. But the fact that correctness matters—that correctness is necessary to being taken seriously as a writer—does not account for the sheer venom that goes into spotting other people's grammatical errors.

Language use is social and conventional. Conforming to the rules is, in a sense, a sign that you agree to be governed by the same conventions that others conform to. Perhaps this is why the intentional sentence fragment has the impact that it does. Really. The gesture makes the writer's style seem daring. It says, "You and I both recognize that I control the standard conventions with sufficient assurance to break them on purpose, not by accident."

Usage: How Language Customs Change

Errors of grammar are relatively stable and locked down. "The eggs was tasty" is wrong; so is "Trump are President" and "Trump is Presidents." But usage, a kind of troublesome and embarrassing cousin to grammar, is a more vexed subject. According to the *Oxford English Dictionary,* usage has to do with "established or customary use or employment of language, words, expressions, etc." Established by whom? Customary within what group? Usage, in short, tends to be less clear cut than grammar.

That is why some dictionaries offer brief paragraphs of discussion from a "usage panel"—a group of experts who weigh in on what is proper and improper in language use. Most of the usage guides you will find at the back of grammar handbooks offer a range of examples of usage. At one end of the range, there are examples in which one form is clearly preferred and another disapproved.

Usage: Examples of Right and Wrong vs. Etiquette

Here is a set of examples, organized on a sliding scale, from clearly distinguished right and wrong to less defensible distinctions.

- **fewer vs. less:** Countable things are fewer: fewer pencils; amounts that can't be counted are less: less support. This is a helpful distinction, one the language needs.

- **good vs. well:** *Good* is an adjective, a part of speech that modifies (describes) nouns and other adjectives. *It was a good movie. Well* is an adverb, a part of speech that modifies a verb or another adverb. *She does not feel well. Good* modifies *movie; well* modifies *feel.* This is another helpful distinction; therefore, most people consider this word choice a matter of right and wrong.

- **can vs. may:** *Can* refers to what one is able to do; *may* refers to what one is permitted to do. *He can spit across the classroom, but according to the teacher, he may not.* Again, this distinction conveys a meaningful difference, although in actual practice, the word *may* is starting to lose its clout—it sounds fussy to many contemporary ears.

- **between vs. among:** *Between* refers to two items, *among* to more than two. *The difference between sushi and sashimi is more easily understood than the differences among sushi, sashimi, and maki.* In this case, we can clearly see that if you used *between* in both cases, a reader would still be able to make sense of the sentence, but the use of *among* is helpful—it lets us know that more than two items are coming. Still, as you can see, this example of usage is less significant, more a matter of good manners, than *can* vs. *may.* Nonetheless, it is arguably a useful distinction.

- **different from vs. different than:** Some say a writer should not use *different than,* because *than* is comparative, but different already signifies that a comparison is coming, so you should always say *different from.* Let's use this example—and there are others like it—as an emblem of a preference for which there is not really much of a reason.

- **ending a sentence with a preposition:** The prescription that one should not end a sentence with a preposition or—if you will—that a preposition is a part of speech you should not end a sentence with, is a case of rather arbitrary usage. In this same category goes the split infinitive— the practice of locating a word inside a *to* + verb construction, such as *to boldly go where no one has gone before.* In a formal setting—an application to law school, say—you would want to be careful to avoid these usages, even though they are not actually wrong.

Why do some guardians of the language insist that we not end sentences with prepositions? Is it snobbery? Etiquette? First, let's admit that etiquette serves a definite purpose, as anyone who has gone out to dinner and had the misfortune to sit next to a food fight will attest. To be understanding, let's assume that the person who enforces usage distinctions as hard-and-fast rules, even when they are not, is a person who wishes to maintain standards in the face of change. And that, too, is a position one may (and can!) respect.

But the fact is that the language is always changing, not just with the addition of new words to the standard dictionaries, but also with the circumstances of usage—"the established or customary use or employment of language, words, expressions, etc." Ultimately, a panel of experts cannot control usage, and that is a healthy thing, allowing a language to evolve over time.

When Usage Begins to Change Grammar

Which brings us back to the issue of grammatical correctness, a subject that impelled this digression into usage in the first place (yes, we know it's a fragment). Usage and, more particularly, changes in usage affect grammar because, although relatively fixed, grammar does not stand still. Some grammatical rules do change when people begin using words differently.

Here are three common examples of how changing usage appears to be inspiring a change in the grammatical conventions of right and wrong. These changes have not yet occurred, but arguably, they are in the process of occurring.

- **possessive apostrophes:** An increasing number of writers simply leave these out. If one writes, *The cars fender was dented* (not car's) or *Max Scherzers slider is the best in the National League* (not Scherzer's), virtually every reader will understand the meaning, though not as quickly as the apostrophe would allow.

- *I vs. me:* especially in prepositional phrases: This one has to do with what grammarians call the case of pronouns. We use one form of a pronoun when it is in the subject and another when it is the object of a verb or a preposition. For example,

  —*My mother and I argue about grammar*—not *My mother and me.* We would not say "*Me argues about grammar.*" *I* is in the subjective case; *me* is in the objective case.

  —*According to my mother and me, grammar matters a lot*—not *According to my mother and I.* We would not say *According to I.* "According to" is a preposition, so you have to use the objective case, as the pronoun in question is the object of the preposition.

Increasingly, we hear native speakers saying things such as *Joe and me are going to get a beer* or *For Jill and I, voting is an undeniable civic duty, virtually an ethical imperative.* In the first example, a speaker might say *Joe and me* because it sounds "natural," that is, unpretentious, as unpretentious as having a beer.

In the second example, a speaker might say *For Jill and I* because (and we're not sure why this is!), the use of "and I" sometimes sounds classier, more high style, and in a sentence where lofty concepts such as civic duty and ethical imperatives occur, you might wish to sound classy. But "I" in "For Jill and I" must be changed to "me," the objective case, because it is the object of the preposition "For."

- **who vs. whom:** This is another version of the pronoun problem. *Who* is subjective case; *whom* is objective case. For example: *I want to know who ate the last slice of pie I left in the refrigerator.* Compare that with *Ask not for whom the bell tolls*—where *whom* is the object of the preposition *for*. Yet increasingly, speakers seem to fear working out the grammar necessary to figure out if the who/whom in question is a subject or an object, so they tend either to eliminate *whom* altogether and just use *who* for every case, or they assume that *whom* is classier, as they do with "and I," and they end up misusing *whom*. Here are examples:

  —*Who is Yu Darvish going to sign with, now that he has become a free agent?* This sentence is grammatically incorrect: we need a *Whom* to be the object of the preposition *with*—*With whom will Darvish sign?*

  —*I read a book by the cognitive therapist whom is most famous for formulating rational emotive therapy.* The loftiness of the topic misleads the writer into using the supposedly classier *whom* even though grammar tells us the pronoun *who* is in the subjective case.

Usage as Cultural Marker

You can think of usage in terms of markers—indicators of something. So, for example:

- usage as marker for informal, conversational versus formal style:

  And then she goes, "That's the silliest thing I've ever heard" versus *And then she says, . . .*

  And some people disallow contractions as too informal.

- usage as marker for social class:

  Where is he at? versus *Where is he?*

  I ain't going versus *I am not going.*

- usage as gender marker:

  Poetess versus *poet*, *actress* versus *actor*, *waitress* versus *waiter* or *waitperson*

  Most people have not heard the word *poetess*—how long before the same will be said of *actress*? (The –*ess* suffix indicating female is now considered sexist by many people because it relegates women to a separate category.)

TRY THIS 12.1: Discover the Rationale for Usage Choices

Research the following pairs of terms. Locate the usage "rules" that govern them, and if you can, uncover the rationale that informs these rules.

Try and/try to
Shall/will
Disinterested/uninterested
Raise/rise

Glossary of Grammatical Terms

adjective   An adjective is a part of speech that usually modifies a noun or pronoun—for example, *blue, boring, boisterous*.

adverb   An adverb is a part of speech that modifies an adjective, adverb, or verb—for example, *heavily, habitually, very*. The adverbial form generally differs from the adjectival form via the addition of the ending "–ly"; for example, *happy* is an adjective, and *happily* is an adverb.

clause (independent and dependent)   A clause is any group of words that contains both a **subject** and a **predicate**. An **independent clause** (also known as a **main clause**) can stand alone as a sentence. For example,

> The most famous revolutionaries of this century have all, in one way or another, offered a vision of a classless society.

The subject of this independent clause is "revolutionaries," the verb is "have offered," and the direct object is "vision." By contrast, a **dependent** (or **subordinate) clause** is any group of words containing a subject and verb that cannot stand alone as a separate sentence because it depends on an independent clause to complete its meaning. The following sentence adds two dependent clauses to our previous example:

> The most famous revolutionaries of this century have all, in one way or another, offered a vision of a classless society, **although** most historians would agree **that** this ideal has never been achieved.

The origin of the word "depend" is "to hang": a dependent clause literally hangs on the independent clause. In the preceding example, neither "although most historians would agree" nor "that this ideal has never been achieved" can stand independently. The "that" clause relies on the "although" clause, which in turn relies on the main clause. "That" and "although" function as **subordinating conjunctions**; by eliminating them, we could rewrite the sentence to contain three independent clauses:

> The most famous revolutionaries of this century have all, in one way or another, offered a vision of a classless society. Most historians would agree on one judgment about this vision: it has never been achieved.

comma splice   A comma splice consists of two independent clauses incorrectly connected (spliced) with a comma. See BWE 2.

conjunction (coordinating and subordinating)   A conjunction is a part of speech that connects words, phrases, or clauses—for example, *and, but, although*. The conjunction in some way defines that connection: for example, *and* links; *but* separates. All conjunctions define connections in one of two basic ways. Coordinating conjunctions connect words or groups of words that have equal grammatical importance. The coordinating conjunctions are *and, but, or, nor, for, so,* and *yet.* Subordinating conjunctions introduce a dependent clause and connect it to a main clause. Here is a partial list of the most common subordinating conjunctions: *after, although, as, as if, as long as, because, before, if, rather than, since, than, that, though, unless, until, when, where, whether,* and *while.*

conjunctive adverb   A conjunctive adverb is a word that links two independent clauses (as a conjunction) but that also modifies the clause it introduces (as an adverb). Some of the most common conjunctive adverbs are *consequently, furthermore, however, moreover, nevertheless, similarly, therefore,* and *thus.* Phrases can also serve this function, such as *for example* and *on the other hand.* When conjunctive adverbs are used to link two independent clauses, they always require a semicolon:

> Many pharmaceutical chains now offer their own generic versions of common drugs; however, many consumers continue to spend more for name brands that contain the same active ingredients as the generics.

When conjunctive adverbs occur within an independent clause, however, they are enclosed in a pair of commas, as is the case with the use of *however* earlier in this sentence.

coordination   Coordination refers to grammatically equal words, phrases, or clauses. Coordinate constructions are used to give elements in a sentence equal weight or importance. In the sentence "The tall, thin lawyer badgered the witness, but the judge interceded," the clauses "The tall, thin lawyer badgered the witness" and "but the judge interceded" are coordinate clauses; "tall" and "thin" are coordinate adjectives.

dependent clause (see clause)

direct object   The direct object is a noun or pronoun that receives the action carried by the verb and performed by the subject. In the sentence, "Certain mushrooms can kill you," "you" is the direct object.

gerund (see verbals)

fused (or run-on) sentence   A fused sentence incorrectly combines two independent clauses with no conjunction or punctuation. See BWE 2.

independent clause (see clause)

infinitive (see verbals)

main clause (see clause)

noun A noun is a part of speech that names a person (*woman*), place (*town*), thing (*book*), idea (*justice*), quality (*irony*), or action (*betrayal*).

object of the preposition (see preposition)

participle and participial phrase (see verbals)

phrase A phrase is a group of words occurring in a meaningful sequence that lacks either a subject or a predicate. This absence distinguishes it from a clause, which contains both a subject and a predicate. Phrases function in sentences as adjectives, adverbs, nouns, or verbs. They are customarily classified according to the part of speech of their keyword: "over the mountain" is a **prepositional phrase**; "running for office" is a **participial phrase**; "had been disciplined" is a **verb phrase**; "desktop graphics" is a **noun phrase**; and so forth.

predicate The predicate contains the verb of a sentence or clause, making some kind of statement about the subject. The predicate of the preceding sentence is "contains the verb, making some kind of statement about the subject." The simple predicate—the verb to which the other words in the sentence are attached—is "contains."

preposition, prepositional phrase A preposition is a part of speech that links a noun or pronoun to some other word in the sentence. Prepositions usually express a relationship of time (*after*) or space (*above*) or direction (*toward*). The noun to which the preposition is attached is known as the object of the preposition. A preposition, its object, and any modifiers comprise a prepositional phrase. "With love *from* me *to* you" strings together three prepositional phrases. Here is a partial list of the most common prepositions: *about, above, across, after, among, at, before, behind, between, by, during, for, from, in, into, like, of, on, out, over, since, through, to, toward, under, until, up, upon, with, within,* and *without.*

pronoun A pronoun is a part of speech that substitutes for a noun, such as *I, you, he, she, it, we,* and *they.*

run-on (or fused) sentence A run-on sentence incorrectly combines two independent clauses with no conjunction or punctuation. See BWE 2.

sentence A sentence is a unit of expression that can stand independently. It contains two parts, a **subject** and a **predicate**. The shortest sentence in the Bible, for example, is "Jesus wept." "Jesus" is the subject; "wept" is the predicate.

sentence fragment A sentence fragment is a group of words incorrectly punctuated like a complete sentence but lacking the necessary structure; it is only a part of a sentence. "Walking down the road" and "the origin of the problem" are both fragments because neither contains a **predicate**. See BWE 1.

subject The subject, in most cases a noun or pronoun, names the doer of the action in a sentence or identifies what the predicate is about. The subject of the previous sentence, for example, is "the subject, in most cases a noun or pronoun." The simple subject of that sentence—the noun to which the other words in the sentence are attached—is "subject."

subordination, subordinating conjunctions "Subordination" refers to the placement of certain grammatical units, particularly phrases and clauses, at a lower, less important structural level than other elements. As with coordination, the grammatical ranking carries conceptual significance as well: whatever is grammatically subordinated appears less important than the information carried in the main clause. In the following example, Microsoft is subordinated both grammatically and conceptually to Apple:

> Although Microsoft continues to upgrade the operating system and special features on its computers, the more stylish and virus-free Apple Macintosh computers continue to outclass them.

Here, "although" is a **subordinating conjunction** that introduces a subordinate clause, also known as a **dependent clause**.

verb A verb is a part of speech that describes an action (*goes*), states how something was affected by an action (*became angered*), or expresses a state of being (*is*).

verbals Verbals are verb forms that look like verbs but, as determined by the structure of the sentence they appear in, they function as nouns, adjectives, or adverbs. There are three forms of verbals.

An **infinitive**—composed of the root form of a verb plus *to* (*to be*, *to vote*)—becomes a verbal when it is used as a noun ("*To eat* is essential"), an adjective ("These are the books *to read*"), or an adverb ("He was too sick *to walk*").

Similarly, a **participle**—usually composed of the root form of a verb plus "–ing" (present participle) or "–ed" (past participle)—becomes a verbal when used as an adjective. It can occur as a single word, modifying a noun, as in *faltering negotiations* or *finished business*. But it also can occur in a participial phrase, consisting of the participle, its object, and any modifiers. Here are two examples:

> **Having been tried and convicted**, the criminal was sentenced to life imprisonment.

> **Following the path of most resistance**, the masochist took deep pleasure in his frustration.

"Having been tried and convicted" is a participial phrase that modifies "criminal"; "Following the path of most resistance" is a participial phrase that modifies "masochist." In each case, the participial phrase functions as an adjective.

The third form of verbal, the **gerund**, resembles the participle. Like the participle, it is formed by adding "–ing" to the root form of the verb, but unlike the participle, it is used as a noun. In the sentence "Swimming is extraordinarily aerobic," the gerund "swimming" functions as the subject. Like participles, gerunds can occur in phrases. The gerund phrases are italicized in the following example: "*Watching a film adaptation* takes less effort than *reading the book* from which it was made."

When using a verbal, remember that although it resembles a verb, it cannot function alone as the verb in a sentence: "Being a military genius" is a fragment, not a sentence. (See the discussion of verbals in Chapter 11.)

Assignments: Nine Basic Writing Errors (BWEs) and How to Fix Them

1. **Chart the BWEs.** Write an example for each of the BWEs, along with a corrected version.

2. **Compose a grammar and style quiz.** Write a paragraph that contains all of the basic writing errors. Not every sentence should contain an error, and you may contain multiple examples of the errors, but make sure you include all nine. Append an answer key in which you identify the errors and provide corrections.

3. **Research online resources.** Go online to different universities and colleges in search of their writing centers, and then look for the ways these websites handle the problem of grammatical correctness. See as an example OWL at Purdue University. Write a brief summary of what you find there.

4. **Circle every punctuation mark.** Take a short piece of writing, your own or someone else's, published or unpublished. Circle every punctuation mark and explain why it is there. This is a useful exercise to do in pairs or in small groups. As a follow-up exercise, you might underline every independent clause and double-underline every dependent clause, circling the subordinating conjunctions.

APPENDIX
Basic Writing Errors (BWEs) Test Yourself Section Answer Key (With Discussion)

Test Yourself 12.1: Fragments (Page 346)

1. EXAMPLE: Like many other anthropologists, Margaret Mead studied non-Western cultures in such works as *Coming of Age in Samoa*. And influenced theories of childhood development in America.

PROBLEM: The second sentence is actually a fragment, a predicate in need of a subject.

POSSIBLE CORRECTION: Like many other anthropologists, Margaret Mead studied non-Western cultures (in such works as *Coming of Age in Samoa*) in ways that influenced theories of childhood development in America.

COMMENT: There are many ways to fix this example, but its original form leaves ambiguous whether the fragment refers only to *Mead*, or to *many other anthropologists* as well. The correction offered includes the other anthropologists in the referent and diminishes the emphasis on Mead's book by placing it within parentheses. Although the correction uses a subordinating *that* to incorporate the fragment into the first sentence, it keeps this information in an emphatic position at the end of the sentence.

2. EXAMPLE: The catastrophe resulted from an engineering flaw. Because the bridge lacked sufficient support.

PROBLEM: The second sentence is actually a dependent clause; *because* always subordinates.

POSSIBLE CORRECTION: The catastrophe resulted from an engineering flaw: the bridge lacked sufficient support.

COMMENT: Because the colon has causal force, this is an ideal spot to use one, identifying the "flaw."

3. EXAMPLE: In the 1840s the potato famine decimated Ireland. It being a country with poor soil and antiquated methods of agriculture.

PROBLEM: The second sentence is actually a fragment, a subject plus a long participial phrase.

POSSIBLE CORRECTION:	In the 1840s the potato famine decimated Ireland, a country with poor and antiquated methods of agriculture.
COMMENT:	The cause of this kind of fragment is usually that the writer mistakenly believes that *being* is a verb rather than a participle that introduces a long phrase (modifying "Ireland" in this case). It would also be correct simply to change the period to a comma in the original sentence.

Test Yourself 12.2: Comma Splices (Page 350)

1.
EXAMPLE:	"Virtual reality" is a new buzzword, so is "hyperspace."
PROBLEM:	This is a comma splice—both clauses are independent, yet they are joined with a comma.
POSSIBLE CORRECTION:	"Virtual reality" is a new buzzword; so is "hyperspace."
COMMENT:	Because the clauses are linked by association—both naming buzzwords—a semicolon would show that association. A writer could also condense the clauses into a simple sentence with a compound subject; for example, "Both 'virtual reality' and 'hyperspace' are new buzzwords."

2.
EXAMPLE:	Many popular cures for cancer have been discredited, nevertheless, many people continue to buy them.
PROBLEM:	A comma splice results from the incorrectly punctuated conjunctive adverb *nevertheless*.
POSSIBLE CORRECTION:	Many popular cures for cancer have been discredited; nevertheless, many people continue to buy them.
COMMENT:	Without the semicolon to separate the independent clauses, the conjunctive adverb could conceivably modify either the preceding or the following clause. This problem is usually worse with *however*.

3.
EXAMPLE:	Elvis Presley's home, Graceland, attracts many musicians as a kind of shrine, even Paul Simon has been there.
PROBLEM:	This is a comma splice—the two independent clauses are linked by a comma without a conjunction. The problem is exacerbated by the number of commas in the sentence; the reader cannot easily tell which one is used to separate the clauses.
POSSIBLE CORRECTION:	Elvis Presley's home, Graceland, attracts many musicians as a kind of shrine—even Paul Simon has been there.

COMMENT:	Although one could justly use a semicolon here, the dash conveys the impromptu effect of an afterthought.

4.

EXAMPLE:	She didn't play well with others, she sat on the bench and watched.
PROBLEM:	Because the second clause develops the first one, a writer might think that it is dependent on the first; conceptually, yes, but grammatically, no.
POSSIBLE CORRECTION:	She didn't play well with others; she sat on the bench and watched.
COMMENT:	If the writer wanted to link the two clauses more tightly, a colon would be appropriate instead of the semicolon.

Test Yourself 12.3: Subject–Verb Agreement (Page 351)

EXAMPLE:	The controversies surrounding the placement of Arthur Ashe's statue in Richmond was difficult for the various factions to resolve.
PROBLEM:	The grammatical subject of the main clause (controversies) is plural; the verb (was) is singular.
POSSIBLE CORRECTION:	The controversies surrounding the placement of Arthur Ashe's statue in Richmond were difficult for the various factions to resolve (or, The controversy… was).
COMMENT:	An error of this kind is encouraged by two factors: the distance of the verb from the subject, and the presence of intervening prepositional phrases that use singular objects—either of which a writer might mistake for the grammatical subject of the main clause.

Test Yourself 12.4: Faulty Predication (Page 352)

EXAMPLE:	The topic of learning disabilities is difficult to identify accurately.
PROBLEM:	The subject of the sentence, "topic," does not match the predicate.
POSSIBLE CORRECTION:	Learning disabilities are difficult to identify accurately.
COMMENT:	The "topic" is not "difficult to identify"—"learning disabilities" are.

Test Yourself 12.5: Pronoun–Antecedent Agreement (Page 353)

EXAMPLE:	Every dog has its day, but all too often when that day happens, you can be found barking up the wrong tree.
PROBLEM:	The plural pronoun *you* that is the grammatical subject of the second clause does not have a plural antecedent in the sentence.

POSSIBLE CORRECTION:	Every dog has its day, but all too often when that day happens, the dog can be found barking up the wrong tree.
COMMENT:	If a writer vigilantly checks all pronouns, the writer will identify the intended antecedent of the pronoun *you* to be the singular *dog*, and will revise accordingly. The singular pronoun *they* can be used to refer to the dog here because the gender of the dog is unknown and does not matter. This use of *they* is supported by both the Modern Language Association guidelines and the American Psychological Association guidelines. The sentence would still be incorrect if the pronoun *it* were used instead of the repeated *dog*, because it could refer to the nearest preceding noun, *day*.

Test Yourself 12.6: Ambiguous Reference (Page 355)

1.

EXAMPLE:	Alexander the Great's father, Philip of Macedon, died when he was twenty-six.
PROBLEM:	A reader can't be sure whether *he* refers to Alexander or to Philip.
POSSIBLE CORRECTION:	Alexander the Great's father, Philip of Macedon, died at the age of twenty-six.
COMMENT:	The correction rewords to remove the ambiguous pronoun. This solution is less awkward than repeating *Philip* in place of *he*, though that would also be correct.

2.

EXAMPLE:	The committee could not look into the problem because it was too involved.
PROBLEM:	A reader can't be sure whether *it* refers to *the committee* or to *the problem*.
POSSIBLE CORRECTION:	The committee was too involved with other matters to look into the problem.
COMMENT:	As with the previous example, rewording to eliminate the ambiguous pronoun is usually the best solution.

Test Yourself 12.7: Broad Reference (Page 355)

1.

EXAMPLE:	The new ordinance restricted rental housing, and the township developed an alternate plan. This was a topic of considerable discussion.
PROBLEM:	It is unclear which of the two topics in the first sentence are referred to by the word "This" at the beginning of the second sentence.
POSSIBLE CORRECTION:	The new ordinance restricted rental housing, and the township developed an alternate plan. This alternative plan was a topic of considerable discussion.

COMMENT:	Usually the best solution for broad reference is to follow the word "this" with restatement of whatever it was in the preceding sentence or sentences that the "this" referred to. As a rule, when you find an isolated *this* in your draft, ask and answer the question "This what?"

2. **EXAMPLE:** The public radio station tweeted the Declaration of Independence on July 4, which was greeted by a barrage of anxious comments. People didn't know what to make of this.

PROBLEM:	The referent of the pronoun *this* is unclear. Precisely what were people confused by: the radio station's original tweet or the response it received from other tweeters?

POSSIBLE CORRECTION: The public radio station tweeted the Declaration of Independence on July 4, which was greeted by a barrage of anxious comments. People didn't know what to think about either the original tweet or the responses it evoked.

COMMENT:	Sometimes a good solution is to eliminate the vague pronoun altogether and substitute clarifying language. In this case, the solution might be to say that the uncertainty of reference was not caused by just one of the options but both.

Test Yourself 12.8: Modification Errors (Page 357)

1. **EXAMPLE:** After eating their sandwiches, the steamboat left the dock.

PROBLEM:	This is a dangling participle—the grammar of the sentence conveys that the steamboat ate their sandwiches.

POSSIBLE CORRECTIONS: After the girls ate their sandwiches, the steamboat left the dock. Or, After eating their sandwiches, the girls boarded the steamboat, and it left the dock.

COMMENT:	The two corrections model the two ways of remedying most dangling participles. Both provide an antecedent (the girls) for the pronoun *their*. The first correction eliminates the participial phrase and substitutes a subordinate clause. The second correction adds to the existing main clause (steamboat left) another one (girls boarded) for the participial phrase to modify appropriately.

2. **EXAMPLE:** The social workers saw an elderly woman on a bus with a cane standing up.

PROBLEM:	Misplaced modifiers create the problems in this sentence, which implies that the bus possessed a cane that was standing up. The problem exemplified here is produced by the series of prepositional phrases—"on a bus with a cane"—followed by the participial phrase *standing up*, which is used as an adjective and intended to modify *woman*.

POSSIBLE CORRECTION:	The social workers saw an elderly woman on a bus. She was standing up with the help of a cane.
COMMENT:	Writers often try to cram too much into sentences, piling on the prepositions. The best remedy is sometimes to break up the sentence—a move that usually involves eliminating prepositions, which possess a sludgy kind of movement, and adding verbs, which possess more distinct movement.

3.

EXAMPLE:	Crossing the street, a car hit the pedestrian.
PROBLEM:	The dangling participle (Crossing the street) does not have a word to modify in the sentence. The sentence conveys that the car crossed the street.
POSSIBLE CORRECTIONS:	Crossing the street, the pedestrian was hit by a car. Or: As the pedestrian crossed the street, a car hit him.
COMMENT:	The first solution brings the participial phrase closest to the noun it modifies (pedestrian). The second converts the participle into the verb (crossed) of a dependent *as* clause and moves *pedestrian* into the clause as the subject for that verb. As in the *steamboat* example, one correction provides an appropriate noun for the participial phrase to modify, and the other eliminates the participle.

Test Yourself 12.9: Possessive Apostrophes (Page 357)

EXAMPLE:	The womens movement has been misunderstood by many of its detractors.
PROBLEM:	The possessive apostrophe for *womens* is missing. The trickiness here in inserting the apostrophe is that this word is already plural.
POSSIBLE CORRECTION:	The women's movement has been misunderstood by many of its detractors.
COMMENT:	Because the word is already plural, it takes a simple "–'s" to indicate a movement belonging to women—not "–s'" (womens').

Test Yourself 12.10: Comma Errors (Page 360)

PAIRED EXAMPLES:	The book which I had read a few years ago contained a lot of outdated data.
	The book that I had read a few years ago contained a lot of outdated data.
PROBLEM:	In the first example, the modifying clause "which I had read a few years ago" is nonrestrictive: it could be omitted without changing the essential meaning of the sentence. Therefore, it needs to be enclosed in commas—as the *which* signals.

POSSIBLE CORRECTION:	The book, which I had read a few years ago, contained a lot of outdated data.

COMMENT:	The second example in the pair is correct as it stands. The restrictive clause, "that I had read a few years ago," does not take commas around it because the information it gives readers is an essential part of the meaning of *book*. That is, it refers to not just any book read a few years ago, as in the first example in the pair, but rather specifies the one containing outdated data. "The book that I had read a few years ago" thus functions as what is known as a *noun phrase*.

Test Yourself 12.11: Spelling/Diction Errors (Page 362)

EXAMPLE:	Its not sufficiently acknowledged that the behavior of public officials is not just an ethical issue but one that effects the sale of newspapers and commercial bytes in television news. When public officials don't do what their supposed to do, than their sure to face the affects of public opinion—if they get caught—because there are dollars to be made. Its that simple: money more then morality is calling the tune in the way that the press treats it's superstars.

PROBLEMS:	The paragraph confuses the paired terms discussed under BWE 9. It mistakes: *its* for *it's* before *not sufficiently* *effects* for *affects* before *the sale* *their* for *they're* before *supposed* *than* for *then* before *their sure.* *their* for *they're* before *sure* *affects* for *effects* before *of public opinion* *its* for *it's* before *that simple* *then* for *than* before *morality* *it's* for *its* before *superstars*

POSSIBLE CORRECTION:	It's not sufficiently acknowledged that the behavior of public officials is not just an ethical issue but one that affects the sale of newspapers and commercial bytes in television news. When public officials don't do what they're supposed to do, then they're sure to face the effects of public opinion—if they get caught—because there are dollars to be made. It's that simple: money more than morality is calling the tune in the way that the press treats its superstars.

COMMENT:	If you confuse similar words, the only solution is to memorize the differences and consciously check your drafts for any problems until habit takes hold.

INDEX

Absolutes, 315
Abstract diction, 327–328
Abstracts
  compilations of, 243
  preparing, 234–235
Abstract words, 13
Academic Index website, 247, 255
Academic writing, ethos of, 133
Academy of American Poets,
  The, website, 248
Acknowledging sources, 214, 215, 231
Active reading, 40
Active verbs, 322–324
Active voice, 301, 324–326
Additive transitions, 296
Ad hominem argument or attack, 93–94
Adjectives
  concrete and evaluative, 326–327
  defined, 366
  experimenting with, 11
  overview, 315
Adverb clauses, 315
Adverbs
  conjunctive, 306–307, 349, 366
  defined, 366
  experimenting with, 11
  intensifiers, 327
  overview, 11
African American Vernacular English,
  351–352
Agency, 172
Agree/disagree writing assignments,
  107–108
Alice's Adventures in Wonderland (Carroll), 79
Ambiguous references, 354–355
American Psychological Association (APA)
  style, 256, 257–258
Analogy
  marking in text, 136
  metaphors, similes, and, 80
  thinking by, 128
Analysis
  appropriate items for, 76–77
  argument compared to, 7–9
  ethos and, 9, 136
  expressive writing compared to, 7
  as frame of mind, 10
  personal associations and, 35–36
  process of, 4–5
  reason for, 3
  rules of, 36
  as search for meaning, 3–4
  summary compared to, 5–6
  things not meant to be analyzed, 76–77
Analytical thesis, 180
Anaphora, 320
"And," 305

Anderson, Sam, "In Defense of Distraction,"
  61, 131
Anomalies, for contextualizing papers,
  283–284
Anticlimax of conclusions, 280
Antithesis, 320, 321
Anything goes school of interpretation,
  77–78
APA (American Psychological Association)
  style, 256, 257–258
Apostrophe errors, 357, 364
Application, 49
Appositives, 315
Archives of periodicals, 252–253
Argument
  analysis compared to, 6, 7–9
  opinion compared to, 12
  overview, 5
  rules of, 155–162
  for significance of key comparison, 109
  writing assignments calling for, 99
Argumentative thesis, 180
Aristotelian model of logical
  argumentation, 156–157
Articles. See also end-of-text article
    citations from websites or databases
  archives of older periodicals, 252–253
  finding sources in, 244–245
Arts & Letters Daily website, 56, 248
Asking "So what?" strategy, 21–25, 70, 109,
  189–191, 195–196
Assessment of own writing, 143–146
Assignments. See topics, responding to;
  writing assignments
Assuming missed point, 106
Assumptions. See also Uncovering
    Assumptions strategy
  framing assumptions of evidence, 154
  naturalizing, 11–12
  Passage-Based Focused Freewriting
    strategy and, 49
Audience
  class members as, 124
  introductions and, 298
  temporarily ignoring, 123–124
Auteur theory, 203
Autobiographical writing, 5, 133
Avoidance of taking position or posing
  problem, 274

Back burner method of revision, 122–123
Backing for warrants, 159
Back pressure, 206
Backspacing URLs, 251
Ballenger, Bruce, "Let's End Thesis
  Tyranny," 182
Bandwagon argument, 94

Bartholomae, David, 54, 227, 228
Basic writing errors (BWEs)
    comma errors, 358–360
    comma splices and fused sentences, 347–350
    misplaced modifiers and dangling participles, 356–357
    overview, 343–344
    possessive apostrophes, 357
    pronoun reference, 353–355
    sentence fragments, 345–347
    shifts in sentence structure, 352
    spelling/diction, that interfere with meaning, 360–362
    subject-verb disagreements, 350–352
Bauerlein, Mark, 25
Beardsley, Monroe, "Style and Good Style," 301
Beck, Aaron, 13
Becker, Alton, 291
Begging the question, 94
"Between" vs. "among," 363
Bias-free language, 332
Bibliographic research, 243, 245–246, 253–255
Bibliographies
    annotated, 243
    APA style, 258
    Chicago style, 260
    CSE style, 261, 262
    purpose of, 236
Binaries
    reductive thinking and, 108
    reformulating, 60–61, 118, 135
    tracking, 58–60
Blau, Sheridan, 44, 46
Blink (Gladwell), 231
Blogs
    interactive, and Google docs, 140
    as sources, 249
Book reviews, 244
Books, finding sources in, 244–245
Booth, Wayne, 159–160
Borick, Christopher, 284
    "A Reason to Believe," 91–92
    "On Political Labels," 61–62
Breaking spell of perspective, 228
Broad references, 355
"But," 305
BWEs. See basic writing errors

Cannon, Kelly, 242
"Can" vs. "may," 363
Case of pronouns, 364
Casey, Emily, 220, 227, 228
Cassill, R. V., 118
Causality, 91, 95
Causes, tracing responses to, 106
Census Bureau website, 247
Challenge to commonly held view, beginning introductions with, 276
Chiasmus, 321–322
Chicago style, 256, 258–260

Childhood experiences, writing about, 135
Christensen, Francis, "A Generative Rhetoric of the Paragraph," 293
Circular reasoning, 94, 150
Citing sources. See also documentation styles
    after quotations, 232–233
    plagiarism and, 237
Claims
    evidence compared to, 150–151
    in introductions, 276, 281
    linking evidence and, 148–153
    marking in drafts, 175–176
    to support deductions, 163
    thesis and, 208–209, 211–212
    without evidence, 148, 149–150
Clauses. See also independent (main) clauses
    adverb, 315
    defined, 302, 366
    dependent (subordinate), 308, 346, 348, 366
    identifying, 309
    nonrestrictive and restrictive, 359–360
    noun, 345
    order of, 313–314
Clichéd expressions and ideas, 144, 209–210
"Clichés" (Ricks), 217–218
Climactic order, 271, 314
Climactic sentences, 316–318, 319
"Closing My Eyes as I Speak" (Elbow), 123–124
Colabroy, Keri, 269, 284–285, 286, 287, 288, 337
Collaborative, analytical writing as, 197–198
Collapsing binaries, 60, 61
Colloquial style, 337–338
Collusion, 237
Colons, 312–313, 347
Comma errors, 358–360
Commas, 305, 310–312
Comma splices, 309, 347–350, 367
Common knowledge, 237
Commonplace books, 53
Communication triangle, 5, 6
Communicative gestures, 76
Comparative summaries, 240–241
Comparative thinking, 128–129
Comparison/contrast formats, 271–272
Comparison/contrast writing assignments, 108–111
Complaint, finding, 54–55, 135
Complements, 304
Complicating binaries, 60
Complications, marking in drafts, 175–176
Compound predicates, 307
Compound sentences, 305–309, 312
Computers, writing on, 124–125
Concessions and refutations format, 272–273

Conclusions
  analyzing, 298
  as expansion of possibilities, 279
  interpretive, 71, 88–89
  leaping to, 10–11, 117, 150
  purpose of, 278–279
  to scientific papers, 286–288
  solving problems in, 279–281
  thesis compared to, 187
  thesis statement in, 204–205
Concrete adjectives, 326–327
Concrete diction, 327–328
Concrete words, 13
Congress.gov website, 247
Conjunctions
  coordinating, 305–307, 367
  identifying, 309
  subordinating, 308–309, 366, 367, 369
Conjunctive adverbs, 306–307, 349, 367
Conner, Ted, 43
Constitutive theory of language, 40
Contexts
  interpretive, 71–76, 87–88, 193–194, 203
  for introductions, 283–284
  limiting, locating personal response
    within, 107
  for meaning, 71–77
Contextual, writing as, 300–301
Contextualizing reading, 41
Contradictions in sources, identifying, 218
Conventional wisdom, thesis as restating,
    209–210
Conversant with material, becoming,
    rather than reading for gist, 38–40
Conversations
  between sources, 225–227
  with sources, 216–218, 227–230,
    238–241
Coordinating conjunctions, 305–307, 367
Coordination, 367
Correctness vs. usage, 362–366
Correlation, 91, 95
Coverage model, 114
Crediting sources, 214, 215, 231
Critical approaches to sources, 228
Critical reading, 43
Critiques, writing, 41–43
CSE (Council of Science Editors) style
  citation sequence system, 261–262
  name-year (author-date) system,
    260–261
  overview, 256
Culmination, 278
Cultivating curiosity, 101–102
Cultural marker, usage as, 365
Cumulative sentences, 318–319
Curriculum, making interpretations
    plausible across, 89–93

Daily writing, 118–119
Dancers, The (Kersh), 74–75
Dangling participles, 356–357
Darwin, Charles, 225

Dashes, 313, 346–347
Databases, subscriber-only, 250, 252,
    253–254
Dearborn, Karen, 207
Debate-style argument, analysis compared
    to, 8–9
Deduction (1 on 10)
  overview, 160–164
  thesis and, 184–185, 186–187
Defamiliarization, 15–16
Definition, beginning introductions with,
    276–277
Definition writing assignments, 111–113
Demonstration
  analysis compared to, 164
  weak thesis statements and, 182–183
Demonstrative pronouns, 316
Dependent (subordinate) clauses, 308, 346,
    348, 366
Deresiewicz, William, "The End of
    Solitude," 36–37
Descriptive approach to responding to
    other writers, 136–140
Descriptive writing, 120–121
Detachment from topics, 104–105
Details
  attending to, 15–18, 17, 117
  as leading to working thesis, 194–195
  making details speak, 151–153
  moving to ideas from, 191–192
Detective, becoming, 36
Dialects, 351–352
Dickinson, Emily, 10
Diction
  concrete and abstract, 327–328
  errors in, as interfering with meaning,
    360–362
  inflated, 338–339
  Latinate, 328–329
Dictionaries, specialized, 244
Difference Within Similarity strategy,
    110–111, 170, 203
"Different from" vs. "different than," 363
Digression, 275
Directional indicators, transitions as, 296
Direct objects, 304, 367
Directory of Open Access Journals website,
    248
Disciplinary conventions
  Doing 10 on 1 strategy and, 168
  organizational schemes, 266–267
Discourse communities, 338, 351
Discussion sections, 286–288
Disraeli, Benjamin, 330
Dobbins, Zachary, 159–160
Documentation styles
  APA, 257–258
  Chicago, 258–260
  CSE, 260–262
  MLA, 262–263
  overview, 255–257
Doing 10 on 1 strategy, 118, 162–163,
    164–168, 174–175, 191

Domain names, 246–247
Do's and Don'ts of Good Writing, 144–146
Douglas, Kate, "The Other You," 230–231
Dowd, Maureen, 129
Drafts
    evolving working thesis in, 188–192
    marking claims, evidence, and complications in, 175–176
    Six Steps for Finding and Evolving a Thesis in an Exploratory Draft, 192–198

"Each," 351
Edelman, Laura, 92–93, 270, 285
Education, banking model of, 39
"Effect" vs. "affect," 361–362
Elbow, Peter
    on audience, 228
    "Closing My Eyes as I Speak," 123–124
    on drafting and editing at same time, 20, 122
    freewriting and, 119
    pointing and, 44
    on private writing, 227
Elements of Style, The (Strunk & White), 301
Ellipses, using to shorten quotations, 233
Embedding modifiers, 315–316
Emphasis and order of clauses in sentences, 313–314
Encyclopedias, specialized, 244
End-of-text article citations
    APA style, 257
    Chicago style, 259
    CSE style, 260, 261
    MLA style, 263
End-of-text article citations from websites or databases
    APA style, 257–258
    Chicago style, 259
    CSE style, 260, 261
    MLA style, 263
End-of-text book citations
    APA style, 257
    Chicago style, 259
    CSE style, 260
    MLA style, 262
End-of-text website citations
    APA style, 257
    CSE style, 260, 261
    MLA style, 263
Enthymemes, 157
Equivocation, 94
Errors. See also basic writing errors
    correction of, 343–344
    grammatical errors vs. usage, 362–366
    patterns of, 343
Essay writing. See thesis
Ethos
    of academic writing, 133
    analysis and, 9, 136
    style and, 334–335
Etymology, 329–330

Evaluating sources, 249–250, 251–253, 263
Evaluative adjectives, 326–327
Everything means principle, 71
Evidence
    Asking "So what?" strategy and, 195–196
    characteristics of, 153–155
    claims compared to, 150–151
    focusing, 172–173
    functions of, 149
    in introductions, 281
    linking claims and, 148–153
    marking in drafts, 175–176
    reciprocal relationship between thesis and, 183–184
    to reformulate thesis, 196
    to support deduction, 162–163
    testing definition against, 112
    without claims, 148
Expletive constructions, 326
Exploratory writing
    overview, 19–21, 117
    Six Steps for Finding and Evolving a Thesis in an Exploratory Draft, 192–198
    thesis statement and, 179, 184
    working thesis evolution in, 188–192
Expressive writing, 5–6, 7

Fact, thesis as statement of, 209
Falconer, Ian, The Competition, 84–85, 87
False analogy, 94–95
False cause, 95
Faulty parallelism, 321
Faulty predication, 352
"Fewer" vs. "less," 363
Figurative logic, 79–82
First impressions, 273
First person, use of, 335–337
First responses, suspecting, 101
First sentences, 145
Fish, Stanley, 72
Five Analytical Moves
    defining significant parts and relations, 16–21
    looking for patterns and anomalies, 25–32
    making implicit explicit, 21–25
    overview, 2, 16
    reformulating questions and explanations, 32–33
    suspending judgment, 16
    using, 36–37
    Whistler's Mother example, 33–35
Five-finger exercise, 121–122
Five-paragraph form
    demonstration and, 183
    outline for, 171–172
    overview, 14–15
    problem with, 168–170
    rehabilitating, 171
Fluency as writer, improving, 116
Footnote-endnote citations (Chicago style), 258–259

Formal essays and Passage-Based Focused Freewriting, 49–50
Formal style, 337–338
Formats. *See also* conclusions; introductions
  for documenting sources, 255–263
  for experimental psychology, 270
  functions of, 266–268
  IMRAD, 185, 268–270
  inferring, 297
  paragraphs, 288–295
  for social sciences, 270
  transitions, 295–297
Forster, E. M., 20
Fortune cookie school of interpretation, 77
Framing assumptions of evidence, 154
Framing quotations, 232
Franzen, Jonathan, "Imperial Bedroom," 63
Freewriting
  descriptive, 120–121
  five-finger exercise, 121–122
  overview, 19–21, 119–120
  Passage-Based Focused Freewriting strategy, 47–52, 70, 102, 216, 238
  single word or phrase, 120
  using, to find and interpret topics, 102
Freshman omniscience, 281
Friere, Paolo, 39
Frost, Robert, 128
Fused (run-on) sentences, 348–349, 367

Gambino, Jack, 12, 23–24, 154–155, 279, 283–284
Gender neutrality and use of "they," 332, 353–354
Generalization
  as habit of mind, 12–14
  hasty, 96
  move to analysis from, 5
Gentlemen Prefer Blondes (film), 223
Gerunds, 304, 369–370
Gladwell, Malcolm, 28, 231
Goal of writer's notebooks, 126
Goldberg, Natalie, 141
Goldzung, Marie, 223–224, 226
Good-bye Lenin! (film), 174–175
"Good" vs. "well," 363
Google docs and interactive blogging, 140
Google Scholar, 249
Google search engine, 248, 252
"Go-to" sentence shapes, 341
.gov websites, 247
Grain
  reading against, 58, 68, 82
  reading with, 40
Grammatical closure, 317
Grammatical errors vs. usage, 362–366
Grammatical tension, 314
Gray, Loretta, 326
Greenblatt, Stephen, 223

Habits of mind
  counterproductive, 9–16
  five-paragraph form, 14–15, 168

generalizing, 12–14
  leaping to judgment, 10–11, 117, 150
  naturalizing assumptions, 11–12
Harper, Molly, 51–52
Hasty generalization fallacy, 96
Hemingway, Ernest, "To the Maestro," 121
Heron, Sean, 47
Heuristic function of formats, 266–268
Heuristics. *See also* Method, The; Notice & Focus strategy
  Asking "So what?," 21–25, 70, 109, 189–191, 195–196
  defined, 117
  Difference Within Similarity, 110–111, 170, 203
  Doing 10 on 1, 118, 162–163, 164–168, 174–175, 191
  for making writing happen, 117–118
  Paraphrase x 3, 45–47, 70, 117
  Passage-Based Focused Freewriting, 47–52, 70, 102, 216, 238
  Pointing, 44–45
  Reformulating Binaries, 60–61, 118, 135
  Seems to Be About X, But Could Also Be (Or Is "Really") About Y, 82–84, 198, 203
  Six Steps for Making a Thesis Evolve Through Successive Complications, 178
  Tracking Binaries, 58–60
  Uncovering Assumptions, 56–58, 68, 218
Hidden meanings compared to implications, 78–82
How, focusing on, 104–105, 113
Hughes, Langston, 50
Humanities
  data analysis in, 89
  introductory paragraphs in, 281–282
  paraphrasing and, 46
  quotations and, 220
Hypotactic sentences, 308
Hypothesis, 178, 187–188, 284

ICANN (Internet Corporation for Assigned Names and Numbers, The), 247
Ideas, move to, 70
Identity terms, 332–333
Illocutionary force, 53
Implication
  in conclusions, 278
  hidden meaning compared to, 78–82
  Paraphrase x 3 strategy as unlocking, 46–47
  Passage-Based Focused Freewriting strategy and, 49
  uncovering assumptions in, 57–58
Implicit, making explicit, 21–25, 41
IMRAD format, 185, 268–270
In Bruges: Finding Hope in the Presence of the Past (Patefield), 199–202
Incoherence, 275
Independent (main) clauses
  commas and, 310, 348
  in cumulative sentences, 318–319

defined, 302, 308, 366
in periodic sentences, 316–318
Indexes, scholarly, 243
Indirect objects, 304
Induction (10 on 1). *See also* Doing 10 on 1
    strategy
overview, 160–168
thesis and, 184–186
Inferring consequences, 160
Infinitives, 369
Inflated diction, 338–339
Inquiry-based writing, 117, 182. *See also*
    exploratory writing
Intensifiers, 327
Intention, as interpretive context, 74–76
Interest, writing as generating, 101–102,
    119
"Interesting," 18
Interlibrary loan, 244–245, 252
Internet Corporation for Assigned Names
    and Numbers, The (ICANN), 247
Internet Library of Early Journals, 252
Internet research, 246–251
Interpretation. *See also* meaning
  anything goes school of, 77–78
  fortune cookie school of, 77
  making plausible across curriculum,
    89–93
  meaning as contextual and, 72–77
  New Yorker cover example, 84–89
  overview, 70
  Passage-Based Focused Freewriting
    strategy and, 49
  plausibility of, 71–73, 89–93
  Seems to Be About X, But Could Also Be
    (Or Is "Really") About Y strategy and,
    82–84
  of statistical data, 90–92
Interpretive communities, 72
Interpretive contexts
  intention as, 74–76
  overview, 71–73
  selecting, 87–88
  specifying, 73–74, 193–194
  for thesis, 203
In-text attributions, 237
In-text citations
  APA style, 257
  CSE style, 260, 261
  MLA style, 262
Intransitive verbs, 304, 322
Introductions
  analyzing, 298
  audience and, 298
  claims in, 276
  examples of, 276–277
  in humanities, 281–282
  purpose of, 273–274
  to scientific papers, 286
  in social sciences, 282–285
  solving problems in, 274–276
  thesis in, 202–204
  working thesis in, 274

Isocolons, 320
"It is," 326
"It's" vs. "its," 360–361
"I," use of, 335–337
"I" vs. "me," 364–365

Jane Eyre (Austin), 58
Jargon, 339–340
Jefferson, Thomas, 47
Journal articles. *See also* end-of-text article
    citations
  archives of older periodicals, 252–253
  finding sources in, 244–245
JSTOR website, 252
Judgment
  leaping to, 10–11, 117, 150
  suspending, 16

Kairos, 54
Keats, John, 14
Key comparison, arguing for significance
    of, 109
Key words
  to link sentences in paragraphs, 290
  quoting when reading, 44–45
  from sources, attending to meaning of,
    220–221, 223
Kolln, Martha, 326
Kozol, Wendy, "The Kind of People Who
    Make Good Americans," 68
Kristeller, Paul, *Renaissance Thought,* 226
Kunstler, James Howard, 59

Lab reports, IMRAD format for, 269
Lakoff, George, 79, 128
Lamott, Anne, 20
Language
  of argument, 159
  constitutive theory of, 40
  customs of, as changing, 362
  figurative, 79–82
  insider, 339–340
  paraphrasing, 45–47
  politics of, 334
  of sources, 220–221
  of text, learning to speak, 39
  transparent theory of, 39–40, 299–300
Lanham, Richard
  Analyzing Prose, 335
  Revising Prose, 322
Las Meninas (Velázquez), 188–192
Latinate diction, 328–329
Leap to judgment, 10–11, 117, 150
Learning communities, 213
Leave It to Beaver (TV sitcom), 75–76
Length of paragraphs, 289–290
Lens
  interpretive context as, 72–73
  reading as, 63–68
  sources as, 239
  thesis as, 183–184
Libraries, reference rooms of, 242, 243, 251.
    See also interlibrary loan

Life, writing from, 132–133
Life Lessons from America's Greatest Writers
(PEN/Faulkner Foundation), 130
Limitations, in conclusions, 278
Limiting context, locating personal
response within, 107
Lincoln, Abraham, "Gettysburg Address,"
341–342
Linking evidence and claims
with deduction and induction, 160–168
overview, 148–153
rules of argument and, 155–162
Linking verbs, 304
Listening exercise, 52–53, 124
Literacy narratives, 118, 146
Local, going, 117, 217
Lodge, David, 15
Logical fallacies
ad hominem, 93–94
bandwagon, 94
begging the question, 94
circular reasoning, 94, 150
equivocation, 94
false analogy, 94–95
false cause, 95
hasty generalization, 96
non sequiturs, 96
oversimplification/overgeneralization,
96
overview, 93
poisoning the well, 96
red herrings, 96
slippery slope, 96
sloganizing, 93
straw man, 96, 225, 272
weasel words, 93, 97
Logos, 9
Louth, Richard, 141

MacGowan, Christopher, 235
Main (independent) clauses
commas and, 310, 348
in cumulative sentences, 318–319
defined, 302, 308, 366
in periodic sentences, 316–318
Making details speak, 151–153
Making writing happen, 117–119
Mantras for writers, 146
Maps of scholarship, 226
Marshall, James, 187, 276
Meaning. *See also* interpretation
analysis as search for, 3–4
as contextual, 71–77
shades of, and word choice, 330–332
as socially determined, 76–77
style as inseparable from, 299–300
Mediator role for disagreement between
sources, 215
Memoirs, 133
Metaphors, 79–82, 129–130
Metasites, 254–255
Method, The (heuristic)
examples of, 27–28

for making summaries more analytical,
103
overview, 117
for poems, 29–31
questions from, 26
reading and, 40
for sources, 218
steps of, 26–27
for text marking, 135
troubleshooting, 31–32
for visual images, 32, 33–35, 86
Methodology, evidence as dependent on,
154–155
Misspellings, 360–362
MLA, 243
MLA (Modern Language Association) style,
257, 262–263
Modifiers
embedding, 314–316
misplaced, 356–357
of phrases and commas, 310–312
Moment, finding, 54–55
More Than Cool Reason (Lakoff and Turner),
79, 128
Moving forward, 21–22
Multiple points of view, consulting and
interrogating, 213

Narrative openings, 277
National Writing Project, 141
Naturalizing assumptions, 11–12
Natural sciences
collaborative nature of work in, 72
as corporate, 288
data analysis in, 89–90
Discussion sections in, 286–288
engaging sources in, 229–230
framing assumptions in, 154
humanities compared to, 282
IMRAD format for, 268–269
introductions in, 284–285, 286
sentence style in, 336–337
thesis evolution in, 187–188
Negative capability, 14
New points, raising in conclusions, 280
New starts method of revision, 122–123
New Yorker, The, cover example
description of, 84–85
making interpretation plausible, 89
making interpretive conclusion, 88–89
The Method strategy and, 86
selecting interpretive context, 87–88
Niesenbaum, Richard, 336
Nineteenth Century in Print, 252
Nonrestrictive modifiers, 311–312
Nonrestrictive phrases and clauses,
359, 360
Non sequiturs, 96
Norling, Frederick, 245, 279
Notice & Focus strategy
interpretation and, 70
for making summaries more analytical,
103–104

overview, 17–19, 117
reading and, 40
for sources, 218
Noun clauses, 345
Noun phrases, 368
Nouns, 368

Obama, Barack, 51
Observations. *See also* Notice & Focus
strategy
exercises for, 120–122
freewriting and, 19–21
inferring implications from, 25
pushing to conclusions, 22
O'Donoghue, Kate, 223
Official Style, 322–330, 332
1 on 10 (deduction)
overview, 162–164
thesis and, 184–185, 186–187
Ongoing analysis of sources, supplying,
221–222
Opaque style, 335
Opinion compared to argument, 12
Organizing papers. *See also* five-paragraph
form; formats
climactic order, 271
comparison/contrast, 271–272
concessions and refutations, 272–273
using 1 on 10, 164
using 10 on 1, 165, 173–175
Orwell, George, "Politics and the English
Language," 334
Overassertive prejudgment, 274
Overcompression, 275
Overgeneralization, 96, 211–212
Overpersonalizing, 11–12
Oversimplification, 96
Overstatement in conclusions, 280
Oxford English Dictionary, 114

Pair of dashes, 313
Pan analogy, 172–173
Paper, writing on, 124–125
Paragraphs. *See also* conclusions;
introductions
coordinate function of, 293–294
identifying structure of, 292, 294–295
lengths of, 289–290
linking sentences in, 290–291
as movement of mind, 291–294
observation → implication → conclusion
model for, 292–293
overview, 288–289
subordinate function of, 294
TRI model for, 291–292
Parallelism/parallel structure, 320–322
Paramedic method, 322
Paraphrase x 3 strategy, 45–47, 70, 117
Paraphrasing sources, 219–221, 237
Paratactic sentences, 308
Parentheses, commas acting like, 311
Parenthetical elements and commas,
358–359

Participial phrases, 368
Participles, 356–359, 369
Passage-Based Focused Freewriting
strategy, 47–52, 70, 102, 216, 238
Passive voice, 301, 324–326
Patefield, James, *In Bruges:* Finding Hope in
the Presence of the Past, 199–202
Pathos, 9
Patterns
of error, 343
of repetition and contrast, looking for,
25–32, 86
"Pause theory" of punctuation, 348
Peer review
one-on-one, 138–140
small group, 137–138
PEN/Faulkner Foundation, 130
Periodic sentences, 316–319
Periods, 312
Personal associations, 35–36, 210–211
Personal home pages of students and
faculty, 251
Personal response
making more analytical, 106–107
writing assignments calling for,
99, 105
Personal writing/essays, 116, 132–135
Perspectives on sources, researching new,
228
Phrases, 368
Physical activity
reading as, 39
writing as, 120
Pitch, finding, 54–55, 135
Plagiarism, 235–238
Plausibility of interpretation, 71–73, 89–93
Pointing strategy, 44–45
Point of view, questioning, 106
Points of departure, sources as, 218
Poirier, Steven, "Progressive Era Women
and Public Sphere Involvement," 226
Poisoning the well, 96
Politics
figurative language of, 81–82
of language, 334
Possession and apostrophes, 357, 364
Post hoc, ergo propter hoc fallacy, 95
Poteet, Ellen, 205
Practical reasoning, 159–160
Predicate adjectives, 304
Predicates, 303, 307, 352, 368
Prejudgment, 274, 275
Preliminary thinking on topics,
215–216, 237
Premises and syllogisms, 156
Prendergast, Catherine, "The Fighting
Style," 295
Prepositional phrases, 368
Prepositions, 363–364, 368
Prescriptive approach to responding to
other writers, 136
Prewriting strategies, 19
Primary sources, 214

Print corollaries for websites, 247
Problematizing, 112–113
Problem-oriented academic writing, 268, 273
Procedural openings, 282–283
Procedural statements, 204
Procrustean, 170
Productive thesis statements, 181, 205–207
Pronouns
case of, 364
defined, 368
inclusive, 333
reference errors, 353–355
relative and demonstrative, 316
Proofreading, 344
Prospectus, informal, 239
Prove/proof, 149
Punctuation marks, 312–313, 344. *See also specific punctuation marks*
Pushing observations to conclusions, 22

Qualifying claims, 153
Queries, 49
Questions. *See also* "So what?" questions
beginning with, 101
to evaluate websites, 249–250
in introductions, 284
phrasing thesis statements as, 207
reformulating, 32–33
unstated, studying wording of topics for, 100–101
using sources to ask, 222–225
Quotation marks in Internet search strings, 252
Quotations, use of
for analysis, 145
in research papers, 231–233
from sources, 219–221
Quoting key words when reading, 44–45

Rabe, Barry, "A Reason to Believe," 91–92
Ranking, 17–18, 70, 109
Reading. *See also* structure of thinking in reading
analytically, 68–69
changing orientation to, 38–40
focusing on individual sentences when, 43–53
against grain, 58, 82
with grain, 40
as lens, 63–68
with others, 52–53
situating rhetorically, 53–56, 104–105
statistically, 92–93
text marking when, 135–136
using Doing 10 on 1 strategy when, 167
writing about, 102
Reasoning
circular, 94, 150
practical, 159–160
Recasting arguments, 157
Reconstruction and reflection of experience, 134
Recursive thinking, 60

Red herrings, 96
Reductive thinking, 108
Redundancy
in conclusions, 279–280
in five-paragraph form, 169
Reference librarians, 242, 243, 251
References lists
APA style, 258
CSE style, 261, 262
Reformulating Binaries strategy, 60–61, 118, 135
Reformulating questions and explanations, 32–33
Relative pronouns, 315–316
Relevance of evidence, 154–155
Representativeness of examples, demonstrating, 165–166
Research. *See also* research papers
bibliographic, 243, 245–246, 253–255
evaluating electronic sources, 251–253
getting started with, 242–243
on Internet, 246–251
Research papers. *See also* sources
abstracts for, 234–235
accumulating perspectives for, 228–229
apprehending viewpoints for, 213–214
maps of scholarship in, 226
quotations in, 231–233
Research sequences, 239
Responding to other writers
description-based, small group peer review, 137–138
Google docs and interactive blogging, 140
one-on-one peer review, 138–140
overview, 136–137
Restrictive modifiers, 311–312
Restrictive phrases and clauses, 359–360
"Revealing," 18
Revision
alternative models of, 122–125
approaches to, 188
conceptual, 192–198
knowing when to stop, 198–199
stylistic, 342
Rewriting drafts, 197–198
Rhetoric
impact on audiences of, 9
situating reading rhetorically, 53–56, 104–105
Rhetorical analysis and noticing, 18–19
Rhetorical awareness, 266
Rhetorical function of formats, 266–267
Rhetorical Grammar (Kolln & Gray), 326
Ricks, Christopher, "Clichés," 217–218
Road map paragraphs, 282–283
Rogers, Carl, 10, 11, 159–160
Ross, Alex, 233
Rules of argument
overview, 155–156
Rogerian argument and practical reasoning, 159–160

syllogism and enthymeme, 156–157
Toulmin model of argument, 157–159
Run-on (fused) sentences, 347–348, 367

Salon.com website, 248
Scholes, Robert, 44
Sciences. *See* natural sciences; social sciences
Sciutto, Mark, 13, 285
Scope of inquiry, reducing, 100, 104
Secondary sources. *See* sources
Second-best example, beginning introductions with, 277
Second person, use of, 336
Seems to Be About X, But Could Also Be (Or Is "Really") About Y strategy, 82–84, 198, 203
Self, writing, 134
Self-evaluation of writing, 143–146
Semicolons, 305, 312, 348
Send-off, 278
Sentence fragments, 309, 345–347, 368
Sentences
    climactic order in, 314
    compound, 305–309, 312
    cumulative, 318–319
    defined, 368
    emphasis and order of clauses in, 313–314
    ending with prepositions, 363–364
    focusing on when reading, 43–53
    identifying clauses and conjunctions in, 309
    linking in paragraphs, 290–291
    modifiers, 314–316
    periodic, 316–318, 319
    proofreading, 344
    punctuation marks, 312–313
    relationship of parts of, 301–302, 344
    shape of, and commas, 310–312
    simple, 301–305
    style of, 299
    subjects and predicates, 302–303
    subordination, 307–309
    unity of, in paragraphs, 289
    verbals, 304–305
    verbs, 303–304
Shaughnessy, Mina, *Errors & Expectations*, 343
Shifts in sentence structure, 352
Shklovsky, Victor, 15–16
Short List of Things That Go Wrong, 144
Similes, 80, 128–129
Simple cause/complex effect fallacy, 95
Simple sentences, 301–305
Six Steps for Finding and Evolving a Thesis in an Exploratory Draft, 178, 192–198
Six Strategies for Analyzing Sources
    attending to language, 220–221
    finding role in conversation between sources, 227–230
    making sources speak, 219–220
    overview, 219

putting sources into conversation with each other, 225–227
supplying ongoing analysis, 221–222
using to ask questions, 222–225
Slate.com website, 248
Slippery slope argument, 96
Sloganizing, 93
Slot-filler mentality, 14–15, 168
Smith, Patrick C., 229
Social sciences
    conclusions in, 286–288
    data analysis in, 89–90
    formats for, 270
    framing assumptions in, 154
    humanities compared to, 282
    IMRAD format for, 185, 268–270
    interpretation of data in, 90–92
    introductory paragraphs in, 282–286
    paraphrasing and, 46, 220–221
    sentence style in, 336
    thesis evolution in, 187–188
Sources. *See also* documentation styles; Six Strategies for Analyzing Sources
    acknowledging, 214, 215, 231
    anxiety about using, 215–216
    conversing with, 216–218, 238–241
    critical approaches to, 228
    evaluating, 249–250, 251–253, 263
    finding, 244–245, 263
    integrating material from, 222, 285–286
    key works from, attending to meaning of, 220–221, 223
    overview of, 213–214
    paraphrasing, 219–221, 237
    plagiarism and, 235–238
    as points of departure, 218
    preparing abstracts of, 234–235
    reliability of, 242
    using analytically, 214–215, 230–231
"So what?" questions
    comparison/contrast and, 109
    conclusions and, 278, 281
    interpretation and, 70, 89–90
    for making implicit explicit, 21–25
    sources and, 222, 224
Specifying interpretive context, 73–74
Spelling errors, 360–362
Splicing quotations, 232
Spot quotes, 223
Square brackets, using in quotations, 233
Standard Written English, 351–352
Starting points for writing, collecting in writer's notebooks, 126–127
Static verbs, 323
Statistical data, 90–93
Stephen, Lesley, 28
Storytelling, 127
"Strange," 18, 24
Strategies. *See* freewriting; heuristics; Six Strategies for Analyzing Sources
Straw man fallacy, 96, 225, 272

Structure, underlying
    of academic writing, 268
    looking for, 103
Structure of thinking in reading
    reading as lens, 63–68
    Reformulating Binaries strategy, 60–61
    Tracking Binaries strategy, 58–60
    tracking thinking through complication
        and qualification, 61–63
    Uncovering Assumptions strategy, 56–58
Style
    analyzing, 340–341
    comparing, 341
    formal and colloquial, 337–338
    as inseparable from meaning, 299–300
    Official Style, 322–330, 332
    overview, 299
    politics of language and, 334
    prescriptive style manuals, 300–301
    tone and, 331–332
    transparent and opaque, 335
Subjects of sentences, 302–303, 368–369
Subject-verb disagreements, 350–352
Subordinate (dependent) clauses, 308, 346,
    348, 366
Subordinating conjunctions, 308–309, 366,
    369
Subordination, 369
Subscriber-only databases, 250, 252,
    253–254
Summary
    analysis compared to, 5–6
    comparative, 240–241
    documenting sources in, 237
    in introductions, 285
    making more analytical, 103–105
    of sources, 219–220
    writing assignments calling for, 99, 103
Syllogisms, 156–157, 158
Sympathetic reading, 40
Synthesis
    comparison/contrast and, 109
    definition and, 112–113
    of multiple points of view, 231
    of sources, 215

Tag phrases, 232
Tannen, Deborah, 64
10 on 1 (induction). See also Doing 10 on 1
    strategy
    overview, 162–168
    thesis and, 184–186
Tenor of similes, 80
Tension in productive thesis statements,
    205–207
Testing adequacy of thesis, 196–197
"Test Yourself" exercises, 344
Text marking, 135–136, 175–176
"Their" vs. "there" vs. "they're," 361
"Then" vs. "than," 361
"There is," 326
Thesis. See also working thesis
    characteristics of, 180–181

in conclusions, 204–205, 278
deductive example of, 186–187
development of, 178–180
evolution of, 182–188
inductive example of, 185–186
interpretive context for, 203
in introductions, 202–204
marking in text, 136
reciprocal relationship between
    evidence and, 183–184
recognizing, 205
Six Steps for Finding and Evolving a
    Thesis in an Exploratory Draft,
    192–198
tracking in finished drafts, 199–202
weak, 181, 182–183, 207–212
wording, 205–207
Thesis-driven writing, problems with, 182
"They," gender-neutral, 333, 353–354
Thinking. See also structure of thinking in
    reading
    comparative, 128–129
    formats and, 266–267
    making visible to readers, 151–153
    recursive, 60
    reductive, 108
    rhetorical, 299
    as writer, 116–117
Third person, 335–337
"This," as pronoun, 355
Three minutes writing prompt, 130–132
Title searches, 252
Tjeltviet, Alan, 187, 222, 245–246, 270, 287,
    336
"To be," forms of, 322–324
Tomine, Adrian, 32
Tone, 331–332
Topics, responding to
    beginning with questions, not answers,
        101
    expecting to become interested, 101–102
    finding analytical potential, 99
    reducing scope, 100
    studying wording for unstated
        questions, 100–101
    suspecting first responses, 101
    writing informally about studies, 102
Toulmin, Steven, The Uses of Argument,
    157–159
Track analogy, 172–173
Tracking Binaries strategy, 58–60
Transitions, 295–297
Transitive verbs, 304, 322
Transparent style, 335
Transparent theory of language, 39–40,
    299–300
Turner, Mark, 79, 128

Uncertainty
    locating area of, 99
    tolerance of, 14
Uncovering Assumptions strategy, 56–58,
    68, 218

University of North Carolina at Chapel Hill
Libraries, 255
Unsubstantiated claims, 148, 149–150
URLs, backspacing, 251
Usage
as changing grammar, 364–365
as cultural marker, 365
defined, 362
rationale for choices, 366
right and wrong vs. etiquette, 363–364
as social and conventional, 362
Uses of Argument, The (Toulmin), 157–159

Vehicle of similes, 80
Verbals, 304–305, 345–346, 369–370
Verb phrases, 368
Verbs
defined, 369
errors in agreement with subjects,
350–352
kinds of, 303–304
"to be," forms of, 322–324
Visual images
using Doing 10 on 1 strategy on, 167
using The Method strategy on, 32, 33–35,
86
Voice, active and passive, 301, 324–326

Wallace, David Foster, 42
Warrants, 158
Weak thesis statements
kinds of, 208
overview, 181, 182–183
recognizing and fixing, 207–212
Weasel words, 93, 97
Websites
by discipline, 254–255
domain names, 246–247
evaluating, 249–250, 251–253
in Google search results, 248
high-quality, 247–248
print corollaries for, 247
quality, finding, 246
subscriber-only databases, 250, 252,
253–254
"What's going on in the field?" searches,
239–240
Whistler's Mother (Whistler), 33–35, 71, 73
Whiston, Anna, "I think my cooking, uh,
sucks," 64–68
WHOIS, 251

"Who" vs. "whom," 365
Why, focusing on, 104–105, 113
Wightman, Bruce, 187, 229–230
Wikipedia, 248–249, 252
Williams, William Carlos, "The Crowd at
the Ballgame," 31
Wisdom, conventional, thesis as restating,
209–210
Words
collecting in writer's notebooks, 128
etymology of, 329–330
focusing on, 145–146
shades of meaning and, 330–332
Wordsworth, William, 15
Working thesis
claim as, 181
details as leading to, 194–195
Doing 10 on 1 strategy to find, 174
evolving, in exploratory drafts, 188–192
formulating, 193–194
in introductions, 204, 274
Works-cited lists, 236
Writers' boot camps, 142–143
Writer's notebooks, 126–130
Writer's workshops, 136
Writing. See also basic writing errors;
exploratory writing; freewriting;
writing assignments; writing
prompts
on computers vs. on paper, 124–125
with others, 52–53, 124
as tool of thought, 2–3
Writing Across the Curriculum program, 3
Writing assignments. See also topics,
responding to
agree/disagree, 107–108
comparison/contrast, 108–111
definition, 111–113
interpreting, 98–99
personal response, 105–107
responding to more analytically, 98
summary, 103–105
Writing center model of peer review,
138–140
Writing Down the Bones (Goldberg), 141
Writing marathons, 141–142
Writing prompts
for personal essays, 133–135
three minutes, 130–132

Zoom analogy, 172–173

A Summary of Tools – Analytical Methods

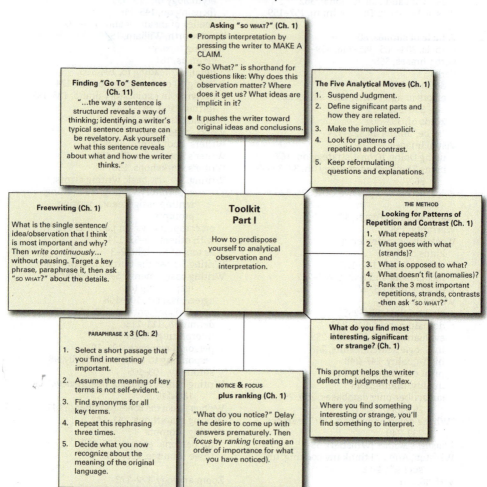

Asking "SO WHAT?" (Ch. 1)

- Prompts interpretation by pressing the writer to MAKE A CLAIM.
- "So What?" is shorthand for questions like: Why does this observation matter? Where does it get us? What ideas are implicit in it?
- It pushes the writer toward original ideas and conclusions.

Finding "Go To" Sentences (Ch. 11)

"…the way a sentence is structured reveals a way of thinking; identifying a writer's typical sentence structure can be revelatory. Ask yourself what this sentence reveals about what and how the writer thinks."

The Five Analytical Moves (Ch. 1)

1. Suspend Judgment.
2. Define significant parts and how they are related.
3. Make the implicit explicit.
4. Look for patterns of repetition and contrast.
5. Keep reformulating questions and explanations.

Freewriting (Ch. 1)

What is the single sentence/idea/observation that I think is most important and why? Then *write continuously*… without pausing. Target a key phrase, paraphrase it, then ask "SO WHAT?" about the details.

Toolkit Part I

How to predispose yourself to analytical observation and interpretation.

THE METHOD
Looking for Patterns of Repetition and Contrast (Ch. 1)

1. What repeats?
2. What goes with what (strands)?
3. What is opposed to what?
4. What doesn't fit (anomalies)?
5. Rank the 3 most important repetitions, strands, contrasts -then ask "SO WHAT?"

PARAPHRASE X 3 (Ch. 2)

1. Select a short passage that you find interesting/important.
2. Assume the meaning of key terms is not self-evident.
3. Find synonyms for all key terms.
4. Repeat this rephrasing three times.
5. Decide what you now recognize about the meaning of the original language.

NOTICE & FOCUS plus ranking (Ch. 1)

"What do you notice?" Delay the desire to come up with answers prematurely. Then *focus* by *ranking* (creating an order of importance for what you have noticed).

What do you find most interesting, significant or strange? (Ch. 1)

This prompt helps the writer deflect the judgment reflex.

Where you find something interesting or strange, you'll find something to interpret.

All quotations are from *Writing Analytically*, 8th edition by David Rosenwasser and Jill Stephen, as selected and arranged by Professor of Biochemistry Keri Colabroy.